Cover photograph: A profile of the head as viewed by a color nuclear scanner, a modern medical research tool. The resulting picture (scan), as shown here, is used to study the brain and other organs. The different colors represent various levels of radioactivity emitted by the head after an injection of a radioactive isotope. This picture also symbolizes an important phase of total health —mental and emotional health.

Book Eight

Health and Growth

In this *Teacher's Edition* for HEALTH AND GROWTH, *Book Eight,* are Teacher's Notes" overprinted on the pupil's pages and a special *Resource Book* at the back.

Note: While this book is written to be easily read by most pupils at the age level for which it was prepared, you may—in some special situations—want to have the text material reread orally by competent readers before group discussion. Such a procedure ensures that *all* youngsters can enter into discussion of content that centers upon the health needs, interests, and curiosities of junior high school pupils. Much information can be gained by all pupils from the illustrations.

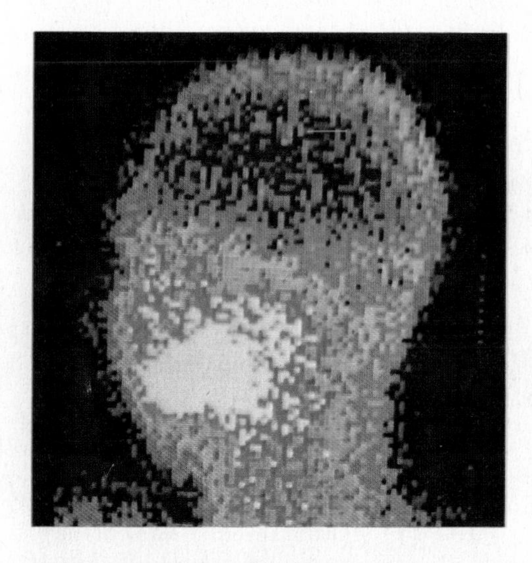

Julius B. Richmond, M.D.
Elenore T. Pounds, M.A.
Gladys Gardner Jenkins, M.A.
Dieter H. Sussdorf, Ph.D.

In consultation with
Irma B. Fricke, R.N., M.S.
Orvis A. Harrelson, M.D., M.P.H.
Norman H. Olsen, D.D.S.
Wallace Ann Wesley, Hs.D.

Designed by Norman Perman
Anatomical Art by Lou Barlow, AMI

Scott, Foresman and Company

Authors

Julius B. Richmond, M.D. Professor of Child Psychiatry and Human Development, Harvard University; Director, Judge Baker Guidance Center; Chief of Psychiatric Service, Children's Hospital, Medical Center; Professor and Chairman, Department of Social and Preventive Medicine, Harvard Medical School.

Elenore T. Pounds, M.A. Writer; lecturer; former Directing Editor, Health and Personal Development Program; classroom teacher; author of *Drugs and Your Safety* and other *Health and Growth Enrichment Booklets.*

Gladys Gardner Jenkins, M.A. Lecturer in Education and Home Economics, University of Iowa, Iowa City, Iowa; former member National Advisory Council on Child Growth and Human Development; author of *Helping Children Reach Their Potential;* coauthor of *These Are Your Children.*

Dieter H. Sussdorf, Ph.D. Associate Professor of Microbiology, Cornell University Medical College and Cornell University Graduate School of Medical Sciences, New York, New York; coauthor of *Methods in Immunology.*

ISBN: 0-673-04863-2

Regional offices of Scott, Foresman and Company are located in Dallas, Texas; Glenview, Illinois; Oakland, New Jersey; Palo Alto, California; Tucker, Georgia; and Brighton, England.

Consultants

Irma B. Fricke, R.N., M.S. Former Director of School Nursing, Evanston Public Schools, District 65, Evanston, Illinois; recipient of the 1971 William A. Howe Award in school health.

Orvis A. Harrelson, M.D., M.P.H. Director of Health Services, Tacoma Public Schools, Tacoma, Washington.

Norman H. Olsen, D.D.S. Chairman of the Department of Pedodontics and Dean of The Dental School, Northwestern University, Chicago, Illinois.

Wallace Ann Wesley, Hs.D. Director, Department of Health Education, American Medical Association, Chicago, Illinois; former teacher at primary through college levels.

Advisors

Thea Flaum, B.A. Former editor, *Safety Education,* National Safety Council, Chicago, Illinois.

Willie D. Ford, Ph.D. Professor, Nutrition and Home Economics, Grambling College, Grambling, Louisiana.

Richard E. Hudson, M.A. Eighth-grade teacher, Blowing Rock Elementary School, Blowing Rock, North Carolina.

Ruth Leverton, Ph.D. Science Advisor, Agricultural Research Service, United States Department of Agriculture, Washington, D.C.

Richard Norgaard, M.A. Health and Physical Education teacher, Mannheim Junior High School, Melrose Park, Illinois.

John D. Withers, Ph.D. Assistant Director of Education, American Institute of Biological Sciences, Education Division, Washington, D.C.

Designer

Norman Perman, B.F.A. Graphic Designer, Chicago; Guest Lecturer, University of Illinois, Circle Campus, Chicago, Illinois; past President, Society of Typographic Arts.

Contents

1 What Are Your Personal Health Concerns?

Teacher's Notes

Unit Overview: Ask teen-agers if they have any theories about why they might have new health concerns and interests quite different from those they had in childhood years. (The teen years are years of rapid growing. Various aspects of this growth lead to new interests and new problems.)

Information in this unit centers around frequent health concerns of young people your age—concerns about growth, overweight and underweight, posture, exercise, skin care, sleep, dental problems, and so on. No doubt you will find some answers to questions you have often wondered about.

Teacher's Notes

Read to Find Out: Talk over the queries here just long enough to give students a chance to commit themselves to some answers. Such commitment helps hold pupils' attention during the unit. They will want to check the accuracy of their tentative answers. Make a note, too, of other queries that are raised by students in the course of the discussion.

How Do You Know If You Are Growing as You Should? Explore what would be meant by the "average height" of a given group of thirteen-year-old boys—or girls. Do students think this "average height" would be a good indication of how tall *all* the thirteen-year-old boys—or girls—in the group should be?

Read to Find Out

1. *How can charts that show only* average *heights and weights be misleading?*
2. *What does* heredity *have to do with your* rate *of growth? With your eventual height?*
3. *How does the* pituitary gland *relate to growth?*
4. *What can a person do about overweight? Underweight?*
5. *What is meant by the statement, "Good posture usually goes along with good health"?*
6. *Why is* acne *chiefly a problem of the teen years? What can be done about acne?*
7. *What are some ways to achieve dental health?*
8. *What are some effects of insufficient sleep?*
9. *Why does a boy's voice change?*
10. *Why are periodic health checkups important?*

Something to Do

Look in the school and public libraries for books and pamphlets such as the following ones on health needs and concerns during the teen years:

American Dental Association. Teeth, Health, and Appearance *(American Dental Association).*

Gallagher, J. Roswell, M.D. You and Your Health *(Science Research).*

Gregg, Walter H. A Boy and His Physique *(National Dairy Council).*

Leverton, Ruth M. A Girl and Her Figure *(National Dairy Council).*

Lubowe, I. I., M.D., and Huss, Barbara. A Teen-age Guide to Healthy Skin and Hair *(Dutton).*

Luce, Gay, and Segal, Julius, M.D. Sleep *(Coward). Paperback.*

How Do You Know If You Are Growing as You Should?

"Am I growing the way I should?" is a question that many young people wonder about. This is of special concern to boys who are shorter than most of their classmates and to girls who are "early growers."

Reassuring answers to the question of whether you are growing as you should can be found in the story of growth variations during the teen years. An understanding of human growth patterns is an important part of this story. Facts about how growth takes place are presented here.

Growth During the Teen Years

Years ago, height and weight studies of young people and adults were concerned mainly with *averages.* For example, the heights of a large number of thirteen-year-old boys were added; then the sum of all their heights was divided by the number of boys in the group. The resulting figure indicated their average height.

Similar studies were conducted to find average heights for people of different ages. Later, additional studies were made to find average weights for people of a given age and height. Findings from studies such as these were made available to the public in chart form.

Over the years, however, it has become apparent that information about average heights and weights can cause confusion. Some people mistakenly believe that the terms *average height* and *average weight* mean the "right" height and the "right" weight. These people do not understand that wide variations from *average* figures are normal and should be expected. (See pages 18–21 for the ranges in height and weight of young people aged thirteen to sixteen.)

Today, physicians and others who give advice about human growth realize that knowing averages is not nearly so important as knowing about the way people of the same age *vary in height and weight.* Research has shown that these variations are normal and that they should be expected, especially during the teen years.

During the teen years, for instance, there may be as much as four years' variation in rate of growth and body build between the most and the least physically mature person of the same age. These differences in growth and body build depend upon many factors, such as the individual's sex, heredity, general health, nutrition, and environment.

After you have learned more about these individual differences in growth, you will no doubt understand what one doctor who specializes in teen-age medicine means by this statement: "Most young people concerned about their size have no real growth problem; *they merely need to know the variations in rate, time, and extent of growth that occur during the teen years.*"

Patterns of Growth

During the growing-up years, each boy and each girl, at his and her own rate, follows the same general growth patterns. As the physical changes leading to manhood and womanhood begin to take place, there is a period of fast growth which is known as the *growth spurt.*

Teacher's Notes

Some discussion leads you may want to try are the following:

"Why aren't all young people the same height at a given age?"

"Can a person control any of the factors that foster most desirable growth for him or her? Explain."

"What is meant by a 'growth spurt'?"

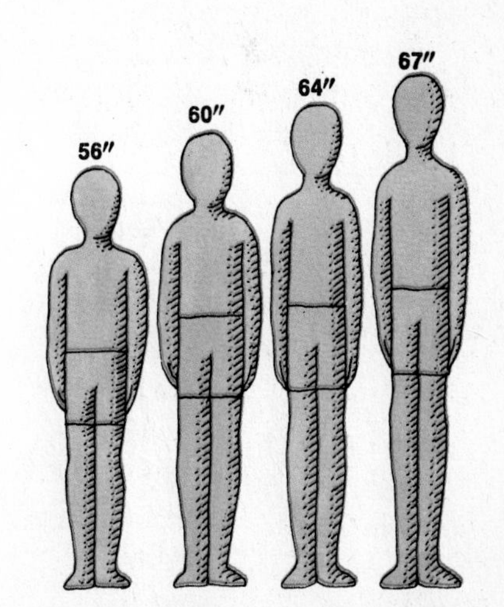

The average *height of these thirteen-year-old boys may not be the actual height of any one of them. The same thing holds true for their* average *weight.*

Teacher's Notes

Such queries as the following may serve as provocative discussion guides:

"What have you learned about how girls grow during the teen years? About how boys grow?"

"What is meant by the terms 'early grower' and 'late grower'?"

"What information have you gained to support the statement, 'The range of heights at a particular age, such as thirteen, is very wide'?" (Refer to charts on pages 18-21.)

Some Things to Do

1. You may want to talk to your parents about family tendencies toward early or late maturing. Family albums may be checked for photos of parents and other relatives when they were thirteen or so. Such pictures often indicate whether parents or other relatives were early or late growers.

2. To learn more about heredity, look in the school or public library for such books as these:

Klein, Aaron. Threads of Life: Genetics from Aristotle to DNA *(The Natural History Press). Advanced.*

Lerner, Marguerite Rush, M.D. Who Do You Think You Are? The Story of Heredity *(Prentice-Hall).*

Randal, Judith. All About Heredity *(Random).*

This rapid growth in height and weight occurs in all boys and girls. However, the age at which it begins, its extent, and the time it lasts vary considerably. It is thought that the growth spurt is brought about at the proper time by the action of the *hypothalamus,* at the top of the *brain stem.* The hypothalamus acts on the body's master gland, the *pituitary.* When the body is ready, the hypothalamus turns on and then turns off the growth processes.

In girls the growth spurt starts earlier than in boys. The spurt may start anywhere from age nine to thirteen or so in girls. The greatest weight gains for girls, however, are usually made in the twelfth or thirteenth year. Most boys begin their growth spurt sometime between eleven and fifteen or sixteen years of age. Boys' greatest weight gains usually occur in the fourteenth or fifteenth year.

Height gains occur at a somewhat slower rate and to a lesser extent in girls than in boys. Weight gains, however, are more dramatic in girls than in boys. During her growth spurt, a girl may gain seven times more weight than she did during the preceding year—often as much as ten to twenty pounds in just one year.

In a boy, during his growth spurt, an increase in height of from four to twelve inches may take place within a single year. Although boys' weight gains tend to be smaller than those made by girls, the gains continue over a longer period of time for boys.

After the growth spurt, there is a gradual slowing down as growth is completed. Much of this growth after the growth spurt involves a change in body proportions. Growth in height is usually ended between ages sixteen and eighteen in girls and between eighteen and twenty or so in boys. When growth stops, boys usually end up being taller and heavier than girls.

The age at which a young person has his or her growth spurt does not determine eventual height and body build. Some boys and girls who are early growers will be tall. Others will be of average height. Still others will be shorter than average. Likewise, some late growers will be tall, others will be of medium height, and still others will be short.

The age at which a person's growth spurt begins, the way the person grows, and the time when growth stops are all individual matters. Usually, though, girls are ahead at the start and boys are ahead at the finish.

Rate of Maturing

A question young people often ask is, "Can I tell in advance whether I will be an early grower or a late grower?"

A young person's heredity offers some good clues about early or late maturing. For example, a boy whose father had his teen-age growth spurt at the age of fifteen *may* also follow that pattern. A girl whose mother was an early grower *may* also tend to reach her full growth at an early age.

There are, however, more scientific ways to find out about a person's rate of maturing. Growth studies of children and young people over many years have furnished useful standards for measuring physical growth. For example, X-ray pictures of the bones of the hand and wrist—showing the growing ends of joints—can furnish accurate information about a young person's rate of development.

Look at the hand-wrist X rays shown at the right. These are X rays of two boys, each boy aged fourteen years and eleven months. In the X ray at the top, you will notice that there is considerable cartilage material around the ends of the small bones. *Cartilage,* sometimes called gristle, is firm and elastic, not strong and rigid like bone. In the X-ray picture at the bottom, much of the cartilage has *ossified;* that is, it has become bony and dense. The bone cells secrete a substance that slowly changes the cartilage into bone. This process takes place as the body matures.

Ratings of these two X rays give the boy whose hand-wrist X ray is shown at the top a bone age, or *skeletal age,* of thirteen years and six months. The boy whose hand-wrist X ray is shown at the bottom has a skeletal age of sixteen years and ten months.

Thus, these two X rays indicate that one boy is relatively slow-growing with several years ahead of him for growth—and that the other boy is skeletally more mature than his actual age would indicate.

Teacher's Notes

This page acquaints students with another way of finding out about a person's rate of maturity—by determining the skeletal age through comparisons of X-ray pictures. These pictures can show the progress in ossification of the growing ends of bones, such as those of the hand and wrist.

Students often ask, "Can eventual height be predicted?" Physicians do have tables based upon a young person's sex, actual age, skeletal age, and present height. Even with the help of such tables, however, eventual height is difficult to predict with complete accuracy.

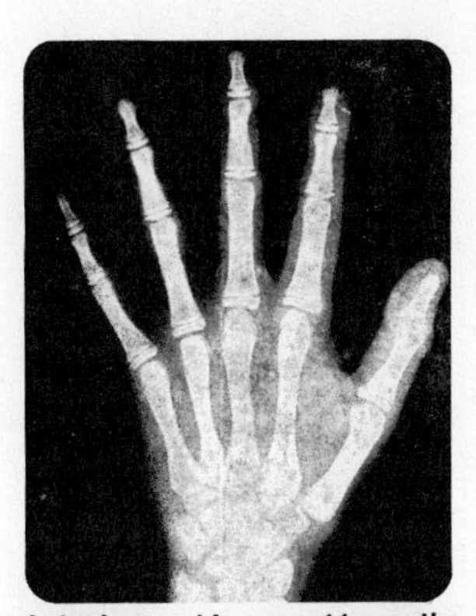

Actual age—14 years, 11 months
Skeletal age—13 years, 6 months

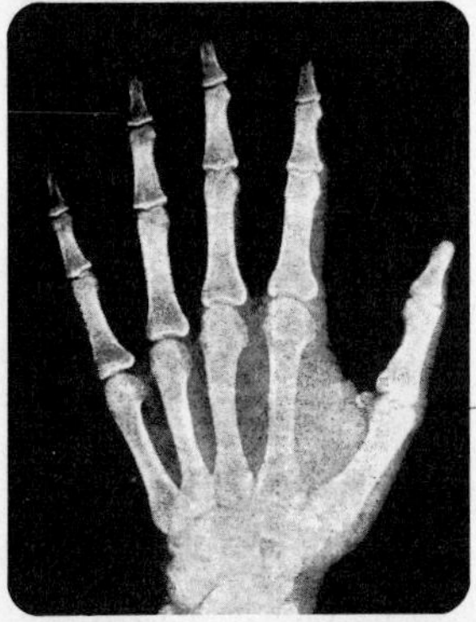

Actual age—14 years, 11 months
Skeletal age—16 years, 10 months

Teacher's Notes

You may want to use such discussion guides as these:

"What are some parts of the body that are among the earliest to reach full growth?" (Feet, hands, brain.)

"What is one clue given in the marginal picture about why a health examination is usually required before teen-agers take part in competitive sports?" (To make sure the heart and other organs are in good condition and are able to withstand the stress of such sports during this period of rapid and uneven growth.)

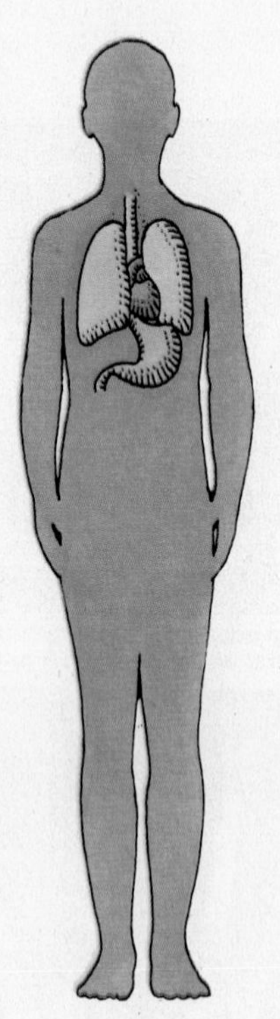

A boy of sixteen may have an almost completely developed framework, but his heart, lungs, and stomach may not have kept pace with his framework. *Now look at page 13.*

Unevenness of Growth

All parts of the body are involved in the teen-age growth spurt. But not all parts of the body grow—or reach their adult size—at the same time. For example, the arms and legs are fully grown long before the trunk is.

During the period from about ten to sixteen years of age, different parts of the body will be growing rapidly at different times. As one part reaches its adult size, its growth stops. Meanwhile other parts of the body continue their growing or begin to grow. This goes on until all parts of the body have reached their full growth. Among the earliest parts to reach full size are the feet, hands, and brain.

This *unevenness* of body growth explains why for a time a young person's feet may seem large and out of proportion to the rest of the body. It explains, too, why the waist may seem high or the legs or arms appear quite long. Some awkwardness may occur during the teen years as a result of the rapid growth of bones and muscles. The lack of proportion may temporarily interfere with smoothness of body movements. The young person will need time to learn to control skillfully the movements of the arms and legs. The lengthened legs may get a person places before he or she expects to arrive. The force of newly acquired strength may cause the young person to knock things over, or the temporary lack of hand coordination may cause him or her to fumble or drop things.

Sometimes, too, the internal organs do not develop as rapidly as the skeleton. The heart, for example, may have an increased burden because it must send the blood over a longer route in the newly lengthened arms and legs. A young person may complain of fatigue or seem lazy because of this temporary imbalance. (See the marginal pictures on this page and on page 13.)

By the time a young person is sixteen, eighteen, or twenty, the slow-growing parts of the body normally catch up with the fast-growing parts. Then the body is in proportion again. Meanwhile, the young person will be growing up in the broadest sense of the term if he or she can accept and be good-humored about annoying aspects of rapid or uneven growth.

The Endocrine Glands and Growth

The story of growth includes the story of the endocrine system. This system of glands has chemical control of the body. *Endocrine glands* are also called ductless glands or the glands of internal secretion. They are termed ductless glands because the *hormones,* or chemical substances, that they produce are not poured through a duct into the hollow organs of the body, as are saliva and the digestive juices. Instead, the hormones are absorbed directly into the bloodstream. The blood then transports the hormones throughout the body, and they function at specific places as needed.

Knowledge about hormones is fairly recent, and current research is continually giving us additional information about them. Present knowledge indicates that there may be as many as several hundred kinds of hormones produced in the body and that a given gland may produce a few or many kinds of hormones. The hormones are used by the glands of the endocrine system to control the body chemically.

The Pituitary Gland

The *pituitary gland,* located in a well-protected place at the base of the brain, is the master gland. (See the drawing on page 15.) It is called the master gland because it directs the work of all the other endocrine glands.

At least eight different hormones are known to be produced by the pituitary gland, and eventually it may be proved that there are more. Some of these pituitary hormones act on other glands of the endocrine system to make them produce their particular hormones. Still other hormones from the pituitary gland act directly on the body's cells.

Among the hormones that act directly on the body's cells is the hormone that regulates growth. The growth hormone influences the growth of the bones, internal organs, and probably other parts of the body. The growth hormone is normally sent into the bloodstream only during the growing-up years. It causes body cells to keep growing and multiplying until adult size is reached. Then the pituitary gland stops making this special growth hormone. After that, a person may become more muscular or fatter but will stop growing taller.

Teacher's Notes

Discuss what the endocrine glands have to do with a young person's growth. Ask this question:
"How do the endocrine glands differ from such glands as the salivary glands?"

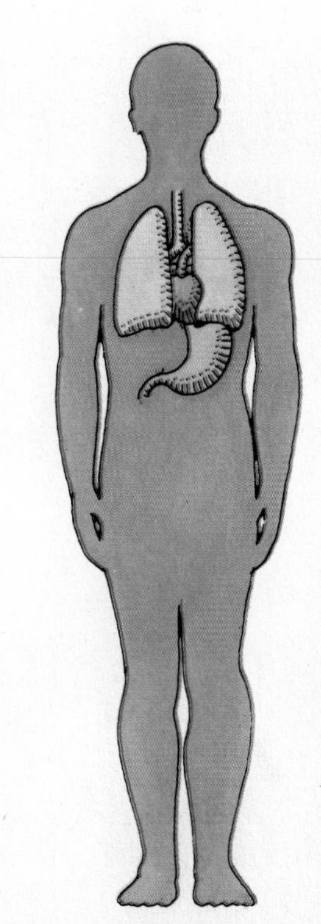

The same boy at twenty will be fully grown physically, with organs such as the heart, lungs, and stomach that are adult in size and in proportion to his framework.

Teacher's Notes

Students are always fascinated by what produces a giant or a midget and they will find the answer here. Stress that these cases are *extremely rare.*

Discuss the significance of the laboratory synthesis of the growth hormone. This hormone is perhaps the most fascinating of the known hormones secreted by the pituitary gland. It not only controls human growth, but it plays a key role in weight control and the body's ability to fight disease. In animal tests, it has promoted faster healing of fractures and has lowered blood cholesterol levels. The feat of the doctor, Dr. Citili, who achieved the laboratory synthesis of HGH, opens the way for it to become, with further refinement, an established medical tool in the near future.

Only rarely does the pituitary gland function abnormally in a person. In rare instances too much of the growth hormone is produced during childhood, causing a person to become a giant. If the pituitary gland produces too little of the growth hormone during childhood, however, a person may become a midget. Midgets are small but well-proportioned adults. If this hormone continues to be produced in adulthood, the person does not get tall, but the bones of the hands, feet, and face increase in size.

The hormones seem to have great influence on each other, so it is very important that they be regulated carefully, or kept in balance. The pituitary gland is also in charge of maintaining this *hormone balance.*

In recent years, medical science has made considerable progress in treating those rare cases in which something is seriously wrong with the hormone balance. In 1971, scientists created a substance called *HGH (human growth hormone),* which is identical to the body's growth hormone. Previous studies of the effects of the growth hormone were hampered by the fact that it could be obtained only from pituitary glands removed from humans after death. Now that an artificial growth hormone is available, it may be increasingly possible to help avoid that very limited number of cases of stunted growth.

Sometimes a young person is worried about the way he or she is growing or developing and will ask a doctor if something can be done to speed up or slow down growth. In most of these instances, the doctor finds that no medical treatment is needed. The young person is growing in a way that is right for him or her, even though it may be a little different from the growth patterns of other young people in the same age group.

Another hormone produced by the pituitary gland has an influence over all the other glands by causing them to speed up or slow down their activity. This hormone particularly stimulates the activity of the reproductive glands—which are *ovaries* in girls and *testicles* in boys. These are the glands that cause boys and girls to develop to full physical maturity. Some of the growth changes produced by this hormone, such as the beard on a boy's face or the rounding out of a girl's figure, are

Do You Know?

1. What do the endocrine glands have to do with a person's growth and development?

2. What are some other names for the endocrine glands?

3. How do the endocrine glands differ from such glands as the salivary glands?

visible. But many of the changes are going on inside the body; they will give boys and girls the physical potential for having children.

The pituitary gland also produces a hormone that helps control water balance in the body. Still another hormone stimulates the adrenals to produce the hormone cortisone.

The Thyroid Gland

The *thyroid gland* is located in the neck, near the windpipe. It produces a hormone called *thyroxin*. This hormone helps regulate the speed at which the activities of the body are carried on. For example, it controls the body's metabolism. In other words, it regulates the speed at which the body uses its supply of food and oxygen to produce heat and energy. If too little thyroxin is produced, body processes slow down. Then the body uses less food, stores fat, produces less heat, and therefore has little energy. If too much thyroxin is produced, body processes speed up. Then there may be an excessive loss of weight; the thyroid gland may enlarge; and the eyes may protrude from their sockets.

The amount of thyroxin that the thyroid gland manufactures also has an effect on how a person acts. If the thyroid gland is overactive, a person becomes jumpy and nervous and is likely to tire easily. If the thyroid gland makes too little thyroxin, a person may be slow and sluggish in his movements. The thyroid may be unable to produce thyroxin if the gland does not contain enough iodine. When there is insufficient iodine, the thyroid cells reproduce. This increase in the number of thyroid cells, or enlargement of the thyroid gland, is called a *goiter*. This problem is rare where people use salt to which iodine has been added.

The Parathyroid Glands

The four tiny glands near or in the thyroid gland are the parathyroids. Their hormone regulates phosphorus and calcium balance in the body. A lack of the proper amount of parathyroid hormone affects the muscles, causing muscle spasms and trembling. Too much of the hormone takes calcium out of the bones—which leaves them soft. Insufficient calcium also weakens the muscles.

Teacher's Notes

After discussion of the various functions of the parathyroids, the adrenals, the pancreas, and the thymus, see if students can supply the technical terms for each of these descriptions:

a. a hormone produced by the islets of Langerhans (insulin)

b. an important hormone closely associated with emotions and produced by the adrenals (adrenalin)

c. glands that produce the substances called hormones (endocrine)

d. glands that produce a hormone needed in the body's use of phosphorus and calcium (parathyroid)

e. disease caused when not enough insulin is produced by the islets of Langerhans (diabetes)

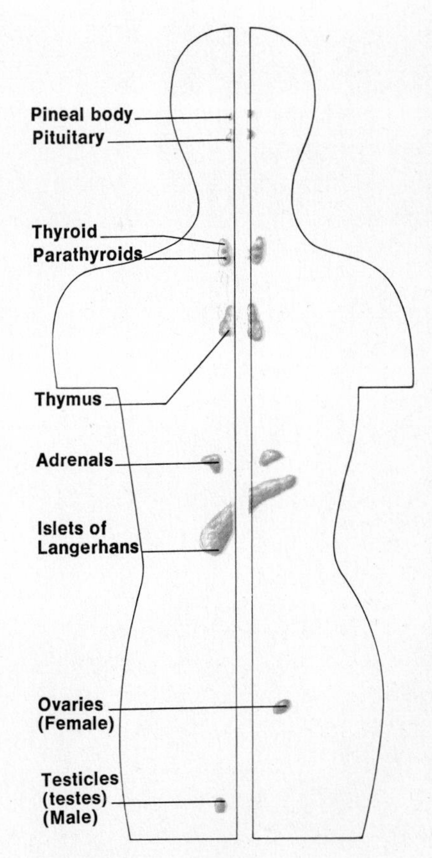

The endocrine glands

Teacher's Notes

Students may want to discuss what medical treatment a person with diabetes is given. In some mild cases, diabetes is controlled by diet alone. In other cases, insulin shots must be given to supply the diabetic person with the insulin the body is not making in sufficient quantity. When shots are used, the insulin has to be injected with a hypodermic needle. Often the person can self-inject the shots. Recently, drugs which can be taken in pill form have proved helpful in treating adults who have mild diabetes.

The Adrenal Glands

The *adrenal glands* are like tiny caps. One is located on the top of each kidney. One hormone that is made by these glands is *adrenalin.* When a person becomes excited or angry or frightened, the adrenal glands pour out more than the usual amount of adrenalin into the bloodstream. This, in turn, stimulates the liver to pour into the bloodstream extra amounts of *glycogen,* or stored sugar. The blood carries the glycogen to the muscles where it is quickly oxidized by the muscle cells to produce extra energy. The increase in the amount of adrenalin also makes the heart beat faster, raises the blood pressure, and increases the breathing rate. All these changes prepare the body for increased effort.

The outer portion, or *cortex,* of the adrenal glands produces the hormone *cortisone,* which is essential to life. Cortisone controls the use of salt in the body. When cortisone is absent or the normal amount is greatly reduced, the blood pressure drops. Weakness or death may follow.

The Islets of Langerhans

The pancreas, which is situated behind the stomach, has two jobs. The pancreas itself makes certain digestive juices, which are poured into the small intestine to aid digestion. But groups of cells within the pancreas form an endocrine gland, the *islets of Langerhans.* This gland makes the hormone *insulin,* which goes directly into the bloodstream. Insulin helps the body use sugar properly. If not enough insulin is produced, a person develops *diabetes.*

Two Mysterious Glands

The *thymus,* located behind the breastbone, has been a mysterious gland for a long time. It is known to produce certain types of white blood cells, but only recently have research workers found that it may be involved in immunity. The gland grows steadily from birth through childhood, then it shrivels and may disappear.

The function of the *pineal body* has been a puzzle for many years. However, medical researchers are currently working on several hormonelike substances present in this gland and may soon remove some of the mystery that surrounds it.

Accepting the Way You Grow

It should be reassuring for you to know about the way boys and girls grow during the teen years. However, just knowing the facts may not ease all your worries about growth.

Consider Ella Mae, a thirteen-year-old. Ella Mae is taller than most of the girls and boys in her class. She dislikes being taller and spends time worrying and complaining about it. Her posture and appearance suffer because she slouches to hide her height.

Or look at Paul. He is shorter than many young people his age, and he worries about it. Sometimes when his friends are looking for more players for a game, Paul walks away. He imagines that he is not welcome because of his size.

What can be done about the feelings that Ella Mae and Paul have about their respective sizes? Remember, many changes will take place before the teen years are over. Ella Mae is an early grower. In a few years other boys and girls her age will catch up with her in height. Paul is short now, but he may have a growth spurt at age sixteen and become as tall as many of his friends. Ella Mae might always be taller than average, however, so she needs to make the most of herself as a tall girl. Paul may suddenly "shoot up" or he may always be a fairly short person. He needs to accept himself as he is—not as he wishes he were.

Think about other aspects of your physical appearance: your body build, the color of your eyes, the shape of your nose and head, the texture and color of your hair. Are these the most important factors in making you accepted by the people you like or successful in what you do? Think of the boys and girls who are well-liked and respected in your school and neighborhood. You will find that among this group there is a great variety in height, weight, body build, and appearance.

Actually, physical appearance is rarely the most important factor in any person's success in life. Determination, friendliness, and trustworthiness are among the many positive personal traits that contribute greatly. You can be any size and still be healthy, happy, and successful in various undertakings of your choice.

Teacher's Notes

Some discussion leads that might be used are the following:

"Why might poor posture be seen in some early-growing youngsters?"

"What advantages do you see in the fact that people differ in body build?" (It would be an uninteresting world if we all looked alike, were the same size, had the same potential for skills, and so on.)

"What are some advantages in being tall? In being short? What famous athletes, both men and women, have been tall? Short?"

"What can help a young person feel better about his or her particular size or rate of growth?"

Some Things to Do

1. Notice the great variety in height and body build among outstanding national or world leaders in such fields as art, music, dramatics, government service, mathematics, and science. Be ready to talk over your observations.

2. Bring in pictures from newspapers and magazines for a bulletin-board exhibit on the theme "It isn't your size but what you are *that really counts."*

Individuality in Growth

Shown below are four pairs of girls, aged thirteen to sixteen. These girls were photographed in classrooms in a given school and reflect typical height and weight ranges. What are the ranges for each pair?

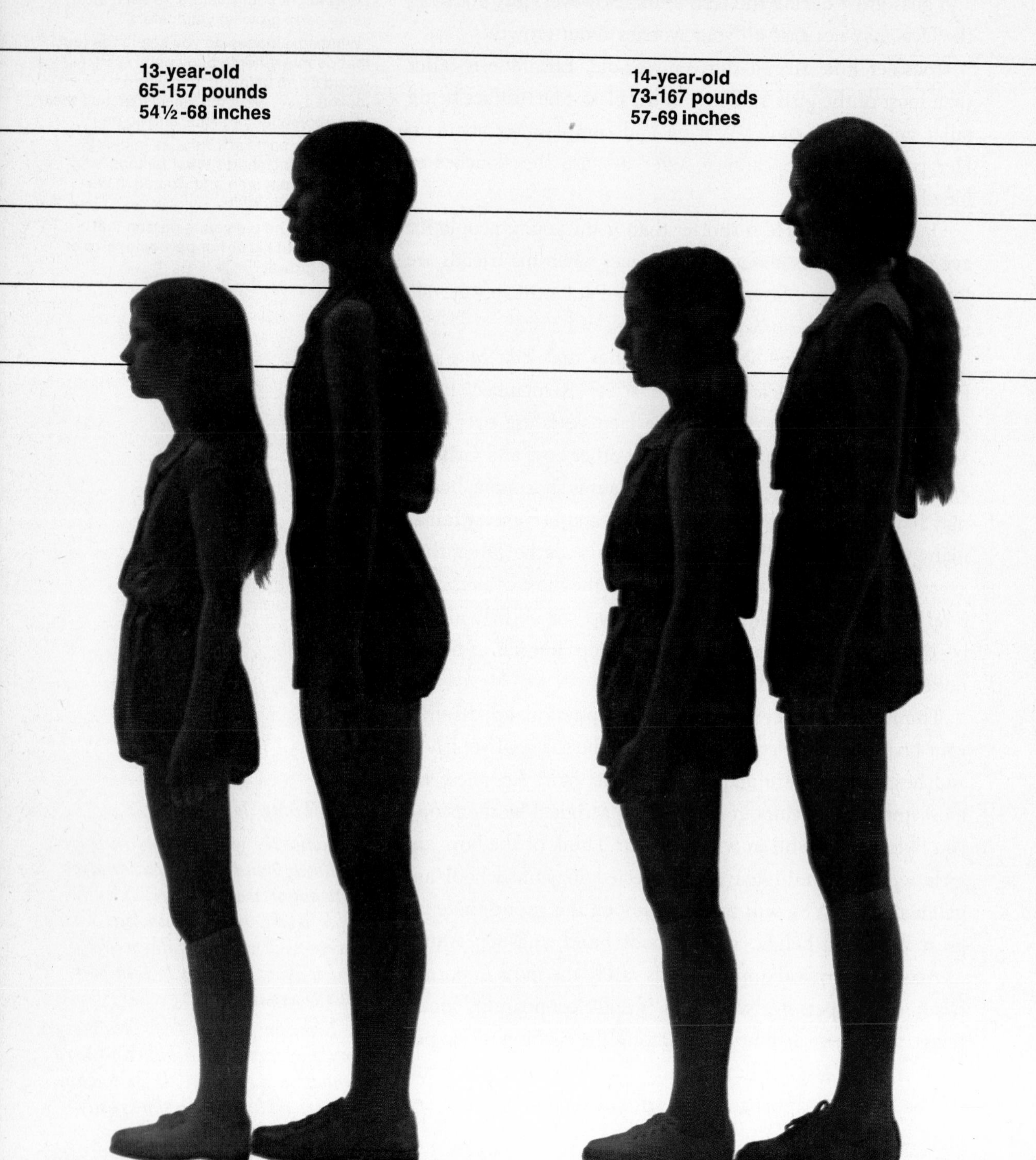

Notice the variations in posture in the girls pictured on these pages. Do you have any suggestions for improvement of posture for any of the girls pictured?

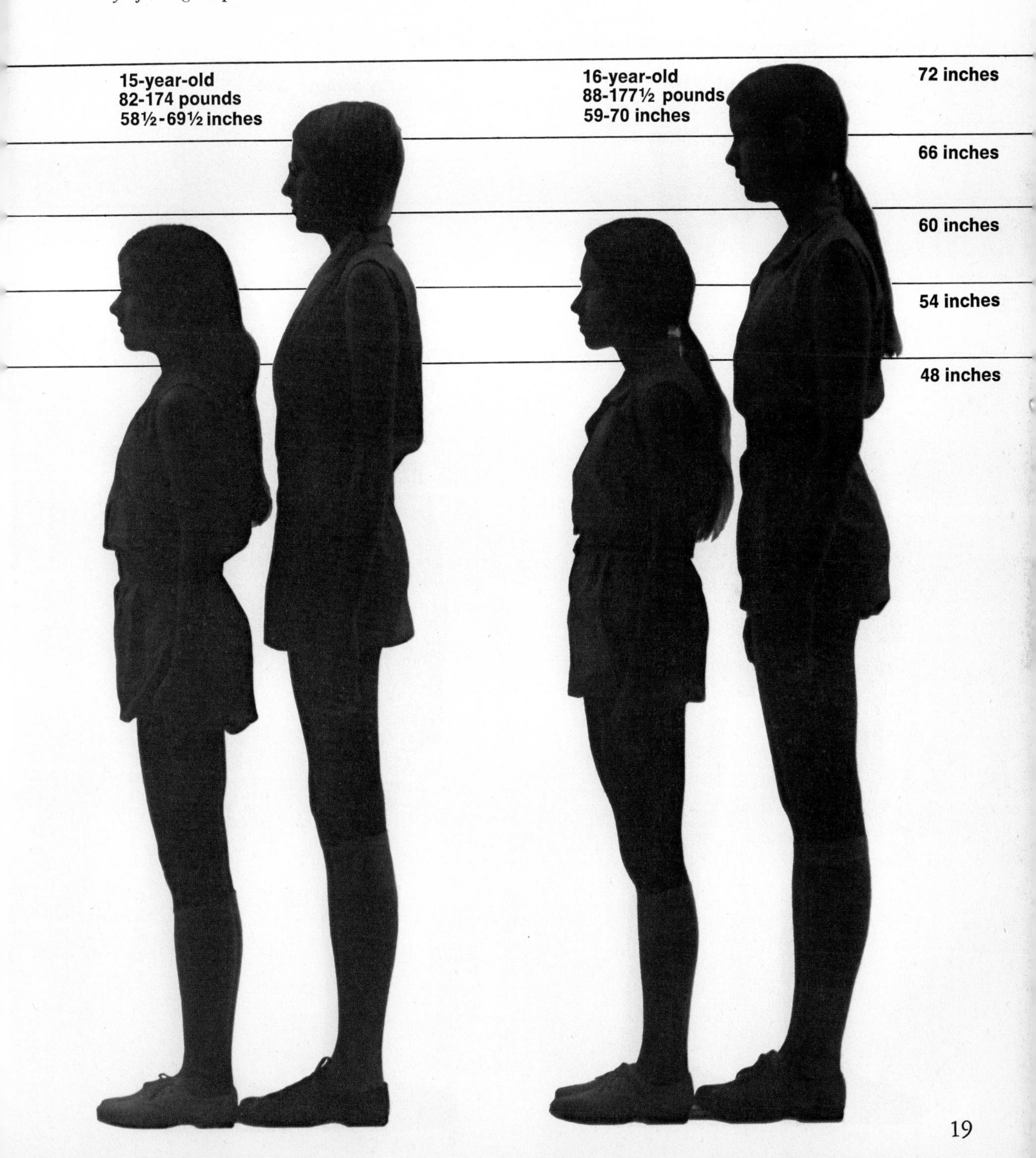

What are the ranges in height and weight for thirteen-year-old boys? For fourteen-year-old boys? For fifteen-year-old boys? For sixteen-year-old boys?

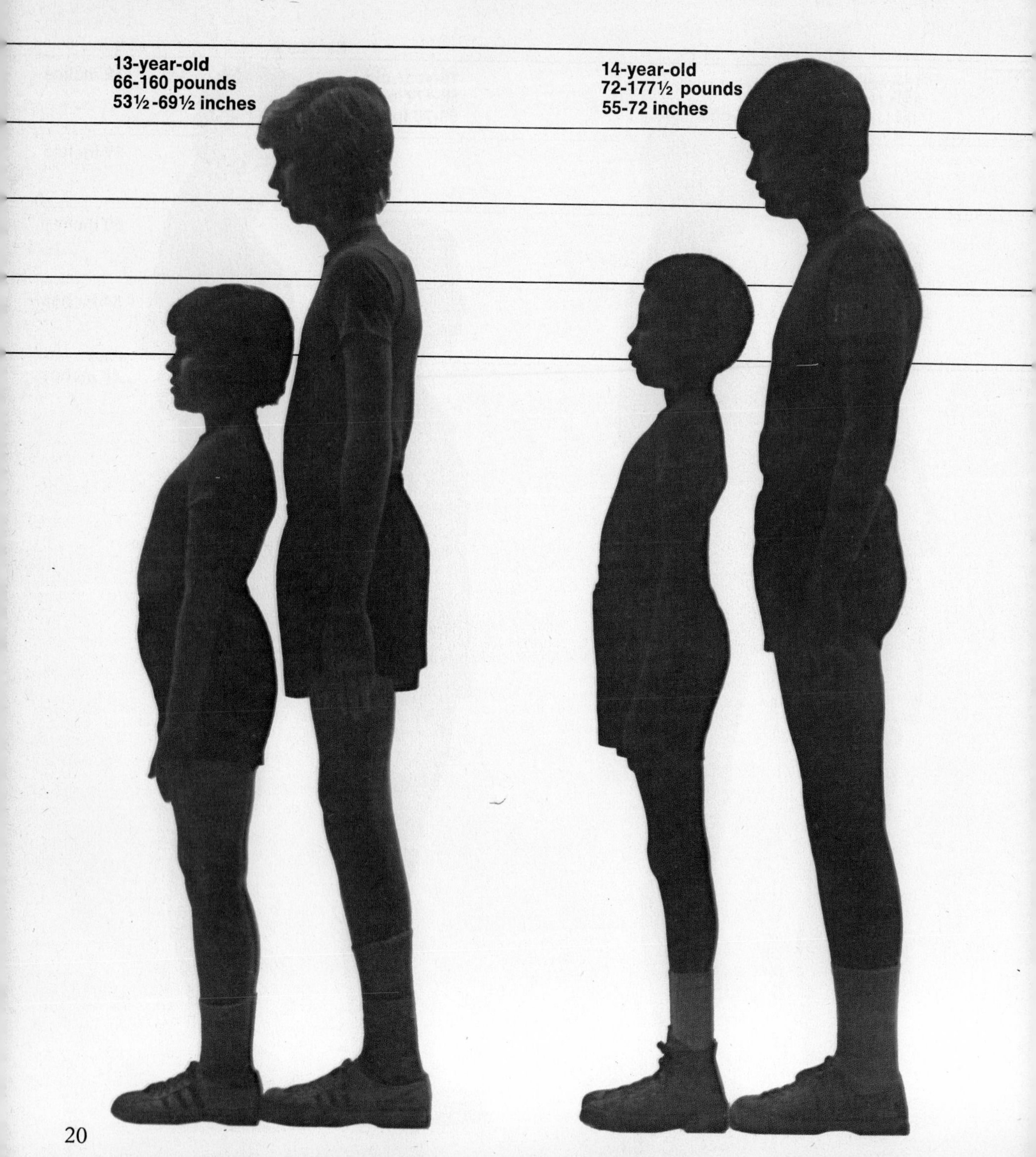

Posture problems are sometimes observed in young teen-agers. What evidences of such problems do you see here? What suggestions do you have for posture improvement in any of the boys pictured?

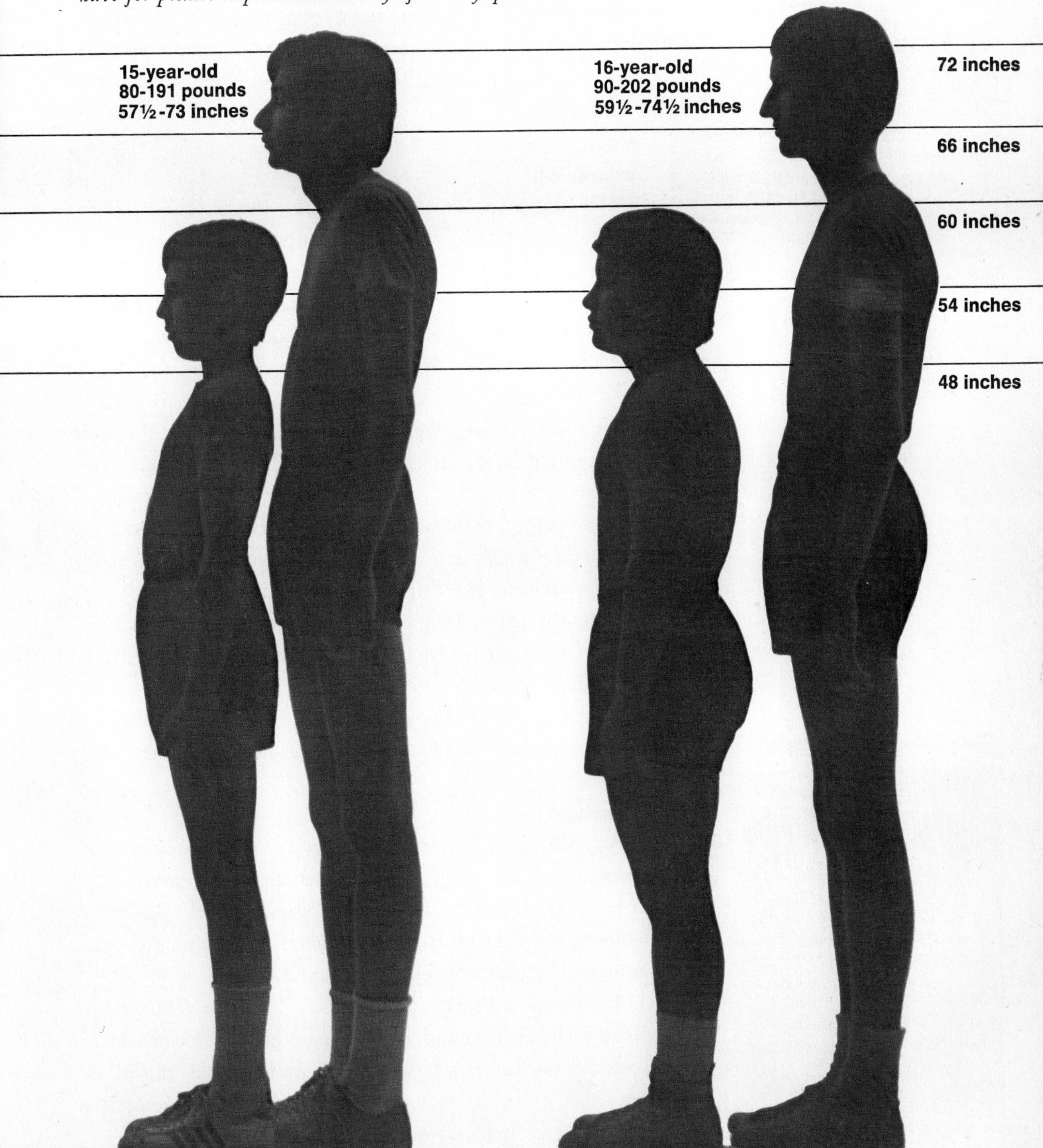

Teacher's Notes

Some conversation guides are the following:

"How can a person be sure he or she really *does* have a weight problem?"

"What are some possible causes of underweight?"

"What are some sensible ways of trying to gain weight?"

"Why is dieting under a doctor's care a wise precaution?"

"What do you think is meant by a 'crash diet'?" (An inadequate diet—such as a banana-and-milk diet or an all-vegetable diet—by which a person hopes to make great losses in weight in a very short time. Crash diets are injurious to health.)

What Can Be Done About Weight Problems?

Doctors who see large numbers of teen-agers in the course of their work observe that many of these young people want to gain or lose weight. All these doctors emphasize that a first step for anyone who is concerned about gaining or losing weight is to have a health examination.

Underweight

The health examination may reveal that a young person who *thinks* he or she is too thin actually is well nourished and weighs enough for his or her particular body build. That person may be "just naturally" thin or slight in build. But he or she may also have good health, an abundance of energy, and no physical condition that needs to be corrected.

On the other hand, some young people really are underweight. In such cases, the doctor will look for causes. Possible causes might be an infection in the body or a glandular disturbance, particularly of the thyroid gland. Still other causes of underweight might be failure to get enough sleep and rest; lack of proper diet; or excessive worry, anxiety, or other strong emotions that are affecting the appetite and digestion.

If poor nutrition seems to be causing the underweight condition, the doctor will doubtless suggest the need for getting an adequate daily diet and for gradually increasing the *amount* of food that is eaten. Some helpful hints for those who are underweight and want to gain weight are given at the left. What are they?

Some Tips for Gaining Weight

Some Tips for Gaining Weight
1. Do not skimp on breakfast.
2. Eat between-meal and bedtime snacks.
3. Eat even if you are not hungry.
4. Drink milk instead of water sometimes when you are thirsty.
5. Take "seconds" at meals.
6. Include foods that are high in calories.
7. Get more sleep than usual for you.

Overweight

A health examination is necessary before a young person takes steps to lose weight. The doctor can determine whether or not there is really a problem of overweight, or whether a temporary weight spurt is taking place. Some young people grow rapidly *outward* before they grow *upward.*

The doctor will give advice about a low-calorie, nutritious diet if such a diet is necessary. Dieting without a doctor's guidance can be dangerous. Without a well-planned, nutritious daily diet, the body may be deprived of essential materials needed for growth and well-being.

Three good meals a day—with meat, milk, vegetables and fruit, and whole-grain or enriched breads or cereals—are still essential for an overweight person, especially a young person who is growing. The foods that need to be eaten sparingly are starches and sweets, and fatty or fried foods.

Poorly planned dieting may end up with a person's craving food, eating more, and weighing more after a short period of unwise dieting. Some helpful hints for losing weight are shown at the right. What are they?

Activity and Overweight

In the physical examination, the doctor will also want to consider how active the young person is. Doctors have discovered that some patients who are overweight do not eat excessively. Often the problem is that the young person is not active enough to cause the body to burn up what is eaten. Hence the excess calories are stored as fat. On the other hand, many young people eat enormous meals; but because they are very active, they have no excess fat.

The fat cells themselves may be a problem for some extremely fat or *obese* people who want to lose weight. There is recent research to indicate that the number of fat cells in the body may have something to do with increased appetite and weight. That is, more fat cells require more "fuel" in the form of food. The number of fat cells in a person's body may be influenced by overweight in infancy and early childhood. This new information about fat cells in the body may account, in part, for the difficulty that obese people have in losing weight through dieting.

Emotions and Overweight

Emotions may play a part in an overweight condition. Prolonged grief, anxiety, a feeling of failure, or other disturbing emotions may lead to overeating as a means of compensating. Young people who are having difficulty staying with a low-calorie diet prescribed by a doctor may have troubles that go beyond overweight itself. Once they are helped to straighten out disturbed feelings—or to cope with the real problems they may have—these persons are more likely to be able to stay on their diets. In fact, they may not even need diets.

Teacher's Notes

Discuss how exercise can help a person lose weight safely. (It causes the body to burn up food that has been stored in the body as fat.)
During discussion, ask:

"What has research shown about why an obese person may need extra 'fuel'?"

"What part can emotions play in a person's being overweight?" (Point out, too, that people differ in their reactions; thus a person who is worried or otherwise upset may react by losing his appetite.)

"What are some sensible things a person can do to control his weight or to help him lose weight?"

Some Tips for Losing Weight

1. If possible, consult a doctor before dieting.
2. Eat slowly and chew thoroughly.
3. Drink milk or water with your meal to fill you up.
4. Cut down on the size of your servings; do not take "seconds."
5. Do not let yourself get famished; then you will be tempted to overeat.
6. Be sure to eat breakfast.
7. Exercise.
8. Take no "reducing" drugs unless a doctor prescribes them.

Teacher's Notes

After study of the text on pages 24, 25, and 28, give students a chance to explain or justify these statements:

Good posture can reduce fatigue.

Good posture makes you look better.

There are individual differences in posture.

Balance is a factor in posture.

Good posture goes along with good health.

Exercise is an aid to good posture.

Posture often reveals a person's feelings.

Poor posture may be related to shoe trouble.

How Can You Improve Your Posture?

The matter of posture improvement is one you may want to consider since it is during the teen years that posture faults often develop. Girls who are early growers, for instance, may begin to slouch to hide their height.

Remember that good posture helps a person look better, feel better, and carry on daily activities with less fatigue. (For pictures of a "basic workout" that can help improve posture, see pages 26–27.)

In any consideration of posture, it should be kept in mind that there is no *one* perfect standing, walking, or sitting posture for everyone. Just as individuals differ in height, weight, and body build, they also differ in posture. One of the reasons is that there are differences in the make-up of the joints—especially those joints which bear the weight of the body in an upright position. There are differences, too, in the structure of the muscles.

Good postures are those in which the general line of the body is graceful and the body weight is so distributed as to give maximum support and cause the least strain. Good postures encourage efficient body movement and functioning. When your posture is good, your body is "in balance"—as in picture C.

Poor postures, however, can be either stiffly erect as in picture A, or sagging as in picture B. Such postures cause tension and strain on the joints, they may be harmful to normal body functions, and they spoil your appearance.

To develop good posture habits, your first step is to be sure you know what constitutes acceptable postures when you are standing, walking, sitting, and carrying heavy objects.

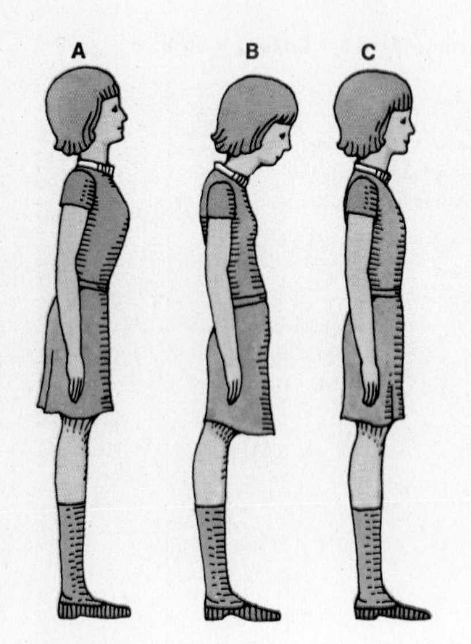

A. Overtense posture
B. Over-relaxed posture
C. Balanced posture

Standing

One way to "get the feel" of a good standing position is to stand with your back to a wall, with your head, hips, and shoulders touching the wall and with your chin level. Place your feet comfortably apart to distribute weight evenly over the heel and ball of each foot. Keep your feet parallel, your toes pointed straight ahead, and your knees slightly relaxed.

If you are standing "in balance," your ear, shoulder, and hip will all be in a straight line. Repeated practice of this stance can help make it automatic and effortless. Then long periods of standing will be less tiring.

Walking

If you are in a good standing position, you will be in a correct position to begin walking. Try to keep your feet parallel, with your toes pointing straight ahead, and let your legs walk for you.

As you step forward, your front leg will provide a new base of support for the weight of your body. As you push off with the toes of your back foot, your weight will transfer forward to the front foot. Thus each time you take a step, your leading leg provides a new base of support. In this way, you are able to maintain the balance that is necessary for a good, easy walking posture.

Sitting

Good sitting postures are especially important. Do you know why? When you are sitting, your body relaxes and your back and leg muscles have a chance to rest.

Sit well back in the chair so that your spine is supported by the back of the chair. If you sit on the edge of the chair or in a curved-back, slumping position, your back is unsupported, and muscle strain and fatigue result.

Odd positioning of legs, arms, and shoulders during long periods of sitting is fatiguing—and often unattractive as well. Generally, it is more restful to keep at least one foot on the floor to balance the body.

If you lean forward when seated—as you may do in studying—bend from the hips, keeping your back comfortably straight. When you are reading on a sofa or bed, be sure that your back is properly supported.

Carrying a Heavy Object

When you carry a heavy suitcase or book bag, try to maintain good body balance. Carry the weight as close to the body as possible and change sides frequently. You can compensate somewhat for the added weight on one side by raising the opposite arm sideward.

Teacher's Notes

After the group has studied the marginal material on pages 24 and 25, volunteers might demonstrate various kinds of posture: balanced posture and not-so-balanced posture; good posture when standing, while lifting a heavy object, and when ironing.

Have students evaluate the chairs in the classroom. Can each person sit back in his seat with his feet on the floor? Is the area provided for writing too high or too low for comfort? What might be done to correct any defects noted?

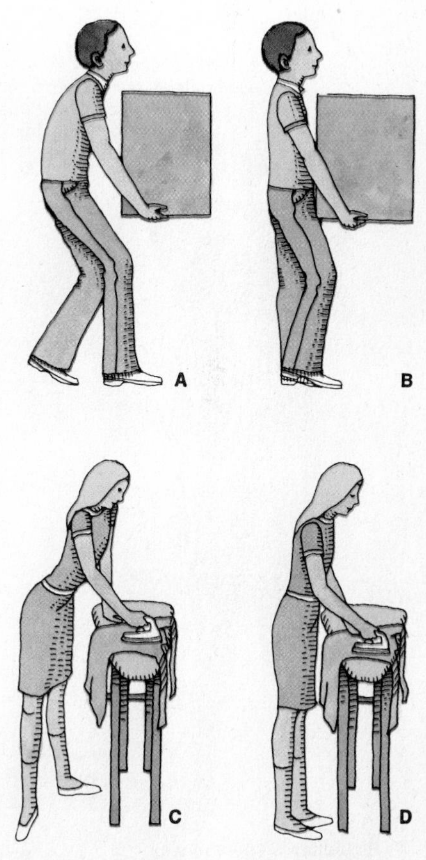

Poor body balance makes tasks harder and more fatiguing than they need to be. Which pictures above show balanced postures?

1 Run in Place 50 slow
Jog in place, raising each foot at least 4″ off floor. Count one repetition each time left foot strikes floor.

2 Twister 5 each way
Starting position: Stand erect, hands on hips. *Action:* Count 1—Bend forward from waist. Count 2—Twist trunk to right. Count 3—Bend trunk backward. Count 4—Twist trunk to left.

3 Robot 20 times
Starting position: Stand erect, hands on hips, feet shoulder-width apart. *Action:* Count 1—Bend trunk to right, reaching hand as far down right leg as possible. Count 2—Return to starting position. Counts 3 and 4—Same action to left side.

The Basic Workout

For good results the exercises should be done five times a week. Try to do all of them without stopping to rest. Perform each exercise correctly to get maximum benefit. Repeat each exercise the specified number of times.

7 Propeller 10 each way
Starting position: Stand erect, arms at sides, feet parallel and 1 foot apart. *Action:* Swing arms sideward and upward in full arcs, crossing them at height of swing and continuing around to starting position. Repeat 10 times in one direction, then reverse direction.

8 Pushup 10 times
Starting position: Lie face down, legs together, hands on floor under shoulders. (Girls should bend knees at right angle with feet raised off floor.) *Action:* Count 1—Push body off floor until arms are fully extended and body is in straight line from head to toes. Count 2—Return to starting position.

9 Run in Place. 25 slow, 50 fast, 25 slow
Jog in place, raising each foot at least 4″ off floor. Count one repetition each time the left foot strikes the floor.

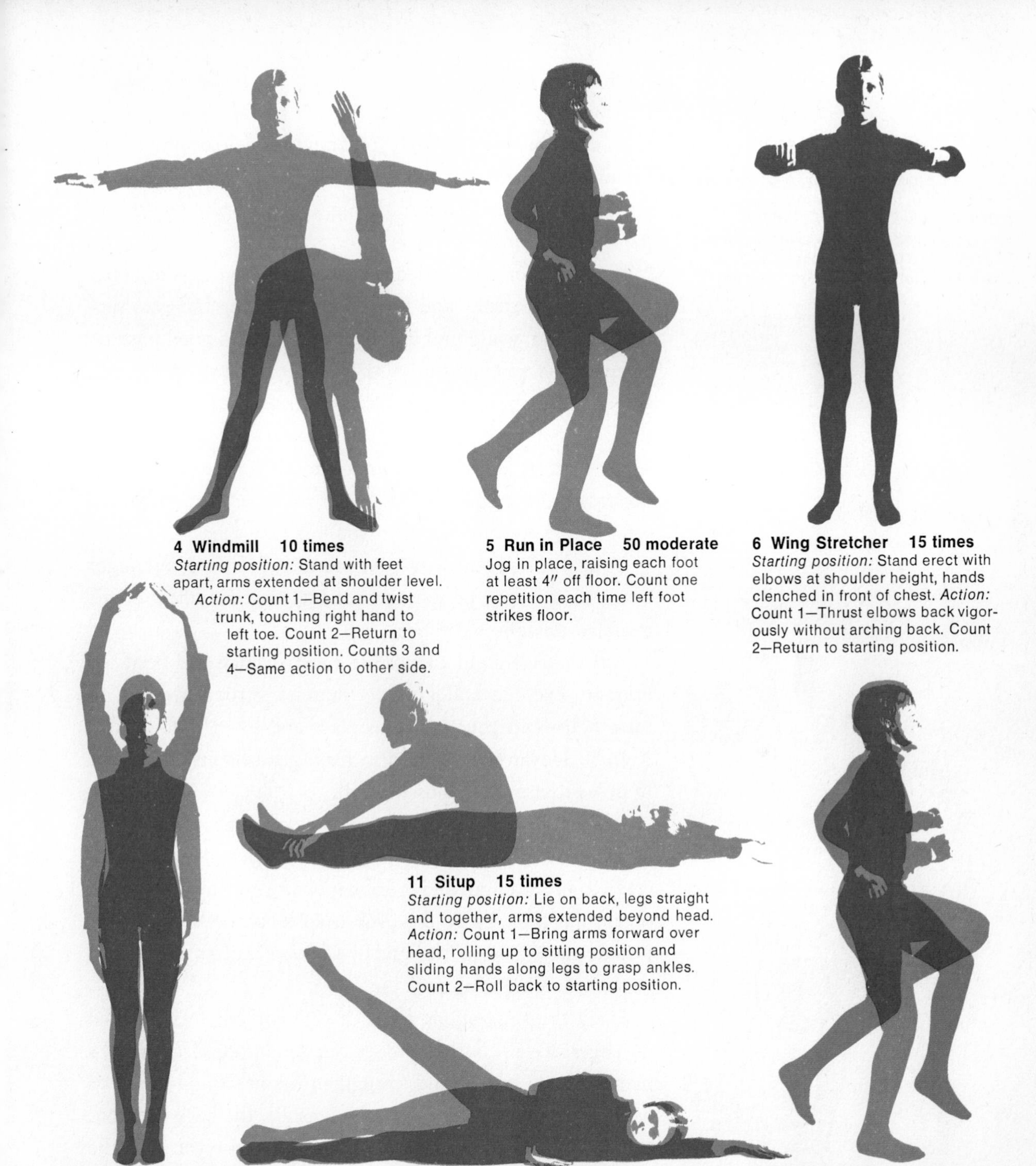

4 Windmill 10 times
Starting position: Stand with feet apart, arms extended at shoulder level. *Action:* Count 1—Bend and twist trunk, touching right hand to left toe. Count 2—Return to starting position. Counts 3 and 4—Same action to other side.

5 Run in Place 50 moderate
Jog in place, raising each foot at least 4″ off floor. Count one repetition each time left foot strikes floor.

6 Wing Stretcher 15 times
Starting position: Stand erect with elbows at shoulder height, hands clenched in front of chest. *Action:* Count 1—Thrust elbows back vigorously without arching back. Count 2—Return to starting position.

11 Situp 15 times
Starting position: Lie on back, legs straight and together, arms extended beyond head. *Action:* Count 1—Bring arms forward over head, rolling up to sitting position and sliding hands along legs to grasp ankles. Count 2—Roll back to starting position.

10 Airlift 10 times
Starting position: Stand erect, feet together, arms at sides. *Action:* Count 1—Lift arms sideward and upward while rising on toes and taking a slow, deep breath. Count 2—Exhale slowly while returning to starting position.

12 Sidewinder 10 each leg
Starting position: Lie on right side, head resting on right arm. *Action:* Count 1—Lift leg as high as possible. Count 2—Lower leg to starting position. Repeat exercise ten times then repeat ten times on other side.

13 Run in Place 50 slow
Jog in place, raising each foot at least 4″ off floor. Count one repetition each time left foot strikes the floor.

"The Basic Workout" from *Vim: A Complete Exercise Plan for Girls 12 to 18 and Vigor: A Complete Exercise Plan for Boys 12 to 18.* Published 1964 by President's Council on Physical Fitness.

Teacher's Notes

Discuss what is usually included in the term *physical fitness.*

If possible, obtain a copy of each of the booklets *Vim: A Complete Exercise Plan for Girls 12 to 18* and *Vigor: A Complete Exercise Plan for Boys 12 to 18.* (For publishing data, see page 27 of the *Resource Book.)* The exercises on pages 26 and 27 are taken from these booklets. The suggestions given are for both boys and girls.

Factors That Affect Posture

Knowing what is involved in good posture and trying to form the habit of using what you know can help improve your posture. You can also try to keep strong and well by following sensible guides for healthful living. *Good posture goes along with good all-around health.*

If you do not get an adequate diet, for instance, your bones will not grow strong and firm. Without strong bones to support you, you would find it difficult to maintain good posture. Sleep affects your posture also. If you constantly fail to get enough sleep, you will feel "droopy" and your posture will show it.

Well-fitting shoes can be an aid to good posture too. It is not easy to have good posture when your feet hurt. What are some things to consider when you buy new shoes?

Your *feelings* can affect your posture at times. How might a very discouraged person move about? A self-confident one?

Exercise, Posture, and Fitness

Any consideration of posture must include the need for exercise. Exercise builds strong muscles. Strong muscles, in turn, help hold your bones in place and so hold your body straight. However, you need to form good habits of balance in order to use these muscles well.

Another benefit of exercise is that of improved physical fitness. Energy needed for physical and mental tasks is increased, and strength and coordination are improved. You can obtain much of the exercise you need by participating in enjoyable games and sports—and by *walking* as often as possible, instead of riding in a car or bus.

Study the suggestions for a "basic workout," as pictured on pages 26–27. Such exercises can condition all the body's major muscle groups and strengthen the heart and lungs, as well as improve posture. For good results, the basic workout should be done at least five times a week. Once you start the exercises, try to continue them without interruption. If you cannot do some of the exercises the number of times called for, do what you can and build up to the recommended number gradually.

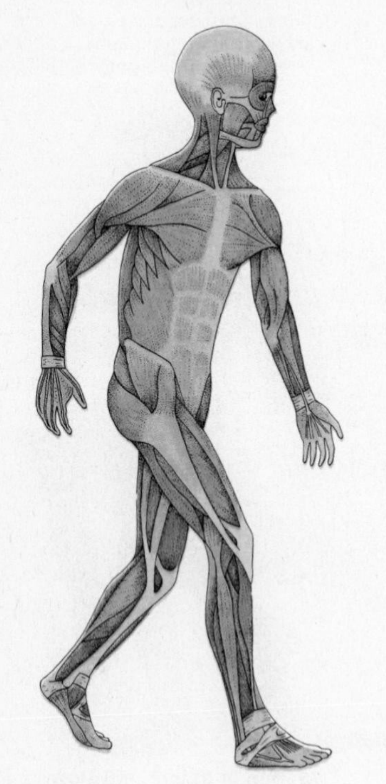

The skeletal muscles cover the skeleton. These muscles, controlled by impulses from the brain, direct the movements of all the bones in the body.

What Can Be Done About Skin Problems?

To understand the skin condition known as *acne,* you need to know first about the structure of your skin. In particular, it is important to know about the increase in activity of certain glands in the skin during the teen years.

The Structure of the Skin

Your skin is arranged in layers. (See the diagram of a cross section of the skin at the right.) The topmost layer is called the *epidermis.* This layer is made up of several rows of cells stacked one on top of the other. The outer row of cells forms a tough protective covering for the body. These tough outer cells of the skin are sometimes called the *horny layer.*

As your skin grows, the cells in the horny layer die and are shed; new ones replace them from below. This shedding usually takes place slowly, but after a sunburn it occurs rapidly and you notice the peeling.

Below the epidermis is the second layer, called the *true skin* or the *dermis.* In it are such structures as blood vessels, nerves, muscles, and glands. You can see in the diagram at the right how some of these different structures would appear if seen through a microscope.

Notice particularly the *oil gland,* or *sebaceous gland.* Oil glands are tiny sacs of oil-filled cells. They are attached to the pits, or *follicles,* from which hairs grow. Oil flows from the oil glands up to the surface of the skin through the *oil ducts.* Some oil glands empty directly onto the surface of the skin.

Below the dermis—and sometimes classed as a part of the dermis—is a layer of connective tissue with many spaces that are filled with fluid and with fat.

Causes of Acne

As you move into your teens, the oil glands in your skin become more active. During this time, they may manufacture much more oil than is needed by the skin.

As you can see in the picture at the right, the oil glands share a common duct with the hair follicles. When too much oil is sent to the surface of the skin, the ducts or their outlets

Teacher's Notes

You might put these true-false statements on the chalkboard and have pupils decide about their correctness. After this, students can study this page and pages 30-31 to verify their ideas.

Acne is 'catching' or contagious. (False)

In acne, there is overactivity of the oil glands. (True)

Blackheads are caused by dirt. (False)

Acne is a common skin disorder, occurring chiefly during the teen years. (True)

Acne appears on the skin where the oil glands are scarce. (False)

Diet, in some individuals, may have an effect on acne. (True)

Acne may be worsened by emotional upsets. (True)

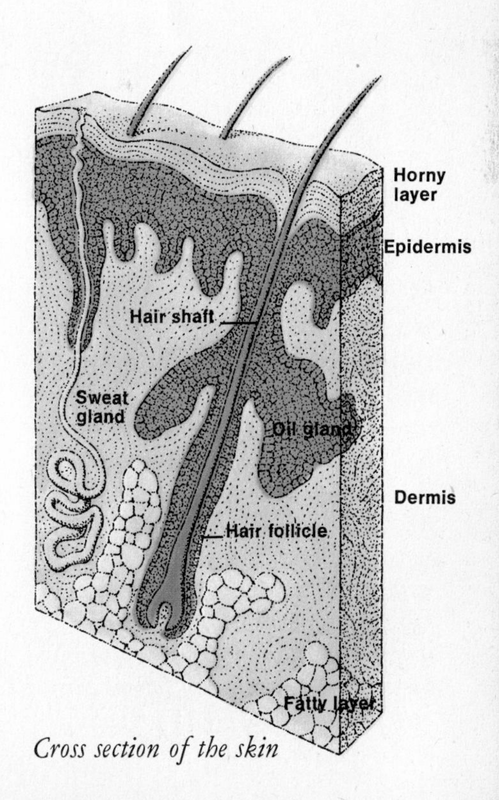

Cross section of the skin

Teacher's Notes

Discuss what causes blackheads and why they darken. Then ask:

"When is it that blackheads become most noticeable?" (When they become swollen, inflamed, and so on.)

List some of the factors that can cause flare-ups of acne in some people. Consider, too, the important way to minimize acne problems, as described on this page. (Wash the face gently many times a day with soap and water to dissolve the oil on the skin and make it drier.)

Do You Know?

What causes chapped skin? Chapping usually occurs in winter when oil glands are less active than they are in warm weather. When skin is not adequately oiled, it gets dry and cracked. Chapping also results when water left on the skin is exposed to cold, dry air and evaporates rapidly. That is why your face and hands should be dried thoroughly before you go out during the winter. Creams and lotions can help prevent chapping by providing needed oil for the skin.

become clogged. Then the oil backs up into the oil glands or their ducts and acne may result. Acne includes *whiteheads, blackheads,* and *pimples.*

Whiteheads are small lumps formed when oil is retained in the oil gland and is not exposed to air on the skin surface. Blackheads are hard plugs of dried oil that protrude from the oil-gland ducts. The dark color of the blackheads is not due to dirt as is commonly believed. Their dark color is due, rather, to a chemical reaction that takes place when the oil plugs are exposed to the air.

Pimples usually begin as a result of irritation and pressure from the plugs of dried oil that block the flow of oil from the oil glands. Bacteria, which are always present on the skin, get in under the plugs and start infections, or pus-pockets known as pimples. Acne may occur on the face, neck, shoulders, and back, where oil glands are most numerous.

Although acne develops as a result of increased chemical activity within the body during the teens, other factors influence it and can cause flare-ups. Thus, anything that reduces general good health—fatigue, insufficient exercise, or infection in the body—may cause new eruptions. There is evidence, too, that excessive perspiration may play a part in acne. Some doctors believe that certain foods and drugs may worsen acne in some people. In some young people, emotional upsets may also cause flare-ups of acne.

Acne is a noncommunicable skin disease. You cannot "catch" it from someone who has it.

How to Care for Acne

There is no short cut to the cure of acne. A doctor can give you the quickest and surest help. In severe cases, a doctor who specializes in skin disorders, called a *dermatologist,* may be consulted to help with the problem.

There are, however, some general suggestions about good skin care and healthful living that will be helpful. Some of these suggestions are given in the material that follows.

Remember that the best methods for keeping acne to a minimum are those that reduce the oiliness and increase the dryness of the skin.

One way to cut down on skin oiliness is to wash the face or other affected areas gently with soap and water—as many as five times a day. The soapy solution helps dissolve the oil and dry the skin. Find a soap that does not irritate your skin.

Avoid eating any foods that seem to make your acne worse. Although acne is not a dietary disease and authorities do not agree on the role of diet in the control of acne, certain foods do seem to worsen acne in some individuals. Foods that are sometimes offenders in individual cases may be chocolate, shellfish, nuts, fried foods, and rich, gooey desserts.

To guard against infection, try not to "pick at" blackheads and pimples and try to avoid squeezing them. Squeezing may spread the infection to neighboring tissues and result in large and painful pimples and eventual scarring.

Some doctors suggest that blackheads be properly removed as an aid in preventing sores. To do this, soften the skin with hot packs—towels soaked in hot water and held against the skin—for fifteen to twenty minutes. Then place the hole of a blackhead remover over each blackhead and use moderate pressure to remove it. Afterwards wash the face with soap and warm water, followed by cold water; then apply rubbing alcohol or witch hazel.

Follow sensible guides for healthful living. Get plenty of sleep, rest, and exercise. Eat an adequate daily diet.

Sunbathing may help dry the skin, but it is wise to start with only a few minutes' exposure daily. Your doctor may recommend a medicated lotion of the type that will help cover up the acne and at the same time have a healing effect on it.

Remember that the teen years are times of new experiences and new emotions. Meeting these new stresses and strains can cause acne to become worse. Try to work through problems that cause upset feelings and to seek counseling help when needed.

Try not to be overly conscious of your appearance. Self-consciousness often results from exaggerated concern over how you appear to others. Others' impressions of you are based not on your skin condition, but on all the qualities that make you *you.*

Teacher's Notes

Some discussion leads are these:

"How might a person determine if a certain food is causing flare-ups of acne?" (A person might note the kinds of foods eaten before the flare-up. If flare-ups repeatedly occur after eating such foods as nuts, shellfish, or chocolate, for instance, he or she might cut down on or eliminate such foods temporarily. The person might then watch to see if this procedure helps prevent an outbreak of acne.)

"What are some sensible guides for the care of acne?"

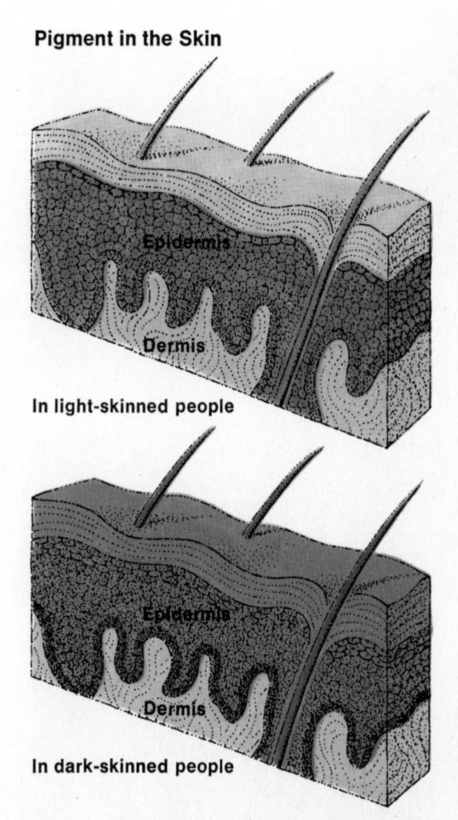

The pigment, *or coloring matter in the epidermis, extends through all layers of the epidermis in dark-skinned people.*

Teacher's Notes

Talk over what is meant by the term *dandruff*, whether or not it is "catching," and how the type most common in the teen years can usually be controlled.

Discuss what causes *warts*, what *not* to do if you have warts, and why no treatment for warts may be needed at all.

During discussion, ask:

"How do *plantar warts* differ from the other kind?"

Have pupils talk over what they have learned about *athlete's foot*.

What Do You Think?

1. Why is it a good idea to wear bathing shoes or sandals instead of going barefoot in locker rooms or around swimming pools?

2. What are some helpful things to do to treat a mild case of athlete's foot?

3. What might lead some people to believe that special "magic" or secret "cures" can get rid of warts?

Dandruff

The frequent shedding of skin scales from the scalp is known as *dandruff*. An overly dry scalp may cause one type of dandruff. For this, it helps to rub a little warmed oil into the scalp an hour or so before you shampoo your hair.

In the kind of dandruff that is most common in the teen years, the scalp is too oily. The dried-up, excess oil and the skin scales form slightly greasy white flakes. You can generally control this kind of dandruff by shampooing the hair frequently, more than once a week or as often as suggested by your doctor. Vigorous hairbrushing is helpful too. Dandruff is not "catching."

Warts

Warts are most common at two periods of life, during the preschool years and again in the teen years. Usually warts appear on the fingers and backs of the hands.

Warts develop as a result of a virus that enters the skin and causes an increase in the number of skin cells. Picking at warts to the point of bleeding can make them spread.

Most warts will disappear without any treatment. They can, however, be removed by a doctor. Warts growing on the sole of the foot are known as *plantar warts*. They can be quite painful and generally have to be removed by a doctor.

Athlete's Foot

A common fungus infection of the feet is *athlete's foot*, or ringworm of the foot. The fungus, or one-celled plant, is often present wherever many people walk barefoot. Moist conditions encourage its growth. For this reason, it is wise to wear your own sandals in swimming-pool and locker-room areas.

Usually athlete's foot is a mild condition that involves itching and some irritation between the toes. In more severe cases, there may be cracks in the skin, blisters, and pus-filled areas.

The same things that help prevent athlete's foot also aid in the treatment of mild cases. Care should be taken to dry the feet thoroughly after bathing or swimming. Foot powder also aids in keeping dry the areas between the toes. Clean socks should be worn daily. In stubborn cases of athlete's foot, a doctor should be consulted.

Dental Checkups

To keep the teeth in good condition, periodic dental checkups are advised—twice a year or as often as the dentist advises. During such checkups the dentist will use instruments to locate any cavities. He will also observe the spacing and condition of the teeth, the health of the gums, and the *occlusion* of the teeth. Occlusion means the way the upper and lower teeth meet when the jaws are closed.

At times the dentist will take X-ray pictures (radiographs). These pictures reveal decay in its early stages, hidden breaks in the teeth, and other conditions that require correction. Dentists are careful to X ray teeth only when necessary, since repeated exposure to X rays may have an effect on growth centers in the teeth.

An important part of the dental checkup involves the cleaning of the teeth by the dentist or by a specially trained assistant who is known as a *dental hygienist.* For cleaning the teeth and removing a hard, yellow substance called *calculus* or *tartar,* a dentifrice containing a grainy paste is used. Calculus can be removed only by the dentist or dental hygienist. Calculus is formed when the plaque on the teeth is not properly removed. *Plaque* is a thin, transparent, sticky layer of harmful bacteria that is constantly being formed on the surfaces of the teeth. Steel instruments called *scalers* may also be used in the removal of calculus. If a cavity is found during the dental checkup, the dentist cleans out the decay so it will not spread into the pulp of the tooth. Then the dentist fills the tooth with silver or other material.

Fluorides and Tooth Decay

In another approach to preventing decay, the dentist may use fluorides to "paint" the surfaces of children's teeth. This topical, or surface, application of fluorides is done at intervals as the dentist sees fit.

Some communities add very small amounts of fluoride to drinking water if fluorides are not already present in the water. Children who drink fluoridated water tend to develop tooth enamel that is harder and therefore more resistant to tooth decay.

Teacher's Notes

Ask students what they could say to someone who doubts that fluoridation of a community's water supply is an effective way to fight tooth decay. Supplement the text treatment on dental research with this information: An experimental liquid-plastic tooth-cavity preventative is being tested on elementary-school children in New York and Montana under a grant from the National Institute of Dental Research. The plastic sealant, if all tests prove favorable, is expected to be useful in helping prevent dental cavities in children. It may also aid handicapped people who cannot brush their teeth and those who do not have access to—or cannot afford—regular dental care.

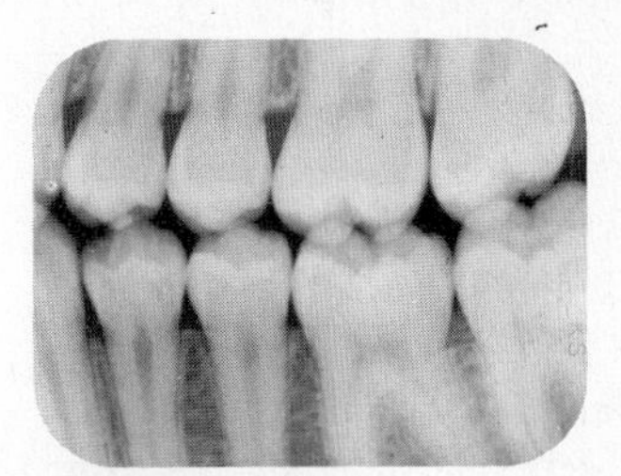

X-ray picture in which no cavity appears

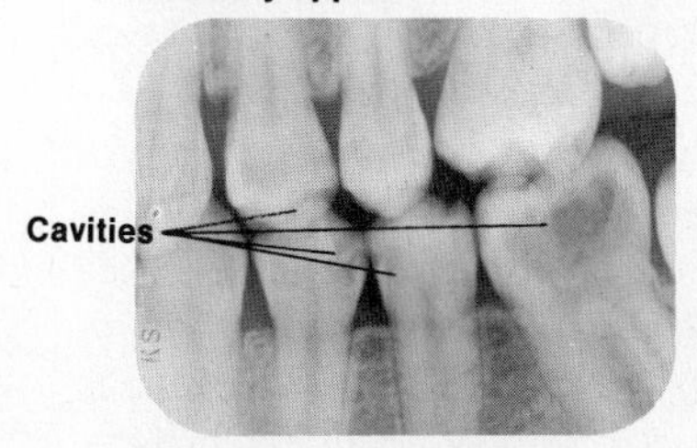

X-ray picture which shows a cavity.

Teacher's Notes

Discuss what is meant by *malocclusion* and what may be some causes of this condition. Then ask:

"What are some reasons why teeth should be properly aligned, if possible?"

Students sometimes ask if the tooth alignment done by an orthodontist lasts "forever." See what information can be found on this page.

Answers to Quiz on Parts of the Tooth

a. Crown—*Part of tooth you can see, the part you chew with*
b. Enamel—*Hard white covering of the crown*
c. Root—*Part or parts of tooth under the gums*
d. Cementum—*Bonelike tissue that covers root*
e. Dentin—*Hard bonelike material under enamel and cementum*
f. Pulp—*Soft mass of tissue in center of tooth*
g. Periodontal membrane—*Cushionlike membrane that lines the tooth socket; it enables the dentist to pull a tooth without injuring the surrounding jawbone.*

Malocclusion

When a person's teeth are poorly aligned so that normal chewing is interfered with or the appearance is affected, the condition is known as *malocclusion.*

Malocclusion may result from hereditary factors, such as the eruption of teeth before the jaw has grown. Or it may result from losing the primary teeth prematurely or from losing one or more of the permanent teeth. For example, when a tooth is removed from one jaw, the opposing tooth from the other jaw receives less pressure and tends to grow outward. Furthermore, the teeth next to the gap left by removal of a tooth tend to drift over to fill the vacant space. (See the drawings on page 37.)

Over the years, unaligned teeth can cause trouble. Malocclusion can lead to faulty nutrition. It is difficult for a person with poorly aligned teeth to chew many of the foods that are essential to good health. Also, tooth decay may result from malocclusion, because poorly aligned teeth are hard to clean.

Poor alignment of teeth can be corrected, however. The branch of dentistry concerned with moving teeth into proper position is known as *orthodontics.* A dentist who specializes in this work is known as an *orthodontist.* Previously, most orthodontic work was begun shortly after the second permanent molars erupted—usually between the ages of eleven and thirteen. Recently, it has been shown that by starting orthodontic care earlier, the teeth can be guided into proper normal position—without waiting for malocclusion to develop.

When the teeth are being aligned, the orthodontist uses gentle pressure by means of wires, bands, tiny springs, and elastic devices to move the teeth into better positions. As a tooth moves, it causes the bone cells it presses against to dissolve, and it allows new bone cells to develop on the opposite side of the tooth. This process is slow, taking from one to three years, because it cannot be accomplished faster than new bone tissue can grow. Even after the positions of teeth have been changed, there is a tendency for the teeth to move back into their former positions unless retaining devices are worn for a period of time.

The drawings below show how poorly aligned teeth can be corrected. The top picture shows poorly aligned teeth, and the bottom picture shows how they were corrected. Some conditions an orthodontist can correct are protruding teeth, overlapping teeth, and widely spaced teeth.

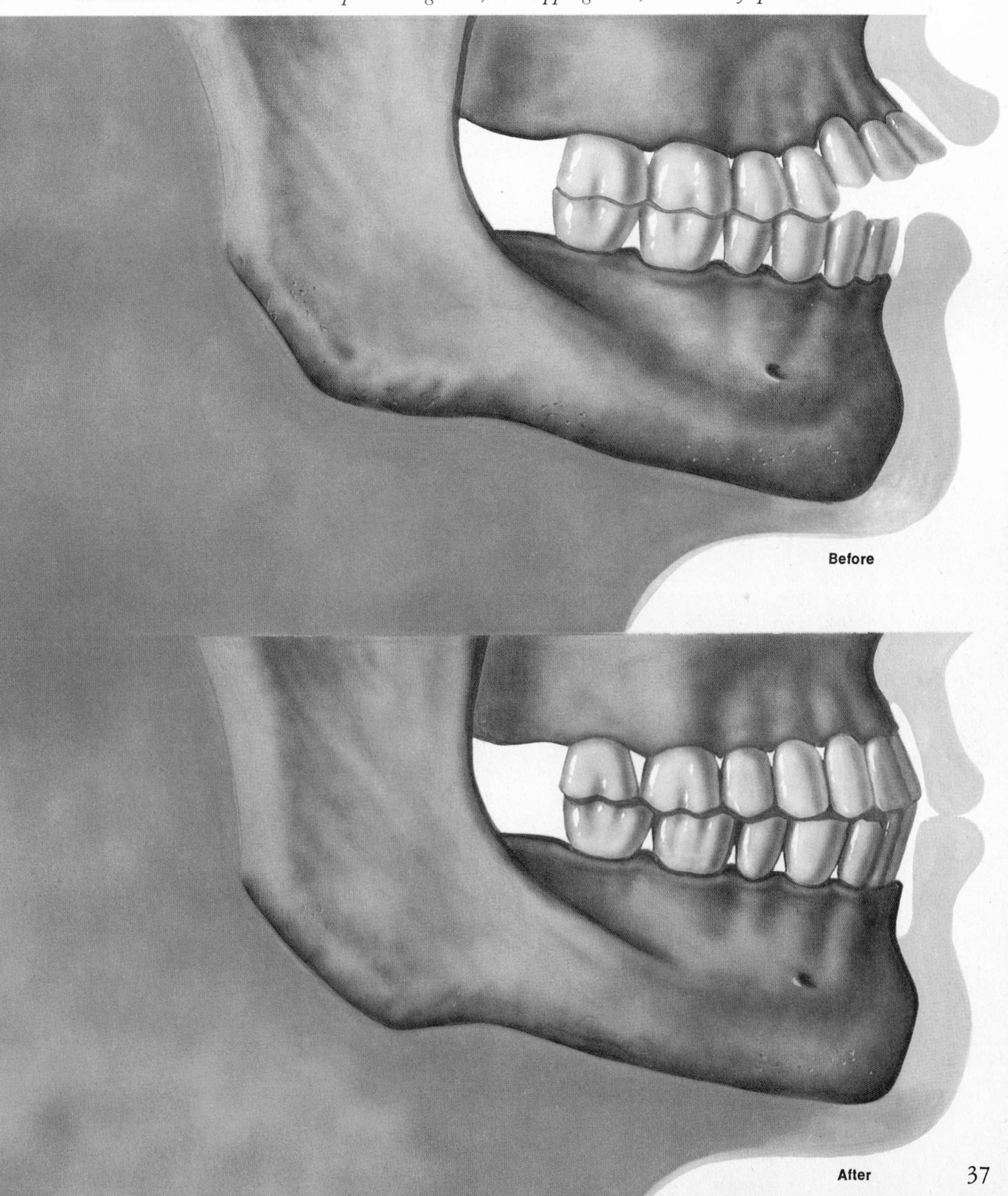

In the drawing on this page and page 39, you can see all the permanent teeth on one side of the jaw.

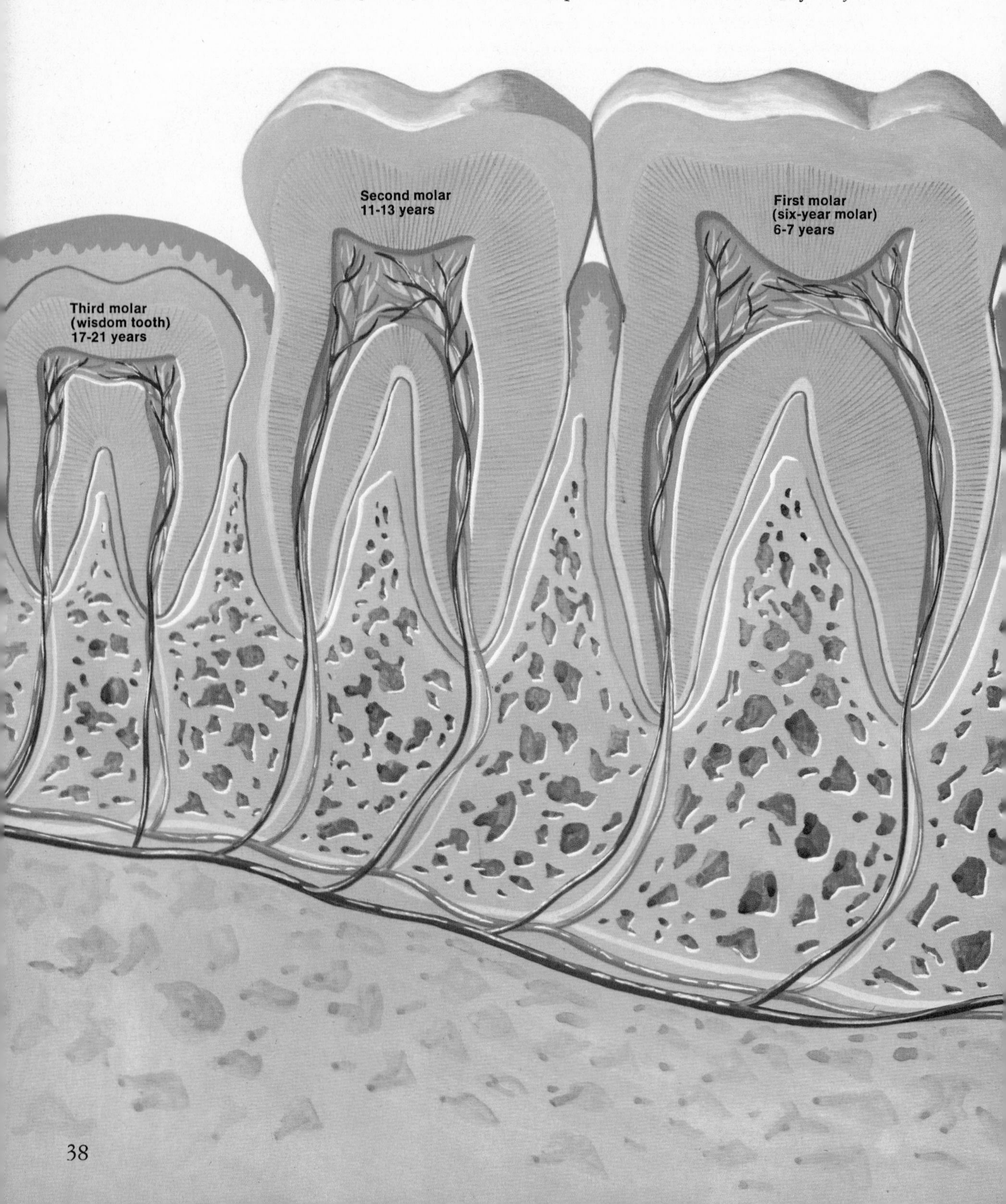

You can also see the ages at which teeth erupt. What teeth come in during ages eleven to thirteen?

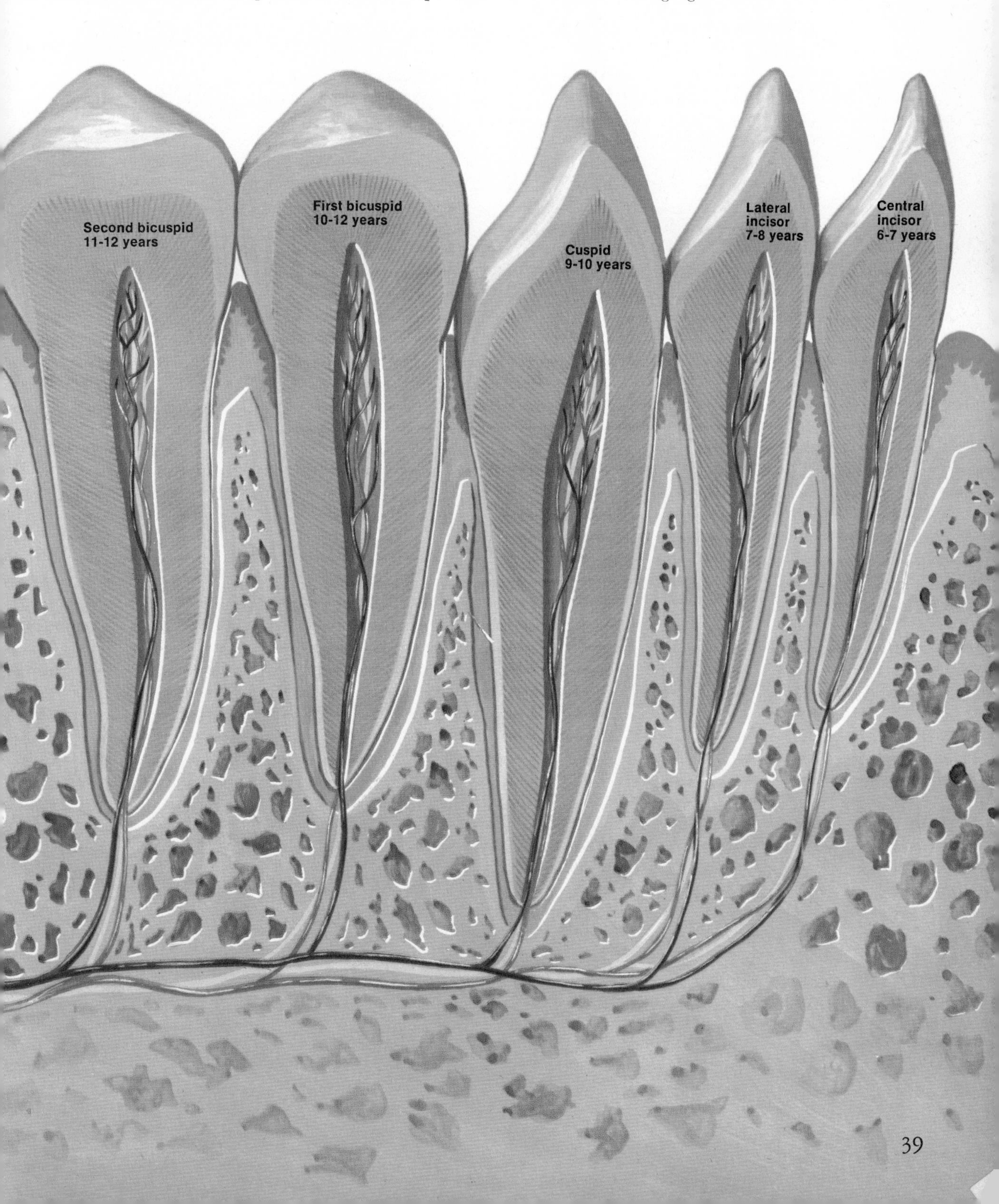

Light passes through the pupil and on through the lens. The lens changes in shape to focus the light on nerve endings in the retina. Nerve impulses are carried from the retina to the brain over the optic nerve. The brain interprets the message—and you see.

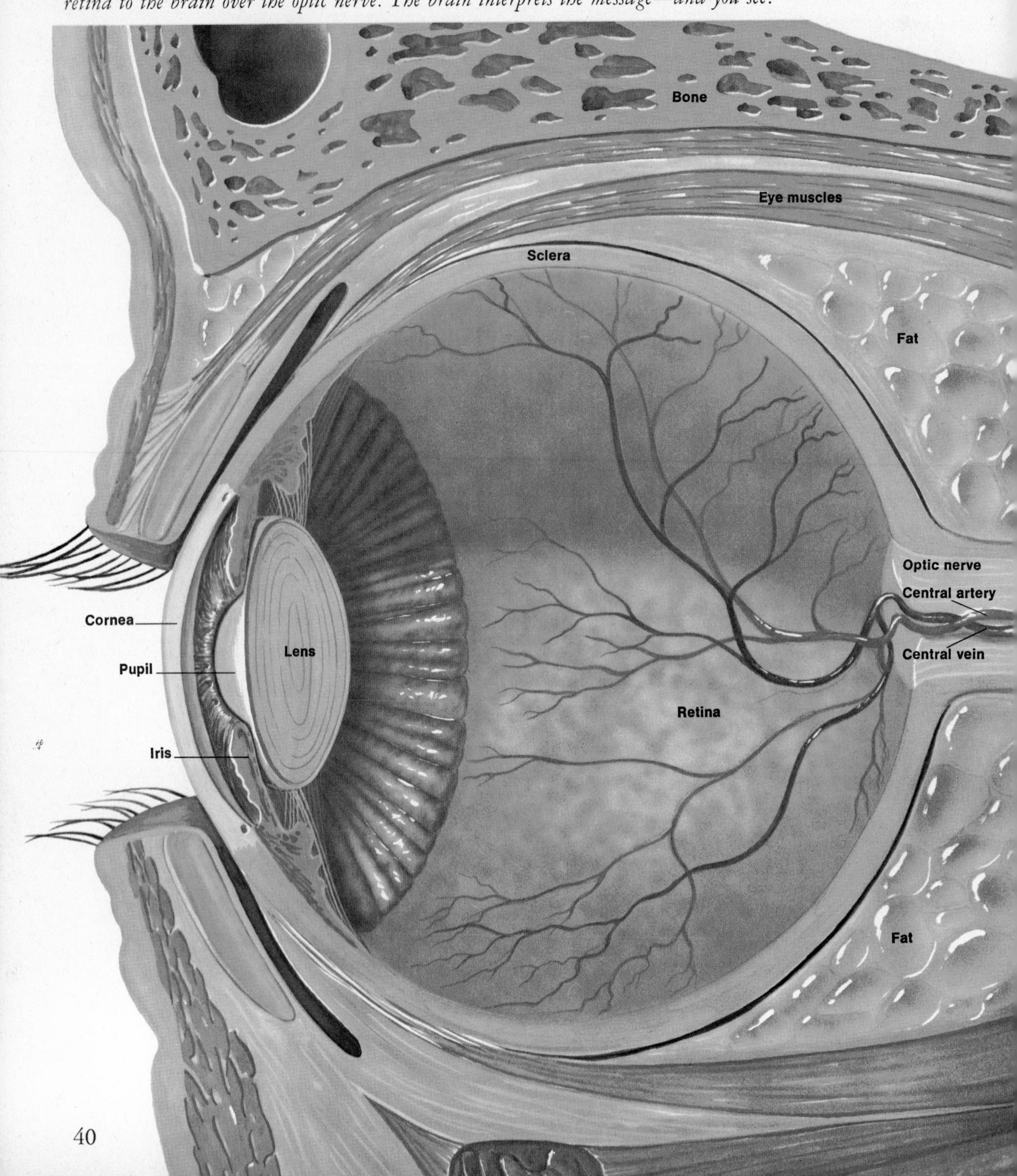

What Causes Near-sightedness and Other Eye Defects?

Teacher's Notes

Many people are confused about *near-sightedness* and *far-sightedness.* See if students can suggest any way to help remember which is which. Discuss what causes near-sightedness, far-sightedness, and astigmatism. How are these difficulties corrected? Ask students what they have learned about contact lenses.

Near-sightedness is much more common than far-sightedness in children and in teen-agers. In *near-sightedness,* the eyeball is too long from front to back. This condition causes the light rays from distant objects to come to a focus in front of the retina—instead of *on* the retina. (See the diagram at the right.) The near-sighted person sees *nearby objects clearly,* but distant objects may appear blurred. Glasses with proper lenses can compensate for this difficulty. For some eye difficulties contact lenses sometimes can be worn in place of glasses. Most contact-lens wearers today are fitted with a very small plastic lens which hugs the cornea. Although some people may have difficulty in adjusting to wearing contact lenses, it is estimated that more than four million people in the United States do wear contacts instead of glasses.

Near-sightedness in the Teen Years

Near-sightedness may become progressively worse during the teen years because the length of the eyeball increases as the eyeball grows. Thus the lenses in glasses may need to be changed each year for several years. However, the degree of near-sightedness generally stops increasing in the later teen years when the eyes have reached their full growth.

Far-sightedness

In *far-sightedness,* the eyeball is too short from front to back, causing light rays from nearby objects to come to a focus behind the retina. (See the diagram at the right.) The far-sighted eye does not see nearby objects well, but it views *distant objects clearly.* However, the eye muscles of some far-sighted persons may be especially effective in helping the eye accommodate to nearby objects. In such cases, the eyesight of these people may be adequate. They may need glasses only for close work to reduce eyestrain. Far-sightedness sometimes decreases or even disappears during the teen years.

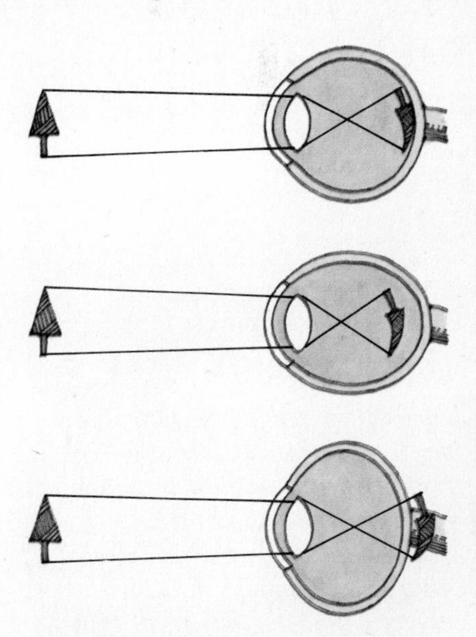

Top. A normal eye
Middle. A near-sighted eye
Bottom. A far-sighted eye

Astigmatism

Another eye defect is *astigmatism.* This difficulty results from irregularities in the surfaces of the *cornea* or the *lens* of

Teacher's Notes

These questions can serve as discussion leads:

"What is the cause of most eye difficulties? How have opinions on this changed over the years?"

"What can *you* do to help care for your eyes?"

the eye. (Can you find the cornea in the illustration of the eye on page 40?) Because light rays cannot focus sharply on the retina, vision is blurred. Astigmatism, however, can be corrected with proper lenses. It is interesting to note that a person may be near-sighted—or far-sighted—and also have an astigmatism.

Causes of Eye Difficulties

Why does a person become near-sighted or far-sighted or astigmatic? In the past, these various defects were blamed chiefly on poor reading habits—habits such as reading for extended periods, reading too-small print, or reading in poor light or position. However, *ophthalmologists,* or physicians who specialize in the care of the eyes, now believe that eye defects are generally hereditary. Thus a person is born with a tendency to become near-sighted, far-sighted, or astigmatic.

Taking Care of Your Eyes

While you cannot alter these hereditary tendencies, you *can* give your eyes proper care and protection. For example, you can seek help in getting corrective glasses or contact lenses when needed. You can also prevent eye accidents, such as those resulting from careless play with sharp sticks, knives, or darts. You can protect your eyes from too much sun or glare by wearing sunglasses. In the event of eye injury, consult an ophthalmologist at once. Medical care is also important if there is any evidence of an eye infection, such as inflamed or watery eyes.

Remember, too, that vision may change during the teen years when the eyeballs are still growing. Because of this, the eyes should be tested each year.

A precaution you can take to prevent eyestrain is to form good habits for viewing television. For example, adjust the set properly so the picture is bright and clear. Do not view television in a dark room; keep a dim light on to avoid sharp contrasts, which make it more difficult for the eyes to adjust. View the screen as nearly from the front as possible and at eye level, or just below. Sit about ten to twelve feet away from the television set. Schedule intervals of rest from periods of television viewing.

Do You Know?

Apart from causing eye fatigue, too much television may keep a person from wholesome outdoor activities, may interfere with his homework, and may keep him from developing satisfying friendships. Excessive weight gains, too, may result from lack of proper exercise—and from the habit of eating continually while watching television.

How Much Sleep Is Needed?

Generally, young people in the teen years need from nine to ten hours of sleep each night. However, sleep needs differ with each individual. Thus *you* may need a little more or a little less sleep than that. The amount of sleep you need also varies somewhat according to your activities during the day.

How can you tell if you are getting enough sleep? A simple test is to check to see if you feel rested and reasonably good-natured during the day. Do not, however, judge by the first hour after you wake up. It is quite normal to feel sleepy then. If the sleepy feeling does not disappear within an hour or so after you are up and around, you have a clue that you probably need more sleep.

Importance of Sleep

Adequate sleep is necessary if a person wants to keep *mentally alert* and to carry on efficiently the kind of work that requires thinking and concentration. Experiments have shown that insufficient sleep causes attention to wander and increases the tendency to make mistakes.

A *good disposition* is fostered by getting the sleep you need. Unpleasantness, irritability, and grouchiness go hand in hand with insufficient sleep.

You can avoid undesirable physical symptoms that often accompany inadequate sleep over a long period. Some of these symptoms are *poor skin color, drowsiness, fatigue, dizziness, poor posture,* and *impaired muscle coordination.*

Energy is conserved, since many body processes slow down during sleep. Although the body rests, the brain continues to be active. In sleep, some parts of the brain are quite active and others are less active. The brain never shuts down completely during sleep. The number of heartbeats is reduced, and the heart gets a chance to relax. Breathing is slowed, and the blood pressure is lowered.

Sleep is important to young people for another reason: In the growing-up years, large amounts of the growth hormone, necessary for proper growth, are secreted from the pituitary gland during sleep.

Teacher's Notes

Discuss individual differences in sleep needs and the importance of sleep. Students often ask, "What makes you go to sleep?" Scientists are still studying this question—and they feel there is much yet to be learned.

We provide good conditions for sleep when we lie down and close our eyes in darkened surroundings. Lying down allows the skeletal muscles of the body to relax; closing the eyes in a darkened room puts them at rest; and quiet surroundings prevent distraction and allow the ears to rest. A peaceful state of mind also promotes sleep.

Do You Know?

1. Are you aware of these interesting facts about sleep?

A third of your life is spent in sleep.

A person can survive starvation for over three weeks, but three weeks' loss of sleep will make him or her act like one who is mentally ill.

2. Why do you think athletes are encouraged to get adequate sleep?

Teacher's Notes

Talk over the advantages of "pacing" oneself—interspersing periods of strenuous or sustained activity with periods of rest and relaxation. Consider the values of hobbies as aids to relaxation. Discuss some of the hobbies that members of the group have. Ask:

"What are some of the various causes of fatigue?"

"What might a person do who feels fatigued most of the time from 'doing too much'?" (Evaluate and perhaps revise some of his scheduled activities. Have a physical checkup if fatigue persists.)

Do You Know?

Following are some causes for constant fatigue:

Overweight—*which puts a strain on the body.*

Lack of exercise—*which hinders the flow of fresh blood through the body and renewal of the zest for living.*

Inadequate diet or use of an unwise diet plan—*which neglects the body's energy needs.*

The presence of infection in the body, a disease such as diabetes or decayed teeth—*which necessitates the help of a physician or a dentist.*

Rest and Relaxation

Of course, you not only need to get sufficient sleep at night, you also need to rest or relax from time to time during each day. Short periods of rest and relaxation give your heart a chance to slow down and can keep you from getting overtired.

In addition to feeling better, you can usually work better if you stop to rest or relax now and then. If, for example, you are doing homework, practicing on a musical instrument, or helping clean house, you may keep going steadily until the job is done. If the job takes too long, fatigue may eventually interfere with the quality of your work.

When you get overtired, your brain and your muscles do not work so well and you do not accomplish as much as when you are rested. That is why, in strenuous games like basketball and football, regular rest periods are given the players. That is also why rest breaks are helpful in offices, in factories, and in plants of various kinds. Sitting around lazily, talking with friends, reading a book or magazine, and listening to music are all good ways of relaxing after you have been especially active.

Some Causes of Fatigue

Almost every young person has *occasional* times when he feels "too tired to move." This is not surprising when you consider how much energy is being used just for growing. Occasional fatigue may also be the result of vigorous physical activity. When you get tired after exercising for a while, your body is signaling that a period of rest is needed to build up a new supply of energy. Generally, though, the tired feeling that comes after a sensible amount of exercise is a good feeling, because your body relaxes. Furthermore, your appetite is stimulated, you sleep well at night, and you wake up refreshed the next morning.

Some young people try to carry a schedule that is too heavy. On top of school studies and homework, they pile club activities, athletics, and so on. These young people may often feel fatigued. Young people who "overload" themselves need to remember that it is important to learn to make wise choices and to plan one's time sensibly.

Why Does the Voice Change During the Teen Years?

For a period during the teen years the voice—especially that of boys—becomes somewhat unreliable. One minute a boy's voice may be deep like a man's voice; the next it may be high like a child's. The larynx and vocal cords are undergoing their growth spurt. The larynx drops to a lowered position in the throat, and the vocal cords begin to lengthen. Because the larynx is not used to its new position, it sometimes moves upward again, causing an occasional break or crack in the voice. As the vocal cords increase in length, the boy's voice begins to take on the deeper quality of a man's voice.

As in all other aspects of growth, there is considerable variation in the time when a boy's voice changes. It may change as early as age thirteen, or not until sixteen or so.

A girl's voice changes, too, while her vocal cords and larynx are growing; but since they do not grow so much or so fast as a boy's, the change in her voice is not so noticeable—except that it becomes lower and richer.

What Can Be Done About Bad Breath?

Bad breath or *halitosis* is not nearly so common among teenagers as some ads for mouthwashes and dentifrices would suggest. Once in a while, there may be breath odors due to strong-smelling foods that have been eaten, such as onions and garlic. These foods contain certain aromatic substances that are absorbed into the blood and are given off from the lungs in breathing.

Other causes of bad breath have to do with bacteria found in the mouth or digestive tract. An infection in the mouth, throat, or nasal cavity may lead to breath odors, as may decayed teeth or digestive upsets.

Frequent brushing and rinsing of the teeth are the most effective ways of keeping the mouth clean and reducing breath odors. Lozenges and products containing chlorophyll may prove helpful, too. If a person persistently has bad breath, he should seek a physician's help.

Teacher's Notes

You might share with students this explanation of how the vocal apparatus works. The voice is controlled by nerves leading from the speech center of the brain. Muscles attached to the wall of the larynx regulate the tenseness of the vocal cords. When you speak, the nerves in the larynx cause these muscles to tighten the vocal cords and draw them close together. The rush of air coming out of the lungs causes the vocal cords to vibrate and make sound. When you whisper, you do not use your voice; the vocal cords do not vibrate. The whispering sound is made as the lips, tongue, and other organs of the mouth partly shut off the flow of air from the lungs.

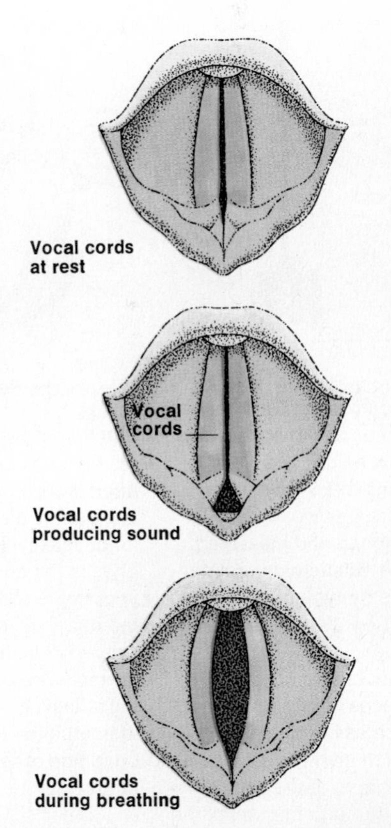

The voice box, when seen from above, shows how the vocal cords look when you are at rest, when you are producing sound, and when you are breathing.

Teacher's Notes
Discussion of what the doctor does during a health examination and why he or she does it may be supplemented by consideration of how to choose a doctor. (See page 98 of this book.)

Why Are Health Checkups Needed?

There are a number of good reasons why periodic health examinations are valuable. Of chief importance is the fact that such examinations often help the doctor find minor troubles. Then he or she can do something about these minor ailments before they become serious.

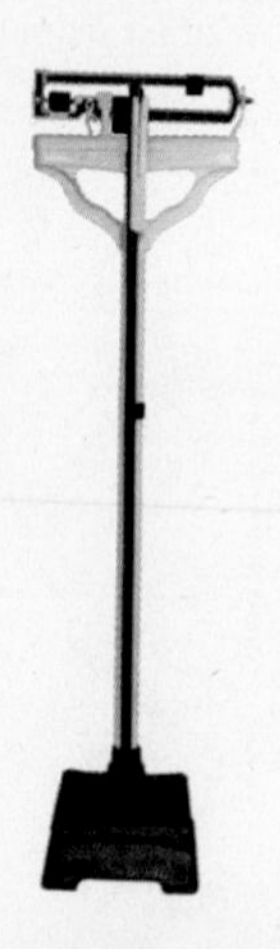

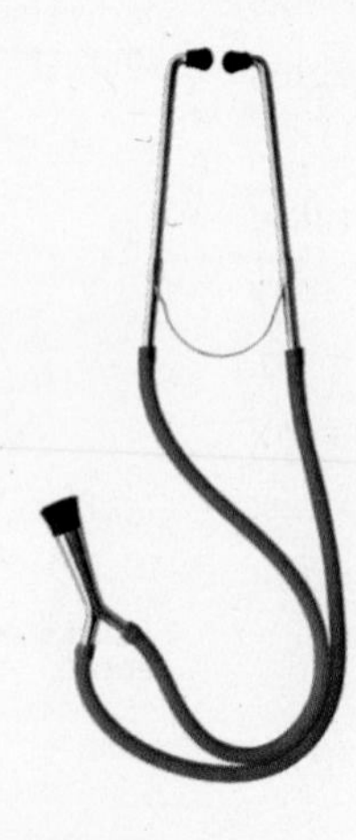

Checks Height, Weight, and Physical Development
The doctor checks to see what height and weight gains there have been since you were last weighed and measured. This will help determine whether you are growing in the way that is right for you.
The doctor notes evidences of any difficulty such as hernia (rupture) which involves a tissue or an organ of the body bulging through the wall of the cavity that should hold it. The doctor also notes the state of development of the reproductive organs.

Checks the Heart and Lungs
The doctor uses the stethoscope and taps the back and chest to listen to the sounds the heart and lungs make. He or she checks the condition of your heart and lungs: Are the heart valves working properly? Is the heartbeat normal? Are there wheezing sounds or other sounds indicating an abnormal condition of the heart or lungs?

Observes Posture
The doctor notes posture, since it gives some clues about general health. He or she searches, in the event of poor posture, for possible causes such as inadequate nutrition, lack of proper sleep or exercise, or bone deformities.

Checks Eyes, Ears, Nose, and Throat
The doctor studies the retina of the eye for early signs of such diseases as diabetes, which may be revealed by the retina's blood vessels. The doctor looks for signs of disease or chronic infection in the eyes, ears, nose, and throat. He or she also checks to see if the eardrums are unbroken and to see if there are accumulations of wax that need to be removed.

When the doctor sees you periodically, he or she is better able to check your physical development and to answer questions you may have. The doctor is also better able to help you if you become ill later—since much information will be at hand about you. For young people your age, an annual checkup is desirable, if possible. The chart on these two pages describes what a doctor does in a health checkup and why these steps are taken.

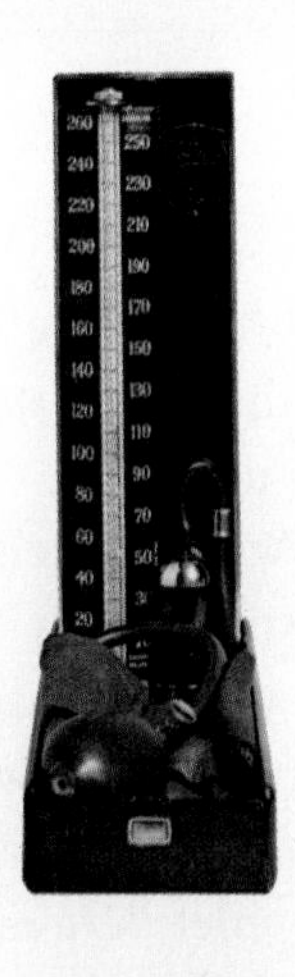

Takes Blood Pressure
The doctor checks the blood pressure at full force of heart's beating (systolic blood pressure)—and at time heart is filling up with blood (diastolic blood pressure)—to see if these pressures fall within normal ranges.

Sends Blood Sample to Laboratory for Tests
The doctor finds out, by blood counts made in a laboratory, if there are sufficient red blood cells in the blood. (A low number of red blood cells may indicate some form of anemia.) He or she looks to see if the white-cell count is normal. (A high white-cell count is a warning that there may be an infection in the body.) The doctor also gets other needed information from various blood tests.

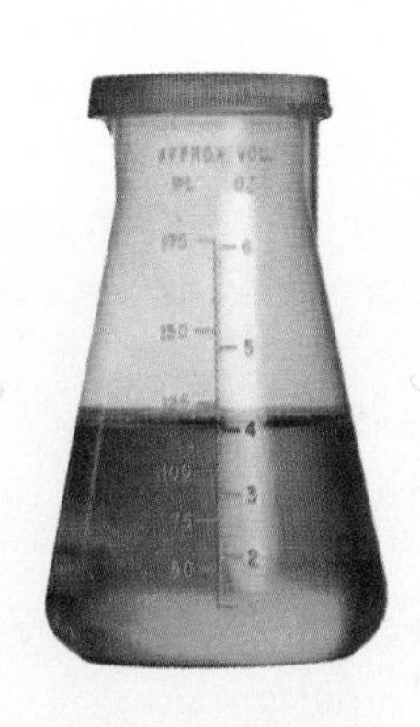

Tests Urine or Sends a Sample to a Laboratory
From the test of the urine, called a urinalysis, the doctor notes how well the kidneys are performing their work of helping remove wastes from the body and of regulating the chemical make-up of the blood.

Checks Immunization Record and Gives Booster Shots
The doctor checks immunization record to be sure you are properly protected against such diseases as tetanus, polio, measles, rubella (German measles), and diphtheria. (See the Immunization Timetable on page 208. For which of these diseases have you been immunized? Is your immunization program up to date? If you don't know, how might you find out?)

Teacher's Notes
Check Yourself: After students have read and thought about these questions, use them as guides for a summary discussion.
Things to Do: Take time to look over the Contents Page of the book and to consider which other units may contain answers to health questions of concern to teen-agers.

Check Yourself

1. Look back at the questions on page 8. How would you answer them now?

2. Is a person's height at age thirteen necessarily an accurate indication of his or her eventual height? Explain.

3. What have you learned about how girls grow during the teen years? About how boys grow during these years?

4. Why is some awkwardness fairly common during the years of rapid growing?

5. Explain the statement: "Often people's *feelings* about growth cause great anxiety."

6. What connection is there between posture and fatigue?

7. What are some things a person can do to help minimize acne problems?

8. How can diet affect the teeth?

9. What is meant by these terms?

a. fluoridation	d. dental hygienist
b. occlusion	e. tartar or calculus
c. malocclusion	f. orthodontist

10. What is meant by near-sightedness? Far-sightedness? Astigmatism?

11. How do you know if you are getting the amount of sleep that is right for you?

12. What is one good reason for having regular health checkups by a doctor?

Things to Do

1. Look for some ads about acne, athlete's foot, dandruff, and bad breath (halitosis). Evaluate the statements in the ads in the light of information found in this unit.

2. Examine your shoes. Are the heels worn unevenly? Are the soles worn unevenly? What clues do you get about how you are walking?

3. A member of your group might write to the American Dental Association (Chicago, Illinois 60611) for the pamphlet *Between You and Me... Is Your Smile.*

Special Research

1. Do some reading about sleep and dreams and then prepare a report for your group. One book you may find useful is *Sleep: The Mysterious Third of Your Life* by Marianna and Jonathan Kastner (Harcourt).

2. Investigate what is being done in the way of automated multitesting laboratories as aids in periodic health checkups. One source of such information is the booklet *From Head to Toe* published by the U.S. Public Health Service, Publication No. 1808. This can be obtained from the U.S. Government Printing Office, Public Documents Distribution Center, 5801 Tabor Avenue, Philadelphia, Pa. 19120.

Teacher's Notes

Pupils may work independently on this review of the unit. Encourage them to reread material in the text when necessary. Tell pupils that any sensible answer which completes the sentence correctly can be considered a "right answer."

Self-Help Review

Use a ruler or a strip of paper to cover the answer column at the right. Read the first item and write the missing word or words on a piece of paper. Then move your ruler or paper strip down to uncover the answer and see if you are right. Go on in the same way with each of the other items. Do not write in this book.

The numbers by the answers show the pages in this book that give information about the subject. For the items you miss, go back and review this information.

1. A doctor who specializes in skin problems is called a ______.	dermatologist 30
2. Girls tend to start the teen-age growth spurt ______ than do boys.	earlier 10
3. The ______ gland produces the growth hormone.	pituitary 13
4. When a person becomes excited or fearful, the ______ glands pour out more than the usual amount of ______.	adrenal 16 adrenalin
5. A boy or girl who is overweight generally needs lots of ______ to cause the body to burn up the food that is eaten.	exercise 23 (activity)
6. In good posture, the body is "in ______."	balance 24
7. In acne, the ______ glands and their ducts become clogged and inflamed.	oil 30
8. Sugars and starches in foods you eat and ______ in the mouth are causes of tooth decay.	bacteria 33

Teacher's Notes

After pupils have taken the test and their papers have been scored, the test items can serve as guides for summary discussion.

Health Test for Unit One

Part I

Copy the following unfinished sentences, completing each blank correctly.

1. The **pituitary** gland produces the hormone that directs and regulates growth.

2. Another name for tooth decay is dental **caries**.

3. A dentist who specializes in properly aligning teeth is called an **orthodontist**.

4. The near-sighted person sees **nearby** objects clearly.

5. An ophthalmologist is a doctor who is a specialist in the care of the **eyes**.

Part II

Copy each number on a piece of paper. After the number write the correct answer, *true* or *false*.

F 6. The term *average weight* indicates the correct weight for a person of a given age.

T 7. The secretions of the endocrine glands go directly into the bloodstream.

T 8. Exercise can play an important part in weight control.

F 9. Dandruff is a communicable disease.

F 10. Blackheads in acne are caused by dirt.

F 11. Athlete's foot comes from taking part in too many sports.

T 12. Warts have been known to disappear without any treatment.

F 13. The hard outside coat of a tooth is known as the pulp.

F 14. A boy's voice changes because his lungs grow and need more air.

F 15. You should consult a doctor only when you are ill.

T 16. Energy is conserved during sleep because many body processes slow down.

T 17. Sweets are a factor in tooth decay.

T 18. Viewing television in a dark room tires the eyes.

F 19. Teen-age boys begin their growth spurt before girls their age do.

T 20. Feelings can affect posture.

T 21. Acne is a noncommunicable disease.

T 22. Fluoridation of a community's water supplies can help reduce dental decay.

F 23. When you are going to lift a heavy box, be sure to bend over to pick it up.

T 24. Frequent washing of the skin with soap and water can help in the care of acne.

T 25. X rays of teeth are taken as a means of treating tooth decay.

Number of Answers	25
Number Right	______
Score (Number Right × 4)	______

2 What Are the Facts About Drug Abuse, Alcohol, and Smoking?

Teacher's Notes

Unit Overview: In the discussion of the message on this page, be sure to emphasize that wise personal decisions about the use of drugs, alcohol, and tobacco can be made only insofar as the individual has at hand accurate and current information on such substances. Remind students to use the Glossary.

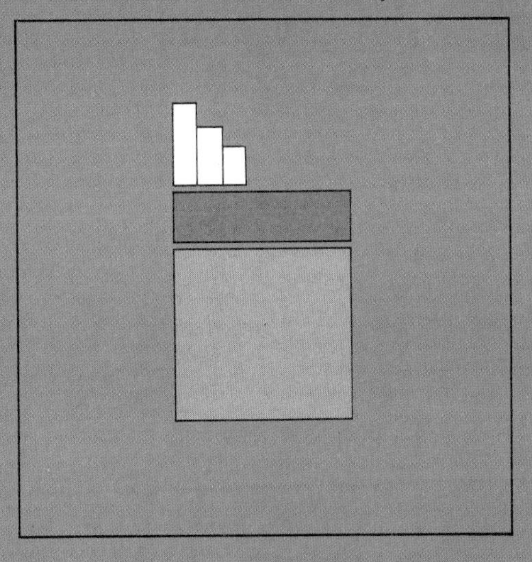

Today there is a wealth of information available about the nature of drugs, about alcohol, about tobacco—and about the effects of these substances on people who use them. Summaries of such information are provided in this unit.

You will want to consider these scientific findings as you build your patterns for living and as you make decisions about the use of alcohol, of tobacco, and of drugs that have a potential for abuse.

Teacher's Notes

Read to Find Out: Discuss these queries briefly—just long enough to give pupils a chance to commit themselves to some answers. Such commitment helps hold students' attention during the unit; they will want to check their tentative answers.

What Drugs Are Often Abused? Talk over some of the beneficial uses of drugs as well as ways in which drugs can be abused.

Stress the difference between *over-the-counter drugs* and *prescription drugs.* (The former can be bought without a doctor's prescription and are intended for minor illnesses and for short-term use; the latter can be purchased legally only with a doctor's prescription.)

Read to Find Out

1. *What are some benefits of drugs when they are properly used?*
2. *What are some examples of* drug abuse?
3. *What is the difference between a* stimulant drug *and a* depressant, *or* sedative, drug?
4. *What is meant by the term* hallucinogenic?
5. *What are some special dangers of* LSD?
6. *What is known at present about the effects of* marijuana?
7. *What does it mean to be* dependent *on a drug?*
8. *What are the medical uses of* narcotics? *What are the dangers of abuse of narcotics?*
9. *How do* alcoholic drinks *affect the nervous system?*
10. *How can* cigarette smoking *affect people's health?*

What Drugs Are Often Abused?

Drugs are chemicals that act on the body's chemistry. Sometimes, as in the case of insulin, drugs replace chemicals the body is not producing for itself. Often drugs help fight infections or improve body functions by speeding up or slowing down the activity of the glands and organs. Drugs of these kinds are bought on the written order of a physician and are called *prescription drugs.* Such drugs can promote and preserve health when they are taken exactly as prescribed. Likewise, the drugs called *nonprescription,* or *over-the-counter, drugs* can be helpful when used as directed on the labels.

On the other hand, drugs can be misused, or *abused.* Drug abuse occurs when people do not follow the directions for the proper use of a given drug. Drug abuse also takes place when people use drugs for purposes other than treating a particular medical condition. For example, a drug abuser is a person who takes a drug for such purposes as for "kicks," for experimentation, to escape a troublesome problem, or to do what others in the group are doing.

Something to Do

Look in the school or public library for such books on drugs and drug abuse as these:

Elgin, Kathleen, and Osterritter, John F. The Ups and Downs of Drugs *(Knopf).*

Greenberg, Harvey R., M.D. What You Should Know About Drugs and Drug Abuse *(Scholastic).*

Houser, Norman W. Drugs: Facts on Their Use and Abuse *(Scott, Foresman).*

Navarra, John Gabriel. Drugs and Man *(Doubleday).*

Drugs, when abused, can injure vital parts of the body, including the liver, kidneys, heart, or brain. Abuse of certain drugs can also lead to a dependence on the drugs. You will learn more about drug dependence later in this unit. The kinds of drugs most often abused are *stimulants, depressants* (sedatives), and *hallucinogens.* In so grouping the drugs, however, it is well to remember that there are many differences among the drugs in each group.

Teacher's Notes

Call students' attention to the source of the information on stimulant and depressant, or sedative, drugs—as indicated in the footnote. Young people, generally speaking, respect authoritative knowledge on any subject. Vague treatments, on the other hand, may arouse suspicion about the accuracy of whatever data is being presented. Discuss kinds of drugs often abused, effects of proper and improper use of stimulants on a user's mood, and some common nicknames for stimulant drugs.

Stimulant Drugs[1]

Stimulants are drugs, usually *amphetamines,* that stimulate, or *speed up,* the work of the central nervous system. They are best known for their ability to combat fatigue and sleepiness. These drugs are also sometimes used to curb the appetite in medically supervised weight-reduction programs. Because stimulants speed up the nervous system, they are often called "uppers"—as opposed to depressant drugs which slow down the work of the nervous system and are known as "downers."

Some of the most commonly used stimulants are known by the trade names Benzedrine, Dexedrine, and Methedrine. Nicknames frequently used by people who abuse these drugs include "bennies," "dexies," "pep pills," "wake-ups," "eye-openers," "drivers," "copilots," and "A's." Slang terms for Methedrine, in particular, are "speed" and "meth."

Effect on Mood

When properly prescribed by a physician, moderate doses of a stimulant drug can check fatigue and produce feelings of alertness, self-confidence, and well-being. In some people, this is followed by a letdown feeling, or depression hangover. Heavier doses cause shakiness, irritability, unclear speech, and tension. Abusers who are regularly taking large doses of stimulant drugs appear withdrawn, their emotions are dulled, and they seem unable to organize their thinking.

Physical Effects

Scientists have found that stimulant drugs introduced into the body trigger the release of a substance stored in nerve

Some Things to Do

1. Watch for programs or commercials on radio and television —and advertisements in newspapers and magazines—that are designed to educate people about the dangers of drug abuse. Be ready to report on the points that are made.

2. Discuss the role of a person's values and goals in influencing his decisions about drug misuse.

---

[1]The material on stimulant drugs and on depressant, or sedative, drugs is adapted from these pamphlets: *Stimulants—Some Questions and Answers,* Public Health Service Publication No. 2097, and *Sedatives—Some Questions and Answers,* Public Health Service Publication No. 2098. Adapted by permission.

Teacher's Notes
Point out that *norepinephrine* is the name of the substance that is stored in nerve endings. Stimulant drugs cause it to be released and to be sent to the higher centers of the brain.
Discuss how stimulants affect the body, what common medical uses they have, and what the term *black market* means. See if students have heard other terms for drug peddlers or pushers, for example, *junkies, dealers,* and *travel agents.*

endings. This substance then concentrates in the higher centers of the brain. As a result, the heart action is quickened and metabolism is speeded up. (*Metabolism* is the body's process for converting food into the chemicals it needs.)

Stimulant drugs also dull the appetite, raise the blood pressure, increase the heart rate, produce palpitations (throbbing heart), cause rapid breathing, and dilate the pupils of the eyes. Abusers may also experience dryness of the mouth, sweating, trembling, sleeplessness, headache, and diarrhea.

Medical Uses of Stimulants

Stimulants were first used as a treatment for colds. These drugs shrink the membranes in the nose and give temporary relief for "stuffy" heads. Nowadays, more-effective drugs with fewer side effects are being used for this purpose. Stimulants are today mainly prescribed for narcolepsy (overwhelming attacks of sleep during normal waking hours), for depression, and for weight control. Use of these drugs for overweight or for any other purpose is advisable only under the close supervision of a physician, because stimulants can produce unwanted reactions. These drugs are too risky for self-medication.

Abuse of Stimulant Drugs

The Food and Drug Administration (FDA) reports that about half the supply of stimulant drugs made by drug manufacturers enters illegal channels, for nonprescribed use. Stimulant drugs are also produced in black-market laboratories, or laboratories not under the supervision of the Food and Drug Administration. Individuals who use drugs produced by black-market manufacturers get the drugs from illegal sources such as drug peddlers or pushers.

Something to Think About

The use of a stimulant drug does not magically do away with fatigue—it merely permits the body to use energy reserves that may suddenly and without warning be exhausted. When the effects of the drug wear off, the body may be in a state of near collapse and the mind may black out. Under what conditions could such a blackout be very dangerous?

Stimulant drugs are misused or abused by people of different ages and walks of life—from the middle-aged businessmen or housewives to truck drivers, students, and athletes. Truck drivers may take them to stay awake on long trips. Students may take them while cramming for exams. Even athletes may take them to pep them up before a game, although sports associations forbid their use. Recent government surveys show, however, that young people are becoming the most frequent abusers of these drugs.

Some people try these drugs for temporary "kicks." Some abusers experiment with both stimulant and depressant drugs, to get a chemical "up" and "down." This practice is, of course, extremely dangerous to health.

The stimulant drugs are usually swallowed as pills, but they can be taken in liquid form by injection into a vein at regular time intervals. This is a dangerous practice known as "speeding." These drugs can also be inhaled or "snorted."

Teacher's Notes

Some leads for discussion are the following:

"*Who* are some of the abusers of stimulant drugs?"

"What is meant by 'speeding'?"

"What is meant by *physical dependence* on a drug? *Psychological dependence?*"

"What kind of dependence is caused by stimulant drugs?"

"Explain the expressions 'uppers' and 'downers.' "

Stimulant Drugs and Dependence

Benzedrine, Dexedrine, Methedrine, and other stimulant drugs do not produce *physical dependence* as do the so-called narcotics. (See pages 57–60.) A person who is physically dependent on a drug craves it and suffers if he does not have it in ever increasing amounts. When he is deprived of the drug, he develops a withdrawal sickness which may involve vomiting and other painful and frightening symptoms.

People who abuse stimulant drugs do develop a *psychological dependence;* they form the habit of using these drugs and develop an uncontrollable desire to take the drugs more and more frequently in order to feel the effects. When a person cannot get the stimulant drugs he has formed the habit of taking, he is likely to become nervous, jittery, excited, or uncomfortable. At times he may become panicky.

Dangers of Stimulant Drugs

Misuse of stimulant drugs can drive a person to do things that are beyond his physical endurance. As a result, he may be left exhausted.

Heavy doses of stimulant drugs may cause mental disturbances that require hospitalization. Such disturbances are usually accompanied by auditory and visual *hallucinations,* or the hearing and seeing of imaginary things. Sudden withdrawal of a stimulant drug from a heavy abuser can result in a deep, suicidal depression. Long-term heavy abusers of stimulant drugs are usually irritable and, like other heavy drug users, show social, intellectual, and emotional breakdown.

Dangers from injections of Methedrine, or "speed," with unsanitary needles include that of contracting a liver disease called *hepatitis.* Injections of "speed" can cause abnormal

Teacher's Notes

Some guides for follow-up discussion are these:

"What are some special dangers of the stimulant drug called 'speed'?"

"What have you learned about the effects of stimulant drugs on long-term heavy abusers?"

"What is the difference between stimulant and depressant drugs?"

"What are some medically sound uses of depressant drugs?"

"By what slang terms are depressants sometimes known?" (Other terms in addition to those given in the text are "double trouble," "bluebirds," "yellows," "blues," "pinks," and "seccy.")

heart rates and may result in mental disturbances and long-term personality disorders. Doses of unaccustomed size may cause death. Even the drug abusers themselves, in some cases, are frightened of "speed." They wear buttons that read "SPEED KILLS" to warn others about this dangerous drug.

Depressants, or Sedative Drugs

Depressants, or sedative drugs, belong to a large family of drugs manufactured for medical purposes to *slow down* the work of the central nervous system. Of these drugs, the best known are the barbiturates.

Barbiturates

The barbiturate drugs are the depressants most often prescribed by doctors. They come in the form of colored pills or capsules. Their color has led drug abusers to use such nicknames as "red devils," "redbirds," "yellow jackets," and "blue heavens." Capsules that are half red and half blue are often called "rainbows." Other slang terms are "goofballs" and "sleepers."

Doctors prescribe the barbiturates widely to treat high blood pressure, epilepsy, or sleeplessness; to diagnose and treat mental illness; and to relax patients before and during surgery. Alone or together with other drugs, barbiturates are prescribed for many types of medical conditions.

Taken in normal, medically supervised doses, the barbiturates mildly slow down the action of the nerves, skeletal muscles, and the heart muscle. As a result, these drugs slow down breathing and heart rate and lower the blood pressure.

Dangers of Abuse of Depressants

Something to Think About

Now and then a physician may give an overweight person a prescription for a stimulant drug. This person may mistakenly decide that if a little of the drug is helpful, increased doses would be more so. By taking more of the drug than the doctor has prescribed, the person may develop a psychological dependence on the drug. Such psychological dependence is very difficult to cure. What guide of major importance can you cite for avoiding such dangers as dependence on a drug?

Authorities consider depressants such as the barbiturates highly dangerous when taken without medical advice and prescription. Because these drugs are commonly prescribed by doctors, many people mistakenly consider the drugs safe to use freely on their own. *Depressant drugs are not safe.* Overdose can cause death.

In heavy doses, the effects of depressants resemble alcoholic intoxication: there is confusion, slurred speech, and staggering. The ability to think, to concentrate, and to work is impaired; emotional control is also weakened. Users may become irritable, angry, and eager to fight someone. Finally, they may fall into a deep sleep.

Barbiturates distort the way people see things, and they slow down reactions and responses. These drugs are an important cause of automobile accidents, especially when they are taken with alcohol. Barbiturates tend to increase the effects of alcohol. Breathing may at times be so slowed that death follows. Also, an abuser of barbiturate drugs may become confused about how many pills he has taken and may die of an accidental overdose. Barbiturates are a leading cause of accidental-poisoning deaths in the United States.

Depressant Drugs and Dependence

Misuse of depressant drugs such as the barbiturates can lead to physical dependence. The body then craves a drug and needs increasingly higher doses for its effects to be felt. If a sedative drug is withdrawn abruptly from a drug abuser, the person suffers withdrawal sickness, with nausea, cramps, delirium, convulsions, and in some cases, sudden death. Therefore, withdrawal should take place in a hospital over a period of several weeks on gradually reduced doses. It takes several months for the body to return to normal.

Legal Controls

Depressant drugs as well as stimulant drugs are regulated by the Bureau of Narcotics and Dangerous Drugs of the United States Department of Justice. *These drugs can be obtained legally only through a doctor's prescription.* Penalties for manufacturing or selling the drugs illegally include fines or prison sentences or both. Merely possessing these drugs illegally can result in arrest for breaking the law.

Narcotics

Narcotics are depressant, painkilling drugs often called "hard drugs." Among the narcotics are *opium* and the drugs made from opium such as *heroin, morphine,* and *codeine. Cocaine,* made from coco leaves, and *marijuana* are classed legally, but not chemically, with the narcotic drugs. Cocaine is actually a stimulant; marijuana is a mild hallucinogen.

Morphine and codeine are used by physicians to relieve pain. Morphine is six times as powerful as codeine and is used

Teacher's Notes

Discuss what is meant by the statement, "*All* drugs are potentially dangerous." Talk over the potential benefits of a depressant drug when taken according to a physician's directions—and the dangers of such a drug when it is abused. During discussion, ask:

"Do depressant drugs lead to any kind of dependence? If so, what kind?"

Discuss, too, the Federal bureau that is in charge of regulating these drugs. Note that *amphetamines* and *barbiturates* are often called "soft drugs" as opposed to the "hard drugs," or *narcotics.*

Something to Discuss

Talk over with your group the various reasons why a person may experiment with or "go on" drugs. What goals might the person be trying to achieve? Could the goals be met in other ways? What do a person's values have to do with his or her attitudes toward drug abuse?

Teacher's Notes
Talk over the *legal* hazards of abuse of depressant and stimulant drugs. Discuss the uses of narcotics—and also the meaning of such terms as *addicted, "hooked," "mainlining."*
Mention that an added hazard of using needles to inject a narcotic drug is that of infection from an unsanitary needle. Many cases of the liver disease *hepatitis* are contracted in this way.

for the relief of severe pain after operations and in other circumstances where extreme pain must be deadened.

Heroin has no medical use in the United States, and its manufacture, sale, and possession are prohibited by law.

Abuse of narcotics can lead to one of the worst possible dangers to physical and mental health, that of *drug dependence,* once called drug addiction. When the abuser gets "hooked," or addicted, the body requires repeated and larger doses of a narcotic drug. The abuser is physically dependent on the drug. The person who is addicted to a narcotic drug such as heroin is not only physically dependent on the drug; he or she is also *psychologically dependent* on it. The abuser comes to depend on the drug as a way to escape facing life.

Heroin is the drug most frequently used by addicts today. Heroin is a white powder that is dissolved in water and then injected into a vein ("mainlining") or just under the skin ("skin popping") with a needle. It may also be sniffed.

The first reaction to heroin is a lessening of worry and tension. Feeling "high" may be followed by a period of sleepiness or even stupor. The drug dulls certain areas of the brain and may reduce hunger and thirst. Because addicts do not feel hungry—and because they spend what money they have on heroin instead of food—hospital care for them must often include treatment for malnutrition.

Withdrawal symptoms appear in an addicted person within 12 to 16 hours after the drug has been discontinued. These symptoms are the same as for other forms of physical dependence. They include sweating, shaking, diarrhea, nausea, and sharp cramps in the abdomen and the legs. The person is in torment unless he or she gets more of the drug—or unless he or she receives treatment for withdrawal symptoms in a hospital.

Young people who become addicted to a narcotic drug such as heroin are groggy a great deal of the time. They do poorly in their studies and have no interest in physical activity. They draw into themselves and often refuse to talk because they are preoccupied with themselves and how to get more heroin.

Drug dependence may lead to a life of criminal activity. The addict's health is too poor and he or she is too unreliable

Did You Know?

1. Tranquilizers *are a class of drugs closely related to depressants or sedatives. Tranquilizers as prescribed by a doctor have the effect of quieting the nerves and reducing anxieties and tensions. These drugs make a person feel at ease but do not put him to sleep as do depressants. Tranquilizers can also be abused. How?*

2. Volatile chemicals *such as airplane glue, gasoline, paint thinner, aerosol sprays, and lighter fluid are depressant substances that can be misused or abused. The practice of sniffing such substances is a dangerous one. A very serious consequence is the effect—often poisonous—of the inhaled fumes on the brain, kidneys, liver, and bone marrow. Even death can result from sniffing volatile chemicals. This is true when such substances are released into a plastic bag and then sniffed.*

to hold a steady job. Yet enormous amounts of money are needed to keep the addict supplied with increasing quantities of the drug he or she craves. For example, an addict may have to spend $25 to $100 or more to buy a day's supply of heroin. He or she may steal or even push drugs to get that money.

Drug addicts cease to be effective human beings. They lose interest in their family, in education, in a job, in appearance. Repeated needle punctures result in discolored scars and tattoo marks on the skin. Drug addicts are likely to die young because they suffer from severe malnutrition and general neglect of personal care. In fact, the life span may be shortened by fifteen to twenty years, according to statistics.

Experimenting with narcotics will almost surely cause a person to become "hooked." Some young people know the hazards but they experiment with addicting drugs anyway because they think they are exceptions and can stop using the drugs without trouble when they want to. They are wrong, however. Nobody can safely "fool" with narcotics.

Treatment of Drug Addicts

Medical authorities know that drug-dependent persons are sick. They need help for their physical and psychological dependence and for their withdrawal sickness. What is more, they need help to keep them from going back to drug use after the withdrawal.

Curing drug dependence is very difficult. Doctors can get addicts off the drug and help them rebuild their health while they are under treatment in a hospital. But the problem comes when the addicts are out of the hospital. The addicts may return to drugs for many reasons. Drugs may have become a way of life for them. They may not have a strong enough personality to enable them to avoid former friends who are still addicts or to make a fresh start in life.

In recent years, various approaches have been tried to rehabilitate drug addicts. One of these approaches involves follow-up treatment in a community clinic. If there is such a clinic in the person's community, he or she can go there regularly for counseling, companionship, and an opportunity to learn new job skills.

Teacher's Notes

Students should know that heroin is an extremely dangerous drug. Dependence, or addiction, is one of its great hazards. Another is the danger of accidental death through an overdose. Heroin is usually mixed with sugar or quinine or some other substance before it gets to the user. It is impossible for a user to know the amount of heroin that is in any given sample. This is because there are no controls over the drug's manufacture; all such manufacturing is an illegal black-market activity. It is possible that a person whose body has developed a tolerance for a certain amount of heroin might buy a sample that contains a higher amount of the drug—and it could kill him. Such deaths are frequently reported in the newspapers.

Did You Know?

Special hospitals and treatment centers exist for the purpose of helping cure drug dependence. These hospitals include two Federal ones—one in Lexington, Kentucky, and the other in Fort Worth, Texas. Treatment is also given in various state and city hospitals and many private hospitals.

There are two major problems in curing drug dependence. One is the shortage of places to help cure addicts. The other is the return of many "cured" addicts to the habit. What factors do you think might lead a so-called rehabilitated addict to return to drug abuse?

Teacher's Notes

Consider with students how a person might become accidentally addicted to a powerful drug such as heroin. (Many young persons do not know about addiction; they think they can easily stop taking a narcotic drug whenever they wish. They need to know that once they are "hooked," they cannot stop taking the drug without suffering misery from withdrawal symptoms. The craving for the drug increases not so much for the pleasure of taking it as to end the intolerable pain and anguish that result from not having it.)

Discuss various rehabilitation approaches for addicts and the different national and international controls over narcotics.

In some communities, "halfway houses" are available where addicts live for up to three years. (See pages 64–65.) The halfway houses are usually run entirely by ex-drug users who work to help newcomers break the drug habit. Experimental efforts also continue on such medical treatments as that by *methadone* —a narcotic commonly used to treat heroin-withdrawal symptoms. Methadone can eliminate an addict's desire for heroin, as well as the "high" effect it produces. Programs of counseling, job retraining, and education must accompany any effective program of rehabilitation.

Narcotics Legislation

In 1914, the United States Congress passed the Harrison Act. This was the first of the Federal laws concerning narcotics. It requires that a doctor who prescribes a narcotic must have a Federal narcotics license. When a doctor administers a drug, a record must be made of the patient's name and address, as well as the doctor's name and address, and reasons given justifying use of the drug prescribed. The Harrison Act has been strengthened by later acts of Congress. For example, the Drug Abuse Control Act of 1970 increased the severity of fines and prison sentences for those found guilty of illegal manufacturing or selling of drugs. This 1970 Act also made provision for an expanded program for rehabilitating drug addicts.

Illegal sale of narcotics can result in heavy fines and long prison terms. A pusher who sells narcotics to someone under eighteen years old is refused parole and probation. If the drug sold is heroin, the pusher can be sentenced to life imprisonment. International treaties and agreements also exist to limit the production and shipment of narcotics from one country to another. The United Nations has two agencies that regulate international narcotics trade and try to prevent illegal drug traffic throughout the world.

Some Things to Think About

1. Most states have laws requiring that facts about narcotics—and about other drugs with a potential for abuse—be taught in the public schools. Why do you think such laws are needed?

2. What facts have you *learned in this unit about narcotics that you did not know before?*

Hallucinogens

Hallucinogens are drugs that can cause hallucinations, visions, or distortions. After a person takes such drugs, the brain interprets in distorted ways the messages of sight, sound, smell, touch, or taste that come to it. The word *psychedelic* is often used in connection with the hallucinogenic drugs. The term psychedelic means mind-altering, and it refers to a state in which there are distorted sensations and intensified awareness of these sensations.

Teacher's Notes

Point out that the manufacture or use of all hallucinogens is prohibited in the United States except for research purposes.

LSD

One of the well-known hallucinogenic drugs is LSD. LSD, which is often called "acid," is a very powerful drug. An average dose of it is about the size of a speck. Yet this speck has an effect that lasts for about eight to twelve hours. Users may take the drug in pill or capsule form, in a sugar cube, or on a cracker or cookie—or they may lick it off some object.

When LSD is taken into the body, it increases the heart rate, causes a rise in temperature and blood pressure, and dilates the pupils of the eyes. Other physical effects may include chills, nausea, and loss of appetite. LSD does not cause physical dependence, however; a person does not build up a tolerance for it or become physically ill when the drug is withdrawn.

One of the dangers of LSD may be a feeling of panic. Users may become fearful that they cannot stop the action of the drug. Then too, days, weeks, or even months after a person has taken LSD he may have a recurrence or "flashback" of hallucinations. At such times the person may fear he is going insane. Accidental death is another hazard of taking LSD. A user often gets the idea that he can float or fly, so he may leap out of a high window, for example.

The effects of taking LSD may be different at different times in the same individual. It is not possible to predict what will happen each time the drug is taken. That is why an LSD user may speak of a "good trip" or a "bad trip."

Other dangerous hallucinogenic drugs are peyote, mescaline, DMT, and STP. Marijuana is a mild hallucinogenic drug, but it is legally classed with the narcotics. It will be discussed in the following section, pages 62–63.

Use of any hallucinogenic drug except by trained research workers is illegal. Hallucinogens are closely regulated by the Bureau of Narcotics and Dangerous Drugs. Federal laws provide strict penalties for those who illegally produce or sell hallucinogenic drugs. Even possessing one of these drugs can cause a person to be fined or be given a prison sentence.

Teacher's Notes

It should be noted just recently a Columbia University research group has uncovered the first direct evidence of cellular damage among habitual marijuana smokers. Tests made by this research group showed that marijuana apparently weakened the body's defenses against disease. White blood cells in marijuana smokers divided (reproduced) 40% less than in nonsmokers of marijuana. These, of course, are initial findings and not yet conclusive.

Marijuana[1]

Marijuana is a mild hallucinogenic drug. It is found in the flowering tops and leaves of the Indian hemp plant. For use as a drug, the leaves and flowers of the plant are dried and crushed or chopped into small pieces. This product is rolled and smoked in short cigarettes or in pipes. Or it can be taken in food. The cigarettes are commonly known as "reefers," "joints," and "sticks." Marijuana is often called "pot," "Mary Jane," "tea," "weed," or "grass."

The long-term physical effects of using marijuana are not yet known. The kind of research needed to learn the results of persistent use is not yet complete or conclusive.

Some obvious and common physical reactions—which differ among individuals—include rapid beating of the heart, lowering of body temperature, and reddening of the eyes. The drug also changes blood-sugar levels, stimulates the appetite, and dehydrates the body. Users may become talkative, loud, unsteady, or drowsy. Coordination of body movements may be difficult.

The drug's effects on the emotions and senses vary widely, depending on the person's individual reactions and on the amount and strength of the marijuana used. The marijuana may be of high or low potency since it is affected by such factors as what kind of soil it is grown on, whether it is a wild variety or is cultivated for smoking or eating, and what portion of the plant is used in the mixture. Also, marijuana is sometimes weakened or adulterated with such substances as tea, oregano, catnip, or with the seeds and the stems of the plant. The social setting in which marijuana is taken and what the user expects to happen to him also influence a person's reactions to the drug.

Something to Think About

Although evidence as yet does not prove whether marijuana causes any lasting physical or mental changes in a user, a stronger cousin of this drug—called hashish*—may well do so. Hashish is the dark-brown liquid or resin that is collected from the flowering tops and seed heads of high-quality hemp plants. When a person smokes marijuana, he has no way of knowing for sure how strong or pure it is—or even whether it is marijuana. It may be hashish. Or it may be a mixture of hashish and some other powerful hallucinogens.*

Usually when marijuana is smoked, the effects are felt quickly—in about 15 minutes. The effects can last from 2 to 4 hours. The range of effects can vary from depression to a feeling of excitement. Some users, however, feel no change of mood at all. In many users, the sense of time and distance often

[1]The section on marijuana is adapted from the pamphlet *Marihuana, Some Questions and Answers,* Public Health Service Publication No. 1829. Adapted by permission.

becomes distorted. A minute may seem like an hour. Something near may seem very far away. Occasionally, uncontrollable laughing or crying may occur. At times, the user may tend to withdraw into himself. He may be unduly suspicious or fearful or anxious.

A person using marijuana may find it more difficult than usual to make decisions that require clear thinking. Doing any task that takes good reflexes and clear thinking is affected by the drug. For this reason it can be dangerous to drive while under the influence of marijuana.

Marijuana does not cause physical dependence. Some scientists think that the drug can cause psychological dependence, however, if users take it regularly. Research workers agree that more studies on marijuana are needed before additional factual statements can be made.

What kind of research is being done on marijuana? The National Institute of Mental Health, an agency of the Public Health Service, is responsible for supporting and conducting research to learn more about this drug and for reporting any new findings on it.

The program of the National Institute of Mental Health's Center for Studies on Narcotics and Drug Abuse includes surveys of how people get the drug, how widely it is used, and what effects different amounts and periods of use have upon people. With the support of the National Institute of Mental Health, scientists are studying how marijuana affects memory, awareness, mood, and physical movement. Studies are also being carried on to learn more about the drug's *long-range* effects on the body and mind.

Meantime you can be thinking over the information you now have about marijuana and about other drugs that can be abused. You can be thinking about the decisions you will want to make, both now and in the future—decisions that are solely up to you.

Keep in mind, too, that if you have good feelings about yourself, you are likely to act in ways that will not cause harm to yourself or others. A mature person does not do things that will be harmful to his or her health and general well-being.

Teacher's Notes

In discussing what research *may* show about the long- and short-term effects of marijuana, you might mention that research *has* shown every other hallucinogenic drug to be harmful. There is likelihood that marijuana will not turn out to be an exception.

In a summary discussion, consider with students various reasons why young people might be tempted to become drug abusers. (Out of curiosity, on a dare, to do what friends are doing, for "kicks," to become more creative, and so on.)

Invite evaluation of the various suggested reasons in the light of what has been learned about drugs and drug abuse.

What Can You *Do About Drug Abuse?*

1. Know the facts about drugs with a potential for abuse—depressants, stimulants, hallucinogens.

2. Protect yourself. Do not let anyone persuade you to experiment with drugs for "kicks."

3. Help others understand the dangers of experimenting with drugs. Speak up if you hear someone say such experimenting is harmless.

4. If you are approached by a drug pusher, report the incident at home and to school authorities.

Gateway House: Drug Rehabilitation Center

Here the University of Chicago collaborates with the State of Illinois to offer treatment which may be helpful with drug abusers and narcotic addicts.

Only those who want to be helped are accepted as members of the Gateway "family." Residents stay a year to a year and a half or longer. They use no drugs and are re-educated for productive lives in society.
Discussion, debates, counseling, job experiences, and hobbies help Gateway residents grow in self-understanding and self-confidence.
All residents share in the work involved in upkeep of the house. Warm human relations are fostered. And the individual is helped to stand on his own feet, to face his fears instead of fleeing from them into drug abuse.

Alcohol and Accidents

About 55,000 people in the United States are killed yearly in highway accidents, and about two million people are injured each year.

The damaged cars here document accidents involving drivers who have "mixed" alcohol and driving.

It has been estimated that nearly two thirds of all drivers involved in accidents have been drinking alcoholic beverages. Drugs also may be a factor in motor accidents.

The effect alcohol can have on a driver's coordination, reaction time, vision, and judgment suggests all too clearly why "alcohol and driving don't mix." Every state has passed laws that forbid an individual's driving while under the influence of alcohol.

Cigarette Smoking and Respiratory Problems

Research in recent years has established the fact that long-time cigarette smoking is a causative factor in the development of two serious lung diseases—lung cancer and emphysema.

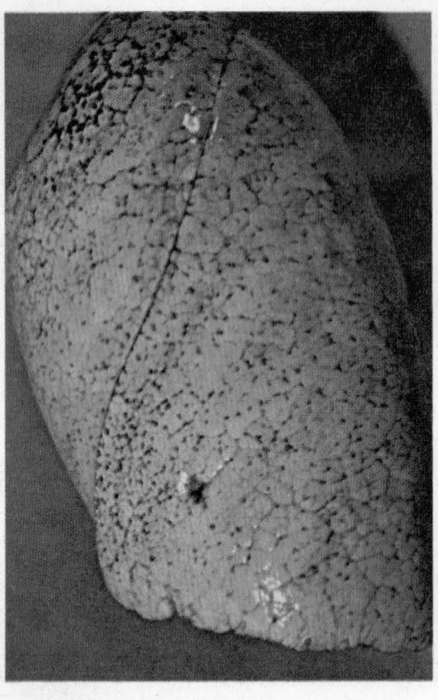

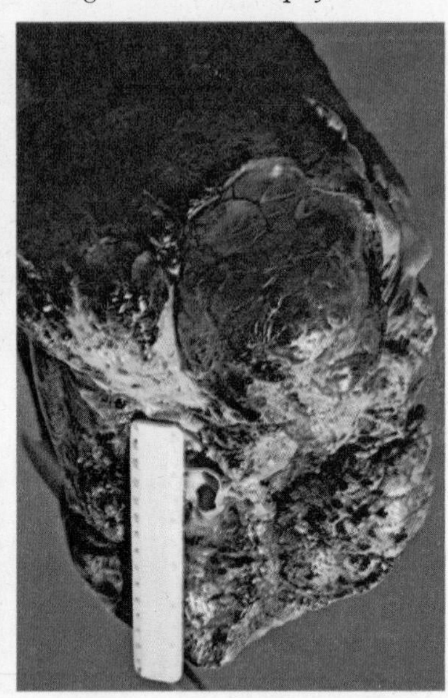

Left. *The normal lung of a middle-aged person.*
Right. *The lung of a middle-aged cigarette smoker. (Inhaled smoke—containing gases and tar—has blackened the lung.)*
Bottom. *Inside the lung of an emphysema patient. (When emphysema develops, the lungs lose their elastic, porous quality. Walls of some tiny air sacs break down. These wall-less sacs join to make larger sacs. In these larger sacs, stale air and smoke are trapped. The lungs cannot get rid of carbon dioxide nor absorb oxygen as they should.)*

Top. *Rapid spread of lung cancer in a patient as shown in X rays taken February 20, March 12, April 7, and April 22.*
Bottom. *View down bronchial tube, showing cancer growth.*

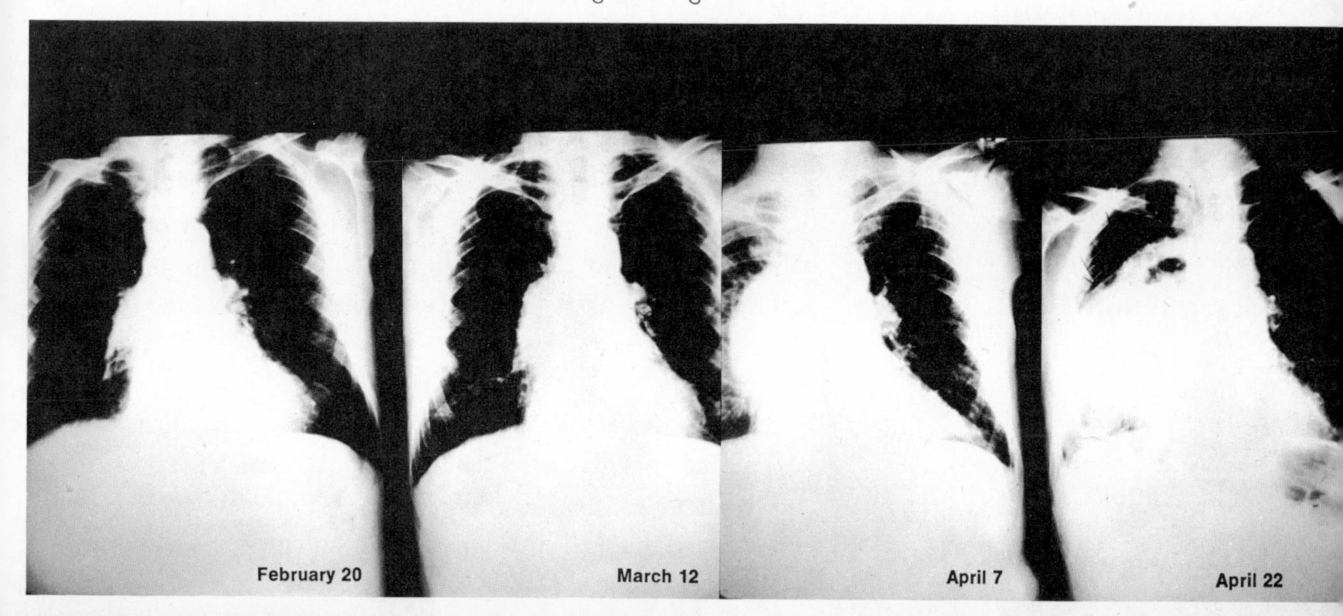

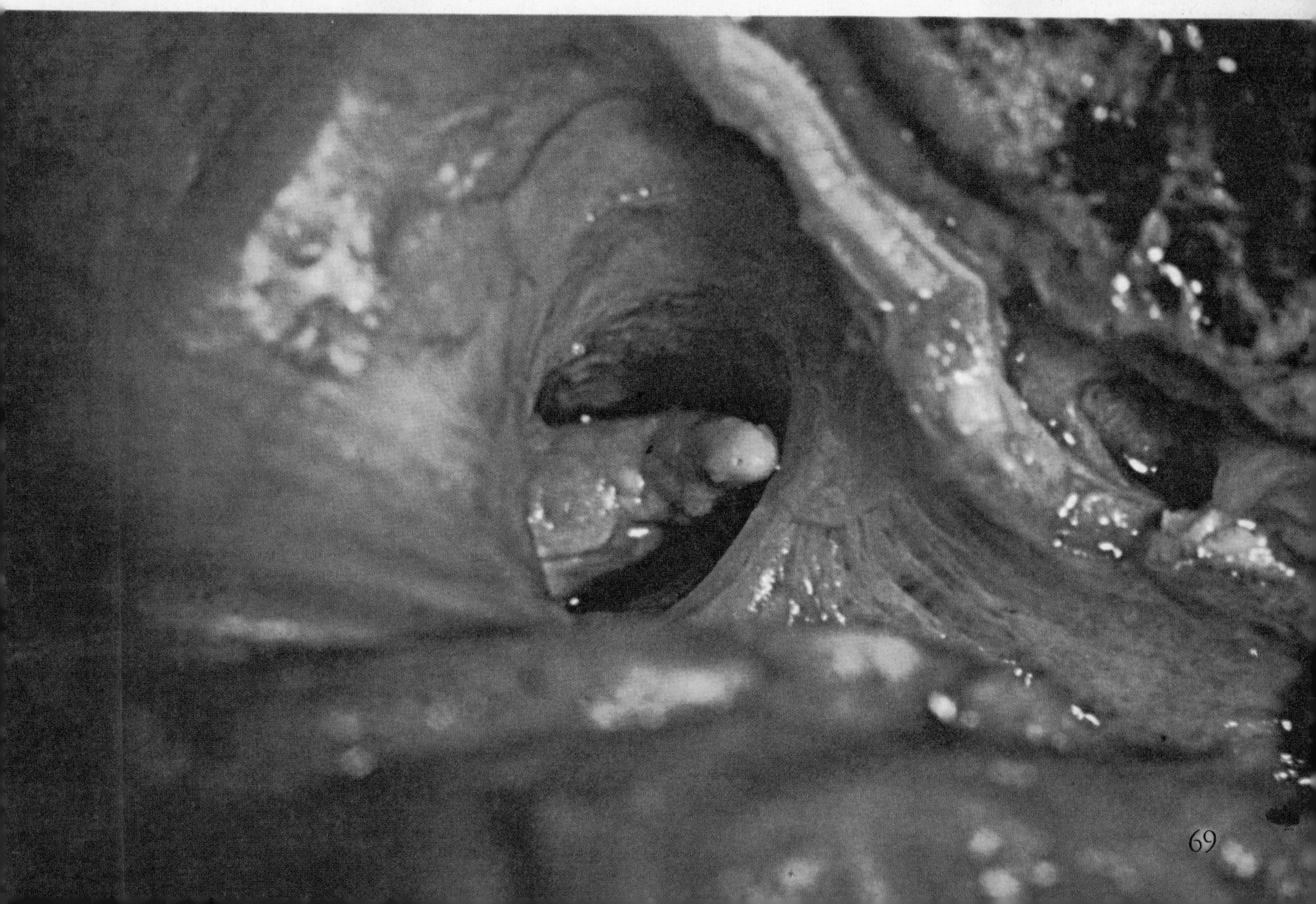

Teacher's Notes

As students discuss the fact that alcohol is a depressant or sedative, you might mention that in past years—before more effective anesthetics were known—heavy doses of alcohol were used as anesthetics for operations and for tooth extractions.

When the general term "alcohol" is used, *ethyl* is usually meant. Another kind of alcohol is *methyl alcohol,* also called *wood alcohol.* Methyl alcohol is a dangerous poison if taken into the body, even in small amounts. Methyl alcohol has uses in industry and in medicine. Rubbing alcohol is an example of a product made from methyl alcohol.

Something to Do

Look in the school and public libraries for materials such as the following about the effects of alcoholic drinks:

McCarthy, Raymond G., and Pasciutti, John J. Facts About Alcohol *(Science Research). Booklet.*

National Institute of Mental Health. Thinking About Drinking *(Sup't. of Documents).*

What Is Known About Alcoholic Beverages?

What *is* an alcoholic beverage? It is any beverage that contains ethyl alcohol. Three common types of alcoholic beverages are beer, wine, and distilled or "hard" liquors such as whiskey, rum, and gin. The alcoholic content of beer is approximately 3 to 6 percent, while wines may vary in alcoholic content from 12 to 14 percent. The alcoholic content of wine may be raised to as high as 18 to 20 percent if the wine is fortified by the addition of more alcohol. Hard liquors have an alcoholic content of from 40 to 50 percent.

The alcohol content of hard liquor is stated on the bottle in terms of "proof." A "90 proof" beverage contains 45 percent alcohol, or half the amount stated in the "proof."

Alcohol in the Body

Because alcohol is burned in the body and produces energy, it can be classed as a food. But it is a very poor kind of food. Actually it is an energy food—nothing more. Alcohol contains none of the vitamins, proteins, and minerals that are necessary to growth and health.

Alcohol is also classed as a drug. Although many people mistakenly think of it as a stimulant, alcohol really is a *depressant,* or sedative. A stimulant causes a speed-up in the activity of body functions; the caffeine in coffee, tea, and cola drinks, for example, is a stimulant. A depressant drug, on the other hand, affects the nervous system in such a way that all functions of the body are slowed down. A depressant makes a person drowsy and dulls the senses.

When alcohol is taken into the body, it does not have to be digested as other foods do. It is not acted upon by the digestive juices but it is absorbed directly into the bloodstream from the stomach and the small intestine.

Within two minutes after alcohol is consumed, some of it starts to enter the bloodstream. Alcohol that is absorbed into the bloodstream is carried first to the liver. The liver oxidizes, or burns, all the alcohol it can handle.

Alcohol that is not immediately oxidized by the liver is carried throughout the body by the blood; thus it reaches all the body cells. The most marked effect, though, is on the nerves and the brain. Eventually, the alcohol is all oxidized—except for a small amount that leaves the body through the breath, kidneys, and sweat glands. It may take anywhere from four to twelve hours or more for the body to get rid of the alcohol completely.

The concentration of alcohol in the blood at any given time is responsible for the effects of alcohol on the nervous system. At the right, you can see one of the devices that can be used to measure the percentage of alcohol in the blood.

In the chart in the margin of page 72 you can read about some of the effects produced by various concentrations of alcohol in the blood. What *are* some of these effects?

It should be noted, however, that no two people react in exactly the same way to equal amounts of alcohol in the body. Nor does the same person always react in exactly the same way every time he drinks alcohol.

There are two factors that speed the absorption of alcohol into the bloodstream and increase the concentration of alcohol in the blood. One is the drinking of alcoholic beverages on an empty stomach; and the other is drinking the beverages hurriedly, as contrasted to sipping them slowly over a long period of time.

Body weight can also be a factor. It takes less alcohol to cause noticeable effects in slight, immature bodies—which is one of the reasons why young people are usually more affected than adults by alcoholic beverages.

Alcohol and Traffic Accidents

The increase in traffic accidents on the highways has become one of the major safety problems in the United States. It has been estimated that from 50 to 60 percent of all traffic accidents involve the use of alcoholic beverages, either by drivers or by pedestrians.

In view of the effects of alcohol on the body, you can see why alcohol can lead to traffic accidents. Safe driving requires good vision, accurate hearing, sound judgment, and quick reactions. Alcohol taken in sufficient quantities impairs all these functions.

Teacher's Notes

Explain that instruments such as the one pictured in the margin are designed to find out if alcohol is present in the blood in sufficient quantities to affect vision, hearing, judgment, and reaction time.

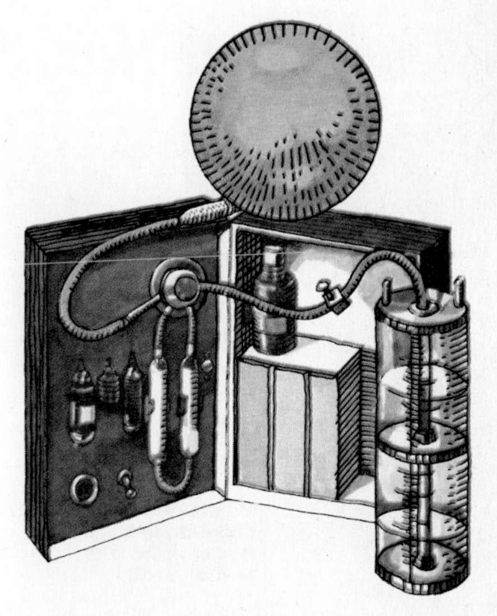

The alcometer *shown here is one of several different types of devices used to help find out, in cases of traffic accidents, if sufficient alcohol is present in the blood to impair driving ability.*
The alcometer analyzes a person's breath to determine the percentage of alcohol in the blood. Other devices analyze the blood, urine, or saliva.

Teacher's Notes

Use such questions as these for discussion leads:

"What is meant by *double vision? Tunnel vision?*"

"What are some *psychological* effects that alcohol may have on a person?"

"Why do you think airplane pilots are forbidden to drink any alcoholic beverage within 24 hours before a scheduled flight?"

"How does alcohol in the body impair various abilities needed for safe driving?"

Alcohol affects a person's ability to see by producing such conditions as *double vision* and *tunnel vision.* When alcohol reaches the part of the brain that controls the optic muscles and nerves, images may be distorted. In some cases double vision occurs. Then the drinker will see two objects instead of one. In tunnel vision, alcohol affects a person's side vision, or the ability to see objects far to either side while looking straight ahead. When the side vision is cut off, a person has a narrowed range of vision. How might these effects on vision contribute to traffic accidents?

What is more, alcoholic beverages have psychological effects on a driver that can result in accidents. Not only is the driver's sense of caution dulled, but he also develops false confidence in his ability to drive. He thinks he is a better driver than he is, and he may take chances that he would not take if he were sober. In an effort to reduce traffic accidents, every state has passed laws that forbid an individual's driving while under the influence of liquor.

Alcoholism

What is alcoholism? It is an illness that involves a person's inability to stop drinking alcoholic beverages or to control heavy drinking. The person who has this illness is known as an *alcoholic.*

Alcohol in Blood	Effects Produced
0.03%	Mild relaxation; slight change in existing mood.
0.06%	Mental relaxation; slight decrease in fine skills; less concern with environment.
0.09%	Exaggerated behavior; talkative; noisy; moody; loss of good judgment.
0.12%	Clumsiness; serious loss of judgment and coordination.
0.15%	Obvious intoxication; grossly incoordinated in all behavior.

Statistics based on average-size person.

Alcoholism is not the same thing as drunkenness. Anyone may get drunk. Some people do it without intending to; others may do it knowingly and frequently. Many people do take alcoholic drinks, especially wine and beer, either with meals or on social occasions without danger if in moderation. Such persons are not considered alcoholics as long as they can control their drinking of alcohol. The alcoholic, however, cannot control his drinking. He is intoxicated often enough to prevent him from leading a normal life.

Although all the causes of alcoholism are not yet understood, medical studies have yielded information about characteristics that many alcoholics have in common. Alcoholics are often people who have difficulty in making satisfying adjustments to life; they use alcohol as a means of running away from problems and difficulties instead of facing them and trying to work them out. There is some evidence, too, that the body chemistry of the alcoholic is different from that of other people—and thus he has physical reactions to alcohol that others do not have.

One of the great hazards in starting to use alcoholic drinks is that it is difficult to know in advance who will be able to control his drinking and who will become an alcoholic. According to some studies, it is estimated that one out of every fourteen persons who begin drinking becomes an alcoholic sooner or later.

Alcoholics are people in need of medical care. They need to be built up physically because they often are suffering from malnutrition. This nutritional difficulty results from the tendency of alcohol, when it is used excessively, to kill the appetite. Alcoholics also need psychological help so that they can learn to face their problems and try to work them out without the use of alcohol. Alcoholics are helped, too, if they have understanding families who realize that alcoholism is an illness and should be so treated.

Under modern treatment a good many alcoholics can be helped to stop drinking *if* they truly want to be helped. But progress is dependent upon the person's willingness to give up drinking alcoholic beverages entirely. The drinking of even small amounts of alcohol almost always results in a relapse into alcoholism.

An organization that has been successful in helping many alcoholics stop drinking is *Alcoholics Anonymous,* or *A.A.* as it is usually called. It began as the result of two alcoholics who designed a plan for helping cure themselves by aiding other drinkers. In this organization, recovered alcoholics work with those struggling to cure themselves of alcoholism. Another important organization is *Al-Anon,* which works with family groups. This organization is for wives, relatives, and friends of alcoholics who band together to offer friendship, hope, and solutions to common problems that occur when there is an alcoholic in the family. Still another organization is the one called *Alateen.* It helps young people who have problems because they have an alcoholic parent.

Teacher's Notes

Talk over some of the characteristics of alcoholics. You might also use these queries to guide the discussion:

"How would you explain the statement, 'Alcoholics are sick people in need of medical care'?"

"Why do alcoholics need to be built up physically as well as psychologically?"

"Can an alcoholic be helped to stop drinking?" (Stress that under proper care—and *if* the person actively cooperates—he can be helped to stop drinking.)

"What is meant by the term *A.A.*? What is the purpose of the organization called *Al-Anon? Alateen?*"

Teacher's Notes

Discuss various kinds of social problems that are connected with the drinking of alcoholic beverages—traffic accidents, alcoholism, absenteeism, and so on. Also have pupils consider what might be meant by the statement, "Drinking is a temporary and inadequate method of meeting problems."

Talk over, too, some of the special hazards of alcoholic beverages to *young* people.

Some Things to Do

1. *Find out about some of the liquor laws in* your *community. For example, check to see if you live in a "dry" community.*

2. *Investigate, too, to see if liquor can be sold on election day during the time the polls are open. If not, what might be a reason?*

Alcohol and the Law

Because the drinking of alcoholic beverages presents many social problems, various states, counties, and cities have passed laws controlling the sale of alcohol within their borders. A number of communities have voted to be "dry"—that is, they have voted that no liquor may be sold there. Sometimes beer and wine may be sold but not hard liquor.

A law that is almost universally found is the one that forbids selling or serving of hard alcoholic beverages to a minor—a person under the legal age as defined by that particular state.

Another frequently found restriction forbids the sale of liquor to a person who is obviously intoxicated. Sales of liquor on Sunday and on election days are also against the law in many places.

Laws about the sale of liquor are enforced by means of licensing. Anyone who makes or sells liquor is required to have a license. If he breaks the liquor laws in his state or local community, his license is taken away from him—and he may suffer other penalties.

Alcohol and Young People

Many young people who experiment with the use of alcoholic drinks are ignorant of the effects of these beverages on immature bodies. A young person may become intoxicated after drinking very little. Why?

Then, too, young people may not be aware of the *psychological intoxication* that occurs even more readily than physical intoxication in beginning drinkers. In this state of psychological intoxication, young people may feel unusually excited. They may do foolish or reckless things or forget their moral standards. They may even endanger the safety of themselves or others.

Now that you have had the opportunity to gain scientific information about the effects of alcohol on the body—and about the problems that excessive drinking can create for the individual and society—you have a realistic basis for making wise decisions about the use of alcohol in the years ahead. These decisions may be among the most important ones you will ever make.

What Should You Know About Smoking?

Not long ago a national study reported that there are fewer teen-age smokers today than there were ten years ago—and that a large number of teen-agers who smoke now plan to join the nonsmokers. What do you think might account for these trends?

One explanation might be that a great deal of information is now available about smoking. Facts have replaced what was only guesswork a few decades ago. What is more, many opportunities exist today for learning the latest research findings about the effects smoking can have on people's health and well-being.

Information of this kind about smoking is presented in newspaper and magazine articles, on radio and television programs, and by means of films and public lectures. In most states, too, the law requires that young people learn about smoking in classes at school.

Some questions that were asked in one junior-high class that was taking part in a smoking-education program are shown below.[1] How would you answer each of these questions?

After you have thought about each question and how you would answer it, check your ideas with the ones given on pages 76–78. Also be ready to suggest other questions that *you* want answered.

1. Do cigarettes really cause lung cancer?
2. How long do you have to smoke before it becomes dangerous?
3. Is smoking harmful if you do not inhale?
4. Are pipes and cigars likely to cause cancer?
5. Are there some here-and-now disadvantages of smoking as well as long-term ones?
6. Why do young people start smoking?
7. What can help a person stop smoking if he already has the habit?

[1]Questions and answers that appear on pages 76–78 are adapted in great part from the article "What Youngsters Need to Know About Smoking" by Dr. Mildred Dubitzky and Dr. Jerome L. Schwartz, from *Parents' Magazine* (November 1968). Reprinted by permission of Parents' Magazine, New York.

Teacher's Notes

Point out that, on the one hand, there are articles and programs telling about the dangers of smoking, but on the other hand there are many newspaper and magazine advertisements that promote cigarette smoking. See if students can describe any such advertisements they have seen. Ask your students to bring in some cigarette advertisements. Consider the various advertisements carefully with the group. Ask such questions as: "What is the advertisement selling?" (Low-tar content, the satisfaction of smoking, the glamor of smoking, or what?)

Note, too, whether various claims are stated plainly or just implied.

Something to Do

A member of your group might write to the nearest branch of the American Cancer Society to ask for a list of their most recent leaflets. Pertinent titles can be ordered, and the leaflets can then be made available for classroom use. (Single copies are usually free upon request.)

Teacher's Notes

Consider in detail what happens when cigarette smoke gets into the lungs. See if students can explain what might cause the well-known "cigarette cough." (The smoker is trying to cough up the mucus and irritating substances that the weakened cilia are unable to move out of the bronchial or other air passages.) Then ask:

"Why—after 1964—do you think many adults decided to stop smoking?"

Do Cigarettes Really Cause Lung Cancer?

In thinking about the answer to this question, it is necessary to consider what is in the cigarette smoke that gets into a smoker's lungs—and what cigarette smoke does to the lungs of a smoker.

Cigarette smoke contains gases, vapors, and particles. *Tar* and a habit-forming drug called *nicotine* are two of the chemical compounds found in the particles. The tar in the smoke breaks down into many separate chemicals, a number of which have produced cancer in animal tissue in controlled scientific studies in laboratories.

When cigarette smoke gets into the air passages of the lungs, the lungs' usual defenses against foreign substances are weakened. Thousands of tiny hairlike *cilia* line the air passageways of the respiratory system. The cilia are covered with a layer of mucus. The cilia lining the passageway below the throat move this mucus up, and the cilia in the nasal passages push the mucus down so that it can be spit out or swallowed. Cigarette smoke, however, weakens and paralyzes the cilia and thus prevents their proper functioning. This means that chemicals from cigarette smoke can accumulate on the lining of the air passages, and they may eventually penetrate and injure the living cells.

Once chemicals from cigarettes damage the cells, cancer cells may begin to develop, to grow, and ultimately to crowd out and destroy normal cells. Many studies have been made of tissue specimens from the lungs of several hundred male smokers. In all the tissue specimens from smokers' lungs, abnormal cells were found; in some, fully developed cancer was discovered.

After careful study of all the scientific evidence, the United States Public Health Service in 1964 made a landmark report. It was called *Smoking and Health.* Among other findings, the report stated, *"Cigarette smoking can cause lung cancer in men; the effect of cigarette smoking far outweighs other factors. The data for women, though less extensive, points in the same direction."* This report and additional scientific evidence obtained in the years that followed have alerted people to the

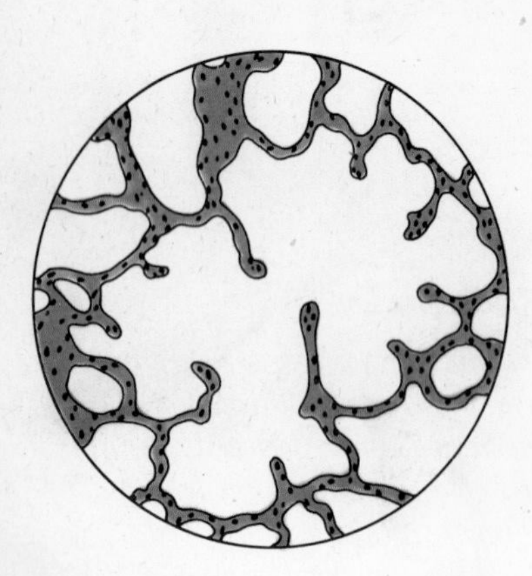

Microscopic view of normal lung cells (magnified 100 times)

very real dangers of cigarette smoking—and have led many individuals to stop smoking or refuse ever to start the habit.

Not only can smoking cause lung cancer, but it can also cause cancer of the throat and mouth. Smoking can be a factor, too, in the development of heart diseases, chronic bronchitis, emphysema, and other illnesses.

How Long Do You Have to Smoke Before It Becomes Dangerous?

The more a person smokes and the longer he smokes, the greater are his chances of developing a serious illness. These figures are provided by the American Cancer Society: Of twenty-five-year-old men, twice as many heavy smokers (two packs a day) as nonsmokers will die before they are sixty-five years of age. The risk of death from lung cancer is about twenty times greater among men who smoke heavily and five times greater among women who smoke heavily than among non-smoking men and women. And the death rate from lung cancer for average smokers (one pack a day) is ten times that of nonsmokers. If heavy smokers stop smoking, however, their chances of becoming ill will go down and keep decreasing the longer they stay off cigarette smoking.

Is Smoking Harmful If You Do Not Inhale?

Smokers who inhale have a greater chance of developing illnesses than those who do not inhale. How far down the cigarette is smoked is also significant, since the impurities are more concentrated in the last third of the cigarette. Most important of all, however, is how many cigarettes are smoked and over how long a period.

Are Pipes and Cigars Likely to Cause Cancer?

For pipe smokers, cigar smokers, and those who smoke both pipes and cigars, the risk of developing lung cancer is greater than for nonsmokers but the danger is still much less than for cigarette smokers. However, the relationship of pipe smoking to development of cancer of the lip appears to be established.

Are There Some Here-and-Now Disadvantages of Smoking as Well as Long-Term Ones?

Yes, there are. Smoking causes shortness of breath, an unpleasant cough, sinus headaches, and a general loss of energy. Smoking irritates the membranes of the throat, nose,

Teacher's Notes

Explain how smoking affects the circulatory system. When smoke gets into a person's body, tiny blood vessels near the surface of the skin contract. The heart then has to beat faster to pump blood through these vessels. The blood pressure rises. The increase in the heartbeat may be as much as fifteen to twenty-five beats per minute—and the blood pressure may rise considerably. The increase in heartbeat and elevation of blood pressure may continue for some time after a person has smoked but one cigarette.

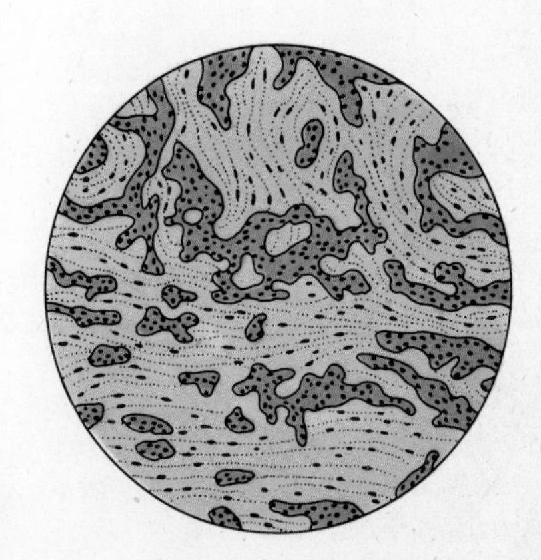

Microscopic view of cancerous lung cells (magnified 100 times)

Teacher's Notes

Students may ask *why* it is difficult for people to stop smoking. One reason is the presence of the drug *nicotine* in tobacco. Nicotine affects the nervous system and contributes to making the use of tobacco a habit-forming practice. You might call attention to the following powerful argument for not starting to smoke during the junior-high years. An American Cancer Society study indicates that if a young person starts to smoke in his teens, the risk of his dying earlier than a nonsmoker is 70 percent. Discuss responses a young person might make if someone asks why he does not smoke.

A recent Public Health Service report showed a marked decline in cigarette smoking among teen-agers. Ten years previously, about one third of the seventeen-year-old boys were smoking, but only one fourth reported doing so a decade later. The trend for teen-age girls decreased similarly.

Figures from American Cancer Society. Used by permission.

mouth, and sometimes sinuses. The sense of smell is eventually affected. A bad taste may be left in the mouth after smoking, which may, in turn, dull the appetite and the enjoyment of food. Smokers tend to have more colds than do nonsmokers. Other disadvantages of smoking include bad breath and tobacco stains on the fingers, fingernails, and teeth.

Moreover, though smoking only a few cigarettes now and then is not likely to give rise to serious symptoms, there is no doubt that it is often impossible for many people to limit themselves to just a few cigarettes. It is difficult to give up the habit once it becomes established. One evidence of this difficulty is the number of antismoking clinics being formed all over the country.

Why Do Young People Start Smoking?

The usual reasons that young people themselves give for smoking are that it makes them feel more relaxed and appear more sophisticated. The risks, however, far outweigh any other consideration. A generation ago, before the hazards of cigarette smoking were known, smoking might have been a rather innocent, if futile, way of seeking a sense of security or social ease. Today, though, it is difficult to believe that starting to smoke is a sophisticated act.

Fortunately, many teen-agers share this view. According to a recent American Cancer Society survey, of the small minority of teen-agers who smoke, less than half believed they would be smoking five years from now, and only one in four had smoked within the previous thirty days.

What Can Help a Person Stop Smoking If He Already Has the Habit?

For most people, the best way to stop is to give up cigarettes all at once. Cutting down on cigarettes gradually seems to work for some people, however. In either case, the first few days or weeks seem to be most difficult. During this period many people find it helpful to chew gum. Keeping busy and active also helps. Many individuals find giving up cigarettes easier if they pamper themselves in some other ways—maybe by spending cigarette money on a paperback, a record, or something else they want.

Teacher's Notes

Check Yourself: After students have read and thought about these questions, use them as guides for a summary discussion.

Things to Do: Other subjects for individual reports are *Smoking and Emphysema* and *Drug Abuse and Crime.*

Check Yourself

1. Look back at the questions on page 52. How would you answer them now?

2. How would you explain these terms?

a. "bennies"

b. "speed"

c. withdrawal symptoms

d. psychedelic

e. pusher

f. heroin

g. "uppers" and "downers"

3. What are some of the dangers of abuse of stimulant drugs? Of depressant drugs?

4. Why does more research need to be done on marijuana?

5. What did you learn about LSD that you did not know before? About marijuana?

6. Why are legal penalties for pushers of narcotics so severe?

7. Why is there a connection between alcoholic beverages and accidents?

8. What is the purpose of Alcoholics Anonymous? Of Al-Anon? Of Alateen?

9. How would you justify this warning on cigarette packages: *The Surgeon General Has Determined That Cigarette Smoking Is Dangerous to Your Health*?

10. Should *all* drugs be illegal? Explain.

Things to Do

1. Make up a slogan that suggests some of the dangers of cigarette smoking—or that might make a young person stop and think before beginning to smoke. One young person offered this slogan: SMOKE, CHOKE, CROAK.

2. Prepare a list of the ways in which drugs can be abused.

3. Make a poster that highlights the hazards of a drug such as LSD or heroin.

4. Suggest some things you think a community—including parents, teachers, and students —might do to fight drug abuse.

5. Think about how you would explain this statement: "Drug dependence is only one aspect of general dependence—of relying on a variety of crutches and on other people to solve problems."

6. Prepare some quiz questions about this topic: The Effects of Alcohol on the Body and on Society. These questions might later be used for an informal quiz session.

Special Research

1. Investigate ways in which smoking is associated with accidental deaths from fire.

2. Write a report on the ways in which smoking can affect the heart.

Teacher's Notes

Pupils may work independently on this review of the unit. Encourage them to reread material in the text when necessary. Tell pupils that any sensible answer which completes the sentence correctly can be considered a "right answer."

Self-Help Review

Use a ruler or a strip of paper to cover the answer column at the right. Read the first item and write the missing word or words on a piece of paper. Then move your ruler or paper strip down to uncover the answer and see if you are right. Go on in the same way with each of the other items. Do not write in this book.

The numbers by the answers show pages in this book that give information about the subject. For the items you miss, go back and review this information.

1. A person whose body craves a drug—and suffers withdrawal symptoms without it—is ______ dependent on the drug.	physically 55
2. An average dose of the drug ______ is the size of a speck.	LSD 61
3. Marijuana often affects a user's sense of time and ______.	distance 62
4. Two narcotics that have medical uses but that are dangerous when abused are ______ and ______.	morphine 57 codeine
5. A dangerous narcotic drug that has no medical use in the United States and is illegal is ______.	heroin 58
6. Narcotic drugs can lead to physical dependence and ______ dependence.	psychological 58
7. Alcohol is a sedative or a ______ drug.	depressant 70
8. It is now known that cigarette smoking can cause ______ ______.	lung cancer 76
9. An organization that works with young people who have an alcoholic parent is called ______.	Alateen 73

Teacher's Notes

After pupils have taken the test and their papers have been scored, the test items can serve as guides for summary discussion.

Health Test for Unit Two

Part I

Copy the first part of each sentence below. Then complete it with the *best* answer.

1. Drugs are chemicals that
a. are always harmful to the body
b. are always helpful to the body
c. may be helpful or harmful

2. Stimulant drugs are
a. often known as "uppers"
b. depressants
c. used for sleeplessness

3. The best-known depressants are
a. hallucinogens
b. Benzedrine and Dexedrine
c. barbiturates

4. LSD is
a. a weak narcotic
b. a powerful hallucinogen
c. a legal drug

5. Cigarette smoking can be a factor
a. in causing lung cancer
b. in encouraging "mainlining"
c. in causing hallucinations

6. The so-called "downers" are the
a. hallucinogens
b. stimulants
c. depressants

Part II

On a sheet of paper, write the term that is suggested by each of the following descriptions:

7. A narcotic that has a medical use. **morphine**

8. A person who cannot or will not stop heavy drinking of alcoholic beverages. **alcoholic**

9. A drug abuser who is physically and psychologically dependent on a drug. **addict**

10. A habit-forming drug in tobacco. **nicotine**

11. Drugs that speed up the work of the nervous system. **stimulants**

12. Drugs that slow down the work of the nervous system. **depressants**

13. An illegal narcotic drug that has no medical use in the United States. **heroin**

14. A person who sells drugs illegally. **pusher**

15. A class of psychedelic drugs. **hallucinogens**

16. A drug that is made from the Indian hemp plant. **marijuana**

17. A slang term for Methedrine. **speed**

18. A drug that may cause recurrent hallucinations weeks or months after a dose. **LSD**

19. An organization that helps alcoholics. **A.A.**

20. Tiny hairlike parts that line the air passages of the breathing system. **cilia**

Number of Answers	20
Number Right	______
Score (Number Right × 5)	______

Part III

Copy the number of each item below. After the number, write *T* if the statement is *True,* write *F* if it is *False.*

T 1. The more a person smokes, the greater is his risk of getting lung cancer.

T 2. Tars from cigarette smoke contain cancer-producing substances.

F 3. Depressant drugs have no medical use.

F 4. Scientific proof of the harmful effects of smoking has been available for fifty years.

T 5. "Pep pills" can be dangerous to people who use them to keep awake while driving.

F 6. Alcohol is digested in the body in the same way all foods are.

F 7. The control of narcotics is a problem that each community must solve on its own.

T 8. Morphine is a drug made from opium.

T 9. Beer is a beverage with an alcoholic content of about 3 to 6 percent.

T 10. Nicotine is a habit-forming drug found in tobacco and in cigarette smoke.

F 11. An alcoholic is a person who likes to take an alcoholic beverage now and then.

T 12. Alcoholism is an illness.

F 13. The liver is the one organ in the body that cannot oxidize alcohol.

T 14. The most common depressant drugs are the barbiturates.

F 15. The more a person weighs, the greater will be the effects of alcoholic beverages on him.

F 16. Research on marijuana is complete and conclusive.

T 17. A person can become physically and psychologically dependent on depressant drugs such as the narcotics.

T 18. A person who abuses a stimulant drug can become psychologically dependent on it.

T 19. Some nicknames for marijuana are "grass," "tea," and "pot."

F 20. Alcoholic beverages rarely, if ever, affect coordination.

F 21. Alcoholic beverages are stimulants.

F 22. The sight area of the brain is not affected by alcohol in the body.

T 23. There is evidence that pipe and cigar smoking is harmful to health.

F 24. Cigarette smoking before a meal quickens the appetite.

T 25. If heavy smokers stop smoking, their chances of getting lung cancer or other smoking-connected illness decrease.

Number of Answers	25
Number Right	______
Score (Number Right × 4)	______

3 Are You Alert to Health Quackery?

Teacher's Notes

Unit Overview: Explore students' ideas of the nature of *health quackery.* (Page 84 will give them a chance to compare their ideas with those provided in the text.) Discuss, too, why people need education in detecting health quackery—and whether students think quackery is something that might ever affect them and their families.

Health quackery is as serious a problem today as it was in the past. People all over the world pay very high prices—in money, health, and sometimes in lives—because they do not always recognize health quacks and health quackery. Even though there are laws that are meant to control quackery, individuals must be educated so that they can protect themselves. In this unit you will gain information that can help *you* avoid many of the hazards of health quackery.

Teacher's Notes

Read to Find Out: These questions arouse interest in the topics to be treated in this unit. Talk over the questions briefly—just long enough to give students a chance to commit themselves to some answers. Such commitment helps ensure that pupils' attention will be held during the study of the unit. They will want to check the accuracy of the tentative answers they have given.

What Is Health Quackery? Students might consider what is meant by such statements as "Health quackery is big business" and "Health quackery can be serious business."

Point out that women as well as men may be health quacks.

Read to Find Out

1. *What is meant by a* health quack?
2. *What example can you give of health quackery that merely involves a waste of money?*
3. *What example can you give of health quackery that can have a serious effect on a person's health?*
4. *What is meant by mail-order "doctoring"?*
5. *How do you explain the term "food quackery"?*
6. *What are some signs of a health quack?*
7. *How can people go about choosing a qualified doctor?*
8. *What is a* food fallacy? *What example can you give of such a fallacy?*
9. *What can you do to find out if you are dealing with a health quack?*
10. *Why are people misled by health quackery?*

What Is Health Quackery?

Each year people in the United States spend more than a billion dollars on worthless treatments for physical ailments, on useless gadgets and devices sold as "cures" for various illnesses, and on ineffective "health aids" of many varieties. In other words, the people in this country spend more than a billion dollars a year for *health quackery*—much of it in the form of food quackery. Many of these worthless treatments and "health aids" are obtained from fakers known as *health quacks.* A health quack is someone who practices medicine without the proper qualifications or who boasts that he has knowledge of "miraculous" remedies.

Perhaps you can recall some examples of quackery that you have read or heard about. What ones come to mind?

Some true instances of quackery are described on pages 85 to 89. As you read these examples, decide which ones involve chiefly a waste of money, which ones endanger health, and which ones endanger life itself.

Something to Do

A member of the class might be chosen to write to the American Medical Association, 535 North Dearborn, Chicago, Illinois 60610, to ask for a list of pamphlets and booklets available on health quackery. A price list should also be requested. Some of the many booklets available from the American Medical Association are Facts on Quacks—What You Should Know About Health Quackery; Health Quackery; Mechanical Quackery; *and* Merchants of Menace.

A "Magic" Machine and a Promise to Cure[1]

"Of course I can cure you," the white-coated man assured his diabetic patient. "The Spectro-Chrome can cure any disease." He pointed to an impressive-looking metal box with a lighted opening on the side. He explained that to cure a disease the rays of light from the box were directed at the ailing parts of the body. To add to the secret magic of the so-called cure, this procedure had to be performed during a particular phase of the moon which was indicated by the patient's disease.

The patient, an elderly man, was impressed by the machine and by the professional manner of the man in the white coat. When the Spectro-Chrome inventor advised him to stop taking his daily insulin shots, the elderly man did not question the advice.

With high hopes, he stopped his insulin shots and instead began daily treatments with the Spectro-Chrome. In a short time he lapsed into a diabetic coma and died.

His death might have passed unnoticed if the Federal Food and Drug Administration (FDA) had not already been on the trail of the white-coated man, Dinshah P. Ghadiali. A native of India, Ghadiali's only qualification was a fake honorary medical degree. But his lack of qualifications did not stop him from prescribing Spectro-Chrome treatments for illnesses ranging from heart diseases to diabetes and cancer.

Ghadiali had invented the Spectro-Chrome over 25 years before, and he eventually sold over 10,000 of them for $475 each. When he was brought to trial, an FDA official demonstrated that inside the Spectro-Chrome was a 1,000-watt light bulb. Colored panes of glass were moved in front of the bulb to "treat" various diseases—red and purple for heart diseases, purple and blue for cancer, and so on.

When all the testimony was in, the Spectro-Chrome inventor was fined $20,000 and put on probation for a few years. Distribution of his machine was halted, but he was never brought to trial for his part in causing the death of the elderly diabetic gentleman.

[1]Adapted from "Quacks—The Would-Be MDs Who Can Harm You" by Barbara O'Connell from *Science Digest* Magazine (January 1969). Reprinted with permission of Science Digest.

Teacher's Notes

The example of quackery here will be better appreciated if students know something about *diabetes.* In diabetes, the body cells are unable to use carbohydrates in the diet because the pancreas does not secrete enough of the hormone *insulin.* Insulin normally aids the body in utilizing sugars and starches. In all but mild cases of diabetes, the patient must take insulin daily by injection. Failure to take insulin regularly in the prescribed dosage can result in a form of unconsciousness known as *diabetic coma.*

Stress that accurate health knowledge is one of our best protections against quackery.

This gentleman, who called himself "Dr." Bokanky, was an old-time dealer in so-called curative herbs. *He was typical of the "medicine men," "herb dealers," and other health quacks of bygone days in our country.*

Teacher's Notes

Discuss some of the factors that contribute to making many arthritis sufferers "fall for" quack aids and cures. In talking over the real-life examples of quackery, invite comments about how the health-quack promoters of such products as the "vrilium" tube and the "Z-Ray" profited by their fakery.

What Do You Think?

1. It has been said that some people go to quacks because the quacks tell them what they want to hear. What evidence of this appeared in the story on page 85 about the quack doctor Ghadiali?

2. It has also been said that quackery is "profitable business." How did the story of Ghadiali confirm this statement?

3. Would you *have been suspicious of Ghadiali? Why or why not?*

Arthritis Quackery[1]

Of all the people who suffer from continuing ailments, those who have arthritis seem most likely to be "taken in" by quackery. For one reason, there is no known cause or cure for arthritis. Although proper medical treatment *can* help arthritis sufferers, many arthritic persons get impatient with a physician's treatment. They decide to look for faster or seemingly "certain relief."

Furthermore, at times the inflammation of the joints, which causes the pain in arthritis, goes away for a few weeks or months or years. But then the pain comes back again. These puzzling aspects of arthritis encourage quackery. If a person is treated by a quack or uses quack products and the arthritis seems to improve, the person mistakenly thinks it is cured.

In the following material you will learn about some of the many kinds of quackery that have been reported in recent years in connection with people suffering from arthritis.

Bracelets and Other Gadgets

Devices peddled or used by quacks to make money at the expense of arthritics have been as simple as copper bracelets and discs of copper or zinc to be worn in the heels of shoes. You can see a photograph of a copper bracelet and other gadgets claimed to cure arthritis on pages 92–93.

The "vrilium" tube was another device which was promoted for a time as a "cure" for both arthritis and cancer. This tube contained a penny's worth of the chemical barium chloride, yet willing arthritic sufferers paid up to $300 for the tube.

"Z-Ray"

The "Z-Ray," which was priced at $50, was purported to be able to restore the health of a person suffering from arthritis by "expanding the atoms" in the body. The tube has been declared worthless. So has another gadget of similar nature consisting chiefly of a plastic lampshade and a light bulb. Its promoters claimed that placing a piece of blue plastic over the lampshade and bathing the affected joints in the glow of blue light would cure arthritis. It would not, of course.

[1]Adapted from *Health Quackery, Arthritis.* Copyright © 1968 by the American Medical Association. Reprinted by permission.

Uranium Treatments

Radiations from uranium have been promoted falsely in devices supposed to be beneficial to people with arthritis. One gadget that sold widely not long ago was the "wonder glove," a mitten selling for $100 that was supposed to be lined with uranium ore. The mitten was, of course, useless in treating arthritis.

Equally useless to arthritis patients is a visit to an old uranium-mine tunnel. This "treatment" has often been advertised at a cost of $10 or more a visit. Such "treatments," warns the Food and Drug Administration, "are not only a waste of time and money for arthritis patients, but any product emitting enough radioactivity to affect functions of the body is dangerous to use without medical supervision." Usually, though, such tunnels advertised to cure arthritis do not even contain uranium.

Mail-Order "Doctoring"[1]

Mail-order quackery is one of the biggest types of fraud dealt with by the United States postal inspectors. Fortunately, certain kinds of doctoring-by-mail have now disappeared. The sale of eyeglasses and dental plates by mail are examples of mail-order doctoring that have been halted by efficient law enforcement and growing public knowledge about quackery. Nonetheless, other schemes and rackets still exist.

Following is an example of mail-order doctoring that had tragic results:

A man and his wife, who had become interested in how the stars and planets influence people, noticed an advertisement in a magazine. It read in part, "Dr. Abn Donahji, Yogi Healer and Clairvoyant Reader, will solve your problems. Send eight questions and $5 with self-addressed envelope." The couple sent the $5 and some questions about astrology to Doctor Donahji, and shortly afterwards the answers arrived. The couple then wrote to Doctor Donahji saying that the wife had cancer and they wondered if he could help.

[1]Adapted from "Mail-Order Doctoring—Still a Menace" from *Today's Health* Magazine (June 1967). Reprinted by permission of the American Medical Association.

Teacher's Notes

Students might discuss and evaluate these recommendations for avoiding arthritis quackery: *Be wary of testimonials (even sincere ones may be due to a temporary ceasing of arthritis symptoms for other reasons); be on guard against anyone who offers a "sure cure" for arthritis; check with a qualified physician before using any unprescribed products for which claims are made.* Point out that modern drugs and treatments are being developed by medical scientists—ones which *can* be of some help to arthritis patients. However, these new drugs and treatments are not normally advertised in popular magazines, in newspapers, or on radio and television.

Something to Think About

Reliable research workers in the area of arthritis state that with most kinds of arthritis, nothing a person eats or does not eat will cause, lessen, or cure pain from arthritis. In the light of this information, how would you evaluate the following arthritis advertisements?

"See an end to all kinds of arthritis troubles: Sip Simms' Sea Water; it's Guaranteed."

"Banish all arthritis pains: Use Uncle Ben's Vinegar and Honey mixture daily."

"No matter what kind of arthritis you have, you'll find relief with Ma Mason's Alfalfa Tablets."

Teacher's Notes

During the discussion of mail-order "doctoring," use such queries as these:

"What *is* mail-order 'doctoring'?"

"What is one reason why mail-order 'doctoring' could be nothing but a fraud?" (The doctor never sees or examines the patients, therefore the doctor could not possibly diagnose their ailments.)

"What was especially dangerous about Donahji's health quackery?"

"What led to Donahji's arrest?"

"What evidence is there in the account of Donahji that indicates many people are easily fooled?"

"What evidence is there that quackery can be profitable to the quacks?"

"What words come to mind when you think of *quacks*? Could you make a crossword puzzle from such words?"

What should a person keep in mind when he or she reads advertisements that claim to do such things as help a person gain or lose weight, grow taller, build muscles, and so on?

Doctor Donahji's answer was reassuring. He told them that he had cured many people of cancer by using his psychic powers. If the couple would send a $5 weekly "donation," he would cure the wife. The man and woman promptly began sending the "donation" each week. From time to time they received letters from Doctor Donahji telling them that the "vibrations" were building up favorably. But within a year the woman died of cancer.

Her life might have been saved or extended if she had been given the right treatment—in time—by a qualified physician. A qualified physician, of course, would have examined her in person. Although all cases of cancer cannot as yet be cured, many of them can be cured or arrested by the prompt use of chemicals, surgery, radiation, or a combination of these various methods.

Inspectors from the United States Postal Service—who can take action against mail frauds involving health products or treatments—began investigating Doctor Donahji. They found that this man, who claimed to be a graduate of the University of Calcutta in India, was really named Donald Wilson. He was born in Iowa and raised in Kansas. He had been an assembly-line worker in Detroit and then a dance instructor in Los Angeles.

Then he had an idea that promised him a great deal of money. He put on a turban, picked up a little information about astrology, changed his name to Dr. Abn Donahji, and offered his services as a spiritual healer, prophet, and marriage counselor. He was popular locally, and he advertised in various publications that brought him nation-wide responses.

The extent of his mail-order medical practice was revealed when, after a full investigation, the so-called Doctor Donahji was arrested for mail fraud. His records contained correspondence with 4,000 persons. These people had been paying the "healer" for such services as mail-order treatment of cancer, heart disease, and multiple sclerosis by "vibrations" and by mysterious "healing powers." His various activities had brought in about $400,000 in his years as "Dr. Abn Donahji." Eventually he was convicted and sent to jail.

Food Quackery

People in this country spend vast sums of money on food supplements, special vitamin preparations, and food fads. Unless a doctor has prescribed them, special food supplements or vitamins are not needed in the diet. Also, people may use such products as "cures" for diseases that need a physician's care. In such cases, the products might be harmful.

Where do you hear about the many food fads and special food supplements? Often you learn about them from acquaintances who are enthusiastic about some particular items. These people often buy products from special stores. Sometimes door-to-door salesmen offer such items for sale. Exaggerated and often false claims about various foods may be found in advertisements received through the mail or in magazines and newspapers.

Regardless of how or where food-quackery ideas or products are peddled, such misleading statements as these are usually given: All diseases are due to poor diet; food supplements are necessary because our food is grown in soil that is too worn-out to supply necessary minerals, vitamins, and other nutrients; most people feel tired because they have a "subclinical" vitamin deficiency that cannot be found in any physical examination. Such statements often sound convincing, but scientific analysis shows that the claims usually go against proven medical knowledge.

Because they are influenced by clever advertising and false information, gullible people buy special food products that are expensive and that do no more for health than ordinary foods found in grocery stores. These people also buy vitamins they do not need—vitamins that are usually plentiful in the ordinary foods of an adequate diet.

Even the term *health* when added to the word *foods* can be misleading because it implies that such products have special health-giving properties. Actually these special foods, in general, contain the same nutrients found in common, everyday foods. For example, yogurt, which is often promoted by self-styled food "experts," has about the same nutritional value as milk. Iodine in the kelp tablets or sea water sometimes offered

Teacher's Notes

Here are some questions that might be used as discussion leads in considering the topic of food quackery:

"What is meant by *food quackery?*"

"Can such quackery be dangerous? Explain your answer."

"How do people learn about special food supplements and various vitamin preparations not prescribed by a doctor?"

"What are some misleading statements that can serve as clues in helping detect food quackery?" (Invite skits of food quackery situations.)

Sea kelp, yogurt, yeast, iodine, blackstrap molasses, and herbs of many varieties do not, *as the food quacks claim, fortify the diet, steady the nerves, pep up the blood, or make the kidneys and bladder work more efficiently. Foods like yogurt, yeast, and blackstrap molasses are good foods in themselves; it is the false claims about them that lead to food quackery.*

Teacher's Notes

Comment, "*You* who are studying this text should be able to protect yourselves against food quackery. Why?"

Review the "Food for Fitness" daily food guide. See if students remember the four groups of foods and the daily servings needed from each group to achieve adequate nutrition. (See pages 116-117 of the text.)

Talk over why many people are willing to spend money on so-called quick and easy reducing schemes. (Losing weight the safe way requires self-discipline and takes time; it is not wise to lose too much weight in a very brief period of time. Thus, it is tempting for some people to try ways of losing weight that are claimed to be rapid and to require little effort or self-control.)

for sale is adequately supplied in seafoods and in iodized salt. Foods grown in special soils are no more nutritious than ordinary foods because the nutritional value of food is influenced very little by the composition of the soil. What is more, most faddish food items, elaborate supplements, and special vitamin preparations are expensive, since their promoters charge high prices for their products. A particular hazard exists when people feel that eating such foods is a safe substitute for having periodic medical checkups. On page 94, you can see a photograph of some quack food supplements that have been confiscated by the Food and Drug Administration.

A safeguard against food quackery is sound nutritional knowledge. If what you eat is planned according to the "Food for Fitness" daily food guide—and rounded out with foods that suit your taste and appetite—you are likely to be well nourished. The four food groups and the suggested number of servings from each group that should be included in the daily diet are shown on pages 116–117 of this book. If people are ill, special diets or food supplements will be recommended, as needed, by their doctors.

Weight-Reducing Products

Frequently, claims are made for certain quack products that they provide a method, a food, a pill, or a machine to reduce weight. Often claims are made that various products or treatments can cause weight loss without any dieting. There is no scientific evidence, however, that any of these products or treatments have a long-term effect—or indeed *any* effect—in weight reduction or weight control. No person, under normal circumstances, will lose excess fat unless he or she consumes fewer calories than are burned up in energy. On the other hand, an adequate diet is essential for maintaining good health and for aiding in weight reduction and control. Because losing weight means using up more calories than you take in, exercise also is an important factor in weight control.

When a large amount of weight is to be lost, the advice and supervision of a physician is essential. For a further discussion of weight reduction, see pages 22–23 of Unit One of this book.

Do You Remember?

1. What are some helpful tips for losing weight? If you don't remember, look back at pages 22-23.

2. What foods are essential for any dieter?

The St. Louis Medical Society's Museum of Medical Quackery

Here and on pages 92 to 94 are exhibits from the museum. Below is a collection of "patent medicines" sold by health quacks in bygone years. Under today's drug laws, medicines are patented to protect property rights—but the term "patent medicine" does not imply quackery. On pages 92 and 93, you can see fake medical devices removed from the market by the Food and Drug Administration.

The Wahl Powersage—a useless device that was supposed to "remove cobwebs from the brain and rejuvenate the personality glands."

Magnetic-Wave Helmet—said by its quack inventor "to stimulate white blood cells to fight disease."

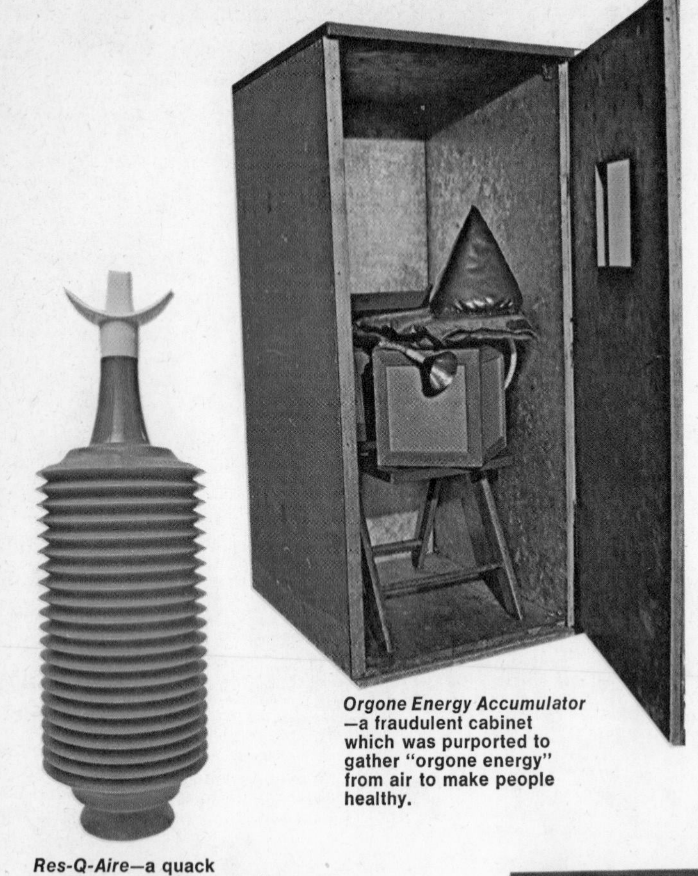

Orgone Energy Accumulator—a fraudulent cabinet which was purported to gather "orgone energy" from air to make people healthy.

Res-Q-Aire—a quack emergency respirator device. It has been found to be very dangerous and should not be used.

Health-Aire—a fake machine that was professed to generate "ionized air" to cure respiratory problems.

Electro-Metabograph—whose quack manufacturer claimed its "radio waves" could "realign vibrations from diseased body parts."

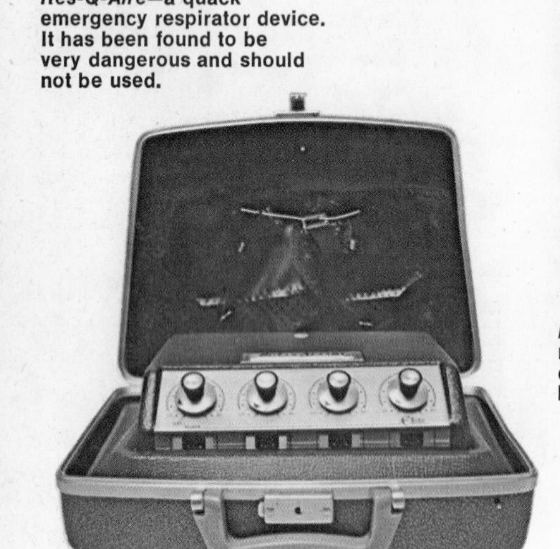

Relax-A-Cisor—which has been confiscated by the FDA. All post offices display notices warning against buying this machine.

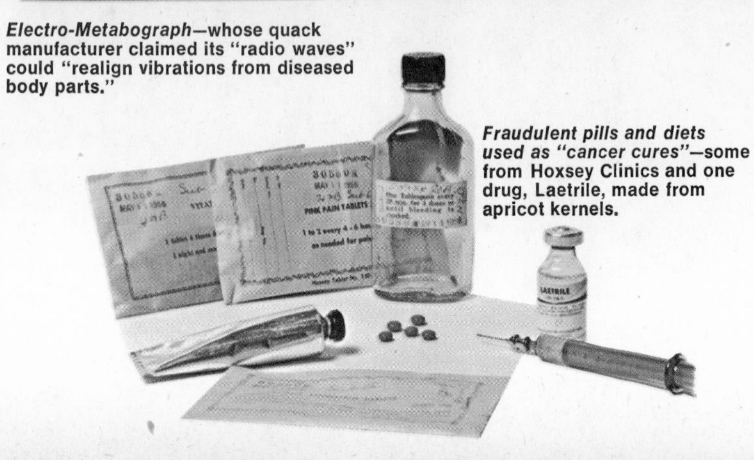

Fraudulent pills and diets used as "cancer cures"—some from Hoxsey Clinics and one drug, Laetrile, made from apricot kernels.

Ghadiali's Spectro-Chrome—which allegedly "cured" diseases by putting different colored lights on the affected areas of the body.

Hollywood Vita-Rol—a useless "aid" for body conditioning, insomnia, constipation, and so on.

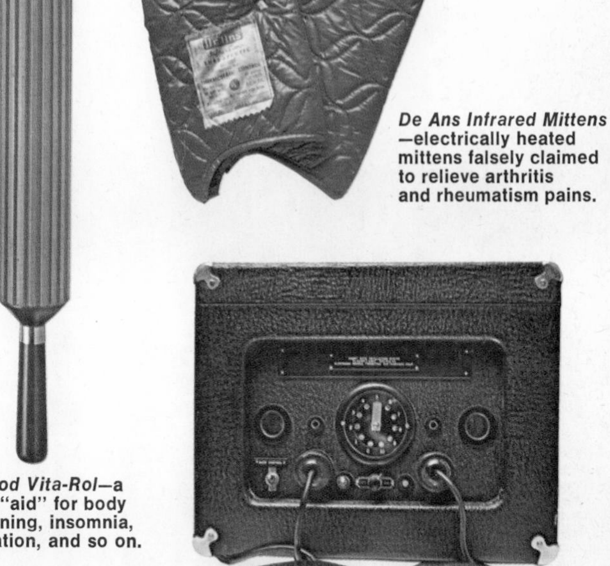

De Ans Infrared Mittens—electrically heated mittens falsely claimed to relieve arthritis and rheumatism pains.

Radionics Device—supposed to "cure" disease by "adjusting disharmony of electronic oscillation."

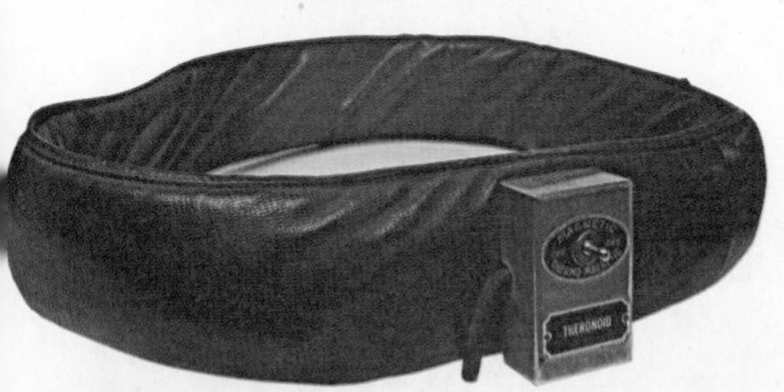

Magnetic-Ray Belt or Horse Collar—falsely claimed "a cure of any disease." It was seized by the FDA.

Micro-Dynameter—a quack machine claimed "to diagnose almost every ailment known."

Master Violet-Ray Generator—sold to gullible people for treament of baldness, arthritis, bursitis, dandruff, acne, and other conditions.

Arden Copper Bracelet—offered for the relief of rheumatism. Millions of people bought it. But the FDA has declared it of no value.

Beautypower—a device that unscrupulous promoters stated would "rebuild underlying muscles" and thus improve the strength and tone of the skin.

All these "food supplements" and other "cure-all" products have been taken off the market by the Food and Drug Administration because of their false health claims.

How Do You Recognize Health Quackery?

Perhaps you wonder why people fall for health quacks and health quackery. There are a good many reasons.

People in this country are becoming more and more conscious of factors that affect their health. There is so much varied information available about foods and health standards that a person may be tempted to look for simple ways to solve complicated problems.

A person may learn that a certain amount of food or vitamin is needed in the diet each day. Then the person thinks, "Well, if that amount is good, then ten times that amount would be better." Thinking of this kind is the result of inadequate knowledge about health and nutrition, and it can have harmful results. Then, too, a person may hear or read about some food or vitamin that offers promise of helping certain problems. He or she thinks, "This product can't *possibly* hurt me, and maybe it *will* do all it claims to do." Such a person is not alert to health quackery and could even fall into the hands of quacks who want to make money selling worthless products.

To a person with no special knowledge about food, nutrition, and health, a health quack may appear to be a qualified person. A quack may have an office and look much as a physician usually does. The walls of the office may display diplomas of various kinds. If examined closely, however, these diplomas usually turn out to be fakes or from correspondence schools or institutions that do not train qualified physicians.

Often the quack is a very smooth talker and a very persuasive salesperson and may use long medical terms to try to impress patients. The quack is apt to claim that without question the illness has been diagnosed and a cure can be guaranteed. It is not unusual for a quack to suggest that a patient stop taking medicines or other treatments prescribed by a physician.

It is important, then, that people learn to detect the signs of quackery. Some guides on how to recognize a quack are given on the next page. After you have studied these guides, be ready to discuss them.

Teacher's Notes

After pages 95 and 96 have been read, volunteers might plan and give brief dramatic skits in which gullible people are being "taken in" by fraudulent advertisements, by word-of-mouth recommendations of health "cures," by inadequate knowledge of nutrition, of arthritis, of safe methods to lose weight, and so on.

Did You Know?

The advances in medicine that have been made in very recent years are often cited as a reason why some people are "taken in" by health quackery. Real-life achievements in medicine are so miraculous that some people are ready to believe almost anything in this field.
One thing to remember, though, is that legitimate medical discoveries are not kept secret for the use of a few people; such discoveries are shared with qualified physicians everywhere.

Teacher's Notes

Students might think about each comment below and discuss whether it was more likely made by a quack or a qualified doctor:

"I can give you the names of fifty people I have cured..."

"You are run-down and have tired blood; what you need is this special Peppo-Nervo tonic..."

"I'll have to make some tests before I can say what the trouble may be..."

"This machine will cure your cancer; don't worry..."

Stress that people must not only learn to recognize the *health quack;* they must also learn to recognize *health quackery* as such. Thus it should be realized that quackery deals with false information no matter in what form it is given—in newspaper or magazine advertisements, on radio or television commercials, on package labels, and so on. To counteract such false information, accurate health knowledge is essential.

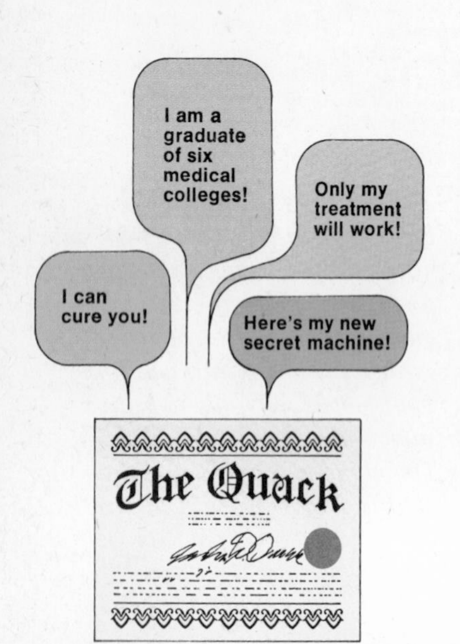

Some Traits of a Health Quack[1]

If you know what to look for, you can help protect yourself and members of your family from health quackery. Here are some of the characteristics of a quack:

1. The quack often uses a special machine that he claims can cure a disease; frequently he has a "secret" formula for a product he sells.

2. The quack may promise or imply a quick or easy cure, or he may talk about "pepping up" your health.

3. The quack advertises, using his "case histories" and testimonials from his "patients" to impress people.

4. He does not use the tried-and-proven methods of medical research and proof. He clamors constantly for recognition of his work by the medical profession, but he avoids a test or refuses to give the information needed for scientific evaluation of his product.

5. He claims medical men are persecuting him or that they are afraid of his competition.

6. He claims that his method of treatment is better than surgery, X rays, and drugs prescribed by a physician. Usually he opposes all immunizations.

What You Can Do

In addition to recognizing signs of health quackery, you can learn about places to go for information if you suspect that quackery is involved. It is especially important to seek such information when you are deeply concerned about your own health or that of someone you love. At such times, you might be less skeptical of a person, product, or method that seems to offer hope—even though it really is a false hope.

You should always remember that a money loss is certain when people turn to quack products or treatments. More serious than the loss of money is the delay in seeking proper medical treatment while relying on an ineffective treatment.

On the next page, there is a list of organizations and agencies that can provide information if you ever have a question involving the possibility of health quackery.

[1]Adapted from *Facts on Quacks.* Copyright © 1967 by the American Medical Association. Reprinted by permission.

Sources of Information About Health Quackery

The following organizations can give you reliable information about health products and services.

American Medical Association (AMA) in Chicago, Illinois. Fighting health quackery in all its forms is an important part of the AMA's work.

The Federal Trade Commission (FTC) in Washington, D.C. Among the functions of the Federal Trade Commission is safeguarding people by seeking to prevent the distribution of false or deceptive advertisements and exaggerated claims about foods, drugs, cosmetics, and so-called healing gadgets.

The Food and Drug Administration (FDA) in Washington, D.C. The FDA administers the Food, Drug, and Cosmetic Act. Its activities are directed mainly toward promoting purity and truthful labeling of consumer products.

United States Postal Service, Bureau of the Chief Postal Inspector, Washington, D.C. The Postal Service seeks to protect the public from the purchase of quack health products through the mails. The bureau's Medical-Fraud Unit checks magazines, pamphlets, and other sources for false claims made to sell quack products and treatments through the mail.

National Better Business Bureau. Although the Better Business Bureau has its main office in New York City, it has 142 local offices to serve the public. The bureau is concerned with truthful representations to the public.

Two other groups, both voluntary agencies, that work hard to keep the public informed about quackery are the *American Cancer Society* and *The Arthritis Foundation.* Both organizations have headquarters in New York City; each has many local, county, and state branches.

Although Federal and state laws do much to protect individuals from health quackery, people themselves have to be on the alert. Even after a health quack has been shown to be practicing illegally, it may take a long time before he is brought to trial. If he is not convicted—or if he is merely fined—the quack is apt to resume his quackery once more. Quackery is a very profitable business, and many quacks are willing to run the risk of arrest because of the promise of rich profits.

Teacher's Notes

Students might check their local telephone directories to see if their communities have Better Business Bureaus. If so, students should realize that questions about quackery can be referred to such bureaus. The local Chamber of Commerce is also of help at times in providing information when quackery is suspected.

Did You Know?

Listed below are fraudulent products seized in recent years—and taken off the market—by the Food and Drug Administration. These examples illustrate types of fraud and deception that still exist today:

Jojuba Oil—"*Can cure baldness, cancer, and kidney disease.*" *(False claim.)*

Life Everlasting Ginseng—"*Effective for treating arthritis, mental confusion, failing memory, and Parkinson's disease.*" *(False claim.)*

Super Pulse Electronic Device—"*Will cure arthritis, hepatitis, and other diseases.*" *(False claim.)*

Teacher's Notes

You might discuss with students why the state requires careful licensing of physicians, nurses, dentists, and so on. (To prevent untrained people from taking advantage of the consumer.)
A special research project might be that of finding out what a physician or dentist must do to be properly licensed in his state.
A Question Box in the classroom in which students can drop their health questions on unsigned papers is a means of "getting at" health queries that might not be asked publicly.
After you have checked the queries, you might make available pamphlets that contain information on matters of concern. Individuals or committees might be assigned the task of looking for answers to various queries of common interest.

What Are Your Questions?

Perhaps you have some questions about health quackery or about situations in which you think you might be spending money needlessly. Some commonly asked questions are shown below. How would you answer them?

After you have tried to answer the questions, check your ideas with the ones given below and on pages 99–101. Also suggest some other questions you would like to have answered. The booklets listed in the margin on page 84 can supply some answers.

1. How can you go about choosing a qualified doctor, especially when you are living in a community new to you?
2. What are over-the-counter drugs and how can they be used safely?
3. What are food fallacies and what are the dangers involved in believing them?

How Should You Choose a Doctor?

If your family does not know a doctor in the community and wants to locate one, these are some things that can be done. You can call the city medical society if you live in a large city; otherwise you can get in touch with the county medical society. Such a medical society will provide some names of nearby physicians. Those who are so recommended will be properly trained and qualified. If a doctor is recommended to you by neighbors or friends, you can still make a further check by calling the city or county medical society to ask about the qualifications of this person. Membership in a medical society is a good indication that the doctor has the proper qualifications to practice medicine.

If you are moving to another community, your present physician may be able to help you. He or she can provide names of doctors from a list of the state's American Medical Association members or from a directory of medical specialists.

Any large hospital, where standards tend to be high, can also furnish names of qualified physicians in your area. Doctors who work in health clinics set up by the city or county health departments will, of course, be qualified.

Something to Know

If you want to find a reputable dentist, you can use somewhat the same procedures suggested for seeking a qualified physician. Your city or county dental society can provide recommendations. Your own dentist or any qualified dentist may also recommend to you the names of several dentists from which to choose.
Low-cost or free dental care may often be obtained in a dental clinic set up by the city or county health department, or in a dental school associated with a university or medical center.

What Are Over-the-Counter Drugs?

Over-the-counter drugs are *nonprescription drugs,* that is, drugs that can be bought at a pharmacy or other store without a doctor's prescription. Among the over-the-counter drugs are those for such ailments as minor colds, minor sore throats, headaches, indigestion, dandruff, and minor injuries. Such drugs are safe if they are used for minor conditions and if they are taken for *temporary relief* and *temporary symptoms.* It is very important that the labels on nonprescription drugs be carefully studied. Information should also be noted on labels of *prescription drugs,* or drugs specially ordered by a doctor. Particular attention should be given to directions about dosage. *Warnings* and *cautions* on the labels of nonprescription drugs should also be heeded. For example, a cough remedy may state, "Be sure to check with a doctor if cough persists beyond three days." What warning is given on the label of nonprescription drugs containing aspirin?

One trouble with nonprescription drugs—as compared with prescription drugs—is that people often take them when they do not need them. For example, many individuals take laxatives that they do not need. Contrary to various advertisements, it is *not* necessary to have a bowel movement every day. Some people may have one only once in two or three days. Individuals differ. Missing a few bowel movements according to one's regular pattern is not a cause for great concern. Generally things return to normal after a few days, and the usual rhythm is resumed. If, however, a person has constipation that persists, a physician should be consulted.

Certain safety practices should be followed in the use of any drugs—whether they are prescription drugs or nonprescription drugs. Some "do's and don'ts" for taking drugs are given below. Be ready to give the reason you think is behind each suggestion.

Never give or take medicine in the dark; be sure you can read the label clearly.

When you are measuring a drug, pay full attention to what you are doing.

Never give or take medicine from an unlabeled bottle.

Teacher's Notes

A question about what is meant by the term "patent medicine" may arise. Following are some comments on "patent medicines" taken from the booklet *Facts on Quacks, What You Should Know About Health Quackery,* published by the American Medical Association:

"At one time health quacks sold what were called 'patent medicines'... improved laws and improved enforcement largely have corrected this situation. New drugs are patented now to protect property rights, but the term 'patent' in connection with medicines does not imply quackery. Drugs that can be purchased over the counter without a prescription are subject to the same strict rules as prescription drugs—and over-the-counter drugs are safe and generally helpful for conditions represented in the labeling when they are used as directed."

Something to Do

Pay particular attention to advertisements on radio and TV for nonprescription drugs. Look for examples of ads that urge people to take nonprescription drugs that they probably do not need.

Teacher's Notes

Following are some additional food fallacies together with the food facts:

Fallacy: Pork is indigestible.
Fact: It is as digestible as other meats.

Fallacy: Fish and celery are "brain" foods, and eating them will make a person more intelligent.
Fact: An adequate daily diet provides nourishment for all the tissues of the body; there is no special food for the brain any more than there is one for an arm or leg.

What Do You Think?

Do you think the following ad is likely to be reliable? "Rid yourself of all acne problems. Use Teen-Tone soap; join the Teen-Tone, clear-skin generation!"

Be sure to store all drugs out of the reach of small children; a locked medicine cabinet is the best place for drugs.

Before measuring liquid medicine, always shake the bottle thoroughly. Why?

Date all nonprescription drugs when you buy them; prescription drugs will be dated by the pharmacist.

Throw away old drugs, especially prescription drugs that have been used for a prior illness; remember that old drugs may change and become ineffective or even harmful.

When you throw away drugs, flush them down the toilet; be sure the discarded containers cannot be reached by children or pets.

What Is a Food Fallacy?

A food fallacy is a mistaken idea or half-truth about food. Many food fallacies that people in this country believed in the past have disappeared as a result of nutrition education. Yet some mistaken ideas and half-truths still persist. Food fallacies may cause poor nutrition practices or lead people to spend money needlessly.

For every food fallacy, there is a food fact. Some common food fallacies with their corresponding facts or corrections are these:

Fallacy: Eating fish four times a week causes a calorie reduction in the content of other foods you eat.

Fact: Fish is nutritious and it is used in most diets, but it has no magical properties. Neither fish nor any food can reduce calories in other foods you eat. Many varieties of fish, though, are low in fat and are lower in calories than other varieties of foods in the meat group.

Fallacy: Onions and garlic are "blood purifiers" and are valuable in the treatment of many diseases.

Fact: Onions have little nutritive value; garlic has practically none. Both are used as food flavorings. Regardless of past statements by food faddists, onions and garlic have no value in treating cancer, high blood pressure, or any other kind of disease.

Fallacy: A diet of skim milk and bananas alone is a good way to lose weight.

Fact: A safe weight-reduction program must provide the nutrients necessary to protect general health. A diet of skim milk and bananas—or any other diet that does not contain enough foods from the "Food for Fitness" daily food guide each day—is not safe or healthful. A few pounds can usually be lost by eating an adequate diet and by cutting down on the size and number of the servings. If more than minor weight losses are desirable, the advice of a physician should be obtained before any dieting is attempted.

Fallacy: Vitamin pills or other vitamin concentrates are needed by everyone.

Fact: An adequate diet, containing enough foods daily from the four food groups, will generally provide all the vitamins needed. People who are ill may at times have a vitamin deficiency that can be corrected by vitamins prescribed by a physician.

Fallacy: Eating grapefruit will cause a person to lose weight.

Fact: No single food has weight-reduction properties. Limitations of the diet to one food will no doubt enable one to lose weight, but the body's nutritional health cannot be maintained on any *one* food.

Fallacy: Pork liver is less nutritious than beef liver.

Fact: Both pork liver and beef liver contain valuable vitamins, minerals, and other nutrients. Pork liver has more iron, and beef liver has more Vitamin A. Both kinds of liver are about alike as to proteins and calories. Pork liver is cheaper but no less nutritious.

Fallacy: Eggs are more digestible raw than cooked.

Fact: The opposite is true. Eggs are less easily digested raw than cooked, but eggs are completely digestible in both forms.

Fallacy: Certain combinations of food make fat, while others cause body fat to melt away.

Fact: It is absolutely impossible for any food combination to cause body fat to be used up. The only exception is that a diet high in protein is known to raise the basal metabolism.

Fallacy: Milk is constipating.

Fact: Milk is not constipating, and in fact its action in the stomach helps in healthy elimination.

Teacher's Notes

One food fallacy that you might want to discuss with students is the one that milk is necessary only for young children. The fact is that the nutrients present in milk, especially calcium and riboflavin, are necessary in the daily diet of people of all ages.

Teen-agers need 4 cups of milk a day. However, milk products like cheese or ice cream can be substituted for part of the milk. It is difficult to provide adequate calcium and one of the B vitamins in the diet if milk and milk products are not included.

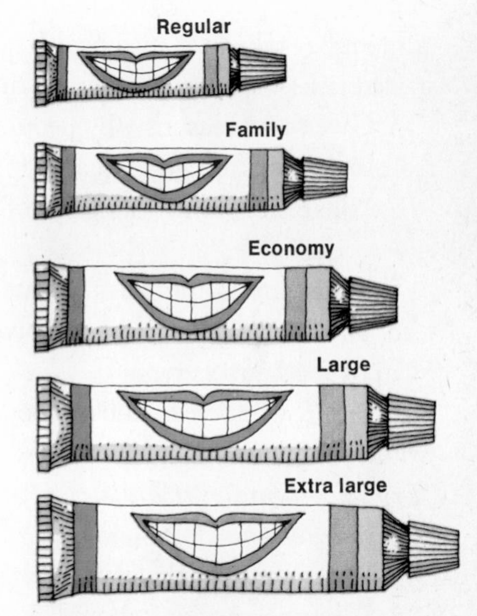

There is a great variety of toothpastes and tooth powders on the market. All of them can aid in cleaning the teeth. And those with fluoride added can be helpful in curbing dental cavities, or caries. If possible, talk with your dentist about the kinds of dentifrices he recommends. Try to figure out, too, what are really the "best buys" in the dentifrices you do purchase.

Teacher's Notes

Check Yourself: After students have read and thought about these questions, use them as guides for a group summary discussion of important ideas in this unit.

Things to Do: Volunteers might prepare a panel discussion in which they talk over what it takes to be protected against health quackery.

Students might also analyze various radio and television advertisements. Is the appeal in the ads to the emotions (irrational) or is the appeal to knowledge (rational)?

Check Yourself

1. Look back at the questions on page 84. How would you answer them now?

2. Why might a person with a very serious ailment be "taken in" by a health quack? What special risks would such a person run?

3. Give some reasons why people who suffer from arthritis often go to quacks for help.

4. What are some dangers of mail-order "doctoring"?

5. What are some sales points that often lead gullible people to be involved in some form of food quackery?

6. From what you know about nutrition, would you judge this to be a food fact or fallacy: *"Try an all-brown-rice diet for two weeks to cure your tension"?* Explain.

7. What are over-the-counter drugs?

8. What precautions should people keep in mind in using over-the-counter drugs?

9. What are some safety guides to observe in connection with *all* drugs?

10. How does the U.S. Postal Service help protect people against quackery?

11. Explain why you think there might be quackery involved in a "reducing" pill that was advertised as "capable of melting away the pounds while you eat all you want."

Things to Do

Below is a list of misconceptions[1] about health frequently found among young people your age. Write a sentence or so telling why each idea listed is *wrong.* Also be ready to tell how you would correct each statement.

a. Good doctors usually advertise.

b. A daily bowel movement is always necessary for good health.

c. Taking vitamin pills guarantees good health.

d. An all-vegetable diet is the best diet.

e. The best doctors always promise to make people healthy.

f. Persons with cancer should go to doctors who guarantee "sure cures."

g. Using reducing pills is the best way to lose weight.

Special Research

Look for an advertisement that you think involves some form of quackery. Cut out the ad; paste it on a sheet of paper. Below the ad, explain why you think some quackery is involved.

[1]From "Certain Harmful Misconceptions of Junior High School Students Attending Public Schools in Metropolitan Areas" by Price Harrison, Jr., and Leslie W. Irwin from *Research Quarterly,* Vol. 35, No. 4. Reprinted by permission of American Association for Health, Physical Education, and Recreation.

Teacher's Notes

Pupils may work independently on this review of the unit. Encourage them to reread material in the text when necessary. Tell pupils that any sensible answer which completes the sentence correctly can be considered a "right answer."

Self-Help Review

Use a ruler or a strip of paper to cover the answer column at the right. Read the first item and write the missing word or words on a piece of paper. Then move your ruler or paper strip down to uncover the answer and see if you are right. Go on in the same way with each of the other items. Do not write in this book.

The numbers by the answers show pages in this book that give information about the subject. For the items you miss, go back and review this information.

1. Food quacks often tell a person he or she has a "subclinical" ______ deficiency.	vitamin 89
2. A very great danger in dealing with a health quack is that a person will ______ getting the proper medical treatment.	delay 96
3. A safety guide in the use of over-the-counter, or nonprescription, drugs is *be sure to read the* ______.	label 99
4. All medicines should be kept where young ______ cannot possibly reach them.	children 100
5. People who want to lose more than just a few pounds of weight should be under the care of a ______.	physician, or doctor 90
6. Drugs that are specially ordered by doctors are known as ______ drugs.	prescription 99
7. If you want to know about qualified doctors in your community, you can call the local or county ______ society.	medical 98

Teacher's Notes

After pupils have taken the test and their papers have been scored, the test items can serve as guides for summary discussion.

Health Test for Unit Three

Part I

Copy the first part of each sentence below. Then complete it with the *best* answer.

1. Health quackery is
a. a serious problem today
b. rapidly disappearing
c. a very recent problem

2. People take the advice of quacks because
a. quacks are so well trained
b. quacks promise "cures"
c. their treatments are always free

3. So-called mail-order doctors
a. rarely if ever see their patients
b. cure people more often than not
c. are members of the U.S. Postal Service

4. Food quackery has to do with
a. ducks and other poultry
b. false claims about foods
c. promoting scientific diets

5. Health quacks
a. rarely, if ever, advertise
b. make use of testimonials
c. are well-trained physicians

6. Over-the-counter drugs are
a. illegal
b. usually cures for serious illnesses
c. meant to relieve temporary ailments

Part II

Copy the number of each test item. If the item is *true,* write *T* after the number; if the item is *false,* write *F.*

T 7. In the United States, huge sums of money are spent on health quackery.

F 8. A copper bracelet can cure arthritis.

T 9. Food supplements are quite likely to be expensive.

F 10. All people who are overweight should buy reducing pills to make them lose weight.

F 11. Everyone needs a laxative every week.

T 12. A health quack is apt to speak of secret formulas or "cures."

F 13. Ads can help you find a qualified doctor.

T 14. The FDA is concerned with purity and truthful labeling of foods and drugs.

F 15. It is always safe to use old drugs.

T 16. Over-the-counter drugs are for minor ailments and temporary use.

F 17. Expensive foods are always the best ones.

T 18. A diet of grapefruit only is a safe way to lose weight.

F 19. Onions can help cure cancer.

T 20. Some quacks can endanger people's lives.

Number of Answers 20

Number Right ______

Score (Number Right × 5) ______

4 What Do You Know About the Science of Nutrition?

Teacher's Notes

Unit Overview: Use the overview to explore students' ideas about what becomes of all the food they eat—and about what is meant by the term *nutrition.* (Nutrition is concerned with the processes involved in changing food into living tissue, resulting in the body's growth, maintenance, and repair.)

You eat about ten to fifteen pounds of food a week, but you do not gain that much weight each week. In your lifetime so far, you have probably eaten several tons of food. But how much do you weigh? Why don't you weigh as much as the food you have eaten? What does your body do with all that food?

You will find answers to these and other questions about food in this unit. You will also learn why you cannot live without food and what it means to be well nourished.

Teacher's Notes

Read to Find Out: These questions stimulate interest in the main topics to be treated in the unit. Discuss them briefly—just long enough to arouse curiosity and to provide a "mind set" for what is to be investigated in the unit.

Why Do You Need Food? Talk over such questions as these:

"What is an *element?*"

"Of what is food made?"

"Of what is the human body made?"

"What is *protoplasm?*"

Read to Find Out

1. *How is food similar to human tissue?*
2. *What are your body's cells made of and why is* DNA *important in their functioning?*
3. *What are four chief* elements *that make up your body?*
4. *What are some reasons why your body must have food?*
5. *How is food* oxidized *in the body?*
6. *What is meant by the term* digestion?
7. *How is food digested in the* digestive tract?
8. *What are the six main classes of* nutrients, *and how do you know whether you get enough of them in your daily diet?*
9. *What are some important uses of* water *in the body?*
10. *What is a* calorie *and how can you find out how many calories are in a certain amount of a particular food?*
11. *What is meant by* metabolism?

Something to Do

Some materials you may want to use for reference—and which you may obtain at the school or public library—are the following:

Arnold, Pauline, and White, Percival. Food Facts for Young People *(Holiday).*

Leverton, Ruth M. Food Becomes You *(Dolphin Handbook, Doubleday). Paperback.*

Mickelsen, Olaf. Nutrition Science and You *(Scholastic).*

Riedman, Sarah R. Food for People *(Abelard-Schuman).*

Sebrell, William H.; Haggerty, James J.; and the Editors of Life *Magazine.* Food and Nutrition *(Time, Inc.).*

Stare, Frederick, and Dwyer, Johanna. Healthy Eating for Teen-Agers *(American Heart Association).*

Why Do You Need Food?

Before you consider just what happens to the food you eat, some important background information can be helpful. Do you know, for example, what you are made of? Do you know what foods are made of? And do you know why you need food?

Your body is made up of many chemical substances, or *elements.* An element is a substance that cannot be broken down chemically into any other known material and still keep its identity. The elements found in your body are the same elements that are found in the ground, in water, and in the air. Of these elements that make up your body, the four chief ones are shown in the margin on page 107. What are they?

In your body, these chemical elements are combined into many kinds of units called *molecules.* These molecules, in turn, combine into living matter called *protoplasm.* Of course, your body—and the body of any other living thing—is not just a mass of protoplasm. The protoplasm is organized into tiny parts called *cells.* Cells are of different sizes and shapes. Nerve cells are different from fat cells, and bone cells do not look at all like nerve, muscle, or blood cells. What gives each of these various cells its characteristic appearance and function? How does it happen that when a cell divides into two cells, both are exactly like the original cell?

The central region, or *nucleus,* of each cell contains tiny, threadlike particles called *chromosomes.* In each chromosome, giant molecules known as DNA (*d*eoxyribo*n*ucleic *a*cid) are found. During cell division, the chromosomes duplicate themselves; the duplicate chromosome (with its DNA) is then passed on to the new cell. DNA directs all cellular activities, and it also carries information about the characteristics of a cell. Thus DNA contains a "blueprint" for all that is passed on by one cell to another. A related substance RNA (ribonucleic acid) serves as a messenger for DNA.

When many cells of one kind are grouped together to perform a common task, they form a *tissue.* Muscle cells form muscle tissue, bone cells form bone tissue, and so on. When human tissue is examined for its chemical make-up and compared with the chemical composition of food, it is found that the human body and food are made up of the same elements.

It is from food that the body gets the substances it needs for building and maintaining body tissues. This is one of the main functions of food in the body. A second function of food is to furnish chemical substances that regulate various body processes, such as promoting the normal functioning of the nerves and muscles.

A third function of food is to furnish chemical substances that the body cells can use for fuel. The slow burning of food in the body cells is called *oxidation.* Oxidation is somewhat like the burning of coal and wood, except that there is no flame. All oxidation is the result of the chemical union of carbon, hydrogen, and oxygen. When any fuel is burned, carbon dioxide and water are made, and energy is set free in the form of heat. The energy supplied by oxidation of food keeps your body warm and enables your muscles to work.

The name given to all the processes by which the body changes food into living tissue and energy is *metabolism.*

Teacher's Notes

Follow silent study with consideration of such queries as these:

"What is the role of DNA in the human cell?"

"What are the names of some elements found both in the human body and in food?"

"What are three important reasons why you need food?"

Chemical Elements in the Human Body

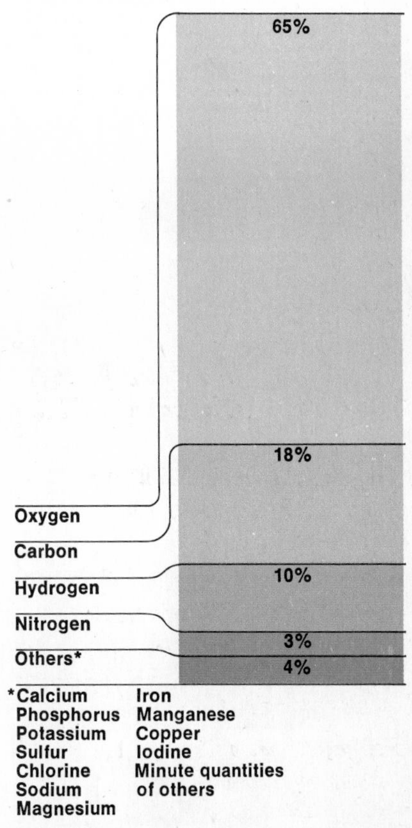

The chemical elements listed above are also the same elements found in food. They are, however, found in different percentages in food.

Adapted from *Nutrition and Physical Fitness* by Jean Bogert, et al. Reprinted by permission of the publisher, W. B. Saunders Company.

Teacher's Notes

Some questions students may consider in connection with this page are these:

"What is meant by *digestion?*"

"What are *nutrients?*"

"Which nutrients have to be broken down chemically before they can be digested?"

"How would you describe the *digestive tract?*"

"Could digestion take place without *enzymes?* Why or why not?"

What Happens to All the Food You Eat?

Now you are ready to find out more about what happens to the food you eat and why you do not weigh as much as the hundreds of pounds of food you have eaten. To find out these things, let us follow the course of some food to see how it is *digested,* or changed into a form your body cells can use.

Suppose, for instance, you have eaten a cheese sandwich on whole-wheat bread. The bread, butter, cheese, and lettuce in the sandwich contain some of the main classes of *nutrients,* or nourishing substances, found in foods. These six main classes of nutrients are *proteins, minerals, vitamins, fats, carbohydrates,* and *water.* Carbohydrates are made up chiefly of sugars and starches.

The approximate nutritive values of whole-wheat bread, butter, cheese, and lettuce have been scientifically determined —as have the values for other common foods. For example, two slices of whole-wheat bread contain the following nutrients: 4.2 grams of protein, 44 milligrams of calcium, 1.0 milligrams of iron, .14 milligrams of thiamin (vitamin B_1), .06 milligrams of riboflavin (vitamin B_2), 1.4 milligrams of the vitamin called niacin, 1.2 grams of fat, and 22.6 grams of carbohydrate.

The minerals and vitamins in the sandwich have to be *mechanically* changed before they can enter your bloodstream to be carried to your cells. That is, the minerals and vitamins must be changed in consistency—or made soft, thin, and watery. On the other hand, the fats, proteins, and carbohydrates in the sandwich must be *chemically* changed before they can be absorbed into the bloodstream. That is, large molecules in the fats, proteins, and carbohydrates must be broken down into different forms or dissolved. The only exceptions are the simple sugars such as *glucose,* which may be absorbed directly from the stomach into the bloodstream. Changes in the food take place in the digestive tract, which is pictured in the margin at the left.

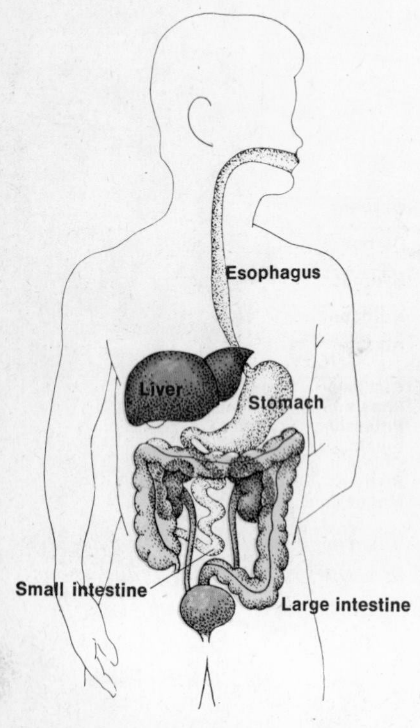

Some parts of the digestive system

The fats, proteins, and carbohydrates need one or more special protein substances, or *enzymes,* to change them chemically. Enzymes are produced by the glands of the digestive tract and are contained in the digestive juices that are poured over the food as it passes down the tract. Each of these juices has its own enzymes, and each enzyme works on just one kind of food.

In Your Mouth

The enzyme in your saliva, for example, acts on the starchy food you have eaten, such as the bread in your sandwich. This action starts in the mouth as soon as the saliva begins mixing with the starchy food.

In Your Stomach

It usually takes food that you have swallowed about five seconds to reach your stomach. There the salivary digestion of starch continues. There, too, gastric juice starts to digest the proteins, such as those in the bread and cheese. Also in the stomach there may be a slight breakdown of the fats contained in the butter and cheese. Muscles in the stomach walls churn the food and mix it thoroughly with the gastric juice.

In Your Small Intestine

In your small intestine, more digestive juices are poured over the partly digested food. One of the juices comes from the walls of the small intestine itself. The enzymes in the intestinal juice help digest proteins and sugars.

Other juices come from nearby organs; pancreatic juice comes from the pancreas and bile comes from the liver. The pancreatic juice contains enzymes that help digest fats, proteins, and carbohydrates. Bile aids in breaking up fats into tiny droplets so that a special enzyme in the pancreatic juice can dissolve the fats more easily.

The digestion of fats, proteins, and carbohydrates is completed in the small intestine. The foods in the sandwich—with the exception of some leftover undigested material—are now in liquid form.

The digested food passes through the walls of the intestine either directly into the bloodstream or indirectly through the lymph. (*Lymph* is a colorless fluid that fills the spaces between the body cells.) This process is known as *absorption*. The digested food is then carried to body tissues and left wherever

Teacher's Notes

Talk over where chemical changes in foods take place in the digestive tract. (Starchy foods begin to be chemically changed in the mouth; chemical changes in starchy foods continue in the stomach; also in the stomach, gastric juices begin to digest proteins; and so on.)
Also let students supply answers to this "Name-It" Quiz:

"What gland produces *bile?*"

"What glands produce *saliva?*"

"What substances make foods dissolve so that they can be absorbed into the body fluids?"

"Where is digestion completed?"

Gland	Juices Secreted	Foodstuff Acted Upon
Salivary glands	Saliva	Starches
Stomach glands	Gastric juice	Proteins
Liver	Bile	Fats
Pancreas	Pancreatic juice	Starches Proteins Fats
Intestinal glands	Intestinal juice	Proteins Malt sugar Milk sugar Cane sugar

Teacher's Notes

Some discussion guides that might be used are the following ones:

"How does digested food get into the bloodstream?"

"What is meant by the term *oxidized?* Is all the digested food oxidized?"

"What happens to food that is not digested?"

"What happens to digested sugars not needed immediately by body cells?"

"There is a book on nutrition called *Food Becomes You* by Dr. Ruth Leverton. What do you think is the meaning of this title?"

cells are growing or need to be repaired—or wherever the different parts of the body need energy to carry on their various functions.

Digested sugars that are not needed immediately by the cells are stored in the form of *glycogen* in the liver and, to a lesser extent, in the muscles. These digested sugars may also be changed into body fat. Digested fats in excess of body needs are stored under the skin and around the organs. You usually think of the food stored under the skin as *fat.*

In Your Large Intestine

Finally, the food materials not yet digested pass into the large intestine, which is about one inch in diameter. When this material, which your body has not been able to break down, first enters the large intestine, it is a watery mass. But soon most of the water is absorbed through the walls of the intestine.

Leftover or undigested material is made up of such things as fruit skins, seeds, outer parts of grain, and the stringlike parts of some vegetables. These undigested materials are usually called *roughage.* There are also bacteria and some digestive juices in the leftover material. All these waste products of digestion, or *feces,* are eliminated from the body through the opening at the end of the large intestine called the *anus.*

Oxidation in the Cells

The blood carries oxygen as well as digested food to the cells of the body. In the body tissues the oxygen combines with and slowly oxidizes the sugars and fats.

What happened to the cheese sandwich we have been tracing is the same thing that has happened to all the food you have eaten throughout your life.

Part of this food has been built into your body and has become a part of you. But most of the food has been oxidized. This process of oxidation produces energy that your body uses day after day.

Now you know why you do not weigh as much as the hundreds and hundreds of pounds of food that you have eaten. What has become of all this food?

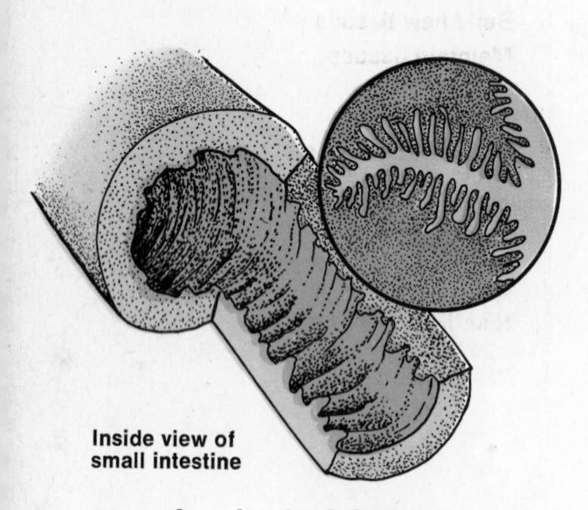

Inside view of small intestine

How does dissolved food pass through the walls of the small intestine? The walls are lined with tiny fingerlike parts called villi. *These villi absorb the digested food and send it into the blood.*

What Kinds of Foods Do You Need?

To be well nourished, you need to eat foods that together include all the nutrients necessary for body growth and repair, for efficient body functioning, and for heat and energy.

There are many different nutrients found in foods, but they all can be classed under the six main nutrient headings discussed earlier: proteins, minerals, vitamins, fats, carbohydrates, and water.

Although most foods contain more than one nutrient, no single food contains *all* the nutrients in the amounts the body needs. *That is why a person needs to eat a variety of foods each day.*

Proteins

Proteins get their name from a Greek word meaning "holding first place." The name is an appropriate one since proteins really do hold first place in the building and maintaining of the body's tissues.

All proteins contain carbon, hydrogen, oxygen, nitrogen; some also contain sulfur or other elements. Proteins can be burned to furnish energy if there are not sufficient sugars and fats in the diet. However, the chief uses of proteins are in building and maintaining body tissues and in helping regulate body processes.

Your cells cannot rely on fats and carbohydrates alone to build tissues. These two nutrients lack the element *nitrogen,* which is present in proteins and is essential for tissue-building. Since proteins furnish your body with the essential building materials, they are often called "body-building foods," or the body's "building blocks."

During digestion, proteins are broken down into simpler substances called *amino acids.* Your body then uses these amino acids to build body tissues. When the amino acids are combined in one way, muscle tissue is built. Another combination of the amino acids forms brain tissue. Still other combinations form hemoglobin (the oxygen-carrying cells in the blood) and various other tissues. A wide variety of protein foods is needed to build all these special tissues of the body.

Teacher's Notes

Review the six main classes of nutrients as introduced on page 108. Discuss the reason why a variety of foods is needed in the daily diet. Talk over, too, why proteins are called "building blocks" and what is meant by *amino acids.*
Then ask:

"Why can't fats and carbohydrates alone build tissue?"

"If a person's diet is deficient in proteins, what are some kinds of foods that might be missing from his diet?"

"What foods have you eaten today that are rich in proteins?"

Foods Rich in Proteins

Proteins help perform these functions:

Build new tissues

Maintain tissues

Supply substances that act as body regulators

Provide small amounts of substances for making enzymes, hormones, antibodies, some vitamins

Furnish energy (if needed)

(Proteins, to properly fulfill these functions, must be part of an adequate diet containing all necessary nutrients.)

Adapted from *Nutrition and Physical Fitness* by Jean Bogert, et al. Reprinted by permission of the publisher, W. B. Saunders Company.

Teacher's Notes
Discuss the advisability of a person's trying to get all the protein foods needed *without* eating any meat, fish, milk, eggs, cheese, or poultry. What problem would be presented?
Consider, too, some of the uses of minerals in the human body. Then ask: "What foods have you eaten today that are rich in minerals?"

Proteins are present in both animal and plant foods. *Animal proteins* are found in meat, fish, milk, eggs, cheese, and poultry. Animal proteins contain all the amino acids needed for health and growth. Proteins that contain all the essential amino acids are called *complete proteins.* Some of these proteins should be eaten every day.

Plant proteins are found in grains, nuts, beans, and peas. Most plant proteins contain a certain number of amino acids that must be supplied in the diet. No one plant protein, however, contains all the amino acids necessary for health and growth. Plant proteins are important in the diet because they help round out the proteins needed for a meal. They are also important to consider in meal-planning, because they are often inexpensive sources of the proteins needed for an adequate daily diet.

Foods Rich in Minerals

Minerals furnish building materials for:
Bones and teeth
Hair, nails, and skin
Soft tissues—chiefly muscles
Nerve tissue
Blood
Glandular secretions

Minerals serve as body regulators to help maintain normal:
Clotting of blood
Oxidation processes
Exchange of body fluids
Functioning of muscles and nerves
(Minerals, to properly fulfill these functions, must be part of an adequate diet containing all necessary nutrients.)

Adapted from *Nutrition and Physical Fitness* by Jean Bogert, et al. Reprinted by permission of the publisher, W. B. Saunders Company.

Minerals

If you look again at the chart on page 107, you will see that your body contains some other elements besides oxygen, carbon, hydrogen, and nitrogen. These other elements are all *mineral elements.* Your body needs to take in varying amounts of these mineral elements, and it must depend upon food to supply them.

The minerals calcium, phosphorus, and fluorine are needed, for example, to make the hard material in your bones and teeth. Calcium is important, too, in helping your blood thicken and clot.

Iron and copper are needed for making red blood cells. Sodium is important in controlling the beating of your heart. Chlorine is required for the hydrochloric acid found in gastric juice—which is made by glands in the stomach wall.

Iodine is needed so that the thyroid gland in your neck can make the special hormone that is essential for cell metabolism. Lack of iodine may cause *simple goiter,* a disease in which the thyroid gland becomes enlarged. Still other mineral elements are also essential. Even though all these minerals are needed in very small quantity, this minute quantity is essential to life.

You get calcium and phosphorus from the milk, milk products, and green leafy vegetables you include in your diet.

Foods rich in iron are liver, other meats, eggs, green leafy vegetables, beans, molasses, nuts, and whole-grain or enriched bread and cereals.

From ordinary table salt and from many meats and fish, you get sodium and chlorine. Seafoods and iodized salt are good sources of iodine in the diet.

Water

Minerals are supplied to the body not only by food but also by water taken from mineral springs and wells. However, water has far more important functions than that of providing minerals. Do you know what they are?

About two thirds of your body weight is water. The fluid part of the blood, which is called *plasma,* contains mostly water. This watery plasma provides the blood's transportation system, which carries food to the body cells and waste materials away from the cells. When it is in the form of perspiration, the water in your body helps regulate body temperature. Perspiration has a cooling effect on the body by keeping the skin cool. The digestive juices also contain water, which helps digest food. Some water is formed, too, when foods are oxidized in the body.

To stay alive, you must have plenty of water. At least two quarts of water a day leave your body—chiefly in urine, in perspiration, and in the moist air you breathe out. You replace this lost liquid partly by the water you drink—usually about five or six glasses daily. You get water, too, from your diet in such liquids as milk and soup. Many common foods, such as fruits, tomatoes, potatoes, and lettuce, are also made up largely of water.

Vitamins

Vitamins get their name from a Latin word meaning "life." The name is a good one for these substances because vitamins are truly essential to growth and a healthful life.

Scientists, for many years, did not know the exact nature of vitamins. The letters A, B, C, and D were given to the first vitamins discovered. Now chemists know the exact nature of the most common vitamins. Scientists can also manufacture many of these vitamins in the laboratory.

Teacher's Notes

Consider the important uses of water in the body and some of the sources of the water that the body must take in daily. You might mention that thirst is one guide in helping us get the water we need each day.

Ask students which they think a person can do without for the longer period of time—food or water? (Food. A person can live for a few weeks without food but only for a few days without water.)

Foods Rich in Vitamins

Some important vitamins:

A

Thiamin (B_1)

Riboflavin (B_2)

Niacin

Ascorbic Acid (C)

Vitamins promote:

Growth

Health and vigor

Nervous stability

Normal appetite

Digestion

Utilization of foods

Resistance to infections

(Vitamins, to properly fulfill these functions, must be part of an adequate diet containing all necessary nutrients.)

Adapted from *Nutrition and Physical Fitness* by Jean Bogert, et al. Reprinted by permission of the publisher, W. B. Saunders Company.

Teacher's Notes

Some questions to start off the discussion after silent study of this material are the following:

"Why are vitamins needed in the daily diet?"

"What are the names of some of the most important vitamins?"

"What foods have you eaten so far today that are rich in vitamins?"

"Which is the 'sunshine vitamin'?"

"Under what conditions should vitamin pills or tablets be taken? Why shouldn't everybody take them daily?"

Foods Rich in Carbohydrates

Carbohydrates (sugars and starchy foods) help perform these functions:

They furnish quick energy

They add flavor (sweetness) to foods and beverages

They furnish some proteins, minerals, and vitamins. (This is especially true of whole grains and legumes.)

(Carbohydrates, to properly fulfill these functions, must be part of an adequate diet containing all necessary nutrients.)

Adapted from *Nutrition and Physical Fitness* by Jean Bogert, et al. Reprinted by permission of the publisher, W. B. Saunders Company.

Instead of the letter names for vitamins, the chemical names are more frequently used nowadays. For example, *thiamin* is used for vitamin B_1, *riboflavin* for vitamin B_2, and *ascorbic acid* for vitamin C.

Scientists are working today to learn more about the vitamins discovered thus far and to find others still unknown. The chart on page 113 shows a few important vitamins and some of their general functions in the body.

You can get most of your vitamins from a variety of foods—poultry, fish, eggs, vegetables, fresh fruits, and whole-grain or enriched breads and cereals. Vitamins, like proteins and minerals, vary in quantity and kind in various foods and they all influence each other. This is why a varied diet is recommended for good health.

One vitamin that babies and young children may not get in sufficient quantity from food is vitamin D. This vitamin is present in only a few foods, but it is made in the body when the skin is exposed to certain invisible rays from the sun. These rays are called ultraviolet rays. In the winter, infants and young children especially may not get enough sunshine; also during any season, clouds, smoke, or smog may shut out some of these ultraviolet rays. Vitamin D can be supplied, however, by fish-liver oil or vitamin-D-fortified milk.

Should you as a teen-ager take vitamin pills or tablets to be sure you get enough vitamins? As a rule, the answer is "no." A healthy person can get all the necessary vitamins from an adequate diet that is properly selected and prepared.

Although synthetic vitamins are available at stores as pills or capsules, these should not be taken unless your doctor recommends them. If you take vitamins without your doctor's advice, you may be spending money needlessly. Your body can make use of only so much of each vitamin. Excesses either are excreted as wastes or may accumulate and be detrimental to your health.

Taking vitamins without medical advice may encourage you to rely on these vitamins to make your daily diet complete—and thus to neglect those foods that contain not only vitamins but other valuable nutrients as well.

Carbohydrates and Fats

Carbohydrates and fats are important because when they are oxidized they produce the energy your body needs to keep warm and do work.

Carbohydrates are the starches or sugars in foods. Many of the starches you eat come from grains such as corn, wheat, oats, rye, and rice. Breakfast cereals, bread, crackers, noodles, spaghetti, and macaroni are all foods made from grains. Potatoes, dried beans, and dried peas also contain much starch.

It is easy to tell some of the foods that have sugar in them, for they have a sweet taste. Candy, honey, corn syrup, and molasses have much sugar. Other foods such as cereals, vegetables, and fruits also contain sugar, but they contain some other nutrients, too. For instance, there are also vitamins and minerals in cereals, vegetables, and fruits.

All oily and greasy foods contain fats. While plants furnish most of our various kinds of sugar, we get fats from both plants and animals. Animal fats come from such foods as butter, bacon, cream, shortening, cod-liver oil, and sausages. Plant or vegetable fats include vegetable oils—peanut, soybean, cottonseed, coconut, corn, and olive oils—as well as vegetable shortenings and margarine.

Carbohydrates furnish the body with the fuel that can be most easily and quickly used. Much of this fuel is in the form of sugar called glucose. All the starches and most sugars in your food are changed to glucose during digestion.

Fats provide more than twice as much food energy as carbohydrates and proteins. A tablespoon of butter, for example, gives you 100 calories. But the same amount of sugar gives you only 40 calories. Fats are the most concentrated form of energy in your diet. However, fats are digested slowly, so that the energy is not released so quickly from fats as it is from carbohydrates. Fatty foods are especially useful when people need extra energy. This could be true in the wintertime when the body might be called on to burn extra fuel to keep the body temperature normal or when people engage in heavy labor. Fats also give a person the feeling that he has had enough to eat.

Teacher's Notes

Discuss the role of fats and carbohydrates in the diet. Then ask: "What foods have you had so far today that are rich in carbohydrates? In fats?" Talk over, too, how a person—even though blindfolded—might determine if a food has sugar in it. How can it be determined whether a food has fat in it? Consider with students which nutrient—fats, carbohydrates, or proteins—contains *more* food energy. Which nutrient gives a person *quick* energy?

Foods Rich in Fats

Fats and fat-rich foods are useful in the diet for such purposes as these:

They provide a concentrated source of body fuel

They supply flavor

They create a feeling that one has had enough to eat

(Fats, to properly fulfill these functions, must be part of an adequate diet containing all necessary nutrients.)

Adapted from *Nutrition and Physical Fitness* by Jean Bogert, et al. Reprinted by permission of the publisher, W. B. Saunders Company.

Teacher's Notes
Discuss why a food guide such as the one on pages 116-117 is *useful* and why it is *flexible*.

How Does a Daily Food Guide Help?

How can you be sure the foods you eat each day include the six necessary nutrients in the right amounts?

A daily food guide is no doubt the best answer to this important question. Such a guide is based on what is known about the body's nutritional needs and about the nutrients present in different foods. The food guide below and on the opposite page is an easy one to use. It points out the main kinds and amounts of foods to eat daily. The foods that contain essential nutrients are put in four groups. What are the groups and how many servings are needed daily from each group?

It is possible to make many choices within these four groups to have *varied meals*. Choices will also permit the selection of well-liked foods, foods that provide for special health needs of individuals, foods within the family budget, foods in season, and foods that reflect regional or ethnic preferences. Notice, for instance, the variety in the menus for a single day, as pictured on pages 123–126.

Food for Fitness—A Daily Food Guide[1]

Vegetable-Fruit Group

Four or more servings. Include—

A citrus fruit or other fruit or vegetable important for vitamin C
A dark-green or deep-yellow vegetable for vitamin A
—at least every other day
Other vegetables and fruits, including potatoes

Count as 1 serving: ½ cup of vegetable or fruit; or a portion as ordinarily served, such as 1 medium apple, banana, orange, or potato, half a medium grapefruit or cantaloupe, or the juice of 1 lemon.

Milk Group

Children under 9: 2 to 3 cups
Children 9-12: 3 or more cups
Teen-agers: 4 cups
Adults: 2 or more cups

Milk can be obtained partly through cream soups, puddings, cheese, ice cream, milk shakes, and the like. Some common portions of various kinds of cheese and ice cream and their milk equivalents: 1-inch cube cheddar-type cheese equals ½ cup of milk; ½ cup cottage cheese equals ⅓ cup of milk; ½ cup of ice cream equals ¼ cup of milk.

[1]Adapted from Leaflet No. 424, U.S. Department of Agriculture.

Some familiar foods are not included in the four food groups because they are almost sure to be a part of your meals anyway. Butter, margarine, sugar, jams, and salad dressings are examples of foods that are omitted from the guide. These foods are often included in recipes or are added to other foods at the table.

Actually, as you have noticed, a food guide provides only a *framework* for the meals of the day, not a complete diet. By choosing at least the recommended number of servings from each food group, you will be assured of the nutritional quality of your diet. You can then add other foods as desired.

Foods from the guide fit easily into meal planning. For example, you can drink a glass of milk at each meal. How might you get the rest of the milk you need?

While you may choose food from each group as part of every meal, this is not necessary. *The important thing is to try to include the suggested amount in each group during the day, in regular meals or in snacks.* It is a good plan, however, to have in each meal some food that is a good source of protein.

Meat Group

Two or more servings

Beef, veal, pork, lamb, poultry, fish, eggs
As alternates—dry beans, dry peas, nuts, peanuts, peanut butter

Count as 1 serving: 2 to 3 ounces of lean cooked meat, poultry, or fish—all without bone; 2 eggs; 1 cup cooked dry beans, dry peas, or lentils; 4 tablespoons peanut butter.

Bread-Cereal Group

Four or more servings

All breads and cereals that are whole grain, enriched, or restored

Count as 1 serving: 1 slice of bread; 1 ounce ready-to-eat cereal; ½ to ¾ cup cooked cereal, cornmeal, grits, macaroni, noodles, rice, or spaghetti.

Plus other foods as needed to complete meals and to provide additional food energy and other food values.

Teacher's Notes
Have pupils use the calorie chart on pages 118-121 to figure out how many calories are in these meals:
Breakfast: ½ grapefruit, 2 slices raisin toast, 2 teaspoons butter, 1 boiled egg, 1 cup cocoa
Lunch: 1 cup vegetable soup, 1 cup macaroni and cheese, 2 lettuce leaves and 1 tablespoon French dressing, 1 apple, 1 cup whole milk
Supper: 1 cup tomato juice, 1 leg fried chicken, 1 medium baked potato, 1 tablespoon butter, ½ cup string beans, cabbage salad (½ cup cabbage, 1 carrot, 1 tablespoon mayonnaise), 1 roll —plain, 1 teaspoon butter, 1 cup baked custard, 1 cup whole milk.
Then ask:
"Does this diet for a day have enough calories for a twelve-year-old boy or girl?" (Yes—about 2,595 calories.)

How Much Should You Eat?

During your junior-high years you may be growing rapidly, and you may have found that your appetite is also growing. Perhaps you start off the day with a good breakfast, and yet by lunchtime you feel "starved." Then after school you may be so hungry that you must have a snack to keep going until supper. At supper you may eat several helpings of the various foods served. By bedtime you might be hungry once more and ready for still another snack.

Are you eating too much? How much *should* you eat?

Eating the foods in the amounts suggested in the food guide on pages 116–117 gives you a diet adequate in nutrients. But even this guide does not tell you *exactly* how much to eat. There is, however, the suggestion in the guide that, in addition to foods from the four main groups, you eat "other foods as needed to complete meals and to provide additional food energy and other food values." These other foods include butter, margarine, and other fats; oils, including vegetable

Approximate Calories in Common Foods[1]

Breads and Cereals	Portion	Calories
Bagel	1	110
Biscuit	1	130
Bread, raisin	1 slice	65
Bread, rye	1 slice	55
Bread, white	1 slice	65
Bread, whole-wheat	1 slice	55
Corn-bread muffin	1	105
Corn flakes	1 cup	95
Corn grits	1 cup	120
Crackers, soda	2 squares	45
Macaroni, cooked	1 cup	210
Macaroni and cheese	1 cup	465
Noodles, cooked	1 cup	105
Oatmeal, cooked	1 cup	150
Pancakes	1	60
Pretzels	5 small	20
Rice, cooked	1 cup	205
Rolls, plain	1	85
Rolls, sweet	1	180
Spaghetti, cooked	1 cup	220
Waffle	1	215

Candies and Desserts	Portion	Calories
Apple Betty	1 cup	345
Cake, angel food	2″ wedge	110
Cake, plain layer (icing)	2″ wedge	320
Cake, pound	1 slice	130
Chocolate fudge	1, 1¼″ sq.	115
Cookies, plain	1, 3″ diam.	110
Custard, baked	1 cup	285
Doughnut, plain	1	135
Gelatin dessert	1 cup	155
Gingerbread	1, 2x2x2″	180
Honey	1 tbsp.	60
Ice cream, vanilla	1 serving	165
Jams, jellies	1 tbsp.	50
Milk chocolate	1 bar	145
Molasses, cane, blackstrap	1 tbsp.	45
Pie, apple or berry	1/7, 9″ pie	330
Pie, coconut custard	1/7, 9″ pie	265
Pie, lemon meringue	1/7, 9″ pie	300
Sherbet	1 cup	235
Sugar, brown	1 tbsp.	50
Sugar, granulated	1 tbsp.	40
Syrup, table	1 tbsp.	55

[1]Adapted from *Composition of Foods,* Agriculture Handbook No. 8. U.S. Department of Agriculture.

oils; sugars; and some grain products. Many of these are ingredients in baked goods and mixed dishes. Your appetite—if not spoiled by too many sweets—can be a fairly accurate guide as to how much of these "other foods" you should eat. It is interesting to know that scientists do have an accurate means of finding out how much food a person *needs*. Scientists know how to measure the energy that different foods provide; and they can measure the energy that human beings require for such activities as sitting, standing, running, and climbing stairs.

You know that when fats, carbohydrates, or proteins are burned or oxidized in the body cells, energy is produced. To find out how much energy a certain food provides, a measure is taken of the heat it gives off when it is burned as completely as possible. This measure of heat given off is taken with an instrument called the *bomb calorimeter*. A small, weighed amount of the food is burned inside a sealed container of oxygen surrounded by water. The heat from the burning food warms the water, and the amount of heat energy given off is measured and expressed in calories.

Dairy Products and Eggs	Portion	Calories
Butter (or margarine)	1 tbsp.	100
Buttermilk	1 cup	85
Cheese, American	1 oz.	115
Cheese, cottage	1 oz.	25
Cheese, cream	1 oz.	105
Cocoa, all milk	1 cup	235
Cream, whipped	1 tbsp.	50
Egg, boiled	1 large	75
Egg, scrambled	1 large	105
Milk, chocolate	1 cup	185
Milk, dried, whole	1 tbsp.	40
Milk, evaporated	1 cup	345
Milk, skim	1 cup	85
Milk, whole	1 cup	165

Drinks		
Chocolate milk shake	1, 8 oz.	500
Cola drinks	1 cup	105
Lemonade	1 cup	75

Fruits	Portion	Calories
Apple, raw	1 medium	75
Applesauce	1 cup	185
Apricots, canned	1 cup	205
Apricots, dried	5 halves	50
Banana	1 medium	90
Cantaloupe	½ melon	35
Dates, dried	⅛ cup	60
Grapefruit	½ medium	75
Grapefruit juice, unsweetened	1 cup	90
Orange, fresh	1 large	105
Orange juice, fresh	1 cup	110
Peaches, canned	1 cup	175
Peach, fresh	1 medium	45
Pear, fresh	1	95
Pineapple, canned	1 slice	95
Prunes, stewed	½ cup	155
Raisins	¼ cup	105
Rhubarb, cooked	1 cup	385
Strawberries	1 cup	55
Watermelon	1, 4x8″ piece	120

Teacher's Notes

Discuss with pupils what they think is meant by "counting calories." Then suggest that they refer to the tables on pages 118-121 to learn more about the calorie count of various foods.

In the field of nutrition, the *calorie*—used to express fuel value of foods—is a heat unit. To visualize a calorie in food and nutrition, imagine one quart of water—about one kilogram—on the stove. To raise the temperature of this water one degree centigrade will require the heat that is expressed as one calorie. The amount of heat energy produced per unit of weight depends upon the kind of food that is burned. As you learned on page 115, a given amount of fats produces more than twice as much energy as the same amount of carbohydrates or proteins. The chart on pages 118–121 shows the approximate number of calories in some common foods.

Scientists, in finding out how much energy a person needs, determine several things. First, the scientists calculate the amount of energy required by a person just to stay alive. That is, they calculate the amount of energy needed to carry on such body functions as breathing during rest but not sleep. The body is never completely at rest, and in fact it must work to live. This minimum amount of energy needed to keep up the body's processes is the body's basal use of energy, or *basal metabolism.*

Meats	Portion	Calories
Bacon, drained	2 slices	95
Beef, chuck	3 oz.	265
Beef, dried	2 oz.	115
Beef, ground	3 oz.	245
Beef and vegetable stew	1 cup	250
Bologna	¼ lb.	250
Chicken, fried	1, 5 oz. leg	160
Chili con carne	1 cup	300
Frankfurter	1	125
Ham, baked	3 oz.	340
Lamb roast	3 oz.	230
Liver, calves	3 oz.	120
Pork chop	3 oz.	285
Pork roast	3 oz.	340

Nuts		
Almonds, shelled	1 oz.	170
Brazil nuts, shelled	1 oz.	185
Cashews	1 oz.	165
Peanut butter	1 tbsp.	90
Peanuts, salted	1 oz.	160
Pecans	1 oz.	200
Walnuts	1 oz.	185

Salad Dressings	Portion	Calories
French dressing	1 tbsp.	60
Mayonnaise	1 tbsp.	90
Olive oil	1 tbsp.	125
Thousand island	1 tbsp.	75

Fish		
Flounder	4 oz.	80
Haddock	1 fillet	160
Halibut	1 steak	230
Salmon, canned	3 oz.	120
Sardines, canned	3 oz.	180
Tuna, canned	3 oz.	170

Soups		
Bean	1 cup	190
Bouillon	1 cup	10
Chicken	1 cup	75
Noodle, rice	1 cup	115
Pea	1 cup	140
Tomato	1 cup	90
Vegetable	1 cup	80

A person's basal metabolism is influenced by height, weight, age, sex, and the secretions of the endocrine glands.

Basal metabolism may be measured by certain kinds of respiration apparatus which determine the calories used per hour for each kilogram of body weight. In addition to such respiration tests, other tests are now available for measuring basal metabolism. One of these tests involves taking a blood sample from the person and having the sample analyzed at a laboratory.

After an individual's basal metabolism has been determined, the energy needed for performance of daily activities can be calculated. Energy output per hour, in calories needed, is being measured in the picture on this page. In the experimental chamber shown here, a young man exercises on a treadmill. The sealed chamber is large enough to permit a test person to live a fairly normal life for several days, while the energy output for various tasks is being measured. Such information helps scientists determine the calories that are needed for typical activities of everyday living.

Vegetables	Portion	Calories
Beans, baked	1 cup	325
Beans, lima	1 cup	150
Beans, string	1 cup	25
Beets	1 cup	70
Cabbage, raw	1 cup	25
Carrots, raw	1 carrot	20
Cauliflower	1 cup	30
Celery	large stalk	5
Corn, on cob	1 ear	85
Lettuce	2 leaves	5
Peas	1 cup	110
Popcorn (no butter)	1 cup	55
Potato, baked	1 medium	95
Potato chips	10 medium	110
Potato, French fried	8 pieces	155
Potato, mashed	1 cup	160
Rutabagas	1 cup	50
Spinach	1 cup	45
Sweet potato, baked	1 medium	185
Sweet potato, candied	1 small	315
Tomato, raw	1 medium	30
Tomato juice	1 cup	50
Turnips	1 cup	45

Experimental chamber from which information can be gained about calories needed for typical daily activities

Teacher's Notes

In talking over the material on this page and on the preceding ones, you might use such review questions as these:

"What is a *bomb calorimeter?*"

"What is a *calorie?*"

"How can you find out how many calories are in foods such as an apple and a glass of skim milk?"

"What is a person's *basal metabolism?*"

"How do scientists measure the amount of food an individual needs?"

The total amount of energy that a person needs for maintenance of body functions and for performance of his daily activities will determine how many calories he needs daily.

How many calories are usually used in typical daily activities? On an average, in one hour, an average-sized man uses up about 100 calories while sitting. He uses 140 calories while standing for an hour and 300 while walking fairly fast. He uses 660 while cycling for an hour and 900 while running fairly fast. Contrary to what many people think, mental activity or hard concentration does not require added food for energy.

Usually a person's calorie needs do not increase or decrease much with outside temperature changes. This is because people generally vary their clothing to keep comfortable and keep their body temperature about the same.

Young people need more food in proportion to their weight than their parents do, because they are using additional energy for growth and for building new tissues. Furthermore, cells of young persons burn fuel much more rapidly than do the cells of older persons.

Tables have been set up based on all the studies of human nutrient needs. These tables show the approximate calorie needs of moderately active people of average size and weight at various ages. A portion of such a table is in the margin at the left. Averages such as those shown must, however, be adjusted to fit any particular individual—with special attention paid to his level of physical activity.

Approximately How Many Calories Do You Need Each Day?

		Calories Needed Daily
Girls	**10-12**	**2250**
	12-14	**2300**
	14-16	**2400**
	16-18	**2300**
Boys	**10-12**	**2500**
	12-14	**2700**
	14-18	**3000**
	18-22	**2800**

Chart adapted from *Recommended Daily Dietary Allowances.* Reprinted by permission of the National Research Council.

Unless you have a problem of underweight or overweight, you probably do not need to count the calories in the foods you eat. But you should eat enough food to keep your body supplied with energy and essential nutrients throughout the day. You should also eat enough to provide nutrients necessary for the weight gain involved in growth. Following the daily food guide will enable you to get an adequate diet.

On pages 123–126 there are photographs of meals that include a variety of foods and methods of cooking. Such colorful and tasty-looking daily menus can all be nutritious even though they differ greatly, one from another.

Different People, Different Menus

Here you can see what Rose Bellini ate one Saturday. Did she get enough foods from the four food groups?

Breakfast
1 glass orange juice
1 cup bran flakes with milk
1 slice Italian bread, butter
1 glass milk

Lunch
1 cup minestrone soup (vegetables with noodles)
2 slices boiled beef (from soup)
1 slice Italian bread, butter
1 slice cheese
1 apple
1 glass milk

Snack
1 glass milk
1 cookie

Supper
1 serving spaghetti
Mixed salad (½ tomato, ½ egg, green pepper slices, oil and vinegar)
1 serving sliced chicken
1 glass milk
1 serving chocolate pudding

James Jones' diet for a day included foods his family especially likes. Did his diet contain enough from the four basic food groups?

Breakfast
1 serving grits, butter
1 serving pork sausage
1 serving scrambled eggs
1 glass milk

Lunch
1 serving ham hocks
1 serving turnip greens
1 serving sweet potatoes
1 serving cornbread
1 serving canned peaches
1 glass milk

Snack
1 glass vitamin-enriched orange juice
1 serving cake

Supper
1 serving rice and ham with "red-eye" (ham) gravy
1 serving turnip greens
1 serving biscuits
1 serving fresh sliced tomatoes
1 large glass buttermilk

Juanita Ortega prepared these meals herself one Saturday. Did they contain enough foods of the right kinds? What are some foods *you* can prepare?

Breakfast

1 serving melon
1 serving omelette
1 glass milk

Lunch

1 serving enchiladas (corn cake with meat filling, cheese, and sour cream sauce)
1 glass milk
1 orange

Snack

2 tacos (meal cake stuffed with meat and shredded lettuce)

Supper

1 serving green peppers stuffed with cheese
1 serving boiled rice
1 serving sliced tomatoes
2 cups hot chocolate

You can see here Stanley Gorski's meals and snacks for one day. Check his diet with the food guide on pages 116-117. Is it adequate?

Breakfast
½ grapefruit
1 serving scrambled eggs
2 servings fresh Polish sausage
1 slice bread
1 glass milk

Lunch
1 bowl chicken-noodle soup
1 luncheon-meat sandwich
1 glass milk

Snack
1 glass milk
3 Kolaczkis (fruit-filled cookies)

Supper
2 servings cabbage rolls (cabbage leaves stuffed with rice, ground beef, and tomato sauce)
1 serving dumplings
1 large serving fresh green beans
1 serving applesauce
1 glass milk
3 Kolaczkis

What Are Your Questions About Nutrition?

What are some questions young people your age often ask about food and nutrition? Listed below are some commonly asked questions. How many of them can you answer?

After you have tried to answer the questions, check with the information given below and on pages 128–137.

If you have questions of your own that are not listed here, where might you find answers to them? What are some other sources of information besides those listed at the right?

1. Why is there so much concern over teen-agers' diets?
2. Just how important is breakfast?
3. Does a person's diet have anything to do with skin troubles?
4. What is a low-cholesterol diet?
5. What is being done to improve nutrition throughout the world?

Why Is There So Much Concern over Teen-agers' Diets?

According to recent nutrition surveys, the teen-ager, especially the teen-age girl, is the least well-fed member of the family. Only about four out of every ten girls and six of every ten boys are receiving as much as two thirds of the daily recommended amounts of nutrients.

The results of such surveys are a cause of concern because in the teen years the body's need for nutrients is great. At no other period, except during infancy, does growth take place at such a rapid rate. Nor is this growth just in height alone; almost every part of the body is growing and developing. Only food can provide enough of all the materials needed for building muscle, bone, blood, nerve, skin, and other tissues during these years of rapid growth. The harmful consequences of inadequate diets may not be evident until several years have passed.

Then, too, many teen-agers are very active from morning until night. In addition to classes, sports, studies, and other school activities, they may have home chores and community activities. To supply the energy needed for all these things, there will be an increased need for calories.

Teacher's Notes

Students may ask about organic farms and farming. Organic farming is that done without any sprays to kill insect pests. Only organic materials are added to the soil. Among these organic materials are grasses, leaves, and chicken droppings. While most farmers in the United States today use some sprays and other man-made materials such as fertilizers, organic farms are becoming more prevalent. Students might discuss why this is so. (To avoid possible pollution of the soil or crops with chemicals that might be harmful).

Some Sources of Nutrition Information

One person from your group might write to one or more of the following sources to ask for a list of available free or inexpensive publications on foods and nutrition:

1. The United States Department of Agriculture, Office of Information, Washington, D.C. 20250.

2. U.S. Government Printing Office, Public Documents Distribution Center, 5801 Tabor Avenue, Philadelphia, Pennsylvania 19120.

3. Your State Department of Public Health at your state capitol.

4. American Medical Association, Council on Foods and Nutrition, 535 N. Dearborn Street, Chicago, Illinois 60610.

As the surveys have indicated, girls especially do not get enough of the right foods for the amount of energy they need. Several reasons may account for this. Many teen-age girls are worried about overweight. These girls may cut down their calorie intake without proper guidance from a physician. As a result, they may endanger their health. Some girls, on the other hand, cut down on their activity and become spectators instead of participants in sports and other activities. This can be detrimental to health and can lead to overweight.

The greatest deficiencies in teen-agers' diets are calcium, iron, and ascorbic acid. One reason for the calcium deficiency is the sharp decrease in amount of milk consumed, especially by weight-conscious teen-age girls who mistakenly try to cut down on calories by eliminating all milk. There is also a lack of sufficient thiamin and sometimes vitamin A in many teen-agers' diets. Insufficient amounts of these nutrients can result in poor teeth, sallow complexion, and lack of stamina.

Number of Teen-age Girls* with Diets Deficient in Specific Nutrients

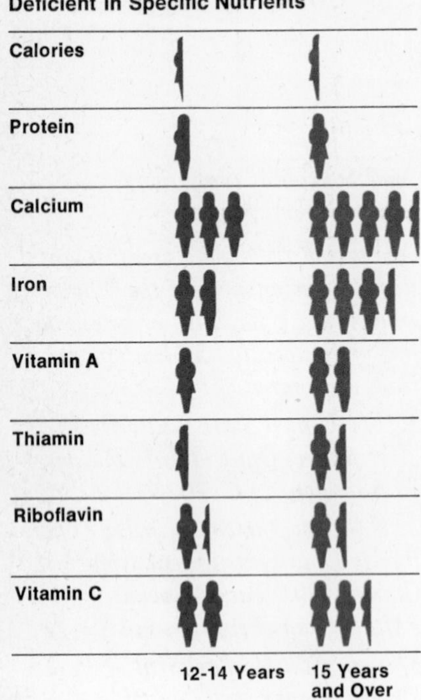

*Number out of every ten in study

Reprinted by permission from Mattie Pattison, Helen Barbour, and Ercel Eppright, *Teaching Nutrition,* Second Edition, copyright 1963, The Iowa State University Press.

Another reason that has been suggested for nutrient deficiency among teen-agers is emotional stress. Growing up involves a certain amount of tension and strain. For one thing, tremendous body changes are taking place. Furthermore, aspects of growing up such as learning to become more independent and taking more responsibility than formerly are not always easy. As a result of this stress, some young people do not eat an adequate diet. Some may lose their appetites and some may eat constantly to ease the pressure they feel. In some cases, stress affects the body's functioning so that it does not use the nutrients supplied to it as effectively as it might. The extent to which stress or tension affects nutrition is still being studied.

The poor diets of many teen-agers may be blamed, in part, on faulty food habits. For example, omitting breakfast is common. The most frequently offered excuses for skipping breakfast are "lack of time," "no appetite," and "not in the habit of eating in the morning." The daily supply of nutrients is likely to be short if breakfast is omitted or is too skimpy.

Even three meals a day cannot be counted on to fulfill all the nutrient requirements during the years of rapid growth. In these years, snacks should be selected to contribute to overall nutritional needs. Milk, ice cream, fruits, milk shakes, hamburgers, and pizzas are examples of nutritious snacks.

If foods have little nutritional value, they are sometimes called "empty-calorie" foods. Since these foods add little to the nutritional value of the diet, it is not wise to choose a diet on the basis of calorie-count alone. "Calorie watching" should be combined with "nutrient watching." Often a low-calorie food that might be substituted for a high-calorie one is not equally nutritious. Such empty-calorie foods as soft drinks and candy bars should be watched especially. These foods may contain few of the important nutrients the body needs. If eaten to excess, such foods can crowd out the nutritious foods that are needed to ensure an adequate diet. Remember, too, that tea, coffee, and soft drinks may crowd out of the diet the milk that is needed during the teen years.

Teacher's Notes

Consider the question of whether or not total skipping of breakfast is an effective way to lose weight. In a study of schoolboys, young men and women, and elderly men, Dr. Kate Daum and her co-workers concluded that the complete omission of the morning meal is ineffective in reducing weight.[1] An effective method for losing weight is, instead, to increase physical activity daily.

[1]Used by permission from Mattie Pattison, Helen Barbour, and Ercel Eppright, *Teaching Nutrition,* Second Edition, copyright 1963, The Iowa State University Press.

Just How Important Is Breakfast?

"Eat a good breakfast to start a good day" is more than an easy-to-remember slogan; it suggests a practice that research has proved to be effective. Studies have shown that students who eat an adequate breakfast are more alert and accomplish more than do those who neglect the morning meal.

Of course, now and then a young person may get up late and have to skip breakfast or eat a very skimpy one. If this happens rarely, little harm is done. But a regular habit of skipping breakfast or eating an inadequate one can be harmful.

There can be a twelve- to fourteen-hour period between supper and breakfast. Then if a person misses breakfast, another four or five hours of fasting is added. A person who has gone without food for sixteen to eighteen hours or so cannot expect to have a full amount of energy for the day's work.

The body is not like a machine that stops running when the fuel tank is empty. When the body needs refueling, it must cut down on whatever activities it can while still maintaining many life processes. Thus the body in need of fuel has to borrow from its cells, skimp along, and "make do" until food supplies arrive. When the body is in need of food, it functions in a below-standard way. Feelings of fatigue and discouragement often occur—just because a person needs food.

Did You Know?

You can use these meal patterns to help you plan an adequate breakfast.

Light Breakfast: *Fruit, Bread, Milk*

Moderately Light: *Fruit, Cereal, Bread, Milk*

Moderately Heavy: *Fruit, Cereal, one or two Hot Foods, Milk*

What foods can you suggest for each breakfast pattern?

Teacher's Notes

Young people sometimes ask, "What can be done if you are not hungry at breakfast time?"
The point might be made that eating or not eating breakfast is a habit. If a person becomes accustomed to eating breakfast, he then feels that he cannot do without it.
Also, heavy snacking at bedtime may lead to little or no appetite for breakfast. Such heavy snacking might well be reduced.

Breakfast is essential for a good start on the important job of getting all the nutritious foods needed to supply an adequate daily diet. If a person eats a poor breakfast, or none at all, he places a special burden on the other meals to supply extra amounts of important nutrients needed. Studies show, in fact, that the young person who skips breakfast does not usually make up later in the day for the nutrients that were missed, especially vitamin C and calcium.

If a young person becomes tired of the usual foods for breakfast, today's nutritionists suggest that he have some new breakfast adventures. Some substitutions that might be made in breakfast menus are a grilled-cheese sandwich, fish, chipped beef in cream sauce, toast and peanut butter, pizza, or a soup made with milk.

Does a Person's Diet Have Anything to Do with Skin Troubles?

There is still much to be learned about the causes of acne, or a pimply complexion, and other kinds of skin difficulties.

Among the probable causes are these: a temporary speed-up in the functioning of the oil glands during the years of rapid growth; unfavorable effects on some people of certain foods in the diet; an unusual amount of emotional stress or upset feelings over a long period.

A number of foods have been studied to find out what effect, if any, they may have on acne. From these studies, some physicians believe that starchy foods, such as potatoes and bread, and sweet foods such as pastries, jellies, and candy make acne worse in some individuals; in others, such foods have little or no effect.

Another group of foods that some physicians believe may make acne worse are fatty foods. Some scientists who have investigated the relationship of fatty foods to acne think that large quantities of fatty foods in the diet may increase the amount of oil produced by the oil glands or may change in some way the characteristics of the oil that is secreted.

Perhaps you have noticed that your skin is worse after you have eaten large amounts of sweet, fatty, or starchy foods. Of course, you would not want to entirely eliminate such foods from your diet; they are essential to adequate meals. But you

Something to Do

You may want to look in the school or public library for books about the skin and its care.
A helpful paperback is The Look You Like: Answers to Your Questions About Skin Care and Cosmetics *(American Medical Association).*

might try eating these foods in *moderate* rather than in *excessive* amounts. From experience, a young person may find that one certain food makes his or her acne worse. Some physicians believe that chocolate, for example, can cause acne to increase. Other foods that at times worsen acne in some people are nuts, shellfish, strong cheese, eggs, milk, ham, and malt. Before omitting a food suspected of making acne worse, a young person should—if possible—discuss the problem with a doctor.

Teacher's Notes

Invite discussion of information students have about food problems throughout the world—and about food problems in their own state or region. Volunteers might prepare reports based on books from the school or public library such as *The Race Against Famine* by Melvin Benarde (Macrae) and *This Hungry World* by Elizabeth Helfman (Lothrop).

What Is a Low-Cholesterol Diet?

Perhaps you have heard some adult speak of being on a "low-cholesterol diet." What does this mean? *Cholesterol* is a fatlike substance found in the brain, nerves, liver, blood, and other tissues. Cholesterol is necessary for life, but it can cause health problems if it is deposited on the walls of the arteries.

Saturated fats—such as those found in animal foods like beef, pork, or lamb and in solid cooking fats such as butter or lard—tend to increase blood cholesterol. *Polyunsaturated fats*—which are mainly of vegetable origin and include vegetable cooking oils such as corn oil and peanut oil—tend to lower blood cholesterol. A low-cholesterol diet, then, would be low in saturated fats. A person on such a diet would attempt to substitute polyunsaturated fats for saturated ones.

There is some research to indicate that teen-agers, as well as older people, should try to watch their cholesterol intake. One way is by cutting down on eggs, though not eliminating them entirely from the diet. Foods low in saturated fat such as poultry, fish, veal and other lean meats; skim milk; and some cereals are fine protein foods. These foods are just as nourishing as pork, beef, and lamb, which are high in saturated fat. Again the idea is to cut down on, not cut out, the latter foods.

What Is Being Done to Improve Nutrition Throughout the World?

More than half the world's population still subsist on diets inadequate for good health. As a result, millions of people suffer from serious shortage of calories; from severe deficiencies of proteins, vitamins, and minerals; and from starvation itself. Food shortage is a problem that will increase as the world population increases.

Did You Know?

Along with getting an adequate diet, you should pay attention to other requirements of healthful living, such as getting enough sleep and outdoor exercise. Such attention may help minimize acne and skin difficulties of other kinds.

Teacher's Notes

Following are some programs that are being undertaken now and that must be expanded in the years to come if there is to be enough food in the future for the people of the world:

Trying to increase the yield of each acre that is cultivated.

Developing new types of seeds that produce hardier crops, greater yields, higher nutrient values, more resistance to drought and various plant diseases, and so on.

(Continued on page 133.)

You have already seen what can happen when your diet does not contain adequate nutrients. But what happens when a person's diet is inadequate from birth—or when nourishment is inadequate even before the person is born? This is a problem particularly in some developing countries. Children suffer most during their years of rapid growing, especially during the years from one to four. After they stop nursing, children are sometimes given soft, starchy foods because they cannot chew the adult foods that supply needed nutrients. A four-year-old child needs about 50 percent more calories and 100 percent more protein per unit of weight than an adult. If both calories and proteins are insufficient for body needs, a wasting-away of tissues due to starvation may occur. The child may fail to grow, and there is sometimes bloating. Miraculous cures can be effected in a relatively short time, however, if additions are made to the diet. These additions to the diet include calories and high-quality protein such as that found in protein-rich milk powder.

In the past few decades, many people and groups have been cooperating to find ways to increase food production in developing countries—and to help developing countries fight diseases resulting from poor nutrition wherever these diseases occur. At times, too, help is needed when disasters strike. Thus there may be floods, droughts, earthquakes, and epidemics of disease. The United States, as well as many other countries, rushes food supplies to countries when such unexpected emergencies arise. Often the food supplies are distributed by non-government agencies such as CARE/MEDICO, the International Red Cross, Church World Service, and Catholic Relief Services.

Above, you can see some of the high-protein foods and beverages that have been introduced throughout the world.

Protein malnutrition is often a problem in the tropics and in other areas where high-carbohydrate diets are common and where protein foods are scarce or are very costly. A widespread protein-deficiency disease is called *kwashiorkor.* To assist in preventing protein malnutrition, efforts have been made to see that milk in powdered form is available to children in areas where protein foods are scarce. In some countries, too, local milk supplies and livestock production have been increased with the assistance of agricultural specialists who have come to share their skills. Work is also being done to develop vegetable sources of protein. These sources provide plentiful supplies of protein which can be produced locally and can be distributed at low cost. For example, soybean products and cottonseed flour are among the new vegetable sources of protein that have been developed. To combat a severe vitamin-A deficiency, which is a major cause of blindness and even death, a vitamin-A supplement along with the protein-rich milk is being supplied to many children in developing countries. To foster interest in eating vegetables, school and home gardens are being encouraged in many areas around the world.

The deficiency disease known as *pellagra*—caused by a shortage of the vitamin *niacin* in the diet—is common in areas where corn furnishes 60 percent or more of the calories in the diet. With the help of various food and health experts, countries with a high rate of pellagra are trying to increase the production and consumption of such foods as meat, dairy products, and peanut products. These foods are good sources of niacin. In some areas, enrichment of corn meal with niacin is proving successful.

A common disease in more than a hundred countries and territories is that of *simple goiter,* a disease caused by a lack of iodine in the diet. In the United States, ordinary table salt is iodized with potassium iodide to prevent goiter. In the countries where crude sea salt is used, potassium iodide does not mix with the salt; but research has found that another chemical substance, potassium iodate, can be used successfully. Thus the cheap and commonly used table salt is again the means for getting iodine into the diet.

Today scientists are helping save millions of people from starvation through the development of so-called miracle grains. Thus farmers in Asia may now harvest *three* crops of miracle rice a year instead of one or two. In addition, wheat varieties have been developed that produce amazingly high yields. Look at the picture essay (pages 134–137) on food problems of the world.

Teacher's Notes
(Continued from page 132.)

Reclaiming desert areas by means of irrigation and creating additional water supplies by desalting sea water.

Developing more efficient animal breeding methods and more efficient feeding to improve livestock production.

Seeking new sources of food—from plants such as algae and seaweed.

Some Things to Do

1. *Use reference books such as* Food for People *by Sarah R. Riedman (Abelard-Schuman) to find answers to queries like these:*
a. Why is crop rotation important in efficient food production?
b. How does soil erosion affect crop production? How can erosion be prevented?

2. *Investigate the work of a group such as the Food and Agriculture Organization (FAO) in helping with food problems around the world.*

Food for Hungry People

Some two thirds of the world's people do not get enough food to eat. A greater supply of food, however, is being achieved in many areas through modern, scientific methods of food production.

Page 134. *India, in recent years, has made massive efforts to cope with problems of starving people—and starving cattle such as those shown on page 134. Many problems result from drought.*
This page. Top left. *A free-food kitchen in India.*
Top right. *The Indian government gives priority to modern agricultural methods. Here experts select seeds for high-quality protein in corn.*
Bottom left. *Famine scene in the Congo—a reminder of food problems that still exist in the world.*

Opposite page. *Here, in Egypt, land that was once desert has been irrigated with water from the Nile River. The result is fertile soil and good crops.*

This Page. Top left. *A Malaysian farmer works in a rice field. A new "miracle rice" has been developed that can help him grow several crops of rice a year where only one crop was possible before.*
Bottom left. *Bountiful harvesting in the United States, a land blessed with favorable agricultural conditions. Even the United States, however, has some problems in seeing that all its people are properly nourished.*
Bottom right. *Scene in the Inter-American Institute of Agricultural Sciences in Costa Rica where students learn about modern farming methods.*

Teacher's Notes

Check Yourself: After students have read and thought about these questions, use them as guides for a summary discussion.

Things to Do: In considering their own daily diets, pupils might check to see if they have any of these common shortcomings: *not enough food in the morning, too many sweets, too few fruits and vegetables, not enough milk, not enough fruits and juices rich in vitamin C.*

Check Yourself

1. Look back at the questions on page 106. How would you answer them now?

2. Which one of the six classes of nutrients is known as "building blocks"? Why?

3. What is your explanation of each of these terms?

   a. element

   b. protoplasm

   c. nutrient

   d. enzyme

   e. glycogen

4. Which of these foods have the best quality of protein: nuts, meat, fish, beans? Explain.

5. Why might a girl your age need more calories daily than her grandmother?

6. What would be some defects in this plan for dieting: "Drink lots of milk and take plenty of vitamin pills daily"?

7. Why do you *not* weigh as much as all the food you have eaten?

8. What part can snacks play in helping you get an adequate daily diet?

9. Why shouldn't you skip breakfast?

10. What are some poor food habits of teen-agers? How can these habits be remedied?

11. What are some serious world food problems? What is being done about them?

Things to Do

1. Use the calorie chart on pages 118–121 to figure out the total calories in these meals: Breakfast: *½ grapefruit, 2 slices rye toast, 2 slices bacon, 1 glass whole milk.* Lunch: *1 frankfurter, 1 serving baked beans* (½ cup), *1 serving cabbage slaw* (½ cup), *2 cookies, 1 serving vanilla ice cream.* Supper: *2 servings fried chicken, 2 corn-bread muffins, 1 serving string beans* (½ cup), *tomato and lettuce salad, 1 serving Apple Betty, 1 glass whole milk.*

Do the meals provide enough calories for a teen-age boy? For a teen-age girl? If not, how could the needed calories be added?

Do the three meals include enough servings as recommended in the daily food guide shown on pages 116–117?

2. Bring in clippings about meal-planning, food research, or other aspects of nutrition. Be prepared to discuss this material.

Special Research

Prepare a written report on one of the topics listed below.

Food for Today's Astronauts
What Hydronauts Eat
New Sources of Food
Solving World Food Problems

Teacher's Notes

Pupils may work independently on this review. Encourage them to reread material in the text when necessary. Tell pupils that any sensible answer which completes the sentence correctly can be considered a "right answer."

Self-Help Review

Use a ruler or a strip of paper to cover the answer column at the right. Read the first item and write the missing word or words on a piece of paper. Then move your ruler or paper strip down to uncover the answer and see if you are right. Go on in the same way with each of the other items. Do not write in this book.

The numbers by the answers show the pages in this book that give information about the subject. For the items you miss, go back and review this information.

1. The same chemicals found in the body are also found in ______.	food 106
2. The slow burning of food in the body is called ______.	oxidation 107
3. The changing of food in the body into energy and living tissue is called ______.	metabolism 107
4. Young people your age need ______ cups of milk every day.	four 116
5. You need ______ or more servings from the Vegetable-Fruit group in your daily diet.	four 116
6. You need ______ or more servings daily from the Bread-Cereal group.	four 117
7. You need ______ or more servings daily from the Meat group.	two 117
8. Food provides the materials your body needs for building and maintaining tissues, for regulating body processes, and for ______.	heat 107 (energy, fuel)
9. Simple goiter can be caused by a lack of ______ in the diet.	iodine 133

Teacher's Notes

After pupils have taken the test and their papers have been scored, the test items can serve as guides for a summary discussion.

Health Test for Unit Four

Part I

Copy the number of each test item. If the item is *true,* write T after the number; if the item is *false,* write F.

F 1. Many foods contain all the nutrients in the amounts the body needs.

F 2. Minerals are the best fuel foods.

T 3. Fats come from both plants and animals.

T 4. Macaroni and rice are starchy foods.

T 5. Vitamin D is the sunshine vitamin.

F 6. A person tends to weigh as much as the food he has eaten.

T 7. Proteins are body-building foods.

F 8. Snacks are harmful.

T 9. Enzymes cause chemical changes in food.

F 10. Everyone should take vitamin pills.

F 11. All digestion of food takes place in the stomach and in the stomach only.

T 12. A very active person needs more calories per day than an inactive one.

F 13. Soft drinks are rich in nutrients.

T 14. Food serves as fuel for the body.

T 15. The burning of food in the body is called oxidation.

T 16. Lack of adequate food may lead to feelings of fatigue or discouragement.

Part II

Copy each number. Beside it write the letter of the best answer for each incomplete statement.

17. When food is oxidized
    a. the body is cooled
    b. heat is produced (underlined)
    c. enzymes are put to work
    d. fat is formed

18. Good sources of proteins are
    a. fruits
    b. meat, fish, and chicken (underlined)
    c. honey and molasses
    d. jams and jellies

19. Some good sources of vitamins are
    a. nuts and other fats
    b. fresh fruits and vegetables (underlined)
    c. corn syrup and molasses
    d. sugar, salt, and water

20. Foods and the human body are made up of
    a. the same chemical elements (underlined)
    b. minerals chiefly
    c. skin and bones
    d. calorimeters

Number of Answers 20

Number Right ______

Score (Number Right × 5) ______

5 How Can You Improve in Your Human Relations?

Teacher's Notes

Unit Overview: Use the message here to start off a preliminary exploration of what is meant by *human relations* and of the pertinence that the subject *human relations* has in the study of human health and well-being.
(*Note:* The common pronouns *he* or *his* refer to persons of either sex except when *she* or *her* is definitely applicable.)

Those who study how people live together—and how people solve problems—tell us that we must learn more about human needs and human relationships. Even if all the problems of health care should miraculously be solved, even if the world should become less threatened by pollutants, people could still destroy themselves if they do not progress in learning how to live with others.

In this unit you will learn more about human relations. You also will find answers to such questions as "Why do people behave as they do?" and "How can people change their behavior?" and "How can we become more understanding of ourselves and of others?"

Teacher's Notes

Read to Find Out: These questions stimulate interest in main topics covered in the unit. Talk over the queries just long enough to give students a chance to commit themselves to some answers. Such commitment helps ensure that pupils' attention will be held during study of the unit. They will want to check the accuracy of their tentative answers.

What Is Meant by Human Relations? See if pupils can recall examples of good human relations that have been reported recently in their local newspaper. Suggest that they bring in clippings of the reports. Discuss the importance of good human relations at home, at school, in the community, and in the world.

Read to Find Out

1. *What are some important* physiological needs *that all people have?*
2. *What are some important* psychological needs?
3. *What part does* motivation *play in people's behavior?*
4. *How may people's* expectations *influence their behavior?*
5. *What are some steps in the* problem-solving method *of coping with a difficult situation?*
6. *What are some of the ways people use to protect their feelings about themselves?*
7. *What is meant by* prejudice? *How does prejudice hurt those against whom it is directed? How does it harm the person who holds the prejudice?*
8. *How would you describe a mentally healthy person?*

What Is Meant by Human Relations?

The term *human relations* refers to the interactions of individuals with each other, or to what goes on between people. Sometimes these relationships are helpful and cooperative. Sometimes they can lead to serious misunderstandings, conflicts, and even wars.

At school, human relations involve what goes on among you, your teachers, and your classmates. At home, human relations involve how you feel and what you do when you are with your parents, your brothers and sisters, or other relatives. In the city or town in which you live, human relations include the ways in which people work, play, talk—the way they react to each other. Some people are encouraging, or *supportive,* in their human relations; other persons may be harmful, or *destructive.* Can you think of a situation in which you noticed someone acting in a supportive way? What happened?

Can you think of any situation in which a person harmed another by his or her attitudes or behavior? What happened? How could the situation have been handled differently?

Something to Do

Look in the school or public library for such books as the following that deal with human behavior:

Alexander, Arthur. The Hidden You: Psychology in Your Life *(Prentice-Hall).*

Goldenson, Robert M. All About the Human Mind *(Random).*

Groch, Judith. You and Your Brain *(Harper).*

McBain, W. N., and Johnson, R. C. The Science of Ourselves: Adventures in Experimental Psychology *(Harper).*

Noshpitz, Joseph D., M.D. Understanding Ourselves: The Challenge of the Human Mind *(Coward).*

Why Do People Behave As They Do?

Behind the behavior of every young person and every adult there is some cause—some combination of circumstances—that led to the kind of behavior which occurred. Sometimes a person knows the reason for the behavior. At other times, the cause of the action is not known or understood. In other words, one is not always conscious of the reasons for one's actions.

Even though people may do the same things, the reasons *why* they do them may be quite different—depending upon the experiences in their own lives. For instance, suppose that three boys have stolen some apples. Bill took them because he was hungry and did not have enough to eat. Ted stole because he was unhappy. He wanted the food because eating it made him feel better. Joe stole because his friends dared him to, and he wanted their approval. Each boy had a different immediate cause for his behavior; yet each was trying to fill an important need.

There are many theories that try to explain why you do the things you do. One theory is accepted by many people who study human behavior. This theory states that you usually act in certain ways because you are trying to satisfy important *human needs.*

Important Human Needs

Social scientists believe that in order to understand human behavior you must know what needs are strong enough to make you want to satisfy them. There is no common agreement on all the needs people may have. There are, however, some needs about which there is rather general agreement. To make progress in improving human relationships, you have to learn how these needs can be met, at least in part, both by individuals and by groups of people.

The physical needs of people are sometimes called *primary,* or *physiological,* needs. The primary, or physiological, human needs are those that must be met if life itself is to continue. What do you think these needs might be? Make a list and then compare your list with the one shown at the top of page 145.

Teacher's Notes

You might ask:

"What advantages do you see in learning about human behavior?" (The more you really know and understand about yourself, the better you can manage yourself and your life. Similarly, the more you understand others, the easier it will be to get along with them comfortably and effectively.)

Discuss, too, the *various* reasons that might underlie such behavior as not doing homework one evening. (The person may be tired, may be confused, may want to do something more interesting, may dislike a teacher, and so on.)

Reemphasize that the same behavior may have very *different* causes.

Something to Think About

What do you think is meant by the statement, "It helps in understanding yourself and others if you try to look beyond surface behavior to causes that may underlie this behavior"?

Teacher's Notes

Consider with students whether there are things *they* can do to help themselves satisfy some of their inner needs. (For example, people can venture into new activities; they can try to create something—through sewing, cooking, painting, building, and so on; they can try to develop a hobby. They might try to learn the joy of reading if they haven't yet experienced it; there are types of reading to fit all tastes and abilities.)

Invite pupils to give examples of times when they have been especially motivated to carry out some activity.

There are other human needs known as *secondary,* or *psychological* needs. They are not called secondary because they are second in importance, but because they are dependent upon life-giving primary needs. A person's first instinct is to stay alive, and therefore energy is usually directed toward survival before there can be concern for feelings. Therefore, if a person is starving or suffering from malnutrition, that person will usually seek food before any of the secondary needs will seem important.

Social scientists are usually in agreement that there are three psychological needs that are of special importance. These three needs are shown on the opposite page. What are they? How would you explain each one?

The effort to satisfy secondary, or psychological, needs is evident in people of all ages. It is one of the forces that pushes people on, or *motivates* them, to do many of the things they do. When any one of these psychological needs is not being adequately fulfilled, a person may feel tense and anxious or frustrated. The person may feel unable to do many things he or she is really able to do. Such unpleasant feelings are common—they may happen to you or to any other person. When your psychological needs *are* being met, you are more relaxed and "at peace" with yourself and with others.

The Importance of Motivation

Motivation plays an important part in your life just as it does in the life of everyone. One explanation of motivation is that it is something such as an inner need or desire or *drive* that causes a person to act in a certain way. Motivation is sometimes called an "energizer of behavior."

Throughout your life you will have many needs, wants, and wishes. Some will motivate you to act in one way and some will motivate you to act in another. In addition to your inner drive toward fulfilling the needs everyone has, you will find that you develop drives to fulfill personal wants and goals. The drive to fulfill personal goals will come out of your interests and your own past experiences. Unlike the universal human needs, these individual wants and goals will vary from person to person.

Some Things to Do

1. Look for examples in the books you read of how people react when some of their human needs are not being adequately fulfilled.
For example, in the book The Year of the Raccoon *by Lee Kingman (Houghton), fifteen-year-old Joey is just an "average" boy among a family of very talented brothers. How do you think this might make him feel? In what ways might his feelings motivate him to act?*
Try to get this book at the library and see how your speculations agree with some things that actually happened.

2. Discuss some of the primary and secondary needs that have not yet been met in many instances in the world today.

Some Needs of All Human Beings

<table>
<tr><th>Primary, or Physiological, Needs</th><th>Secondary, or Psychological, Needs</th></tr>
<tr><td>Air That Is Safe to Breathe</td><td rowspan="2">The Need for Love
Every person needs to be able to give love and to receive love from others. He or she needs to belong to some kind of family group and to have some close friends. Everyone has a need for affectionate, warm, kindly relationships with other people. A person who does not have such relationships often feels left out, unwanted, or rejected. Such a person may spend a whole lifetime in search of love and affection.</td></tr>
<tr><td>Water That Is Pure Enough to Drink</td></tr>
<tr><td>Food of the Right Kind and Amount</td><td rowspan="2">The Need for Self-Respect
Every person needs to feel that he or she is of worth and is a useful and necessary person. He or she has a need for self-respect. This involves the opportunity to achieve what one can achieve and the appreciation from others for the efforts and contributions that are made, however large or small.</td></tr>
<tr><td>Clothing for Protection</td></tr>
<tr><td>Sufficient Sleep</td><td rowspan="2">The Need to Be Oneself
Each person has a need and a desire to be himself or herself and to have the opportunity to do those things that he or she can do. Each person usually wants to make the most of himself or herself as a person.</td></tr>
<tr><td>Adequate Shelter from the Elements</td></tr>
</table>

Teacher's Notes

You might ask:

"Why might a young person drop out of school at age sixteen? What might motivate another young person to stay on and graduate from high school?"

"What are some *circumstances* that might motivate you to get up early on a Saturday morning and help clean the house?"

Your *individual* wants and goals will depend in part upon the values and interests you have acquired through the years. For one person in your group, a goal may be to become an honor student; for another, the goal may be to play on the basketball team. One of you may want to earn money to buy a pocket radio now; another may prefer to start saving money for a college education in the future. But whether your goal is toward something now or something in the future, if you want it very much, you will be motivated to try to achieve it. If your motivation is not very great, however, you may stop trying when things become difficult. Then, perhaps, you may substitute some different goal.

Motivation and Circumstances

Sometimes your motivation is strong, and sometimes it is weak or barely existent. For instance, if you are hungry and food is put before you, your hunger will motivate you to eat. If you have just had a big snack at a friend's house, however, you will have no motive to eat this same food.

Suppose you have been told to clean out the garage on a Saturday morning. You may start out half-heartedly, complaining of feeling tired. Your motivation is weak and arises from your fear of your parents' displeasure if you neglect the job. Then a friend comes along and says a ball game is going to start soon at the park. Your tiredness may then vanish. You may finish up your job in a hurry and take off for the park with plenty of energy. Can you think of some other examples where strong motivation played an important part in getting a job done?

What Do You Think?

1. Joan kept putting off washing her hair one Friday evening, even though it was in need of shampooing. Mary, on the other hand, eagerly set about the job of shampooing her hair that same evening.
What circumstances might cause Joan to act as she did? What might be motivating Mary's behavior?

2. When the school Science Fair was announced, Joe started thinking about a project for it. Phil said he doubted that he could be bothered planning an entry.
What might be motivating each boy to behave as he did?

Motivation and Expectations

Motivation also depends in part upon your expectations. Do you expect to succeed or fail? If you expect that you will succeed or have a chance of succeeding, you are more likely to work eagerly toward a goal or to accept a challenge.

If, on the other hand, you have met *many* situations in which you were not successful or were not able to do as well as you would like to have done, you may not try very hard to succeed. Your motivation may be weak because you are afraid you will not be successful.

You may want to do better in school, for example, but because of past experiences you may feel that it is no use. So why try? You may have no motivation to sit down and work out an assignment. You are discouraged before you start. In such a case, it would be a good idea to talk to a teacher, explain your problem, and ask for help. Such help might enable you to regain your confidence so that you *can* succeed.

You should keep in mind that there is no disgrace in failure if you have tried to meet a goal. Failure can be a step toward success if it is used to find out the things that you *can* do. Failure can become a part of motivation. Many fine scientists, for instance, fail and have to go back and begin over again on some project they are pursuing. Sometimes through their failure they are also successful because they have learned what does *not* work. Often knowing what you cannot do is as important as knowing what you can do. Occasionally, too, when you fail at one thing, you find at the same time something else you are successful in or something that unexpectedly interests you or excites your curiosity. Can you think of a time when you failed at something, but through that failure found something else you could do?

The fact that you have a motive and want to achieve a particular goal does not mean that you always will be able to do so. It *does* make it more likely that you will be able to move toward your goal. If you are motivated with a real desire to achieve something, you will focus your attention much more completely on what you are trying to do. At times you may have to change a goal somewhat so that you have a chance of reaching it in several steps instead of one. Sometimes, also, you may have to learn—and be realistic about—what you must do to achieve the goal toward which you are motivated.

Behavior Is Learned

Often, the way in which you try to fulfill a need or goal may not be desirable. You may have to *learn* a better way. At times, you may need help in becoming aware that what you are doing is not the best way to reach your goal. Parents, teachers, older brothers and sisters, and youth group leaders are among the people who can often give you help in changing your

Teacher's Notes

Some questions that might be discussed are these:

"Can you think of an example of a real person—or character in a book—who achieved his goal because of his great desire to achieve it? Tell about it."

"How might a person find help in discovering what is needed to achieve a particular goal?"

"What example can you think of where a person might have to take *several* steps to reach a goal important to him?" (If he wants to get a full-time summer job, he may have to take a part-time or low-paying one during the preceding year; this will help him build up work experience and job references, for instance. Or he may have to get some work experience through volunteer work.)

What Do You Think?

Suppose you are tutoring a young child who is having some trouble with arithmetic. Which of these approaches would be likely to get the best results? Why?

a. Tell the youngster that he has been doing poorly and he will have to try lots harder if he expects to make progress.

b. Start out with some very easy work and praise the youngster every time he gets something right.

Teacher's Notes

Some discussion guides that might be used are the following:

"What examples can you give of behavior you have learned?"

"What kinds of behavior does a person tend to continue?"

"How would you explain what is meant by *conscience?*"

"Why do you think parents are concerned about the kinds of friends their daughters and sons have?"

behavior. Keep in mind always that *learned behavior can be changed* if your motives for wanting to change that behavior are strong enough.

In general, you tend to continue the kinds of behavior that bring you satisfaction. Behavior that brings about unpleasant results is the kind you may try to discontinue. Can you think of ways you have learned to behave because the results are pleasant? Can you think of ways you are acting that make you uncomfortable—ways you would like to change for some more satisfactory ones?

Most of the ways in which you try to fulfill your needs and achieve your goals were learned as you were growing up. For example, you have learned from your relationships with other people—how they treat you and how they respond to you. You have learned from your parents and from the standards they have tried to teach you. You have learned from the examples, the attitudes, and the ideas of your friends and your teachers. Also you have learned from television and radio programs, from books and magazines, and from the many experiences you have had.

Over the years, you have been learning your sex role, or what you feel is expected of a boy or girl, a man or woman. You have been learning the attitudes, standards, and values you hold. Your prejudices have been learned too; and so have many of the ways you behave in certain situations.

From all your experiences and in all these ways, you have been learning how to make choices about the kind of behavior you want for your own. As you have grown, you have learned the kinds of behavior that are considered acceptable or unacceptable in the part of the world in which you live.

Sometimes you consider all the possible ways to act and decide that the way you learned is not the best way for you and for all concerned. Gradually you have developed a *conscience,* which gives guidelines when you must decide which is the best way to act. By the time you are eighteen or so, you should have chosen, and in good part acquired, the kinds of behavior you want to make your own—behavior that becomes a part of your own special personality.

You Learn from:

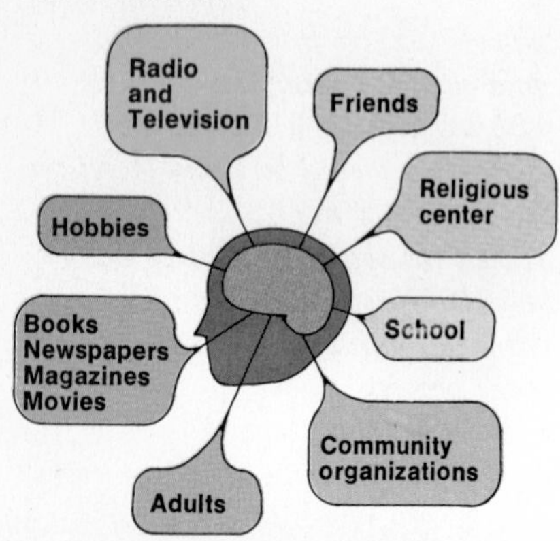

How Can You Meet the Demands of Life?

Neither you nor anyone else goes through life without meeting some problems and without having to make some difficult choices. Sometimes you will make mistakes and cause your own problems. It is important for your own personality development that you face up to your mistakes honestly. Then it is far easier for you to solve the problem you yourself caused and to avoid similar problems in the future. In addition, all people at one time or another find themselves in situations which are not of their own choosing but which must be met.

Young people, through no fault of their own, are faced with problems that may at times seem almost overwhelming. The problem may be a family crisis—possibly illness or divorce, or perhaps the necessity of moving and thus being in a strange community. Also, having a physical disability presents problems. Still another difficult problem is that of being in a school or community in which you are not well received. This might be because your outward appearance is different or because your language or family background or religion is not just like that of a majority of those around you.

Many young people have these or other difficult experiences to meet. Although a situation may seem hard or unfair, you should try to develop the strength and courage to face the problem. Do *your* best to become an understanding person, even when the odds against you are great. Work steadily to improve conditions when it is possible. Try to make at least one or two good friends with whom you can enjoy doing things and with whom you can talk things over.

Becoming bitter makes it more difficult for you to work out your problem. Bitterness also prevents you from finding the many things in life that you can do and enjoy in spite of the difficulties and unkindnesses you may have to face. Courage to meet your difficulties can come from the realization of this fact: *It is the kind of person you are trying to become, with your own goals and values, which will help you achieve a desirable life—in spite of problems that seem almost impossible to solve.*

Teacher's Notes

In discussing the values of facing and trying to work through problems instead of avoiding them, you might point out that *each problem we face and work through with reasonable success leaves us stronger and better able to handle the next difficult situation that comes along.* Running away from problems or merely becoming bitter or belligerent about them deprives a person of useful experience in learning to cope successfully with difficult situations.

Something to Do

You can find help in meeting your problems through reading the biographies of people who have had difficulties to face and have found ways to meet them. Here are a few books of this kind that you might want to look for at the library:

Baker, Rachel. The First Woman Doctor: The Story of Elizabeth Blackwell *(Messner).*

Cavanah, Frances, Editor. We Came to America *(Macrae).*

Eaton, Jeanette. Lone Journey: The Life of Roger Williams *(Harcourt).*

Frank, Anne. Anne Frank: Diary of a Young Girl *(Doubleday).*

Hughes, Langston. Famous American Negroes *(Dodd).*

Keller, Helen A. The Story of My Life *(Doubleday).*

Sterne, Emma Gelders. Mary McLeod Bethune *(Knopf).*

Teacher's Notes

Students might discuss the following descriptions of people who are reasonably able to meet life's demands. They are from the pamphlet "Mental Health Is 1, 2, 3," National Association for Mental Health:

They plan ahead and do not fear the future.

They welcome new experiences and new ideas.

They try to think for themselves and make their own decisions.

They do something about their problems as they arise and accept their responsibilities.

Steps in Problem Solving

Think through what the problem really is.
Write down some possible ways of meeting or solving the problem.
List some people who might be able to help, if help is needed.
Evaluate the various solutions; decide which solution to try first.
Number the other suggestions in the order they might be tried.
Cross out those that do not seem sensible—on second thought.
Be sure the suggestions listed can be carried out in the real situation.

Problems Can Be Met

The problem-solving approach is a healthy, mature way of trying to handle difficult situations. Keep in mind, though, that before you can do anything about a problem, *you first must be willing to admit that the problem exists and that you will act to solve it.* Once you have faced the fact that you have a problem, there are helpful steps you can take to solve it. Some of these steps are listed at the left. What are they?

There will be times when you cannot solve a problem or meet a situation in ways you would like. There are times when you may have to learn to live with a difficult situation. Part of learning how to meet life is to recognize when you can do something about a problem and when you cannot. There is a quotation you may have heard, expressing the wish for "the serenity to accept the things I cannot change, the courage to change the things I can, and the wisdom to know the difference." This is a mature goal, and it is an approach that can be learned. For instance, if you have a physical handicap, you can learn to accept it and live with it—and find those things you can do despite the handicap.

In addition to helping you meet serious problems, the problem-solving approach can also be applied to some of the situations you may have to face day by day. There will be many times when what you would like to do and what it is necessary or possible for you to do will be very different things. How would you use the problem-solving steps in these situations?

The person you want most for a best friend prefers someone else to you.

You want to convince your parents that you are able to make more mature decisions on your own than you used to.

You want to be liked by and stay friends with those in a group who are doing things you do not want to do—such as smoking or shoplifting.

You have trouble controlling your temper and often find yourself shouting at people or having tantrums.

You will find some common problem situations pictured on pages 151 to 154. Try the problem-solving approach in answering the questions on each page.

Some Problem Situations: What Would You Do?

Situation One: *Joel is having trouble with his schoolwork. His test grades get lower and lower. How might Joel meet this situation?*

Situation Two: *Tom is afraid he will not make the school basketball team. For one thing, he is shorter than most of the fellows who are trying out. How might he meet this situation?*

Situation Three: *Inez would like to stay in her present community —where her friends are—but her family is moving to another city. What can she do to make the best of this situation?*

Situation Four: *Amy discovers a pimple on her face and she is worried about how to handle this skin ailment. What can she do about the situation?*

Some Ways in Which We Protect Ourselves

The problem-solving approach is an effective method to use in meeting situations you find difficult. There are, however, other ways everyone uses at times to meet or react to a situation. Often you use these other ways of reacting to situations when you are not really aware of what your difficulty is or why you are not at ease or why you are feeling anxious and upset.

Everyone wants to feel comfortable and at ease. So everyone attempts to protect himself from uncomfortable thoughts or feelings. Often a person protects himself without thinking about it or even realizing what he is doing. He is unaware of why he is acting in a particular way. All of us guard ourselves and our feelings about ourselves and our behavior. The various ways in which we do this are sometimes called *our ways of defense.*

Some of the common ways in which we defend ourselves are by *rationalization, compensation, daydreaming, repression and suppression, displaced aggression, projection,* and *denial.* These various ways are explained on pages 156 to 162. You will want to take time to study the explanations carefully.

As you read about these various ways of defense, remember that all people use some of these forms of behavior some of the time. Such responses explain a lot of our own behavior as well as the behavior of others. If you decide that you have occasionally used some of these ways of making yourself feel comfortable, you do not need to be worried. Such behavior can help individuals cope with the feelings of inferiority, failure, and anxiety that everyone has from time to time. There *is* cause for concern, however, if a person overuses these defense mechanisms, as they are sometimes called. It is important to balance their use with the ability to face up to problems and to life as it really is. The defense mechanisms often tend to cover up problems that should be faced directly and worked out.

Defense mechanisms are tools with which people may try to protect their own opinions or feelings about themselves. If you realize that, you will be helped to understand some of the things you do and some of the reasons why other people may act in certain ways.

Teacher's Notes

Perhaps students may wonder of what use it is to know about various ways we have of protecting our feelings about ourselves—especially when many of our motives are *unconscious.* For one thing, seeking to understand why one frequently acts in a particular way can be the first step in trying to change the behavior if that behavior is not constructive. Then, too, even though responses to certain situations are unconscious ones, a person can work toward changing these responses if he tries to understand what is in back of his feelings and actions. It may take a while, but many times it can be done.

Ways We Protect Ourselves

Rationalization
Compensation
Daydreaming
Repression and Suppression
Displaced Aggression
Projection
Denial

Rationalization

Rationalization is a method by which people justify the way they think or feel or act. A person may defend himself by words or thoughts rather than by actions. Rationalization is a way of finding reasons for one's behavior that are not the real reasons. An excuse is given for behavior that it is hoped will satisfactorily explain what has been done. Usually this happens when someone thinks his behavior is unacceptable. Therefore he must think of excuses for the behavior to protect his opinion of himself.

Here are some examples of rationalizations, along with suggested real reasons for the behavior:

"I couldn't do my homework because the teacher didn't make the assignment clear." (Real reason: I wasn't paying attention in class when the assignment was given.)

"I didn't make the team because the coach doesn't like me." (Real reason: I missed too many practice sessions to be eligible for the team.)

"I did not paint a picture as good as Mary's because my brushes were too old." (Real reason: Mary has always been a better painter than I am.)

"My report was poor because I had a headache the day I gave it." (Real reason: I didn't start writing it until the night before and so did not rehearse it.)

"I didn't win the race because the lane I had to run in was too bumpy." (Real reason: I was up too late the night before the race and was tired.)

"I didn't bring a cake for the party because my mother wouldn't let me bake one." (Real reason: I forgot about the cake until the day of the party and I didn't have time to do any baking.)

When an individual rationalizes, he is *alibiing* to cover up his own failure to carry out a task or to act appropriately. He justifies his acts to escape facing the truth that *he* was responsible for his behavior. Often when a person rationalizes, he is not aware of the underlying reasons that are causing him to excuse his behavior.

What examples can you give of rationalizing your actions?

Compensation

Compensation has to do with the way a person makes up for an actual or imagined lack of some particular skill or ability. Compensation is one of the most commonly used mechanisms of defense. Every one of us at times tries to develop ways to make up for what we do not have or cannot do. We substitute something we can do for something in which we cannot be successful.

Below are some examples of people using compensation—as a wholesome response to a situation.

A boy who thinks he has weak arm and shoulder muscles works at weightlifting to develop greater muscle strength.

A boy who does not have much athletic ability compensates by developing his hobby of photography.

A blind person develops with training an unusual sense of touch in the fingertips and thus can rapidly read the raised printing of Braille.

A girl who worries about being awkward joins a "Y" class in modern dance so that she will become more graceful.

Sometimes, though, people overdo their efforts to compensate for some real or imagined handicap. If the boy who is doing weightlifting, for instance, talks excessively or brags about his weightlifting, he would then be *overcompensating.*

Sometimes, too, people compensate by trying to cover up frightening or disturbing feelings and giving the impression that they are feeling the opposite way. Blustering is another way of covering up fear. Actions and behavior that are "over-polite" may be a cover-up for hostile feelings.

When a person feels inferior about something, he may bully others or act as if he is better than they are. He does this to make up for his inferior feelings and to cover up the feelings of doubt he may have about himself. Feelings of inferiority in some area may be based largely on the fact that the person has been unable to do what he felt others expected of him.

If you find you are overcompensating, you might ask yourself if you *really* need to feel inferior. Perhaps you can balance your strengths against a weakness. You may not need to feel so downhearted about yourself.

Daydreaming

Through daydreams a person withdraws into wishful thinking. When he does this, he may escape from a difficult situation or a world in which he cannot achieve all the things he would like to achieve. He escapes by imagining himself to be wonderful, capable, or endowed with all the things he wants. He can create his own world.

Sometimes the daydreamer will see himself as a hero who achieves great things. A shy girl may see herself as an actress or a beauty queen. A boy who is feeling left out may see himself as a football star or a popular singer.

Some daydreams, however, are not pleasant ones. They may involve fantasy in which a person feels guilty or unhappy or imagines that he is being punished. Such daydreams may at times indicate that help is needed for the troubled person. The amount of daydreaming a person does is often related to the number of difficulties he faces in real life and his need to find relief from them.

Daydreams are not always an escape from reality. Many people daydream because it is pleasant to do so. What a person daydreams about today may lead to real accomplishments in the future. A young person may in fantasy see himself as successful in the work which he really wants to do. He may be imagining himself in a future situation which is attainable for him. Then his daydreams may motivate him to *work hard* to achieve his goal.

Daydreams may be a pleasant and relaxing part of life if they do not prevent one from recognizing the difference between fantasy and reality. If daydreams become more satisfying than real life—if they cause a person to ignore his obligations and responsibilities or neglect the demands of everyday life—they are controlling the daydreamer instead of vice versa.

Daydreaming is a part of everyone's life. To daydream can be normal and healthy. But if the daydreaming is used as a too-frequent escape from meeting real-life situations, it can be damaging.

Can you think of some healthy examples of daydreaming? Some unhealthy examples?

Repression and Suppression

Repression is a complicated way of protecting one's feelings. Repression occurs when a person protects himself from recognizing something that has occurred—or from acknowledging a painful or unacceptable thought or feeling. He unconsciously prevents himself from thinking about it or facing it. Thus, thoughts or impulses which the person has been taught are inappropriate may not even come into his consciousness. If they did, he would feel guilty and anxious because he had such thoughts or because he acted on them. He may inhibit or hold back such thoughts, or he may apparently "forget" his actions.

Someone may have had a severely upsetting experience that was too much for him to face. Such an experience may be repressed so that he does not recall it. Sometimes actions are repressed that were not severely upsetting but deeply embarrassing. Everyone at times acts in some foolish way. If the behavior causes anxiety and more than normal concern, sometimes the incident is repressed and not recalled.

Repression is a complex process that cannot be consciously controlled. Repression occurs without a person's even realizing that it has happened.

At times, though, someone may consciously put out of his mind certain thoughts, ideas, or unpleasant things which have happened to him. He refuses to let himself think about them. When he does this, he is using suppression rather than repression, because he is aware of what he is doing. He is saying to himself, "I will not think about this." We all use suppression from time to time.

When either suppression or repression takes place, the feelings and anxieties do not just disappear. They may come out in various physical symptoms such as these: constant headaches, bitter or sarcastic responses to others, irritability, anxiety, or depressed feelings that a person cannot explain.

When something has been repressed—or if one suppresses too many of his thoughts or feelings—sometimes a trained person is needed to help. Such a person may provide guidance in understanding and handling the upset feelings.

Displaced Aggression

Displaced aggression takes place when a person expresses his feelings by hitting out at someone or something that had little or nothing to do with the situation. Here are some examples of displaced aggression:

A boy is angry at a small brother at home who keeps getting into his belongings and destroying them; on the way to school the boy bullies a young child he chances to meet.

A girl feels unhappy because someone in her "crowd" has made a critical comment about her appearance; in turn, she makes fun of a classmate outside her group—one who had nothing to do with the comment.

A boy is angry at a teacher who has scolded him for not doing his homework; at home that evening he becomes unreasonably angry with his mother when supper is late.

Displaced aggression can involve either a misplaced physical attack or a less direct attack through unkind remarks or through gossip. This defense mechanism is often used when an individual knows that a direct attack on the person who aroused his anger would not be permitted—or would bring undesirable consequences. For example, the boy who was angry at his brother knew that hitting was prohibited. The girl who was angry about having her appearance criticized by one of her "crowd" did not want to show her anger to that person—for fear she might be dropped from the group. So instead, she took out her anger on someone who had nothing to do with the situation. The boy who was angry at his teacher could not shout at her without getting into further difficulties.

Displaced aggression occurs when a person is frustrated and takes out his frustration on someone who was not involved. Such frustration can occur when a person does not know whom he should blame for a problem. So he chooses a *scapegoat.* Scapegoats are people or groups who are blamed for things they did not do. Sometimes the displaced aggression is a conscious act—a person knows he is displacing his aggression. Sometimes a person hits out without considering what he is doing or why.

What example of displaced aggression can you think of?

Projection

Most of us have qualities, impulses toward certain kinds of behavior, and feelings that we are unwilling to face in ourselves. We are unwilling to face them because we have learned that they are not acceptable. As a result, we may unconsciously credit someone else with the feelings that really are our own. Thus, unfriendly or hostile people are very likely to attribute unfriendly or hostile feelings to others who may not have those feelings at all.

Bill felt hostile toward Peter. Bill hit Peter, started a fight, and then claimed, "He had it in for me. He was going to hit me. I had to hit him." But Peter had approached Bill in a friendly manner and did not feel hostile toward him.

Sometimes one may project his feelings onto others because he has a great need or wish to believe that these people have the feelings he wants them to have. Such projection may prevent recognition of the real situation. For example, a boy or girl "falls in love" with someone. He (or she) may then attribute similar feelings of affection to the other person—even though there may be no evidence that the other person has any romantic interest at all.

In another form of projection, a person may express a very high opinion of himself. He then indicates that everyone else has the same opinion about him—because he needs to believe that this is true.

Projection differs from most of the other ways in which we defend ourselves in that its use can harm other people. If a person projects blame or feelings on another which are really his own, he may feel free to then launch an attack on the other person. He may gossip about him or charge him with motives—such as jealousy—which he himself is feeling. Sometimes it is not only individuals but groups that can come under such unmerited attacks.

Projection may protect a person by making him less anxious about himself and about his thoughts or faults than if he had to face up to them directly. It protects his self-esteem. Everyone projects a little at times. However, excessive projection prevents facing up to problems and working toward change.

Denial

One of the most frequent ways in which we try to protect our feelings about ourselves is by refusing to recognize a problem or by refusing to recognize facts which are unpleasant or painful if we accept them as true. We deny that a situation exists. Unfortunately such denial, whether it is conscious or unconscious, can keep us from facing a situation and doing something about it.

A student may be failing in schoolwork but keeps insisting that everything will be all right by the end of the semester. At the end of the semester failure does come. This failure might have been avoided if the student had been willing to face the problem, work harder, and perhaps ask for help. Or a young person may be having a real problem and be in danger of getting into serious trouble because of the actions of those with whom he is associating. He may say to himself, "They are all right. Everything will be fine. I won't get into trouble." But he does get into trouble along with his friends.

In such cases, the individuals are not deliberately pretending that things are all right. Rather, they are dismissing the risks from their thoughts and attention. They ignore the realities of the situation because they do not want to believe that they exist.

Most people use denial many times in their lives instead of facing facts. Denial becomes serious if it prevents a person from facing a situation that can be really harmful and one for which he could obtain help.

A person may be afraid to face a dangerous situation, for instance, yet deny that he is afraid. This is sometimes called "whistling in the dark." He denies his fear to keep up his courage. This can at times be a helpful form of denial. But suppose he denies his fear by maintaining that the situation is not dangerous. He would then be using denial to keep him from admitting to himself that he must ultimately face the situation. As another example, some people realize that they have a serious health problem that must be met. However, they deny the seriousness until it is too late to receive the treatment they should have had.

How Can You Improve in Your Relationships With Others?

The person who is growing toward emotional maturity and toward increased effectiveness in human relations is one who tries to understand that there are reasons why people behave as they do. You can become more understanding if you keep in mind that other people are much like you. They have the same emotional needs that you have.

Everyone feels uneasy or unhappy or dissatisfied when one or another of these emotional needs is not being fully satisfied. People may at times behave in undesirable ways to try to make up for various unmet needs.

It helps, then, in improving human relationships, if you try to *know* other people before you decide you do not like them. Once you try to know a person, you may begin to understand some of the reasons for his or her actions. You may find you really like the other person and that the boasting or some other annoying trait is just one of many qualities—one that may be outweighed by other qualities. You may come to understand something about another person's needs that are not being fully met. Perhaps then you can help that person meet some of these needs by showing genuine interest and concern.

So begin to give the other person a "break." If you can, help someone else. Remember that everyone, just like you, has a need for kindliness, friendliness, and self-respect. The following description of people who feel kindly toward others offers suggestions about how to improve your human relations.[1]

> *People who feel kindly toward others* are able to give love and to consider the interests of others.
>
> They like and trust others, and take it for granted that others will like and trust them.
>
> They respect the many differences they find in people.
>
> They do not push people around, nor do they allow themselves to be pushed around.
>
> They feel a sense of responsibility toward others.

[1]From "Mental Health Is 1, 2, 3," The National Association for Mental Health, Inc. Reprinted by permission.

Teacher's Notes

Discuss some reasons why it matters whether we try to improve in our human relations. For example, a person is hindered in many of the things he or she wants to do now and later in life if his or her relationships with others are poor. Perhaps students can give some examples. For instance, a player fails to make the team because he or she cannot cooperate with team players; a person may lose a job because he or she cannot get along with co-workers.

Something to Do

There are many fine books about young people who are growing in their understanding of themselves and others. Some books of this kind that you might want to look for at the library are these:

Bishop, Curtis. Fast Break *(Lippincott).*

Clark, Ann Nolan. Santiago *(Viking).*

Fritz, Jean. I, Adam *(Coward).*

Low, Elizabeth. Hold Fast the Dream *(Harcourt).*

Rabin, Gil. False Start *(Harper).*

Van Leeuwan, Jean, Editor. A Time of Growing *(Random).*

Teacher's Notes

As boys and girls discuss prejudice, you might well point out that recognizing the value of each individual does not mean that we have to *like* every other person. But it does mean that we should *respect* every person as an individual and accord him or her the same rights and privileges we ask for ourselves. Thus we should respect the *feelings* of others—we should try to understand the other person and to avoid hurting his or her feelings. For example, we may choose our best friends for out-of-school activities, but we have a responsibility for working cooperatively with others at school.

Feeling Kindly Toward Some but Not Toward Others

There are some people who are able to feel kindly only toward individuals like themselves. These people feel less kindly toward persons who may for some reason appear "different." Such people lump together in groups all those who seem different. The "difference" may be a physical characteristic such as the shape of the eyes or the color of the skin—or it may be a difference in ideas or religious beliefs. These people also assume that a person who has a characteristic which seems "different" will think, act, and feel as do all others who have that same characteristic. Furthermore, these people tend to assume that ways which are not like their own are inferior. There are people in our country and in many parts of the world who have unfriendly feelings toward those who are "different" from themselves.

Such people forget that every person deserves to be judged on his or her own merits and that there are fine persons and less admirable persons among all races, nationalities, and religious groups, and within all communities. Certain people make up their minds about others before they know them as individuals. These opinions are formed on the basis of feelings about the groups to which the other persons belong. Such prejudging of others before the facts are known about them is called *prejudice.*

Calling classmates "odd" because their interests differ from those of the majority is an example of prejudice. Excluding classmates because of outward differences that have nothing to do with their value as individuals is another example.

Something to Think About

All people are affected by the way they are treated by others. People who are used to having others act toward them in a friendly manner learn to respond in a friendly manner themselves. But people who are made to feel they are inferior may come to consider the world an unfriendly place—and may act in hostile ways. How we respond to other people helps influence their actions as well as their feelings about themselves.

Psychologists have found that one of the causes of prejudice against others lies in a feeling of personal inadequacy or insecurity. Some prejudiced people boost their own self-images by setting themselves up as superior to others.

Prejudice may also be a habit, a way of thinking that is passed down from one member of a family or community to another. This kind of prejudice can be changed when the members of the family or community really begin to think about what their prejudice means. Then they may realize that prejudice against certain people can be destructive to those people.

The person who is constantly made to feel inferior may have a hard time maintaining the self-confidence needed to develop talents and strengths. Such a person may become discouraged and feel that there will not be an opportunity to develop personal talents as fully as possible because the kind of opportunities and education that are needed cannot be obtained. Then, abilities are left undeveloped and are lost not only to the individual but also to the world.

Prejudice is damaging not only to the person against whom it is directed but also to the person who holds the prejudice. The person who holds prejudices is harmed because he or she is likely to gain a false sense of superiority. Such a sense of superiority is based not on what the person is or what has been accomplished but on the fact that the individual belongs to a certain group or race or nationality.

The prejudiced person attacks others for their shortcomings and in so doing is able to avoid looking into his or her own personal shortcomings and doing something about them. Even more serious, there is nurturing of the habit of making judgments that are not based on facts. This type of habit hinders the growth and development of one's personality.

Learning to Communicate with One Another

Part of learning how to understand other people is learning how to talk with them and how to listen to them. Many of the problems and misunderstandings that arise among people develop because they find it hard to really communicate with one another.

Communication is a "two-way thing." It is essential to listen carefully so that you get the real meaning of what another person is trying to say. Many people talk *at* one another instead of *with* one another. Think of the people with whom you have talked today. With how many people do you think you have *really* communicated?

Sometimes your feelings get between you and what you are trying to communicate. How might this occur? You might, for example, be so angry or so upset that you are unable or unwilling to make your point clearly or to listen to what the other person is saying.

Teacher's Notes

Some discussion guides are these:

"What can cause a person to change a prejudice?"

"How are people affected when they are victims of prejudice?"

"How are those who hold prejudice harmed?"

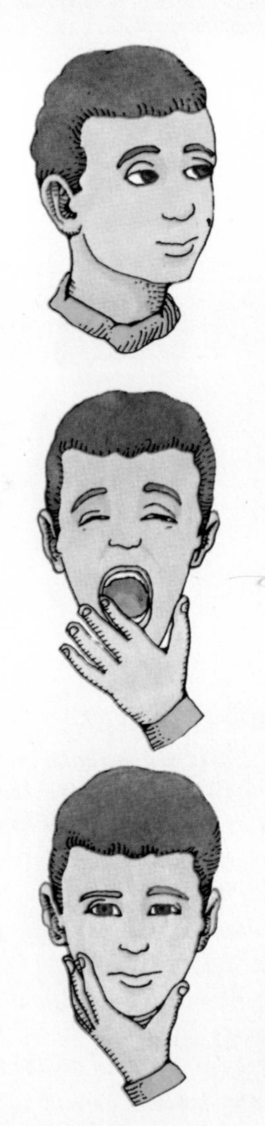

How are ideas being communicated here without use of words?

Teacher's Notes

Mention that it often helps if, when we are not sure what the other person means, we *restate* his position and then ask "Is this what you mean?" or "Is this what you were saying?"

Students might work in small groups to plan and later present skits in which they show examples of people who are communicating well through words and those who are not.

Skits might also be given in which *actions* and not words give clues about the kind of ideas or feelings that are being communicated.

Sometimes you may be so sure you are right that you will not listen to another person's point of view. Suppose you have had difficulty lately in communicating with your parents. Suppose you have had a misunderstanding with a good friend. Or you and a teacher may not have understood one another. In each of these cases, how do you think things might have been different if the persons involved had really listened to one another?

Real communication is a shared experience. It is a mutual awareness of ideas, of points of view, and of feelings. Each of the persons trying to communicate must be willing to listen and must try to hear what the other person really has to say. Even more important, each one must try to understand what the other really means.

Communication is not always verbal. You can and do communicate with other people through your behavior. If you turn your back on someone or refuse to sit next to someone in the lunchroom or make signs to a friend that someone else is not wanted, you are communicating in a forceful way. If you have a friendly attitude, you are also communicating your feelings —your interest, your desire to be friendly.

It is worth thinking about the ways in which your actions may convey your feelings to another person. There is an old saying that "Actions speak louder than words." What situation can you think of where this has been true?

What Do You Think?

How would you evaluate each of these definitions of mental health given by young people your age?

"Mental health means the way you think and act."

"Mental health is how your brain works."

"A person with good mental health can make his own decisions; he is not unhappy or depressed all the time."

"Mental health is something you have or don't have. There is nothing you can do about it."

What Is Good Mental Health?

In this unit, as you were learning about understanding yourself and others, you were also learning about mental health.

No doubt you have often heard the term *mental health*. You have probably seen television programs or read articles on the subject. Think about what you have read and heard and what you have learned. Then see if you can suggest a definition of mental health.

Compare your definition with those shown at the left—which were given by some young people your age. Which definitions come closest to describing what *you* think is meant by mental health?

Did you decide that mental health is not an easy term to define? Even those who are specialists in the field of mental health do not define it in exactly the same way. Usually the term is explained in reference to *good* mental health. Some commonly accepted ideas about good mental health are the following ones:

Good mental health involves the ability to feel comfortable about yourself, kindly toward other people, and able to meet life's demands.

People have good mental health when they can manage their emotions and feelings in ways that do not hurt themselves or others.

Good mental health consists of the ability to face things as they are, to find activities that interest you, and to try to work out your problems.

"Emotional maturity" is one way to describe good mental health. A person's emotional maturity can be indicated by the way he or she gets along with others—and by the quality of his or her relationships at home, at school, on the job, and in the community.

A mentally healthy person does not expect others to think, look, or act the same as he or she does; a mentally healthy person appreciates differences in others.

Some people have better mental health than others, and all people have ups and downs in mental health just as they have in physical health.

Your present mental health is built on all the things that have happened to you since you were born and on how you have reacted to them. Your future experiences and your own willingness to change and grow will also influence your mental health. This means that it is possible for you to work to improve your mental health throughout your lifetime. As you continue to increase your understanding of yourself and other people, you will be working toward the goal of improved mental health.

Some aids to good mental health that are applicable to everyone are shown in the margin at the right. What are these aids?

Teacher's Notes

Consider with students the advantages of achieving good mental health. Expand the discussion to include mention of the relationship between physical and mental health. Thus when one is reasonably happy and satisfied with himself and the world, his body functions more efficiently: he sleeps well, his food is digested properly, he does not feel tense and "tied in knots," and so on. There is much truth in the old statement, "To have a healthy body, one must have a healthy mind."

Some questions to use for discussion guides are these:

"Is a person's mental health always the same? Explain."

"What has brought about *your* present state of mental health?"

"What can help you work toward improved mental health?"

Some Aids to Good Mental Health

Family and Friends
Good relationships with family, friends, and others around you can make your life rich and satisfying.

Talking Things Over
Talking things over with friends and with others you trust helps relieve worry and tension.

Work
A job—or some regular organized activity such as attending school—helps provide an outlet for energy and gives a feeling of usefulness.

Play
Some individuals find their most enjoyable recreation in sports and games; others find pleasure and a sense of achievement in hobbies.

Personal Values
All individuals need to work out the personal values by which they want to try to live.

Teacher's Notes

Check Yourself: After students have read and thought about these questions, use them as guides for a summary discussion.

Things to Do: Students might make a glossary of some psychological terms used in this unit: *drive, motivation, mental health, daydreaming, compensation,* and so on.

Check Yourself

1. Look back at the questions on page 142. How would you answer them now?

2. Suppose three people are trying out for a staff position on the school paper. What *different* reasons might be motivating each one?

3. How can a person's expectations affect whether or not he achieves a task?

4. What example can you give of a kind of positive behavior that is *learned?*

5. What can motivate a person to try to *unlearn* some form of behavior?

6. What ways of protecting yourself are brought to mind by each of these situations?

a. A boy comments, "I could have been elected to the Student Council but everyone knew I didn't want to be on it."

b. A young person who got a poor grade on a test throws his books on his locker shelf, bangs the door shut, and kicks the locker.

c. A girl who finds it difficult to share her possessions criticizes others for not being more generous.

d. A person who often has an earache says, "Oh, it really isn't anything—not anything at all."

7. What can help you communicate more effectively with another person?

Things to Do

1. Work with one or more classmates to dramatize situations in which a person is using a defense mechanism. The audience can then name the mechanism.

2. Write a paragraph or so suggesting some things a person can do to work toward good mental health.

3. Be ready to discuss how prejudice can influence the mental health of a person against whom the prejudice is directed.

4. Explain why you think a community that has parks, playgrounds, hobby groups, and the like is playing a part in improving the mental health of people who live there.

5. See if you can communicate some attitudes to the group by actions rather than words.

Special Research

1. Investigate *stereotyped thinking* and ways it can affect human relations. One source you might use is the chapter entitled "How We Think" in the book *All About the Human Mind* by Robert M. Goldenson (Random).

2. Write a report on improving human relations in the classroom.

3. See if there is a Human Relations Council in *your* community. What does it do?

Teacher's Notes

Pupils may work independently on this review. Encourage them to reread material in the text when necessary. Tell pupils that any sensible answer which completes the sentence correctly can be considered a "right answer."

Self-Help Review

Use a ruler or a strip of paper to cover the answer column at the right. Read the first item and write the missing word or words on a piece of paper. Then move your ruler or paper strip down to uncover the answer and see if you are right. Go on in the same way with each of the other items. Do not write in this book.

The numbers by the answers show pages in this book that give information about the subject. For the items you miss, go back and review this information.

1. Some physiological human needs are air, water, food, ______, ______, and ______.	clothing, sleep, shelter 145
2. Some psychological human needs are the need for ______, the need for self-______, and the need to be ______.	love, respect, oneself 145
3. A person who is making alibis for his behavior is ______.	rationalizing 156
4. A person who tries hard to make up for some real or imagined handicap is ______.	compensating 157
5. When a person withdraws into wishful thinking, he is engaging in ______.	daydreaming 158
6. Forming opinions about a person without really knowing him is a form of ______.	prejudice 164
7. Sometimes we communicate through words and sometimes we communicate through ______.	actions 166
8. "Emotional maturity" is a term that is often used in describing good ______ ______.	mental health 167

Teacher's Notes

After pupils have taken the test and their papers have been scored, the test items can serve as guides for a summary discussion.

Health Test for Unit Five

Copy each number on a piece of paper. After the number, write the correct answer, *true* or *false.*

F 1. When people do the same thing, they always do it for the same reason.

T 2. Sleep is a primary human need.

T 3. Strong motivation makes it more likely that a person will achieve a goal he has set for himself.

T 4. If a form of behavior brings you satisfaction, you are likely to want to continue that kind of behavior.

F 5. Bitterness is an aid to achievement and good human relations.

F 6. All human problems can be solved in exactly the ways we want them to be solved—if only we try hard enough.

T 7. A person who has many excuses to offer for his behavior is rationalizing.

F 8. People are born with prejudice.

F 9. The only way to communicate with others is through words.

T 10. An indication of a person's mental health is the way he gets along with others.

F 11. A person either has or does not have good mental health; there is nothing he can do about improving his mental health.

F 12. The person most likely to have good mental health is the one who is rich and is not obliged to take any responsibility.

T 13. If you feel capable and confident about a task you must do, you are apt to be more successful than if you feel timid and fearful about that task.

T 14. All of us need to belong to some kind of family group and to have at least a few close friends.

T 15. There is no disgrace in failure if you have tried hard to meet a goal.

F 16. When you are faced with a serious problem, it usually helps to try to pretend the problem does not exist.

T 17. A person who constantly brags about his good grades at school may be overcompensating for a lack of some other ability.

T 18. There is no harm in some daydreaming unless it becomes a person's constant method of escaping reality.

T 19. A prejudiced person is often one who feels insecure or inadequate.

T 20. A person who is mentally healthy faces his problems and tries to work them out.

Number of Answers	20
Number Right	______
Score (Number Right × 5)	______

6 How Much Do You Know About Safety and Accident Prevention?

Teacher's Notes

Unit Overview: Use the message here to explore students' ideas about safety education—and about whether there is any real need for them to spend time on a safety unit. Ask provocative questions on some topics covered in the unit—on hyperventilating, hunting safety, safe-car design.

Did you know that accident rates for young people your age are higher than the accident rates for younger groups? This is due partly to the fact that you are participating in an ever widening range of activities.

Learning how to take part *safely* in the many things you need to do and the things you enjoy doing is one of your important tasks in growing up. No one else can carry out this task for you. Keeping safe, of course, is basically a do-it-yourself job. This unit, therefore, features in the main a do-it-yourself approach.

Teacher's Notes

Read to Find Out: Discuss these questions briefly—just long enough to start students thinking and speculating about the answers. Such a procedure helps ensure holding pupils' attention as they study the unit; they will want to check the accuracy of their tentative answers.

What Is Involved in Living Safely? Discuss some of the aids that people have to keep safe in daily living: safety signs; safety posters; guard railings; safety built into the design of equipment being operated at home; safety workers such as policemen, crossing guards, safety engineers in factories; and so on.

Read to Find Out

1. *What are some safety practices that might prevent* swimming *accidents?* Boating *accidents?*

2. *How might many* home accidents involving firearms *be avoided?* Hunting accidents involving guns?

3. *What are four or five major causes of* motor-vehicle *accidents?*

4. *What are some important reasons for* always fastening your safety belts *when you are riding in a car?*

5. *What examples can you give of* looking ahead to prevent accidents at home?

What Is Involved in Living Safely?

Suppose that you are taking part in a panel discussion on the topic "Living Safely." What ideas would you present to explain what must be done if a person is to live safely as well as enjoyably? Compare your ideas with those below—ideas that were actually offered in a panel discussion held by some young people your age.

"You have to know the important safety practices that apply to the activities you participate in."

"You need to know *why* safety guides are good ones. Knowing the why's helps you remember."

"You have to *use* the safety knowledge you have in everyday living. Unless you use what you know, you won't keep yourself very safe."

In the material that follows, you will be helped to learn or review many important safety practices. And, just as significant, you will find out the *why*'s behind the practices. There are problem situations to consider. There are also answers presented so that you can check your safety knowledge. You can easily guess the next step—the most important step of all. It will then be up to *you* to use this knowledge to help you live safely and enjoyably.

A Quiz About Emergencies

Near the telephone at home there should be a list of emergency telephone numbers. What should some of these numbers be? Check your ideas with the answers at the left on page 174.

What Do You Know About Water Safety?

The beach that you see below does not look very hazardous, does it? What safety aids are visible in the picture?

It may surprise you to know that for students of junior-high age, water accidents are a major cause of accidental deaths. Drowning as a result of swimming or boating accidents accounts for about one fourth of all accidental deaths to young people between the ages of twelve and fourteen.

What safety guides, if followed, might help eliminate accidents to swimmers? What safety guides should boaters keep in mind? Check your ideas with the ones on pages 174–175.

Teacher's Notes

Discuss which, if any, safety guides on this page are new to your students. Then ask:

"If young people *know* most of these safety guides, why do you think water accidents happen so frequently among those your age?" (Such causes as these may be mentioned: carelessness, overestimation of one's strength or skill, foolhardiness, the feeling that "nothing will ever happen to me.")

Review important ideas on the page by asking these *why* questions:

"*Why* should swimmers leave the water as soon as a storm threatens?"

"*Why* is it thought that you should wait an hour after a heavy meal before going swimming?"

"*Why* is safety instruction essential in using snorkels and face masks?"

Answers to the Quiz on Page 172

List of Emergency Telephone Numbers

1. The fire department

2. The police department

3. The nearest hospital

4. Your doctor

5. The nearest poison-control center

6. The nearest neighbors

7. Places where family members can be reached when they are not at home

Swimming

Did you think of the following safety guides for swimmers?

Swim only in supervised areas. (Few drownings occur in lifeguarded areas; less than 2 percent occur each year in supervised pools.)

Never swim alone, even in a lifeguarded area. (Use the buddy, or partner, system. A lifeguard cannot watch every swimmer, but you and your buddy can watch each other.)

Know your limits. (Poor swimmers should stay in shallow water. Good swimmers should take care not to go out too far or to risk chilling or fatigue. Cold water creates a shock to the body, which lessens a swimmer's strength.)

Use floating devices only if permitted and only where you would be safe even without them. (Floating devices are easily upset. These devices tempt the poor swimmer to float out into deep water where trouble could occur if the floating device overturned.)

Avoid hyperventilating, or taking several deep breaths, before swimming underwater. (Hyperventilating, or "overbreathing," reduces the supply of carbon dioxide—which is necessary to trigger the urge to breathe. Therefore, a hyperventilated underwater swimmer has no warning of the need to take a breath. The oxygen in the blood may reach a low level, and the underwater swimmer may suddenly lose consciousness. Hyperventilation is the suspected cause of many unexplained drownings of good swimmers.)

Use snorkels and face masks only after instruction by a qualified teacher. (Unless you have been taught the proper skills, you may swallow water when you try to breathe.)

Wait at least one hour before going into the water after a heavy meal. (It is thought that there *may* be a connection between a person's eating a heavy meal and later getting stomach cramps, which might disable a swimmer or cause the swimmer to panic. Light snacks do not count.)

Leave the water as soon as a storm threatens. (The most dangerous time for lightning is before a storm breaks. Water attracts lightning, and an electrical charge may be conducted to a swimmer across several hundred feet of water.)

Boating

Did you think of any of the following ways to help prevent boating accidents?

Take out a motorboat only if you know you can handle it safely. (Take a course in boating instruction before attempting to operate a motorboat. Six out of ten boating drownings happen to people in open motorboats.)

Always wear a life jacket when you are in a boat, or have one at hand where you can reach it immediately. (About half the people who drown while boating have a lifesaving device in the boat but cannot get to it when they need it.)

Avoid overloading the boat. (The Coast Guard advises, "If the boat looks or feels overloaded, it probably is; so don't take the boat out." Most boats have a small plate that tells the maximum number of persons and weight they can carry safely. However, this passenger and weight limit is not a reliable guide if there are waves or if the water is rough.)

Do not take out a leaky boat.

Be sure to balance the load in the boat. (Improper loading makes a boat unstable and hard to manage. Keep the weight *low* and in the *middle.* Passengers should sit only on seats, not on the bow, stern, or sides.)

Go boating only in good weather, when the water is calm. (Small boats often cannot withstand rough waters.)

If you are in a boat that capsizes, stay with it and wait for help. (Nearly all boats will float, so hang on to the side of the boat and let the water support most of your weight. Or, if the boat is flat-bottomed, slide part of your weight on to the bottom of the overturned boat at the rear end of the boat; you can then use your legs, which are still in the water, to kick your way toward safety. In no case should you try to swim to shore; it is hard to judge distances in the water. Also, it is easier for rescuers to spot a boat than a lone swimmer's bobbing head.)

If someone falls from a boat in which you are a passenger, grab him and hold on to him if possible. Or throw him a rope or life preserver if one is at hand. (Try to get him into the life preserver before helping him into the boat. Bring him over the boat's stern or bow—to avoid overturning the boat.)

Teacher's Notes

Continue the discussion by asking these *why* questions on boating safety:

"*Why* is safety instruction in handling a motorboat essential?"

"*Why* should overloading a boat be avoided?"

"*Why* is it dangerous to change seats or move around in a small boat?"

"*Why* should you stay with a boat that capsizes?"

"*Why* should the load in a boat be balanced?"

"*Why* shouldn't you bring a person from the water into the boat over the sides?"

Discuss this concept often stressed by safety experts: "If you should ever have trouble in the water—or if someone with you gets into trouble—it is important to keep your head." Panic is the cause of many drownings.

What Should You Do?

1. If you get a cramp in your foot or leg while swimming, roll over face down in the water and knead the cramped area. A cramp is caused by a contraction in the muscle, and gentle pressure and massage will relieve it.

2. If, while wading, you step into a hole or a drop-off and find yourself in water over your head, remember that you are only one or two steps from safety. Turn around and go back, thrusting yourself up and forward with your arms.

How Much Do You Know About Firearms Safety?

Did you know that accidents with firearms occur very frequently among young people your age? In fact, age fourteen is the peak year among young people for deaths by firearms.

Accidents with firearms that occur among young people are about equally divided between hunting accidents and home accidents. *What safety precautions are being practiced by the hunters in the picture below? How might these precautions prevent firearms accidents to the hunters?* Compare your ideas with the guides given on page 177. Check, too, the causes of—and ways of avoiding—*home accidents with firearms.*

Firearms Safety: Hunting

Did you think of the following safety guides as ones that might prevent *hunting* accidents?

Take a course in safe gun-handling. (Some states require teen-agers to have passed such a course before granting them a hunting license.)

Wear some fluorescent orange or red clothing. (These are the most visible colors. About one thousand hunters are shot every year because some other hunter does not see them or mistakes them for game.)

Carry a gun with the muzzle pointed away from yourself and your companions. (Accidental discharges *can* happen. Walk side by side with your companions, too. You should be able to control the muzzle's direction, even if you stumble.)

Do not fire at a flat, hard surface or over water. (Bullets can ricochet, or bounce, off the surface and hit someone.)

Never climb a tree or fence with a loaded gun. (Lay down your gun before going over or under a fence.)

Load a gun only in the field or woods. (Carrying a loaded gun is dangerous.)

Release the safety on the gun just as you are ready to fire. (The safety is a protection until that point.)

Firearms Safety: At Home

The following situations are ones which could—and unfortunately often do—lead to firearms accidents at home: *preparing to clean a gun, dropping a gun or knocking it off a rack or other support, showing a supposedly unloaded gun to a friend, engaging in foolish horseplay with a supposedly unloaded gun.*

Here are some basic gun-safety guides that can help prevent accidents with guns in the home:

Check to make sure any gun is unloaded before it is brought into the house; check again before a gun is cleaned.

Treat every gun as if it were loaded; many accidents occur because someone is "sure" a gun is not loaded.

Never keep a loaded gun in the house; store firearms and ammunition in separate places, and keep them locked up.

Never point a gun at anyone or at yourself.

Teacher's Notes

Following are some frequent causes of hunting accidents: *victim is out of sight of the shooter, victim is mistaken for game, victim moves into line of fire, shooter stumbles and falls and discharges his gun, shooter accidentally discharges gun while climbing over a fence, trigger of gun catches on brush or other object.* See if students can formulate safety guides that might prevent such accidents.
Expand the discussion to cover prevention of gun accidents at home.

Something to Do

Someone in the group might write to the National Safety Council, 425 N. Michigan Avenue, Chicago, Illinois 60611, to obtain copies of these Safety Education Data Sheets:
Happy Hunting
Firearms

How Much Do You Know About Auto Safety?

Did you know that about 50 percent of all fatal accidents involve motor vehicles? What is more, an appalling number of other less serious accidents also are associated with automobiles and other motor vehicles. *The picture below suggests something that can cause accidents. What do you think it is?*

What do you think are some other frequent causes of motor-vehicle accidents? Check your ideas with pages 179–180.

Although you have not yet reached driving age, it is not too early for you to begin thinking ahead. What ideas are given on pages 181–183 to help you become a good driver?

Some Causes of Motor-Vehicle Accidents

Sometimes motor-vehicle accidents happen because the car driver—or a pedestrian who gets in his way—is *emotionally upset.* When a person is angry, worried, or otherwise upset emotionally, he may become careless and more likely to have an accident. Being familiar with safe ways of driving or with safety guides for pedestrians is not enough in itself to prevent accidents. When a person is upset emotionally, he may not apply the safe practices he knows. At such times, he would do well to avoid driving if at all possible.

For safety reasons, then, as well as for other reasons, it is important when you are upset emotionally to try to get your troubles straightened out if you possibly can. Talking over your problem with someone who is understanding and who may be able to help is one way to start working through problems and getting rid of upset feelings. The problem-solving method described on page 150 can be helpful too.

Did you decide that other frequent causes of motor-vehicle accidents might be the following?

Speeding or traveling too fast for road conditions.

Disregarding traffic signals.

Risk-taking.

Failing to yield the right of way.

Driving under the influence of alcohol or other drugs.

Engaging in horseplay that might distract the driver.

Driving a car while sleepy or unusually tired.

Use the items listed above to help you formulate some guides for safe driving.

The Importance of Safety Belts

Even if a car accident should occur, injuries to the passengers can be minimized. How can this be accomplished?

The single most effective action a person can take to save himself from injury or death in a traffic accident is simply this: *Fasten the safety belts.*

Safety belts are lifesavers because they keep car passengers from smashing against the hard interior of the car or from being thrown out of the car. Smashing against the interior of the car is sometimes called the "second collision."

Teacher's Notes

In passing, you and your students might talk over such behavior as drag racing and other forms of risk-taking. Ask: "What might account for such behavior?" (A desire for power or to do what the others are doing, accompanied by the feeling that "nothing will ever happen to me." Also sometimes people speed up or act aggressively on the road because of temporary anger.)

Consider, too, some reasons why pedestrians may become involved in motor-vehicle accidents. (They cross into the street from between parked cars, they do not observe traffic signs, they get out of the car on the street side, they do not keep *left* when walking on roads where there are no sidewalks, and so on.)

Some Things to Do

1. Make a list of safety guides for bicycle riders or drivers. Put a check beside the safety practices that are the same for both bicycle drivers and car drivers.

2. Discuss what part manufacturers' advertisements relating to speed and horsepower of motor vehicles might play in causing highway accidents.

Teacher's Notes

After discussing the importance of using safety belts, invite students' ideas of what can be done to encourage more people to form the habit of *always fastening them.* Ask pupils to recall any campaigns on radio or TV they have noted about the use of safety belts. Discuss the findings of research engineers at such centers as Cornell University on the effects of impact on persons inside colliding cars.

Engineers at Cornell University have studied what happens inside a car when there is a collision at a speed of only eighteen miles per hour. The driver first hits the steering wheel, and then the top of the windshield. The passenger next to the driver, in the "death seat," flies into the windshield and then falls out the door. Passengers riding in the rear are hurled over the front seat and into the dashboard.

Many people believe they could brace themselves with their arms to keep from going through the windshield. However, to brace oneself in a sudden stop at only thirty miles per hour requires that a person put up a force of 2,250 pounds. That is about equal to doing pushups with the weight of fifteen people on top of you.

Some people who use safety belts on expressways often neglect to use these safety devices while driving at low speed around the neighborhood. Yet safety belts are vitally necessary at such times. National Safety Council figures show that half of all auto deaths occur at speeds of forty miles per hour or less. And 80 percent of all auto accidents happen within twenty-five miles of home.

Would safety belts trap you if the car caught fire or was submerged underwater? Only a half of 1 percent of all auto accidents involve fire or submersion. Even then, safety belts keep the occupants from hitting against the interior of the car and being knocked unconscious. Thus they are able to unfasten the belts and escape from the car.

Safety belts should be adjusted to fit snugly. A child who is too small for a lap belt needs a harness that is anchored, like a safety belt, to the car structure. A child's car seat which hooks over the front seat was proved dangerous in tests conducted at the University of California. The seat tears loose in a crash and throws the child against the dashboard. Children between the toddler age and those large enough for a seat belt should have a car seat held by a safety belt. Such seats are available from auto manufacturers.

Everyone should wear safety belts at all times when riding in a car. The National Safety Council estimates that this procedure could save ten thousand lives *each year.*

Did You Know?

Carbon monoxide, *a colorless, odorless gas, is present in the exhaust fumes of all automotive engines. An idling engine in a closed garage will produce enough carbon monoxide to cause unconsciousness or even death. Never start a car or keep the motor running in a closed garage.*

Becoming a Good Driver—When the Time Comes

An eventful day may be waiting for *you* in just a few years. It is the day when you drive a car on your own for the first time. You will start the engine, step on the gas pedal, and pull away from the curb—all alone.

Do you think you will be prepared to meet the challenge of driving when that day arrives? That depends a great deal on the ideas and feelings about driving that you are forming right now, and on the training and information you possess before you go out on your own in a car.

When you get behind the wheel, you will assume a more awesome responsibility than you have ever had before. Driving a car puts immense power in your hands. You will be *fully responsible* for controlling a powerful machine. It is a machine that contains several thousand pounds of metal, it is driven by hundreds of horsepower, and it is capable of inflicting terrible damage.

Motor-vehicle accidents are one of the most serious problems in the United States. On the average, a human life is lost every ten minutes in a highway accident. A disabling injury occurs every sixteen seconds, which is about the amount of time it will take you to read the next few paragraphs. The cost of auto accidents is estimated at more than twelve billion dollars a year. This amount includes property damage, medical expenses, lost wages, and insurance costs. Such a vast sum of money is easier to grasp once you realize what it will buy: twelve billion dollars is enough money for four million young people each to purchase a brand new three-thousand-dollar automobile.

You have probably heard it said that teen-age drivers have "more than their share" of accidents. The meaning of this expression is clarified by the chart at the right. In this country, 10 percent of the drivers are teen-agers. Therefore you would expect that they would be involved in 10 percent of all auto accidents. However, as shown in the graph at the right, teen-age drivers account for some 16 percent of the total traffic-accident fatalities—that is half again more than "their share."

Teacher's Notes

Teen-agers are at a time of life when their strength and physical abilities are at a peak. Their sharp vision, quick reaction time, and smooth coordination make them the age group best suited to meet the physical demands of operating an automobile. Have students discuss why, despite this, teen-agers have more than "their share" of accidents. (Lack of experience, attitudes toward driving—such as "nothing will happen to me," sheer amount of time spent riding around in cars, and so on.)

Teen-age Drivers and Accidents

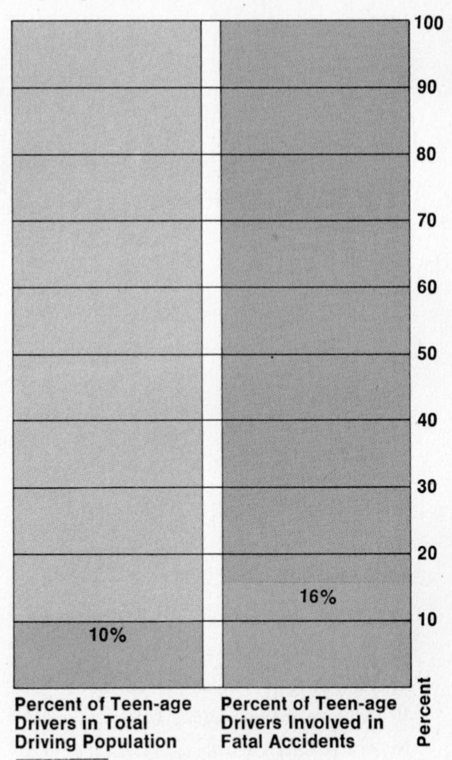

Figures from National Safety Council.

Teacher's Notes

Consider with students some of the factors other than the ones mentioned on this page that might play a part in the driver's responsibility for a car accident. (Insufficient knowledge about rules of the road or about safe driving practices, the unwise use of medication that induces drowsiness, poor reaction time, and so on.)

Each year more teen-agers die as a result of auto accidents than are killed by all diseases combined. A total of four and a half million teen-age drivers are involved in motor-vehicle accidents. That is as many people as populate the entire state of Georgia.

To prepare yourself to be an accident-free driver, you can start now to build your understanding of the traffic-accident problem.

When any particular accident is described, you may hear that the *cause* of the accident was a "dangerous driver" or "bad brakes" or a "slippery road." Such simple explanations are inaccurate, however. An accident almost always has a combination of causes.

Consider this for example: Eighteen-year-old Bob Halda was driving sixty miles an hour on a superhighway when a light rain began to fall. Suddenly he noticed something blocking the road ahead. Bob hit the brakes, and the worn tires on his car began to skid. Bob lost control of the car and it went off the road and hit a light pole.

What were the causes of Bob's accident? Among them were the rain, the worn tires on his car, the speed at which he was driving, and his inexperience in handling skids. Can you think of other possible causes?

When scientists examine the traffic-accident problem, they see it as composed of three major factors: the *driver,* the *driving environment,* and the *machine.*

The Driver

Who is the *driver?* Is the driver a person with little driving experience? Someone who is tired? Tense? Under the influence of alcohol or another drug? Unable to see properly? All these and many other factors play a part in determining whether or not a driver will have an accident. For this reason, many of the safety programs designed to reduce traffic accidents are aimed at the driver.

Television and radio messages and commercials, as well as newspaper and magazine advertisements, explain the dangers of driving after drinking alcoholic beverages. They also warn against driving to "let off steam" or to "show off."

Something to Think About

What do you think are some reasons why *teen-agers have more than "their share" of auto accidents? What are some factors that can help reduce accidents among teen-age drivers?*

Driver-education courses for teen-agers and driver-improvement programs for adults are designed to provide drivers with knowledge about the driving task. Such instruction also attempts to teach the techniques of safe driving behavior.

Safe driving means attempting to be one step ahead of the other driver. When you are driving, you never take anything for granted—you always try to anticipate the most unsafe thing the other driver or pedestrian can do. This is called "defensive driving." It means you are always looking ahead for what *might* happen. You do not just watch the car in front of you; you watch several cars ahead and to both sides of you, and you are always alert to possible dangers.

Teacher's Notes

Invite conversation about safety-education messages for drivers that students have noted on radio or TV or that they have seen in newspapers or magazines.
Discussion of advertising that encourages dangerous driving, such as high-powered "muscle" cars, "power-to-pass" gasoline ads, and so on, might also be initiated.

The Driving Environment

The driving environment includes such things as the type of road, weather conditions, signs, and lighting. To improve the driving environment, road engineers have designed better lighting systems, highly visible signs, and divided superhighways that make head-on collisions unlikely. New roads are built with curves instead of the long straight stretches of road that encourage "highway hypnosis" and put drivers to sleep.

Engineers are now experimenting with traffic signs that break easily upon crash impact, with roadway barriers that collapse like a telescope when hit, and with highway guardrails that have built-in shock absorbers. The purposes of all such devices are to cushion the force of the crash impact and to lessen the severity of injuries to passengers.

The Machine

To make sure that cars are kept in good driving condition, vehicle-safety checks are required by some states. Tires, steering, brakes, lights, and so on, are checked for proper maintenance. Does your state have such safety checks? Can you suggest some ways in which owners can make sure their vehicles are safe to drive?

Safety belts, padded dashboards, collapsible steering wheels, and shatterproof safety glass are among the many elements of auto design that reduce injury to car passengers in case of a crash. Some interesting new designs for safety aspects in cars of the future are shown on pages 184–188.

Did You Know?

Driver-education courses for high-school-age students include information on traffic laws, on the operation of a car, on physical forces (gravity, friction, and so on) that control driving, and on mature driving practices.
However, taking a driver-education course will not, by itself, make you a good driver. What else will be needed?

Experimental Safe-Car Design Programs

Extensive efforts are being made, under the sponsorship of the U.S. Department of Transportation, to develop a prototype experimental safety car. Contracts have been awarded to Fairchild Industries, General Motors Corporation, and AMF Incorporated. On these two pages are views of a model safety sedan that is being designed by Fairchild Industries.

Protection of occupants in crashes—crashworthiness—is being given the highest priority by the companies that are developing the prototype cars. Designers are also considering all safety aspects of a car, such as handling, braking, lighting, visibility, and fire prevention.

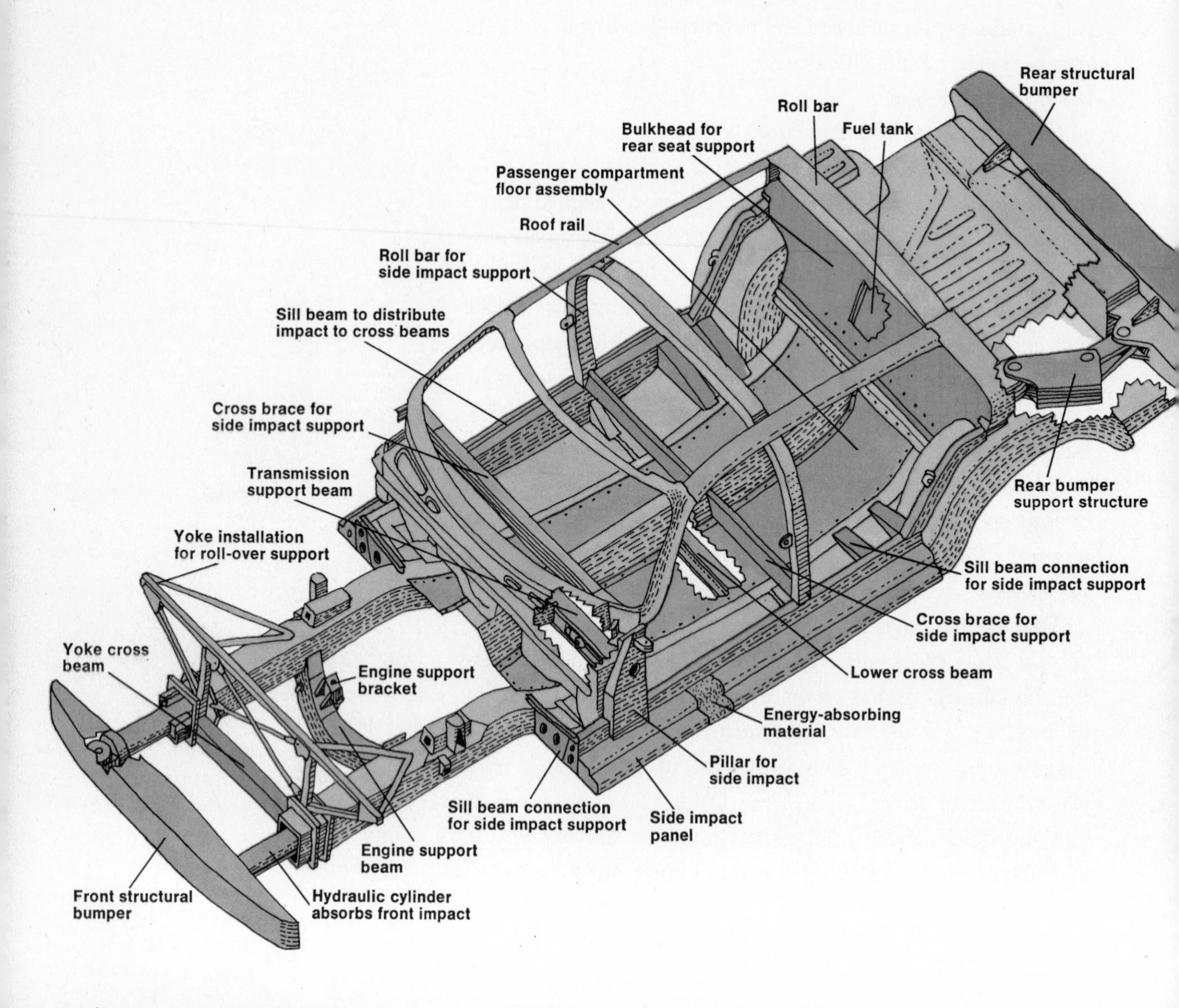

The brakes on this experimental car will minimize stopping distances, prevent skidding, and provide good emergency braking. Special supports aim to minimize injuries in front and rear crashes at 50 miles an hour—as well as injuries in side and roll-over crashes. Driver visibility is stressed, and innovative rear viewing includes a periscope. A special tank design protects the fuel tank from spillage and fire. The interior compartment makes effective use of padding and other energy-absorbing materials. Also used are airbags at each seating position. These airbags protect the passengers in high-speed crashes.

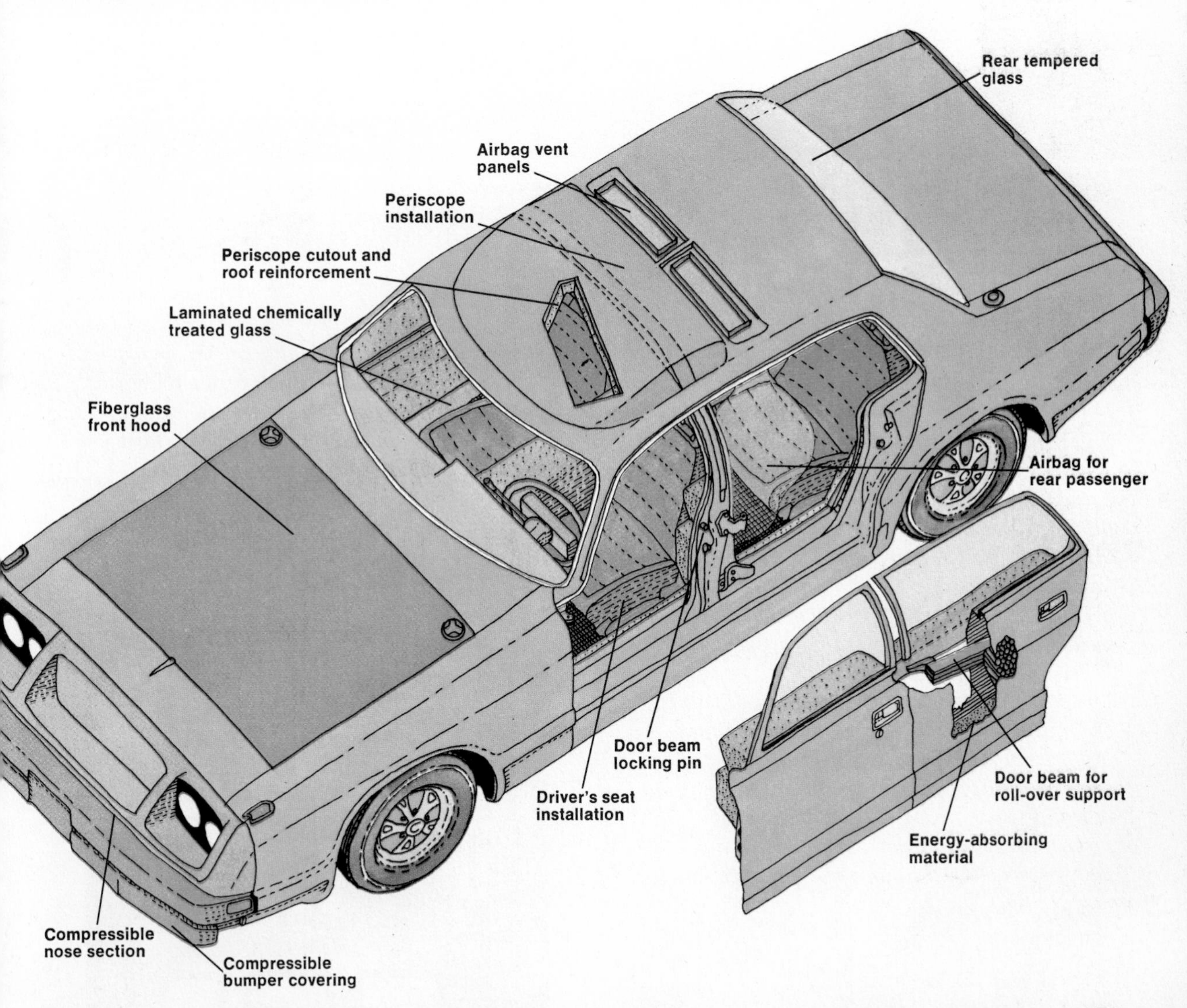

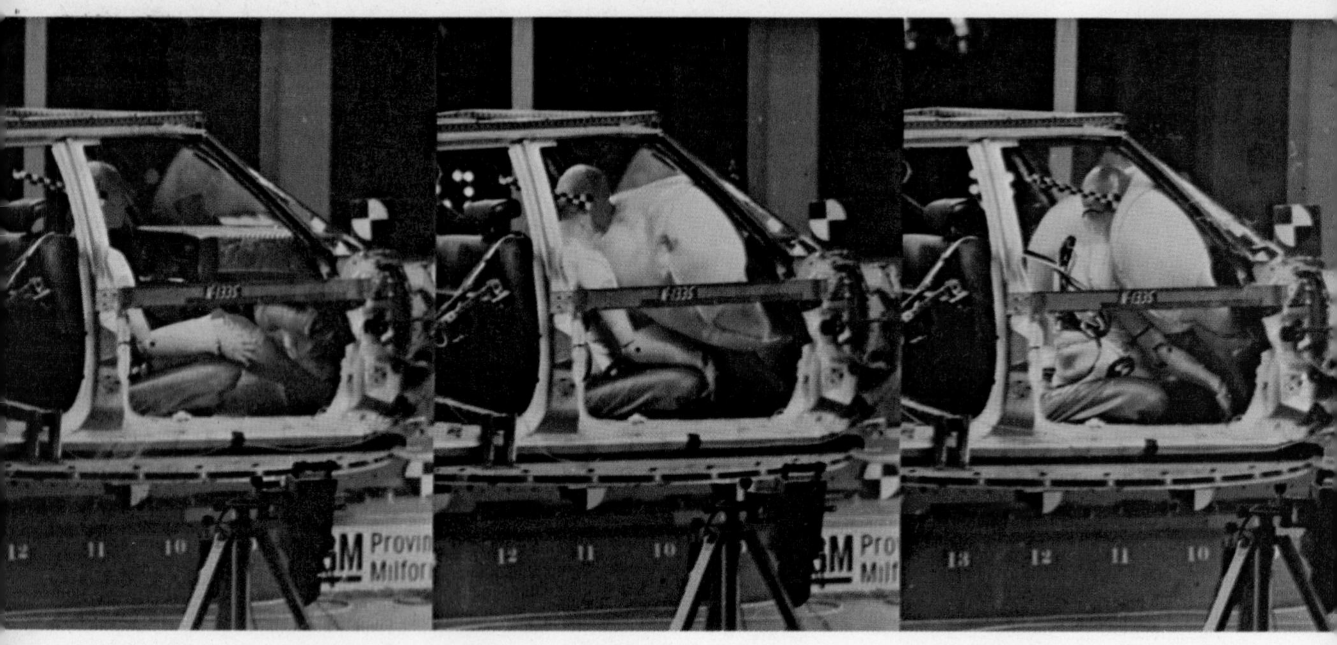

Here and across the top of page 187, an experiment is being conducted on the impact sled as a high-speed motion-picture camera photographs the action during split-second impact.

Experimental Testing Programs

Testing programs of existing cars and of the prototype safety cars are conducted by both universities and corporations. At General Motors Corporation, many experiments are carried out at their extensive laboratories and proving grounds.

Among the most valuable pieces of car-safety laboratory equipment is the impact sled, developed by General Motors. The impact sled nondestructively simulates crashes at speeds up to 70 miles an hour.

Complete cars—or parts of cars—can be tested on the sled. Valuable information is obtained about what happens at different speeds to such things as airbag-restraint systems, belt-restraint systems, head restraints, steering wheels and columns, instrument panels, and most importantly, the "dummy" passengers.

Below. *A head-on view of a car on an impact sled. Impact test data—collected from the crash under controlled conditions—are recorded on magnetic tape (in foreground) and are later put on a computer for further study.*

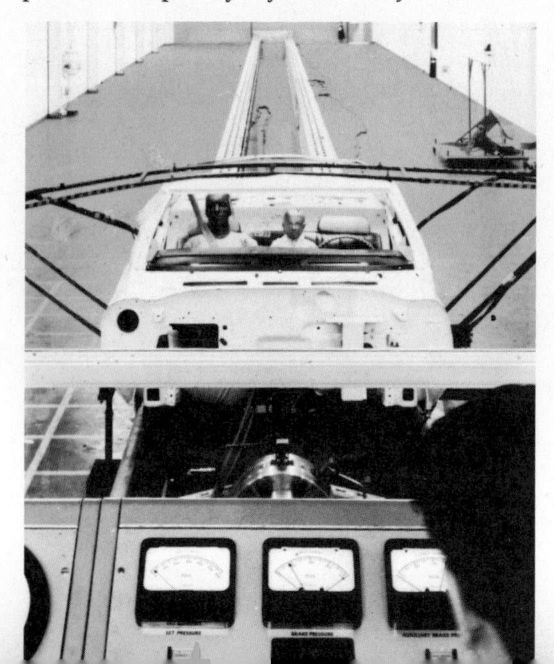

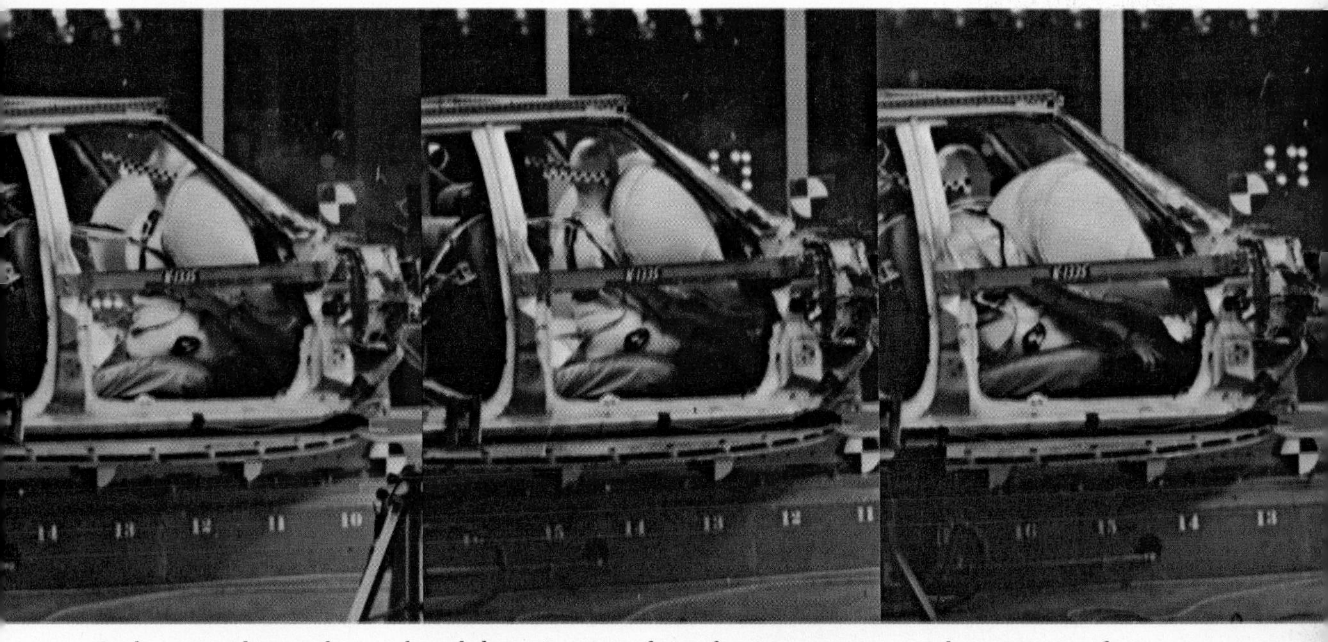

Such tests as the one shown above help engineers perfect safety improvements on the prototype safety car. In this experiment, tests are being made on the experimental airbag-restraint system.

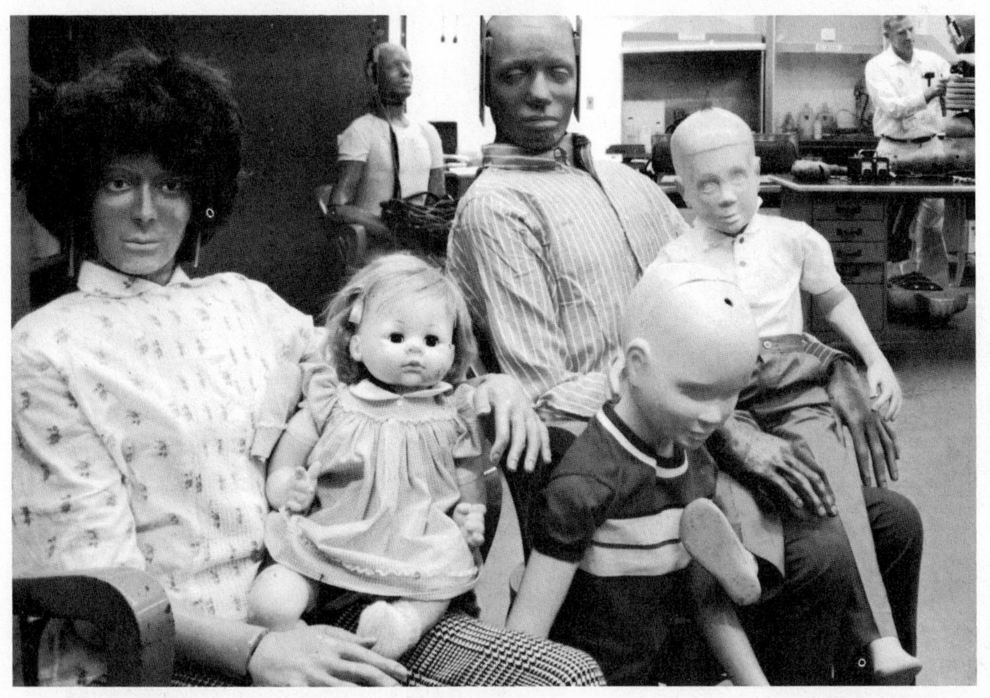

Here you see a "family" of General Motors' test dummies waiting their turn for more testing.

Above. *Another test of a car's safety involves a full-scale collision. Here crash-testing is being done at General Motors' Barrier Building.*
Below. *A new car is tested at a proving ground to see how it stands up to rough road conditions.*
Right. *A water trough is used to test a car's ignition system, the effects of water on its brakes, and so on.*

Do You Know What to Do in Emergencies?

As you have learned, there are many things you can do to help "safety-proof" yourself. You can find out as much as possible about safe ways of doing things, and you can try to form the habit of using these safety guides.

No matter how careful you are, however, there will be times when you or others around you will require first aid. There will also be emergencies that will require you to think and act quickly. In such situations, you will need to have proper knowledge at your fingertips. You may have to be quite sure of your knowledge so that you can do what is necessary calmly and perhaps without anyone to advise you.

The quiz below will give you an opportunity to check your knowledge of what to do in several different first-aid and emergency situations. After testing yourself, check your ideas with those on pages 190–193.

What Should You Do?

What should you do if—

1. You think you have been in contact with poison ivy?
2. You think your fingers are frostbitten?
3. You suffer a mild burn on your hand?
4. You bump your arm and bruise it?
5. You have hiccups that are hard to stop?
6. A dog bites you?
7. You accidentally come too close to someone who is spraying a chemical substance on some weeds and some of the spray gets in your eyes?
8. You are with friends on a hike and one person is bitten on the leg by a snake you believe is poisonous?
9. There is a fire in the oven at home?
10. The grease in a frying pan catches fire?
11. You are with a friend who has been injured in a bicycle accident and the injured person begins to show symptoms of shock? (Someone has gone to get a doctor.)
12. The area you live in is threatened by a flood?
13. A hurricane warning is issued?
14. There is warning of a nuclear explosion?

Teacher's Notes

Students might test themselves with the quiz on this page and then check with the answers on pages 190-193. As an alternate, the class or small discussion groups might talk over each question in turn, offering tentative ideas. Then, after silent study of appropriate material from pages 190-193, they might talk over *correct* emergency procedures.

Something to Do

Look in the school or public library for such books as these about emergencies:

Bendick, Jeanne. The Emergency Book *(Rand McNally).*

Bry, Benjamin, M.D., and Annette F. In Case of Emergency *(Doubleday).*

Teacher's Notes

After each emergency described on the page (and on following pages) is discussed, take time to consider ways —if any—in which the emergency might have been avoided. Thus, wearing protective gloves might prevent frostbite, using a potholder might prevent a mild burn, and so on. Be sure to review safe procedures around dogs such as not petting a strange dog, not teasing a dog, and not trespassing where there are *Beware of Dog* signs.

For reference during study of this section, make available if possible the series of four booklets: *Basic First Aid, Books 1, 2, 3,* and *4* (Doubleday & Co., Copyright 1971 by the American National Red Cross, Washington, D.C.)

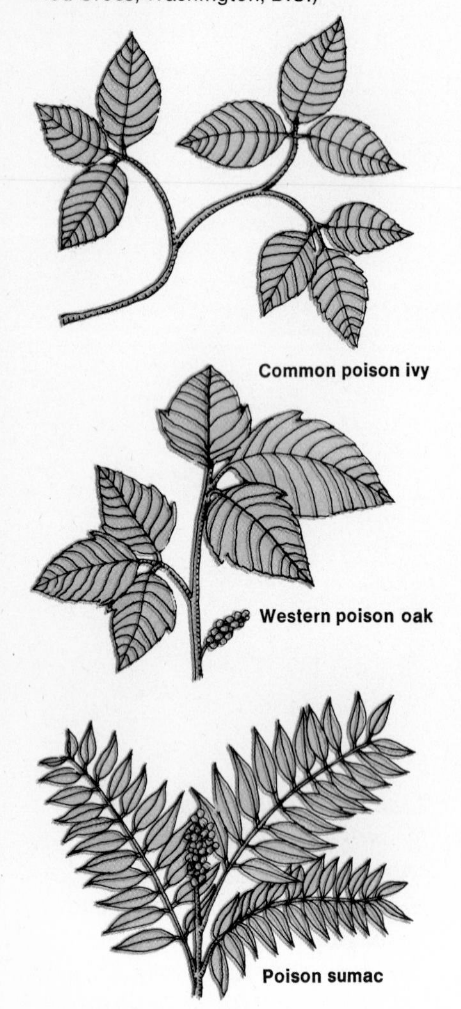

Some poisonous plants

Contact with Poison Ivy

If you think you have been in contact with poison ivy (or poison oak or sumac), bathe thoroughly with soap and hot water. Rinse, repeat soaping, and rinse again. Then sponge with rubbing alcohol. Make a complete change of clothes, because the oil from the plant may be on your clothes and may give you further contact with the poison. If a rash appears, a calamine lotion may be used. Learn to recognize poisonous plants. See the pictures at the left.

Frostbite

Cover frostbitten part with your warm hand or a piece of woolen material. *Do not rub* since rubbing increases the risk of tissue injury. Get indoors as soon as you can and soak the frostbitten part in lukewarm (not hot) water. Wrap yourself in warm blankets, and take a warm drink. Sometimes you can be suffering from frostbite and not be aware of it. A symptom of frostbite is grayish-yellow skin, which results from the frozen tissue.

A Mild Burn

For a mild burn with no blisters, immerse the burned part in comfortably cold tap water at once. Add ice now and then to cool the water. Continue until you can remove the burned part from the water and not feel pain.

A Bruise

Apply ice or cold cloths immediately to a bruise to reduce swelling and to relieve pain.

Hiccups

Sometimes you can stop hiccups by drinking water very slowly. A half teaspoon of baking soda might be added to the water. Another good remedy is to lie down for a while.

Dog Bite

Wash the wound thoroughly with soap and water. Apply a sterile pad and bandage; *then see a doctor promptly.* If possible, identify the dog that did the biting so it can be watched by a veterinarian for two weeks to see if it has rabies. If the dog does have rabies, you must be given rabies shots. This procedure should also be followed with the bites of other animals, such as squirrels, raccoons, and rabbits.

Chemicals in the Eyes

If a chemical gets in your eyes, the first thing to do is wash out the eyes with clean water. Pour water into inner corners of the eyes and allow it to run over the eyeballs and under the eyelids until at least a quart of water has been used. Get a doctor's help as quickly as possible.

Snake Bite

Bites from poisonous snakes will usually result in immediate pain and swelling of the bitten area.

Get the care of a doctor as soon as possible. The sooner the victim receives *antivenin,* if needed, the better. If the victim will be under medical care within twenty to thirty minutes, no further first aid is ordinarily advisable.

While waiting for or en route to medical help, *get the victim to lie down and keep quiet.* Body movement speeds circulation and spreads the venom more rapidly through the body. If medical aid is delayed and if it is possible, apply a cold wet cloth—or ice wrapped in a cloth—to the bite. This will ease the victim's discomfort and pain.

If the bite is on an arm or leg, *tie a rubber band or cloth band two inches above the bite, between the bite and the heart.* Make the band tight enough to stop the flow of blood near the surface of the skin, but not tight enough to stop all blood flow. After five minutes, remove the band. If the bite is not on an arm or leg, the band cannot be used, but the other steps are the same: *Get medical help* and *keep the victim lying down.*

If the snake is not poisonous, treat the bite like any other cut. Stop the bleeding and wash the wound with soap and water. See a doctor as soon as possible in case a tetanus shot is needed.

Fire in the Oven

In the event of a fire in the oven, turn off the source of heat. Close the oven door until you obtain some fire-fighting material. A good way to smother a small fire is to pour table salt on it. Shutting the door until you get the salt keeps the air out of the oven and thus avoids fanning the flames. Keep the oven clean and free of accumulated drippings as a means of avoiding oven fires.

Teacher's Notes

Make a special point of finding and posting pictures of any poisonous snakes in your area.

Some safety guides concerning snakes are these: If you are in poisonous-snake country, wear boots; watch where you step, sit, or put your hands; remember snakes generally will not bother you if you do not disturb them; a rattlesnake cannot strike more than a couple of feet from where it is coiled, so just step back a few feet if you see one.

A snake-bite victim should *not* be given alcoholic drinks.

Something to Remember

Do you know what to do if you should be in a theater or other public building when a fire breaks out?
Keep calm. Walk to the nearest exit. *If there is a jam at the exit, do not panic. Look for another means of escape.*
Make a habit of locating the nearest exit when you are in a theater or other public building.

Teacher's Notes

A good way to remember how to treat shock is that you want to act in response to the symptoms you detect in the victim. He is cold, so you cover him. His face is pale, so you elevate his feet to encourage the flow of blood to his head (*unless* it interferes with his injury or he is having trouble breathing). He may be losing blood, so you replace the fluid with sips of water or other liquid except alcohol. (However, you do not give liquid to an unconscious person or semiconscious person because he may choke on it or breathe it into his lungs.) The victim's injury has put a strain on his heart, so you keep him lying down and quiet. Since you do not want to add another shock to his system, you do not move him. Because he is anxious about his injury, you try to reassure him.

Did You Know?

If you are indoors *during an electric storm, stand away from metallic objects such as the sink, radiator, or bathtub. These objects are connected to metal pipes that attract electricity. If you are* outdoors *during an electric storm, avoid any position that makes you higher than the surrounding area. In this way you will not be a target for lightning.*

Grease Fire

If grease in a frying pan suddenly catches fire, smother the fire by sprinkling a generous amount of baking soda on it. Or put a cover on the frying pan and quickly put it on a cool part of the stove. The baking soda—or the cover—helps smother the flames.

Do not put water on flaming grease, for water makes the fire more intense and spreads it about.

Shock

Shock is a depressed state of most of the body functions. It is brought on by the failure of enough blood to circulate through the body following an injury. Symptoms usually develop gradually. The symptoms include these body changes: *skin, pale, cold, moist, and clammy; eyes, vacant with dilated pupils; breathing, shallow and irregular; pulse, weak, irregular, and rapid; nausea; faintness or even unconsciousness.*

First-aid procedures are as follows:

Keep the injured person lying down.

Elevate legs twelve to eighteen inches by putting pillows or coats under them. (This will encourage the flow of blood to the head.) Do not raise the legs if head or chest is injured.

Keep injured person only warm enough to prevent chilling. It is better that the person be slightly cool rather than overheated.

If the victim is conscious and you are certain there is no abdominal injury, give him water in sips.

Get medical aid as soon as possible.

Remember that, if untreated, shock could cause death even though the injury itself might not be fatal.

Floods

There are several hazards of floods. These hazards include being marooned or drowned by flood waters and becoming ill from water or food that has been contaminated by flood waters which often contain sewage.

Important guides in the event of a flood are these:

Pay strict attention to flood warnings—if told to evacuate your home, do not delay.

Boil your drinking water until community supplies are safe.

Hurricanes

A hurricane is a round cone of whirling air. The center of the cone, called the eye, is an area of dead calm. But the whirling air around the eye blows at high speeds—speeds capable of uprooting trees, destroying crops, and blowing massive buildings to pieces.

Some sensible precautions to take when a hurricane forecast is issued are these:

Keep tuned to local radio and television stations for the latest information and instructions.

If warned to do so, leave low-lying coastal areas that may be swept by high tides or huge waves.

If you do not have to evacuate your home, board up the windows and brace the doors. Store inside the house any objects such as garbage cans and porch furniture that might be blown about and cause serious damage.

Nuclear Explosion

A nuclear attack is an unthinkable catastrophe, which everyone hopes will never occur. Civil Defense authorities, however, believe that everyone should know how to protect himself as well as possible. Therefore a protection system has been planned so people will know what to do in the event of a nuclear attack.

In the event of a nuclear explosion, trained weather and radiological experts would estimate the path and speed of *radioactive fallout,* tiny pieces of dust and debris that are radioactive. Information would then be broadcast over the nation's disaster- and emergency-information system. This emergency-information system is called *Emergency Broadcast System,* or *EBS.* It is part of a warning system that Civil Defense authorities have set up in case a nuclear attack should ever occur.

Immediately upon hearing the warning signal, known in a community as an ALERT SIGNAL, people should turn on their radios. Since 1963, all certified radio stations have been authorized to broadcast over their normal frequencies if there is a nuclear attack. Civil Defense authorities will then use these frequencies to give instructions over the radio for survival of our population.

Teacher's Notes

Point out that hurricanes never happen suddenly. The U.S. Weather Bureau provides information on a hurricane—and experts start reporting on it—days in advance. This gives people time to prepare and to heed the warnings and instructions given over radio and television.

A *tornado,* on the other hand, usually forms and disappears within an hour. When there is a tornado warning, if a person has a storm cellar, or a cellar, he should get into it. At any rate, he should stay inside if possible. The tornado funnel sucks up trees, machinery, cars, and so on—these objects may be thrown through the air or be overhead, ready to drop. A person is more likely to be hit by an object as it flies through the air, rather than having it just *drop* on him. If a person is caught outside in a tornado, he should seek shelter in a low place such as a ditch. He should cover his face with a cloth to protect himself against dust, which could suffocate him.

Above is a photograph of Hurricane Ginger taken from a satellite.

Teacher's Notes
Check Yourself: After students have read and thought about these questions, you might use the queries to guide a summary discussion of important ideas in this unit.
Things to Do: Special reports might be made, by way of review, on mouth-to-mouth artificial respiration.
Special Research: A survey might be made by some students of especially hazardous places in their own community —quarries, unguarded railroad crossings, abandoned buildings, and so on.

Check Yourself

1. Look back at the questions on page 172. How would you answer them now?

2. What advice would you give to someone who is planning to buy hunting clothes?

3. What have you learned about the Emergency Broadcast System?

4. What might lead you to suspect that your fingers were frostbitten? What would you do if they were?

5. Finish this safety slogan:

For a mild burn
Try this advice
Use some ______ ______,
Or a piece of ______.

6. What is one way to help identify poison ivy?

7. What happens inside a car when there is a collision? What safety practice is suggested by these facts?

8. What emergency first aid should be given in case of a poisonous-snake bite?

9. When can shock occur? What are the symptoms and first-aid procedures?

10. What are some hazards of floods?

11. What should be done when grease in a frying pan catches fire? When there is a fire in the oven?

Things to Do

1. Write a paragraph about an accident you had recently or one you know about. Try to analyze the cause of the accident and suggest how it might have been avoided.

2. Make up some slogans giving safety tips for swimmers or boaters. For example:

To keep safely afloat
Don't overload the boat.

3. Try to make a safety acrostic, using the letters of your first name as starters for safety suggestions. Your suggestions might include auto-safety ideas, water guides, or gun-safety tips. Here is a sample acrostic about gun safety by a boy named Ned.

N ever point a gun at anyone.
E nroll in a gun-safety course.
D on't keep a loaded gun in the house.

Special Research

1. Prepare a report on items that should be included in a home-safety or car-safety kit. Use the American National Red Cross manual to help you—or use your *Girl Scout Handbook* or *Boy Scout Handbook.*

2. Find out from the police department and prepare a report about local regulations on use of BB guns and air rifles.

Teacher's Notes

Pupils may work independently on this review of the unit. Encourage them to reread material in the text when necessary. Tell pupils that any sensible answer which completes the sentence correctly can be considered a "right answer."

Self-Help Review

Use a ruler or a strip of paper to cover the answer column at the right. Read the first item and write the missing word or words on a piece of paper. Then move your ruler or paper strip down to uncover the answer and see if you are right. Go on in the same way with each of the other items. Do not write in this book.

The numbers by the answers show the pages in this book that give information about the subject. For the items you miss, go back and review this information.

1. An important rule for persons riding in a car is to wear ______ ______ at all times.	safety belts 179
2. To put out a grease fire in a pan, smother it with a ______ or with some ______ ______.	cover 192 baking soda
3. After a flood, you should ______ your drinking water.	boil 192
4. Never go swimming ______; use the ______ system.	alone, buddy 174
5. Many gun accidents happen because people mistakenly think the gun is not ______.	loaded 177
6. It can be dangerous for a person to drive a car when he is ______ upset.	emotionally 179
7. A symptom of frostbite is ______-______ skin.	grayish-yellow 190
8. One cause of boating accidents is ______ the boat.	overloading 175
9. It is not enough to know safety practices; a person must be sure to ______ them.	use 172

Teacher's Notes

After pupils have taken the test and their papers have been scored, the test items can serve as guides for summary discussion.

Safety Test for Unit Six

Part I

Copy the first part of each sentence below. Then complete it with the *best* answer.

1. A good treatment for a bruise is
a. application of hot cloths
b. application of cold cloths
c. firm bandaging of the bruise

2. Sometimes you can stop hiccups by
a. scaring a person
b. rubbing the abdomen
c. drinking water slowly

3. In case of shock, have the victim
a. lie down
b. put his head between his knees
c. stand up

4. If there is a fire in the oven,
a. close the oven door
b. open the oven door
c. close oven door, pour salt on fire

5. In case a chemical gets in your eyes,
a. let tears wash it out
b. wash with lots of water; see a doctor
c. try an eyewash

6. If grease in a frying pan catches fire,
a. turn up heat under the pan
b. put a cover on the pan
c. put water on the fire

Part II

Copy the number of each item below. After the number, write *T* if the statement is *True;* write *F* if it is *False.*

T 7. A dog-bite victim should receive prompt medical attention.

F 8. Flood waters are usually pure.

T 9. Poison ivy has three glossy leaves.

F 10. Safety belts help only at high speeds.

T 11. A bite from a poisonous snake is usually accompanied by immediate pain.

T 12. Shock often accompanies severe injury.

T 13. "Overbreathing" before swimming underwater is an unsafe practice.

T 14. If you are in a boat that overturns, you should stay with the boat.

F 15. Hunters should wear green for safety.

T 16. Emergency Broadcast System has been set up to warn people of a nuclear attack.

F 17. Air mattresses are always safe water toys.

F 18. In a storm, a swimmer is safe in the water.

F 19. Only small children under age six ever get hurt in gun accidents at home.

T 20. A safety rule with guns is "Treat every gun as if it were loaded."

Number of Answers	20
Number Right	______
Score (Number Right × 5)	______

7 How Is Medical Knowledge Advancing?

Teacher's Notes

Unit Overview: Use the message here to start preliminary discussion of the fascinating advances being made in the field of medicine today. Ask students to suggest some of the medical advances they believe have occurred in *their* lifetime. Ask how they can go about checking their ideas.

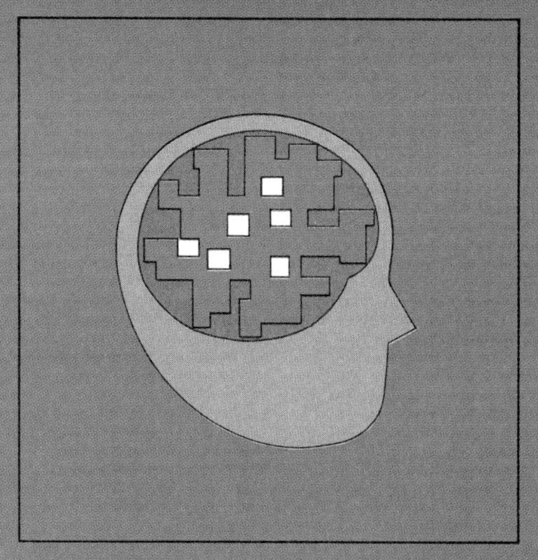

Medical progress in recent years has been dramatic. Advances have been made in the development of new drugs, in surgery and anesthesia, in the use of new medical tools for the diagnosis and treatment of disease, and in many other areas. One notable result has been the increase in the human life span—from an average of forty-seven years, which was the life expectancy of a child born in the United States in 1900, to about seventy years today.

In this unit you will learn about some of these fascinating developments. You will discover, too, where progress is needed and where it may be expected in the near future.

Teacher's Notes

Read to Find Out: These questions stimulate interest in the main topics to be treated in the unit. Discuss them briefly—just long enough to give students a chance to commit themselves to some answers. Such commitment can be a factor in holding pupils' attention during the unit. Boys and girls will want to check the accuracy of the tentative answers they have proposed.

What New Drugs Have Been Developed? Discuss with pupils some of the beneficial uses of drugs and some of the sources of drugs used in primitive times. During discussion, ask:

"How do you think people discovered that certain plants had beneficial uses as drugs?" (By chance.)

Read to Find Out

1. *What contribution to the beneficial uses of drugs came as a result of the work of* Paul Ehrlich *in the early 1900's?*

2. *Why were the discoveries of the* sulfa drugs *and the* antibiotics *important?*

3. *What are some highly useful drugs that have resulted from research in the field known as* endocrinology?

4. *What progress has been made in* immunization?

5. *Why are surgeons today able to perform more complicated surgery than they could a century ago?*

6. *Why was the discovery of* radium *important to medicine?*

7. *What progress has been made with medical* transplants? *What is one factor that often hinders successful transplants?*

8. *How would you describe a mentally healthy person?*

9. *What is meant by the term* mentally retarded? *What are some causes of mental retardation?*

10. *What progress is being made in preventing and treating mental retardation?*

Something to Do

Look in the school and public libraries for books about advances in medical science. Here are some books you might enjoy:

Poole, Lynn and Gray. Electronics in Medicine *(McGraw-Hill).*

Rosenberg, Nancy, and Snyderman, Reuven K., M.D. New Parts for People: The Story of Medical Transplants *(Norton).*

Rosenberg, Nancy, and Rosenberg, Lawrence, M.D. The Story of Modern Medicine *(Norton).*

Simon, Harold J. Microbes and Men *(Scholastic).*

Simon, Tony. The Heart Explorers *(Basic Books).*

Sylvester, D. S. The Story of Medicine *(St. Martin's Press).*

What New Drugs Have Been Developed?

Since primitive times, drugs have been used for such purposes as treating diseases, healing sores, and relieving pain. Some of the earliest drugs came from plants that had been found, more or less by chance, to have medicinal value. Many drugs obtained from plants are still used today. Among the drugs derived from plants are quinine, opium, caffeine, ephedrine, and digitalis.

In the twentieth century, however, tremendous advances have been made in the use of drugs as medicines. The German bacteriologist Paul Ehrlich had set the stage for these advances early in the 1900's. He worked in the laboratory using extremely systematic procedures. He wanted to find new drugs that would head straight for their target in the body and kill certain bacteria without harming body tissues.

Ehrlich conducted careful trial-and-error tests of hundreds of chemical compounds. One of the successful drugs he developed was nicknamed "606" because 606 experiments were made to obtain the proper compound. In 1910, he used this drug, "606," successfully to destroy the germs of the venereal disease *syphilis.* Because he was the first to conduct an organized search for chemicals to treat infectious diseases, Ehrlich has been called the "Founder of Chemotherapy."

Teacher's Notes

Some follow-up discussion leads are the following:

"What was Paul Ehrlich's role in aiding progress in the wise use of drugs?"

"What was the contribution of the sulfa drugs to medicine?"

"What is meant by 'side reactions,' or 'side effects,' of drugs?" (Sometimes drugs have effects on the body other than those intended; for example, a drug may fight an infection but it may also—at times, and in some individuals only—cause such symptoms as headache, dizziness, drowsiness, and upset stomach. Drugs should be used exactly as a doctor directs or as the container specifies. Side effects of a drug that a doctor has prescribed should be reported at once to the doctor. A person should *immediately* stop taking a nonprescription, or over-the-counter, drug that produces unexpected side reactions.)

The Sulfa Drugs

No doubt the most important step forward in modern drug history came in the 1930's with the development of the *sulfa drugs.* The sulfa drugs were originally discovered in Germany and then perfected in France. These sulfa drugs accomplished wonderful things in curing some infections. For example, before the development of the sulfas, people who contracted streptococcus infections were often doomed to death. It seemed that medical science could do nothing to fight these infections. But the sulfa drugs performed almost miraculously in halting this once-fatal type of infection. The sulfa drugs were frequently—but not always—effective in checking many other types of infection. However, some patients were sensitive to sulfa drugs and developed harmful side reactions to them.

The Antibiotics

Sulfa drugs were followed shortly by *antibiotics.* Perhaps the best known of the antibiotics is *penicillin,* a substance which fights bacteria and which is made from a mold. This drug was discovered in 1928 by the British scientist Dr. Alexander Fleming. However, little was done with penicillin at first. This was because Fleming could not produce the large quantities of the mold that would be needed for drug experimentation on large numbers of human beings.

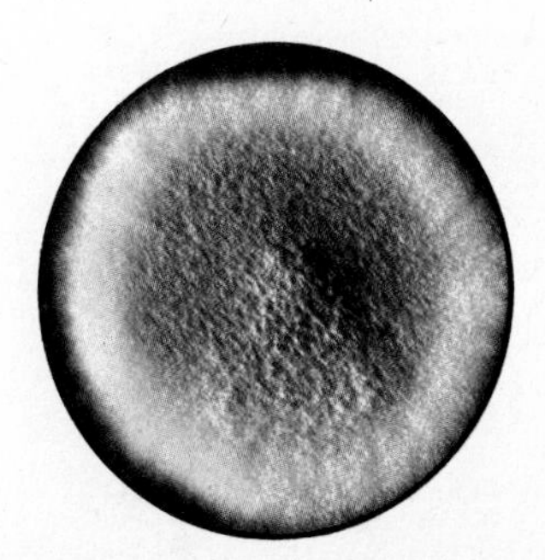

Penicillin, *produced by the mold pictured above, was the first of the antibiotics. The word antibiotic means "something that acts against life." The antibiotics act against germ life.*

It was not until World War II, when new types of drugs were needed to treat infections of wounded soldiers, that penicillin was used extensively. In 1943, the United States government made available scientific help, chemical factories, and materials, and a method was found to produce penicillin in large quantities. By 1944, there were sufficient quantities of the new drug for use with civilians as well as with the soldiers.

Teacher's Notes

Ask students why they think the search continues for new antibiotics. (Because a given microorganism can develop strong resistance to a particular antibiotic. The physician needs to have a broad range of antibiotics at his or her disposal. If one antibiotic proves to be ineffective, another can be tried.) Discuss some of the new kinds of drugs —and their functions—that have been discovered in the last fifty years or so. In discussing tranquilizers, it might be noted that physicians may occasionally prescribe these drugs for mentally healthy persons—to relieve tension in times of great stress.

(*Note:* Many drugs come from plants, such as the two shown below. Atropine is used as a muscle relaxant; digitalis is used as a heart stimulant.)

Atropa belladonna (Drug: Atropine)

Foxglove (Drug: Digitalis)

Investigate the sources of some drugs that have been found useful over the years. For example, see what you can find out about the two drugs that come from the plants shown above.

Although penicillin proved to be very useful, it could not fight off all types of bacteria. It also produced harmful side reactions in some patients. Research scientists, however, had gained additional clues to find other drugs that *might* combat bacteria-caused diseases. Since penicillin was developed from a mold, scientists concluded that other drugs might also be made from molds.

In 1944, Dr. Selman Waksman and his co-workers at Rutgers University were looking for promising molds and other organisms in the soil. Their investigations led to the development of the germ-killer called *streptomycin.* This drug has been especially helpful in the treatment of tuberculosis.

From that time on, laboratory research has continually yielded new antibiotic drugs. The future will no doubt see many more of them. To date, none of the antibiotics or sulfa drugs have proved consistently effective against virus-caused diseases such as colds, influenza, and mumps. The search for effective virus-killing drugs is continuing.

Tranquilizers and Energizers

Another important group of drugs that have been developed in recent years are the ones called *tranquilizers.* These drugs have proved especially useful with persons who are emotionally disturbed. Tranquilizers are not a cure for mental illness. They do, however, calm disturbed patients so that other forms of therapy may be used more effectively.

Energizers are another group of modern drugs. These drugs, too, are helpful in treating people with emotional disorders—especially people who feel constantly depressed. In contrast to the tranquilizers, energizers elevate a patient's mood and stimulate him to be more active.

Both tranquilizers and energizers should be used only under a doctor's direction, since they sometimes have harmful side effects. Some of these drugs, when abused, can be physically addicting. An overdose in some situations can be fatal.

Other Recent Developments

The human body is so complicated that many different drugs are needed for many different problems. There is a new drug, for example, that can reduce high blood pressure.

Another interesting drug that has been developed lately—and that is being successfully used in some cases—is one called *methadone.* This drug is sometimes used by physicians to treat those addicted to heroin. The drug seems to reduce some of the cravings a "hooked" person has for heroin; it can also help reduce the pains of withdrawal from heroin. When addicts are treated with methadone under close supervision, they can often be helped to resume a normal life in their community. The emotional problems underlying the person's drug dependence are not cured by the drug, however, and the problems must still be treated by other means.

Some other effective modern drugs are those made from hormones. You will read about these drugs on pages 202–204. The discovery of each of these and of the many other new drugs has been part of a constant search for ways of coping with disease. There is dramatic evidence of the progress that has been made thus far. Most of the prescriptions a doctor writes today call for drugs which were discovered or manufactured within the past few decades. These modern drugs have saved millions of lives and have prevented untold suffering.

Safety Factor in New Drugs

The public is protected from any new drugs that might be harmful or ineffective. Formal permission to market a new drug must be obtained from the New Drugs Section of the Food and Drug Administration (FDA) in Washington, D.C. Along with the request for permission, the applicant must submit carefully prepared data about the new drug, including detailed reports of all the clinical studies made on it.

Once a new drug has been accepted, the FDA still keeps watch over it, conducting follow-up studies of doctors who have prescribed the drug. If any shortcomings are noted, physicians are warned. In the event that serious harmful effects appear, the drug is withdrawn from sale.

After a new drug has received approval from the FDA and is on the market, it is evaluated by the American Medical Association's Council on Drugs. In the weekly *Journal of the American Medical Association,* doctors are given a full evaluation of the drug.

Teacher's Notes

In discussing the drug *methadone,* be sure the term "addict" has been clarified. Students can use the Glossary for help. They can also read pages 60-61 of the text. It should be noted that methadone is still being used somewhat experimentally in treating drug addiction. The person using the drug methadone also develops a craving for this drug; but many scientists think methadone does not have the harmful physical or emotional effects of heroin. What is more, methadone is a drug that can be used legally. In some communities daily doses are given at a local clinic, so that the addict can function as a normal person. It is important that close supervision be maintained and that job retraining and counseling accompany the methadone-maintenance treatment.

Teacher's Notes

Discuss what is meant by the term *endocrinology*. Review the names of *all* the endocrine glands (pineal, pituitary, thyroid, parathyroids, thymus, adrenals, islets of Langerhans in the pancreas, and the female and male reproductive glands —ovaries in the female, testicles [testes] in the male). Refer back to the marginal picture on page 15 in Unit One. Other names for the endocrine glands are *ductless glands* and *glands of internal secretion*.

The substances the endocrine glands produce, or secrete, are called *hormones*.

Ask these questions:

"Which particular glands have been useful in the development of a drug for diabetics?"

"What is the story behind the development of this drug for diabetics?"

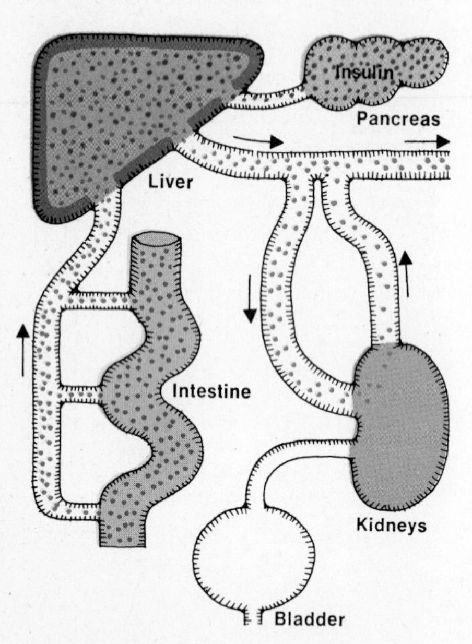

Nondiabetic condition: *Glucose, derived from sugars and other carbohydrates in foods eaten, goes to the liver from the intestine. When normal amounts of insulin are produced by the islets of Langerhans in the pancreas, much of the glucose is stored as glycogen in the liver. The liver releases only enough glucose into the bloodstream to meet the needs of the body.* *Now see page 203.*

What Is Hormone Therapy?

Some very effective modern drugs have resulted from research in *endocrinology,* that is, the study of endocrine glands and their hormones. Information about the endocrine glands is found in Unit One.

Among the well-known hormone drugs are *insulin, cortisone,* and *ACTH.* The stories about the development of these hormone drugs are interesting ones. These accounts give evidence that progress in developing a new drug takes time and effort. Progress often involves the work of many people, and each person contributes something to the final achievement.

Insulin

An important step forward in the use of hormone drugs took place in Canada in the 1920's. Two research workers named F. G. Banting and C. H. Best were studying secretions of the pancreas in the hope of finding a treatment for *diabetes.* Many other workers were doing similar studies elsewhere.

Diabetes, a disease in which the body cannot make proper use of sugar and starch, was known to have something to do with the pancreas. It was greatly feared since the only known treatment for it was a near-starvation diet, and even with a controlled diet many patients died.

By experimenting with dogs, Banting and Best found a way to extract the secretion of the islets of Langerhans, a gland formed by small groups of cells lying within the pancreas. Later, the two researchers extracted this same secretion from cows. They found that this secretion—which was actually the hormone *insulin*—revived animals dying of diabetes.

The next step was to find a way of purifying this extract and putting it into commercial production. In this task a brilliant biochemist, James B. Collip, was of great assistance. Finally, in 1922, in the Toronto General Hospital, the new product was tried on a fourteen-year-old boy who was dying of diabetes. The boy was given gradually increasing doses of insulin by injection. As a result, he did not die but was restored to reasonably good health for as long as the insulin injections were continued.

From this time on, the dread disease of diabetes could be controlled. In diabetic patients, the islets of Langerhans do not produce enough insulin, which is needed to break down carbohydrates—sugars and starches—in the diet. With the discovery of synthetic insulin, a diabetic person could be given the *manufactured* form to supplement the insulin made in the body. Study the drawings on pages 202 and 203.

Today oral drugs have been developed that for some patients can supply insulin. Oral forms of insulin are used chiefly for older patients who develop diabetes late in life or for those who have mild cases. Many persons must still use insulin injections. With insulin and a controlled diet, most diabetics can now live almost normal lives.

Teacher's Notes

Discuss with students the meaning of the various anatomical and medical terms used: *adrenal glands, adrenalin, medulla, cortex,* and *cortisone.* Students may have heard of Addison's disease, named after Thomas Addison—the British doctor who discovered it. In this disease, a lack of adrenal-cortex secretion causes a weakening of the muscles. A cortical extract is used to treat the disease.

Cortisone and ACTH

Another dramatic advance in the use of hormone drugs came with the discovery of *cortisone* and *ACTH.* The discovery of cortisone, and indirectly of ACTH, grew out of research on the adrenal glands. Scientists knew that the adrenals manufacture or secrete *adrenalin.* This hormone helps produce strong bodily reactions when a person is excited. Have you ever had the experience of getting extra strength seemingly from nowhere to enable you to meet a sudden emergency such as running from danger? This strength came from the extra amount of adrenalin your adrenal glands secreted.

Scientists suspected that the adrenal glands had other functions in addition to the secretion of adrenalin. Further research led to the discovery that each adrenal gland is really two glands in one. There is the core tissue, or *medulla,* which produces adrenalin; and an outer tissue, the *cortex,* whose functions are not yet clear. When scientists found that animals could not live without the cortex of at least one adrenal gland, they suspected that one or more hormones produced by the cortex were essential to life itself. They then set out to discover what mysterious part the cortical hormone named *cortisone* played in the body.

You may have heard the story of what happened when Dr. Philip Hench of the Mayo Clinic, Rochester, Minnesota, used cortisone for the first time. He obtained the cortisone from the

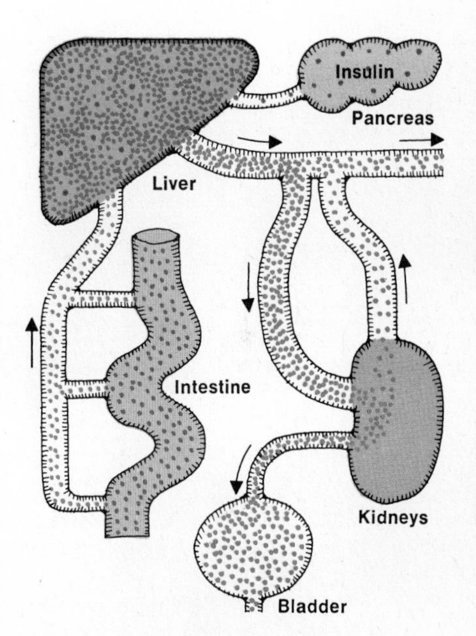

Diabetic condition: *When an insufficient amount of insulin or no insulin is produced by the islets of Langerhans, much less of the glucose entering the liver is changed into glycogen. Excess glucose floods the bloodstream. A large proportion of the excess glucose is removed from the circulation by the kidneys. The glucose is then eliminated from the body in urine.*

Teacher's Notes

Some research on hormones and cancer has shown that in some cases one of the male hormones tends to inhibit cancers peculiar to women. One of the female hormones has also proved useful in some patients in slowing the growth of cancers peculiar to men.

Invite discussion of how students can keep abreast of new developments in hormone therapy. (Through magazine or newspaper articles by qualified medical experts; through TV programs sponsored by reputable health groups such as the American Medical Association and the American Cancer Society.)

adrenal cortex of slaughtered cattle and gave it to fourteen patients suffering from rheumatoid arthritis. All of Dr. Hench's patients had severe cases. Some were so crippled they could not move. Yet after being treated with injections of cortisone for about three days, they were able to discard their crutches and wheelchairs and walk. Stiff joints became supple, and bent knees began to straighten out. Swelling and pain disappeared. Appetite and weight increased.

The relief lasted as long as the injections of cortisone were continued. When they had to be stopped because of a drug shortage, the symptoms of the disease reappeared. Cortisone did not cure rheumatoid arthritis, but it gave remarkable relief. Doctors hailed it as a landmark in medical history.

About this time, a use was found for ACTH, a hormone made by the pituitary gland. ACTH could be used to stimulate a patient's lagging adrenal glands to produce the amount of cortisone his body needed. Scientists were able to produce this only in small quantities, however. It was not until a few years later that research workers found a way to make both cortisone and ACTH artificially in the laboratory.

Careful studies of the long-range effects of cortisone and ACTH on patients indicated that continued use of these powerful hormones nearly always led to harmful side effects. Some of these side effects were growth of facial hair, skin rashes, and digestive disorders. So these drugs are now given cautiously and in limited amounts for short periods of time. In addition, newer and more powerful versions of the drugs have been developed. The new drugs, given in very small doses, have cut down significantly on the side effects.

Further experimentation with cortisone and ACTH has indicated that these drugs can control diseases other than rheumatoid arthritis. They are also useful in the treatment of some severe skin ailments, rheumatic fever, gout, and asthma.

What Do You Think?

1. *What are some of the uses of* cortisone *and* ACTH *in medicine?*
2. *What are some of the drawbacks of these two drugs?*
3. *What is one area in which hormones as drugs may prove beneficial to mankind in the future?*

Other Types of Hormone Therapy

Recently hormones have been found to be useful in slowing the growth of certain types of cancers. Many scientists believe that what is now known about medical uses of hormones is only a beginning—and that significant discoveries lie ahead.

What Progress Has Been Made in Immunization?

Teacher's Notes

Talk over the meaning of these specialized terms: *immunization, vaccination, antibodies, phagocytes, communicable disease.*

Discuss where the special substances called *antibodies* are produced in the body. Students may locate the lymph nodes and the spleen in the marginal picture. Lymph vessels are also pictured, but it is in the *nodes* that some antibodies are produced. The nodes are small glands that occur along the lymph vessels. These nodes also trap and remove some bacteria and force other foreign particles from the lymph stream.

So far you have been reading about drugs and about hormone preparations that are used in the treatment of diseases *after* the diseases have started. Progress has also been made in another area—that of preventing certain diseases by making the body resistant to them *before* they occur. This type of treatment is used especially against diseases caused by bacteria and viruses. The method by which the body is made resistant or *immune* to an infection is called *immunization.* When vaccines are used to immunize, the process is called *vaccination.*

Antibodies and Immunity

The human body has a specialized system of cells and tissues whose job is to give protection against foreign invaders such as bacteria and viruses. As soon as these harmful microorganisms enter the body, substances called *antibodies* are manufactured in special body tissues—which include the spleen and the lymph nodes. These antibodies are carried throughout the body by the blood. (See the picture at the right.)

Antibodies have the unusual ability to attack invading microorganisms by causing a chemical reaction on the microorganisms' outer surfaces which destroys the invaders. The dead microorganisms are then surrounded and made to disintegrate by scavenger cells called *phagocytes*—some of which are white blood cells. The killing and breaking up of invading microorganisms in the body usually marks the beginning of recovery from an infectious, or communicable, disease.

As you know by now, each infectious disease is caused by a different kind of microorganism—smallpox by the smallpox virus, diphtheria by the diphtheria bacterium, and so on. But did you know that for each kind of infectious microorganism the body produces a *special* kind of antibody? Antibodies that are produced to fight a particular kind of infectious organism circulate throughout the body for a long period of time. As long as these antibodies are present, an individual is immune to a new attack by the bacteria or viruses that caused their production. As a result, most boys and girls have such diseases as mumps and measles only once.

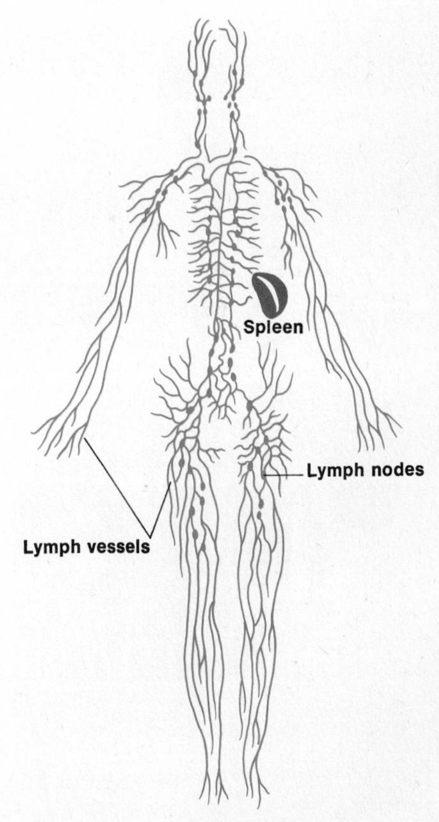

Some places in which antibodies are manufactured are shown in the diagram. What are they?

Teacher's Notes
Discuss the term *immunology*. Ask:
"What was one of the truly significant discoveries in the field of immunology?"
"What have you learned about a form of immunization that was practiced over 2,500 years ago?"
Note that it is only recently that smallpox vaccinations have not been routinely required in the United States. However, travelers who go to areas of the world where smallpox is still a problem must be immunized against the disease. Also, smallpox vaccinations are still desirable in many underdeveloped areas of the world.

One of the most important discoveries in *immunology*—the science that specializes in the study of immunity—was that a microorganism can cause the production of antibodies even though it has lost its ability to produce disease. This loss of the ability to cause disease can be accomplished either by weakening or by killing the microorganism through chemical treatment or other means. Thus, by injecting an individual with weakened or killed microorganisms, he can be made immune without becoming seriously ill.

From China to Jenner's England

Smallpox was a feared disease for thousands of years. About half the people who contracted the disease died and the rest were left blind, disfigured, or crippled. In former times, few persons reached adulthood without some signs of having had the disease. There was, however, one cause for hope in conquering the disease. It was known that a person who had lived through the first attack of smallpox would be resistant to a new attack. Records show that as early as 590 B.C.—over 2,500 years ago—the Chinese made use of this knowledge. To protect a person against smallpox, they placed into the patient's nostrils tiny pieces of smallpox scabs from an infected individual. The person treated in this manner usually developed a very slight case of the disease and afterward was immune to smallpox.

Free smallpox vaccination given in Paris (1890). Today smallpox is rare in developed countries, and widespread vaccinations are no longer required.

Not until the early eighteenth century was a similar method of immunization against smallpox introduced in Europe. Here it found great support, especially in England. Unfortunately, some of the inoculated individuals died from the disease instead of having only a mild infection.

At this time, however, English farmers—whose cattle often suffered from a similar infection called cowpox—made some far-reaching observations. They noted that milkmaids who were in frequent contact with cows often became infected with cowpox. Cowpox produced only a few sores on their hands and it was never fatal. But surprisingly, it was noted, too, that these milkmaids did not get the human disease, smallpox.

An English physician, Edward Jenner, made use of these observations. He saw in them a way to provide immunization against smallpox. Later his method was called vaccination, a term that came from the Latin word *vacca,* which means cow. Jenner scratched some fluid from the sore of a person infected with the mild cowpox into the skin of a healthy eight-year-old boy named James Phipps. A few weeks later, Jenner intentionally infected the boy with fluid from the sore of a smallpox patient. The boy did not develop smallpox! As a result of this experiment and Jenner's untiring efforts, large-scale vaccination against smallpox was introduced all over Europe.

Teacher's Notes

Discuss with students the purpose of immunizing with booster shots and revaccinations. Smallpox vaccination, for example, does not confer permanent immunity and revaccination is necessary every five years in areas where such vaccinations are required. Booster doses are also required for diphtheria, whooping cough, tetanus, and polio.

Vaccines as Tools for Medical Progress

Vaccination against smallpox was eventually introduced on a worldwide scale. Thus an end was brought to the once-common epidemics that had claimed millions of lives through the ages. Successful vaccination against smallpox indicated that, with the use of appropriate vaccines, protection against other infectious diseases was possible.

Following Jenner's work, many other methods were developed for the production of effective vaccines. Vaccines have been made from live microorganisms whose disease-producing ability has been weakened or eliminated by various procedures. Some types of vaccines today consist of whole, killed bacteria or viruses. Other vaccines contain parts of microorganisms that have been made to disintegrate mechanically. Techniques for vaccination also vary nowadays. Vaccination against smallpox still follows Jenner's skin-scratch procedure. Other vaccines, however, are injected into the skin. Still others are given orally in syrups or in sugar cubes.

In addition to smallpox, vaccines have been developed against such epidemic-producing diseases as cholera, typhoid fever, typhus, and yellow fever. Diseases against which children in the United States are routinely immunized are diphtheria, whooping cough, tetanus, and poliomyelitis. Measles is another important childhood disease against which vaccination has been successful in recent years. A vaccine has been developed also for German measles, or rubella, a different disease from ordinary measles. There is now available a one-shot vaccine for mumps, measles, and German measles. See the immunization chart on the next page.

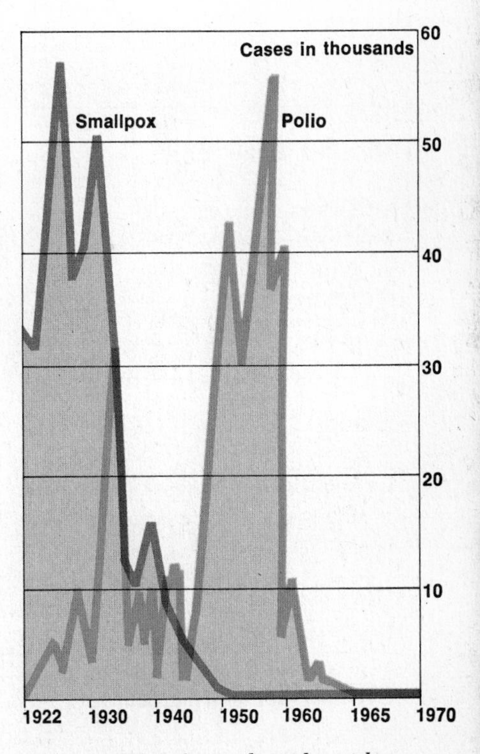

Notice in the chart above how the number of cases of polio and smallpox have declined in the United States since the 1920's.

Statistics from the National Center for Disease Control, Atlanta, Georgia.

Immunization Timetable

Disease	First Inoculations	Booster Doses
Diphtheria **Tetanus** **Whooping Cough** (Pertussis) (All three are combined in one DTP shot until age 6.)	At age of 2 months, 4 months, and 6 months. A fourth dose is given at 15-18 months. A fifth dose is given at 4-6 years.	At age of 14-16 years and every 10 years thereafter, "adult type" doses of tetanus-diphtheria toxoid are given, with pertussis vaccine omitted. Tetanus toxoid is given as recommended by physician at time of an injury.
Polio (Poliomyelitis) Trivalent Oral Polio Vaccine or TOPV	At age of 2 months. Two more doses of TOPV are given at two-month intervals. Another dose of TOPV is given at 15-18 months.	Another dose of TOPV is given at age of 4-6 years.
Measles (Rubeola) Live-virus measles vaccine (Inactivated measles virus vaccine no longer recommended.)	At age of 12 months. Gamma globulin (Immune Serum Globulin) may be given after exposure if live vaccine is not advisable.	None, unless first vaccine was administered before 12 months of age.
Mumps Live-virus mumps vaccine	Single doses after 12 months if given with measles and rubella; may be recommended by physicians for children nearing puberty, adolescents, and adults who have not had mumps.	
German Measles (Rubella) Live rubella virus vaccine	Between age of 1 year and puberty.	

"Immunization Timetable" has been read for accuracy and approved by the American Academy of Pediatrics.

What Progress Has Been Made in Surgery?

Surgery has been practiced since ancient times. The oldest known surgical procedure was called *trepanning.* In this operation a hole was cut in the skull. Evidences of this surgery—no doubt performed with a sharp stone for a cutting tool—were found in the skeletons of men of the Stone Age. This operation was also used by the Aztecs and the American Indians. It might have been performed to relieve pressure from a fracture or to remove foreign objects from the brain. It may have been used, too, for magical reasons, such as letting out "evil spirits" from the head when a person showed signs of mental disturbance.

Surgery in the Middle Ages

In the Middle Ages, surgeons were often barbers as well, or they had barbers for their assistants. Both surgeons and barbers performed the procedure known as *bloodletting,* in which a vein was opened to let the blood out. People were often bled as a preventive health measure. Bloodletting was also thought to aid in the treatment of some diseases. Actually, of course, bloodletting weakened the patient.

One of the most famous surgeons of the Middle Ages was a Frenchman, Ambroise Paré, who lived in the 1500's. He developed a special dressing for reducing wound infection which was much less painful than the customary use of boiling oil. Paré also introduced a better and more humane way to control the severe bleeding that occurred when a limb was amputated. The practice up until his time had been to close the wound by searing the edges with a white-hot poker. Paré used an idea he had found in the writings of Galen, who lived about A.D. 200. It was a method so simple that it had been largely ignored over the centuries—the method of tying off a bleeding vessel after amputation of a limb.

Surgery Before Anesthesia Was Discovered

Surgery as we know it today, however, is a development of the last hundred years or so. Before the discovery of anesthesia in the 1840's, surgery was limited to operations that could be performed in very short periods. This was because operations

Teacher's Notes

To add to the information given in the text, you might mention that the Babylonians practiced surgery over 4,000 years ago. They had rules for setting fees. They also exacted certain penalties from an unsuccessful surgeon. If a patient died, the surgeon's right hand was cut off!

Egypt has often been called the "cradle of surgery." This term may be used partly because the records from Egypt are more complete than are those from China and India, where civilizations were also highly developed. Medical tools, drawings, and instruments found with Egyptian mummies indicate that surgery was practiced as early as 1900 to 1350 B.C.

Teacher's Notes

Discuss anesthesia's role in making possible the rapid advances in surgery. Then ask:

"What is one interesting story connected with early attempts to use anesthesia?"

Students might write newspaper articles —or just headlines—such as those that might have been written about early progress in anesthesia.

were so painful that patients could stand only those of short duration. The usual methods of relieving pain up to that time involved the use of heavy doses of alcoholic beverages or of drugs such as opium. But these methods blotted out the pain only briefly, and operations had to be performed in haste with patients screaming in agony. Many people preferred to die rather than have an operation. The operations performed were mainly amputations and the cutting out of external tumors. Difficult surgery, such as cutting into the chest or abdomen, was rarely attempted.

Anesthesia—a Great Step Forward

The discovery of *anesthesia,* a means of bringing about absence of sensation in the entire body or in a part of the body, was one of the milestones in medical history. After this discovery, progress in surgery could advance more rapidly.

The credit for the discovery of anesthesia has been disputed through the years. However, it *is* certain that much of the early experimentation with anesthesia took place in the United States in the 1840's.

One of the experimenters was W. T. G. Morton, a Boston dentist. He experimented with *ether,* a colorless, sweet-smelling liquid. Before he began to drill, Morton applied the ether on and around the patient's teeth. For very brief periods the ether made the gums insensible. Later, Morton asked one of his patients to inhale small quantities of ether which had been poured into a handkerchief. The patient fell into a deep sleep and Morton pulled his tooth—probably the first painless extraction.

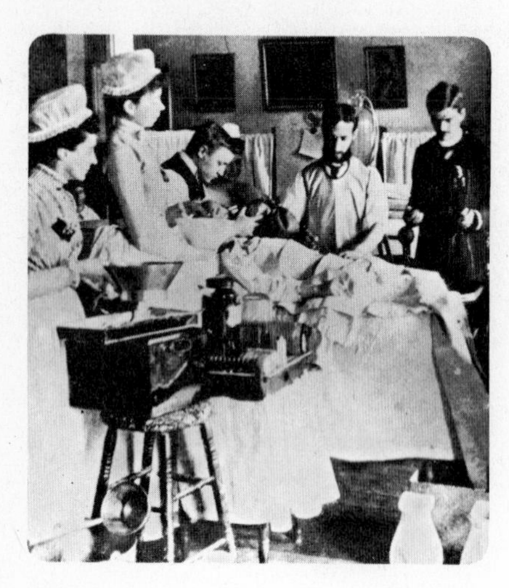

The home surgery of the 1800's and earlier is in remarkable contrast to the surgery performed in modern hospitals.

It occurred to Morton that if ether could prevent the pain of having a tooth pulled, it could also prevent the pain of another kind of operation. So he asked a noted surgeon at Massachusetts General Hospital to try out ether during an operation. This was done; and the operation, performed in 1846, was a success. Upon awakening from the anesthetic, the patient said he had felt no pain.

Other operations with the use of ether confirmed that it was indeed a wonderful discovery. Thus a new era began—while patients slept, doctors could work slowly and carefully.

Development of the medical specialty called *anesthesiology* has made anesthesia safer than ever before. The trained anesthetist now has at hand machines that provide instant reports on the patient's pulse, blood pressure, and heart action during surgery. At a moment's notice, emergency procedures can be performed. Anesthesia has advanced far beyond the technique of dropping ether onto a cloth held over the face. Some modern advances in anesthesia are described here:

Spinal anesthesia. In this procedure, the anesthetic is injected into the spinal cord at various levels, leaving the patient conscious but free from pain in the area where surgery is to be performed.

Intravenous anesthesia. With this method, an anesthetic such as Pentothal is introduced into a vein—causing the patient to fall asleep peacefully and rapidly and to awaken without realizing he has been asleep or has had an operation.

Nerve block. In this technique, an anesthetic is injected around a certain nerve at an accessible point—paralyzing the nerve that carries sensations from those areas to the brain and anesthetizing extensive areas of the body.

Hypothermia. With this technique, the body temperature is reduced to the low 80's Fahrenheit. Hypothermia is a valuable present-day accompaniment to anesthesia. The condition is something like hibernation. The metabolic rate, or all the processes of living, are slowed down and the individual is enabled to withstand pain he could not otherwise tolerate.

Cryosurgery. This is a type of surgery done at below-freezing temperatures. Thus the organ or tissue to be cut out is first frozen solid with a special cooling instrument and then removed painlessly. Cryosurgery has been used to remove tonsils and to remove cataracts from the eye.

Electrical anesthesia. This kind of anesthesia is now being used experimentally. With it, a current is sent through an amplifier connected by electrodes to a patient's temple. Within thirty to sixty seconds the patient is asleep and the operation may begin. The patient remains unconscious as long as the current is on, and he wakes up within thirty to sixty seconds after the current is turned off.

Teacher's Notes

Talk over with students the many advances that have taken place in surgery in very recent times. Six specialized techniques for anesthesia are discussed briefly on this page. Discuss the significance of continued surgical advances to students and to their families.

A volunteer might investigate and report on the training required for an anesthesiologist, or anesthetist.

Teacher's Notes

It should be noted that, in the years after Lister, it was found that germs in the air were not one of the major dangers in the operating room—as Lister had thought. Instead the chief hazard came from germs on the hands and clothing of the surgical team or on the instruments and bandages. Today the gowns, caps, masks, gloves, and instruments of the surgical team are treated with steam to make them *sterile,* or germ free.

Antisepsis: Another Step Forward

While anesthetics were being developed, another great step forward in surgery was being taken by an English doctor, Joseph Lister, in the 1860's. Lister was very much disturbed over the high death rate of people who had undergone surgery. In the hospital at Glasgow, Scotland, where he worked, he noted that patients almost always suffered complications after surgery. They had such infections as blood poisoning, abscesses, and gangrene. At least a third of all the patients who had operations died from infections of their wounds.

The studies of Louis Pasteur in France suggested to Lister that bacteria were causing the infections in surgical wounds. Lister then began to experiment with ways to prevent infections following surgery. He was concerned with destroying germs already present in wounds. Lister eventually decided to use a chemical called carbolic acid which he sprayed on the wound and into the air to fight infection. He called his method *antisepsis.* As a result of his methods, the death rate among surgical cases in his hospital dropped dramatically.

One of the disadvantages of using strong antiseptics such as carbolic acid on wounds was that these substances also destroyed body tissue. In today's hospital, Lister's method of antisepsis has been largely replaced by a technique called *asepsis.* This word means *absence of infection.* Asepsis involves sterilizing all objects or substances that come into contact with the operating area during surgery. With this procedure, bacteria are not allowed to enter surgical wounds.

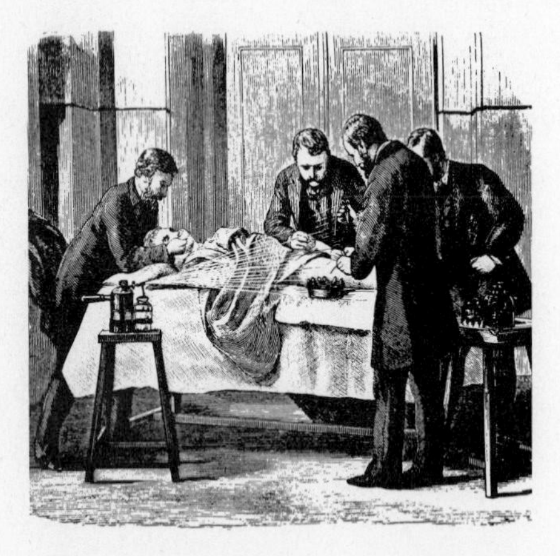

The photograph above shows the use of Lister's carbolic spray during an operation (antiseptic surgery, 1882). What is the difference between the technique of antisepsis and that of asepsis? Why do you think surgeons use sterile instruments, gloves, and masks during surgery today?

The smelly, flesh-destroying antiseptics of the past are used today only to sterilize sharp instruments and to cleanse the skin. But in using antiseptics to fight infection, Lister took a first step in revolutionizing surgical practices.

Improved Instruments

Improved instruments and machines have also made advances in surgery possible. A major discovery was that of the *X ray* in Germany in 1895 by Wilhelm Konrad Roentgen. With X-ray pictures, surgeons were able to see inside the human body; to study the heart, lungs, stomach, and other internal organs; and to prepare effectively for surgery.

Other types of instruments that have been developed over the years enable the surgeon to look directly into various cavities and organs of the human body. For example, the *bronchoscope* is a lighted tube used to examine the lungs; it may also be connected with forceps and other instruments which permit operations inside the lungs. The *cystoscope* is a lighted tube used to examine the urinary bladder and operate on it. (See the drawings at the right.)

Still other modern medical instruments are known as *scanners.* The brain scanner, for instance, is used to "see inside" the brain and find the exact location of a brain tumor that is to be removed by surgery.

In recent years it has become possible by means of the *heart-lung machine* to remove all blood from the heart. This removal occurs for a limited time while surgery is performed inside the heart to repair imperfect partitions or damaged valves. The mechanical heart-lung machine is electrically operated. The machine receives "used" blood which normally would be delivered to the heart, exposes the blood to oxygen the way it would be exposed in the lungs, and returns the oxygenated blood through a tube back to the general circulation. In this way the heart is freed from pumping blood during surgery.

It is now possible, also, to use devices called *pacemakers* to keep damaged hearts beating. One type can be implanted in the human body to maintain a patient's heartbeat. This transistor device is implanted in the body in front of the left kidney and is linked to the heart by wires and platinum nodes. The electrical impulses keep the damaged heart beating. One of the problems in the use of pacemakers has been the relatively short life—and the need for frequent replacement—of the batteries that supply the electrical energy. Research is underway to design batteries that may last as long as twenty-five years.

Another device that aids the surgeon is the *mechanical heart massager.* Formerly, if the heart stopped during surgery, it had to be massaged by hand. This is an exacting and tiring process. The mechanical massager works speedily and reliably to keep the patient alive.

Teacher's Notes

This is a good time to encourage study of the photos in the picture essay on pages 221-226. Students can look especially for some of the improved instruments and equipment that make complicated types of surgery possible today.

See also the explanation of a scanner on the front endsheet of this book.

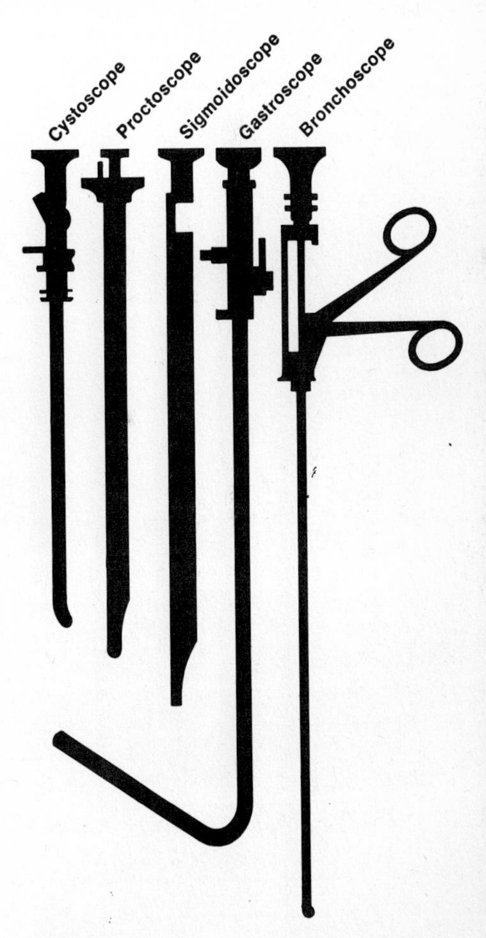

These instruments enable doctors to see inside the body. What are the instruments? What do you know about them? If you do not know how these instruments are used, look in the Glossary.

Teacher's Notes

A dramatic example of progress in surgery can be found in the field of heart surgery. Not so many years ago medical students were taught that the heart could never be operated on. Today dozens of intricate operations on the heart can be performed by specially trained surgeons. Among these operations is one in which faulty or damaged heart valves are replaced with artificial valves. Of course, there are heart transplants also; these will be discussed later in the unit.

In the discussion of *microsurgery*, it might be mentioned that the magnifications used are great—16 times normal in some situations, 40 times normal in others. Microsurgeons have done intricate operations on the ear, on various nerves, on the brain, and on the spinal cord.

Some Things to Do

1. Bring in clippings from newspapers or magazines about new surgical instruments or techniques.

2. If the book The Story of Modern Medicine *by Nancy Rosenberg and Lawrence Rosenberg, M.D. (Norton) is available, you might read the two chapters on surgery called "The Birth of Modern Surgery" and "Progress in Surgery."*

Still another device to aid in heart operations is the *heat exchanger,* which can lower or raise body temperature before and after surgery. With this machine, through tubes attached to an artery, a patient's blood is circulated through a cylinder of coils surrounded by a water jacket. To reduce body temperature—an essential procedure during open-heart surgery—ice water is used to surround the coils. To raise blood temperature after surgery, warm water is used around the coils.

There are, of course, many other recently developed instruments available to help in the treatment and study of patients before, during, and after surgery. For example, there are machines that monitor and record a patient's blood pressure, heartbeat, and respiration. (See page 223.) There are delicate electronic devices, far more sensitive than the surgeon's eyes or hands, that help him in finding exactly the right spot in certain brain operations. Other remarkable instruments are constantly being perfected.

Courses are now being offered at universities in biomedical engineering. These courses indicate how closely medical men and engineers are working together to improve the practice of medicine through the development and use of electronic instruments and mechanical devices.

Improved Surgical Techniques

Another great advance in surgery has been the development of ever more complicated surgical techniques. In recent years surgeons have been able to operate on all parts of the body. In some instances, surgery is made possible by the new technique of *microsurgery*—surgery under high-powered magnification.

Today's surgeon can remove several feet of diseased small intestine, sew the remaining parts together, and the body will function normally thereafter. With similar success, he can remove three fourths of a stomach, take out a lung or kidney, and perform delicate brain operations—and still have his patient survive to lead a nearly normal life.

An exciting development in modern surgery has been the invention of the "light knife." This instrument, also known as a *laser,* produces a light beam so powerful that it can cut through tissue just as the surgeon's knife does. But in contrast to the steel knife, the laser beam makes bloodless incisions, because the blood vessels it cuts are immediately sealed by the intense heat of the light beam. The laser knife is especially well suited for cutting into sensitive body areas where ordinary surgery could cause dangerous bleeding. Thus the laser has been used for removing a variety of tumors and for performing eye surgery.

So many varieties of surgery are possible nowadays that a number of specialties have developed. One surgical specialty is that of *ophthalmology,* which deals with diseases of the eye. For example, a common eye difficulty known as cross-eyes, or *strabismus,* can now be corrected by an eye-muscle operation.

Orthopedic surgery is used to correct various deformities or diseases of the bones, muscles, tendons, cartilage, ligaments, and so on.

Another fascinating field of surgery is *plastic surgery.* It deals with removing scars and blemishes and with correcting defects present at birth or resulting from diseases or accidents. It is possible for a plastic surgeon to remodel a facial structure or to make an entirely new nose or ear when the original one has been destroyed. New jaws can be built out of living bone, cartilage, and flesh.

Some other surgical specialties include those of the ear, nose, and throat; the chest; and the brain. Great progress in recent years has been made in all these fields.

Transplants

A goal toward which much medical research has been directed is that of exchanging diseased or worn-out tissues or organs for artificial substitutes or healthy living replacements.

Progress in transplants has been made, especially in connection with tissues that are transplanted for short-term periods. Tissue needed for only a short time can serve its purpose before being rejected by the body. Thus blood—which may be considered a tissue—can be transferred from one person to another if the blood is properly matched. Or the blood may be separated and the various parts used for transfusions or other injections. Transfused blood, though, merely bridges the gap until the body can make additional blood of its own.

Teacher's Notes

You may wish to add some information about the laser beam, or "light knife." The invisible ray does not hurt. Students might discuss who is likely to be in the operating room at the time of an operation: for example, one or more surgeons, the family doctor, the anesthetist, a surgical resident on the hospital staff, a surgical nurse and several other nurses, and possibly interns in teaching hospitals.

Teacher's Notes

Ask students what advances in the field of transplants the following words bring to mind: *cornea, bone, Teflon, blood.* If the book *New Parts for People: The Story of Medical Transplants* by Nancy Rosenberg and Reuven Snyderman, M.D. (Norton) is available, a volunteer might report on the chapter entitled "Ready When You Need It." This chapter—on tissue banks and other banks—tells, for example, how at the Massachusetts Institute of Technology bone is sterilized by a powerful beam of radiation before it is stored. The giant accelerator that produces this beam is over fifteen feet high.

A person with scarred or clouded corneas in his eyes may be given clear corneas if the transplant takes place within forty-eight hours after the death of a donor of the clear corneas. In some cases, dehydrated corneas—which can be stored for many months—can be used.

People suffering from the disease called *leukemia* may be aided temporarily by receiving transplants of bone marrow from the bones of others. Bone transplants have often been used, also, to bridge fractures that would not unite, to replace sections of large bones damaged by bone tumors, to fuse joints, and to remodel jaws and noses. Another advance in transplants is the development of a bone-building material made from the bones of calves. Eventually the human bone used in transplants may be replaced by this new bone substitute.

Weakened portions of blood vessels can be replaced too. Artery grafts have a high rate of success because the effectiveness of arteries does not depend on their being alive. At first, human arteries were processed for this purpose and stored in freezers until used. Today, though, it has been found that plastic arteries—made of Teflon, Dacron, and other synthetics—can be used effectively.

For such medical uses, "banks" of various kinds of tissues have been successfully established and are in constant use. The most common and best-known type has been the blood bank. In it, blood can be stored for future transfusions. A recent advance—that of freezing blood before storing it—makes it possible to store blood for about two years or longer. Other banks for tissue replacement are eye-cornea banks, bone banks, and cartilage banks.

The challenging goal of the future, however, is the transplanting of *whole organs.* If a patient has a diseased *pair* of organs, such as the kidneys, a donor can often be found who is willing to give up one of his healthy kidneys to the patient. With the remaining kidney, the donor will still be able to live a normal life. Things are more complicated if an unpaired organ, such as the liver, needs to be substituted. The only possible replacements then are an artificial organ, an organ from a person who has just died, or an organ from a living animal.

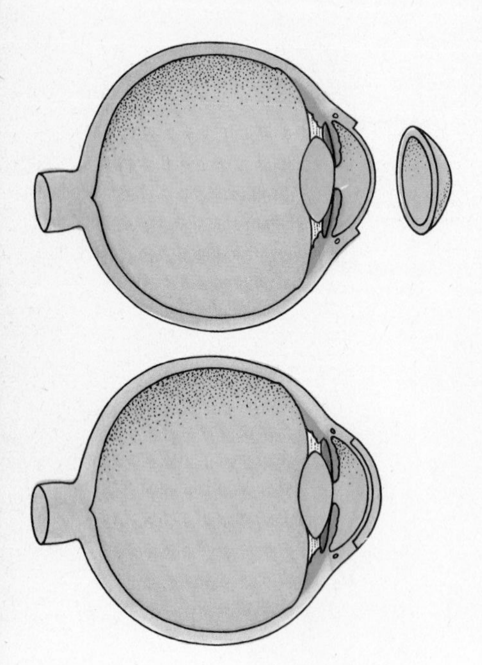

The cornea *is the transparent cover over the front of the eye. A cornea can be transplanted from the eye of a donor to a patient who has a scarred or cloudy cornea.*

Some organs that have been transplanted and have, in some instances, functioned for various periods of time are shown in the diagram at the right. What are they? What specific cases of organ transplants do you recall reading about?

The surgical techniques used in organ transplants generally do not present any serious problems. But successful surgery alone does not ensure survival of the organ transplanted. Since the transplanted organ is a foreign tissue, the body of the patient receiving it reacts against the transplant—just as the body reacts when bacteria or viruses invade the bloodstream. This reaction is sometimes called the *immune response.* The reaction of the body has as its goal the destruction of the transplanted tissue. The immune response is less severe, however, and may even be absent if the donor is a close blood relative of the recipient. Thus, a kidney transplanted to a patient from a brother or sister has a better chance to survive than one transplanted from a distant relative or even a stranger. The most successful "takes" have been between identical twins, and the least successful ones have been between human recipients and animal donors.

Earlier, large doses of X rays were given to the recipient to suppress the rejection of the transplants. More recently, irradiation has been replaced by powerful drugs that have a similar effect but are less harmful to the patient. Drugs can be more carefully regulated in dosage and they are less apt to destroy the body's disease-fighting ability.

The major aims of current research in organ transplants are to make the recipient tolerant toward tissue from unrelated donors and to find ways of using artificial organs to replace diseased human tissue.

There is, however, a special kind of transplant that can usually be done with sure success. This kind of transplant is one that an individual gives to himself. For example, a brown birthmark, called a *nevus,* can be removed from an individual's face and replaced with skin taken from that person's abdomen. The body has a way of recognizing its own tissues and organs and does not reject them when they are moved from one part of the body to another. Such transplants are called *autografts.*

Teacher's Notes

How successful are transplants such as kidney transplants? It has been reported that three out of every four persons receiving kidney transplants from living donors are alive a year after their operations—and less than 5 percent are lost during each of the next two years. Heart-transplant recipients have not fared so well. This low survival rate could be due—in addition to the major factor of the body's rejection of foreign tissue—to patients' poor health *before* their hearts were replaced. Their previous heart disease has often caused damage to such organs as the liver, lungs, and kidneys. A "new" heart cannot bring about good health in such cases.

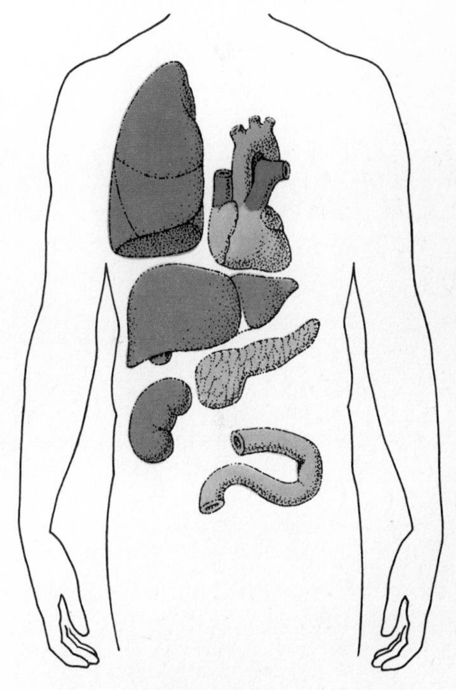

Among the organs that have been transplanted—with varying degrees of success—from one person to another are kidney, lung, liver, heart, pancreas, and sections of the small intestine. In all cases of such transplants, permission has been given to the surgeons. Such permission is given either by patients themselves or by relatives immediately after patients with organs usable for transplants have died.

Teacher's Notes

The following questions might be used as discussion leads:

"What was the medical significance of Roentgen's discovery?"

"What do you think is meant by the term *radioactive?*" (See Glossary.)

"What comparison can you make between the elements *uranium* and *radium?*"

What Progress Has Been Made in the Use of Radiation?

The story behind the use of radiation for medical purposes actually started in 1895, when Wilhelm Konrad Roentgen, a professor at a German university, first reported his discovery of a new kind of ray. The newly discovered rays, he reported, could penetrate the human body and make it possible for doctors to see inside it. Since he did not know what these new rays really were, Roentgen called them "X rays"—X being the unknown quantity.

Use of X Rays

At first, X rays were used to locate bullets from gunshot wounds or to determine whether or not a bone was fractured. Later it was found that X rays could be used to study the heart, lungs, stomach, intestines, and other organs of the body. X rays could be used in this way if patients first were given chemicals that would cause the organs to become visible on X-ray films.

Still later, X rays were found to be useful in treating skin diseases and some cancers. Until atomic radiation, however, X rays were not successful in reaching deep-seated cancers in the body. There was always danger of damage to surrounding healthy tissue.

Radium

A short time after Roentgen's discovery, a French scientist discovered that the element *uranium* was capable of giving off rays similar to X rays. This observation marked the discovery of *radioactivity.*

Then, in 1898, the French scientists Marie and Pierre Curie discovered an element which proved to be a million times more radioactive than uranium. This was the element *radium.*

Radium proved to be of immense value in medicine. Until about 1900, the only known way to treat cancers was by surgery—which is still an important way to treat the disease. But some cancers are so deep in the human body or have spread so rapidly that operations to remove them cannot be performed successfully. After radium was discovered, it was found that the penetrating rays given off by this element could destroy cells. Furthermore, it was found that the rays given off by radium destroyed cancer cells more effectively than normal cells. So ways were found to focus these rays directly on the cancerous cells without reaching the surrounding cells. For example, a tiny amount of radium was placed in a special radium "needle" or tube and inserted in the area of the cancer. In some cases—but by no means in all of them—the cancer was destroyed or its growth was slowed down.

Teacher's Notes

Radioactive isotopes have made it possible for hospitals to afford high-energy radiation therapy. Not only are there economic advantages in the radioactive isotopes, but they also provide a choice of radiation energies. In recent years, radioactive isotopes have proved valuable in diagnosing anemia and a number of other illnesses, in scanning for brain tumors, and in checking the function of various organs of the body.

Atomic Radiation

In 1945, with the bursting of the first atom bomb, the so-called nuclear age began. A wealth of new information on radioactivity gradually became available. Medicine has been able to take great strides forward in the last few decades as a result of new tools and techniques that have had their origin in atomic developments.

One of the first instruments to undergo some changes was the standard X-ray equipment. Synchrotrons, betatrons, and other high-voltage machines were designed by physicists. These machines have been found useful in sending X rays into the deepest parts of the body in the treatment of various kinds of cancers.

Radioactive Isotopes

Atomic scientists also began to make a whole new group of radioactive materials. They put common elements such as cobalt, carbon, gold, phosphorus, iodine, and sodium—which are not naturally radioactive—into the atomic reactor. In the reactor, some of the atoms in these elements capture the nuclear particles that are flying about. In this way *radioactive isotopes* of the elements are formed.

When isotopes are made radioactive, they give off rays similar to the rays given off naturally by radium. For example, Cobalt 60 is a radioactive isotope of the metal cobalt. Cobalt 60 gives off radiations so powerful that their penetration of body tissues is about the same as that of the radiation from a three-million-volt X-ray machine. Cobalt wafers used in a Teletherapy Unit are over three hundred times as radioactive as the same amount of radium. You can see such a Teletherapy Unit at the right.

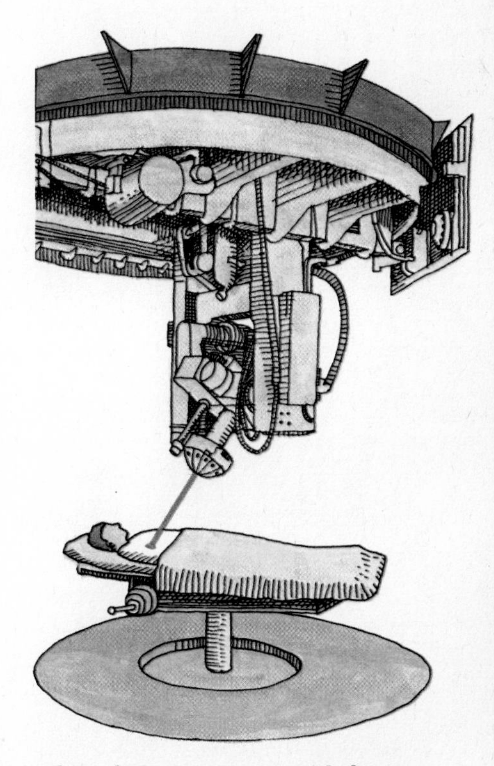

The Cobalt-60 Rotation Teletherapy Unit shown here is an important weapon against some kinds of cancers. Why?

Teacher's Notes

One of the great steps forward in man-made limbs has been the development of an artificial muscle that can relax and contract just as a real muscle can. When this "muscle" is incorporated into an artificial arm and hand, the ability to grasp with thumb and two fingers can be brought about. This ability to grasp makes possible such actions as eating and writing with the hand and arm. See the picture on page 224.

While certain radioactive isotopes, such as Cobalt 60, are very effective in treating some forms of cancer, other radioactive isotopes are used widely as investigative tools, or *tracers.* For example, elements in the food a person eats can be made artificially radioactive. Then Geiger counters and other instruments can be used to trace these radioactive elements wherever they go in the body. By such means, knowledge is being broadened about exactly what happens in foods when they are changed in the body to tissue and energy. In somewhat the same way, doctors are learning about the function of certain organs of the body. If the doctor needs to know the rate at which the thyroid gland stores iodine, for example, he or she gives the patient some radioactive iodine. Then a Geiger counter can measure the rate at which the gland works.

In similar fashion, the course of sugar can be traced through the body by putting radioactive carbon in the sugar molecule. New knowledge that is being gained will increase understanding of diabetes, the disease that results from the body's inability to handle sugar and starch adequately.

Radioactive isotopes also help provide exact information about how various drugs act in the body—how they are used, where they accumulate in the body, and how long they remain active. Such problems were much more difficult to solve before the discovery of radioactive isotopes.

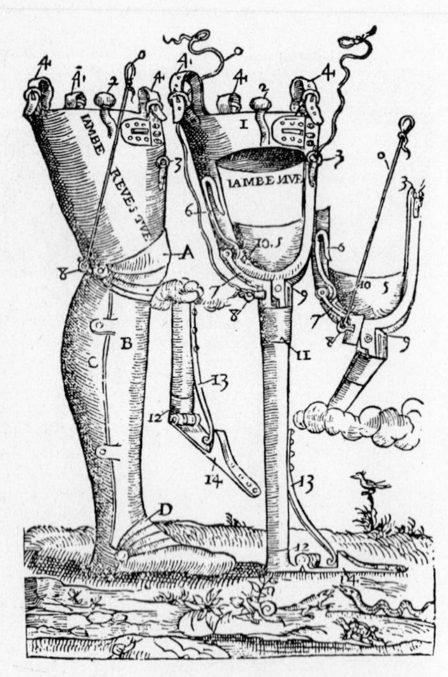

Here are drawings of artificial legs invented by a French surgeon, Ambroise Paré, in the 1500's. Artificial limbs of today are a vast improvement over those of the past. (See photograph of present-day artificial arm on page 224.)

What Progress Has There Been in Developing Mechanical Aids?

In recent years, there has been remarkable progress in developing or improving mechanical devices that can help people overcome such handicaps as poor hearing and loss of limbs.

For example, artificial limbs have changed a great deal since the days of Captain Hook in *Peter Pan* and Long John Silver in *Kidnapped.* Today, artificial legs are made of lightweight plastic instead of wood and metal. Some artificial legs are attached by suction and have knees that bend by means of elastic straps. Some of them work almost as well as real limbs do. On page 224, you will see a man-made arm pictured. Notice the mobility permitted in this artificial arm.

Modern Medical Tools and Research Help Doctors Help Their Patients

Below is a picture, or scan, of a normal brain made by a newly developed color scanner. The scanner moves a radiation-sensitive device back and forth over a patient's head and locates diseased areas, if any.

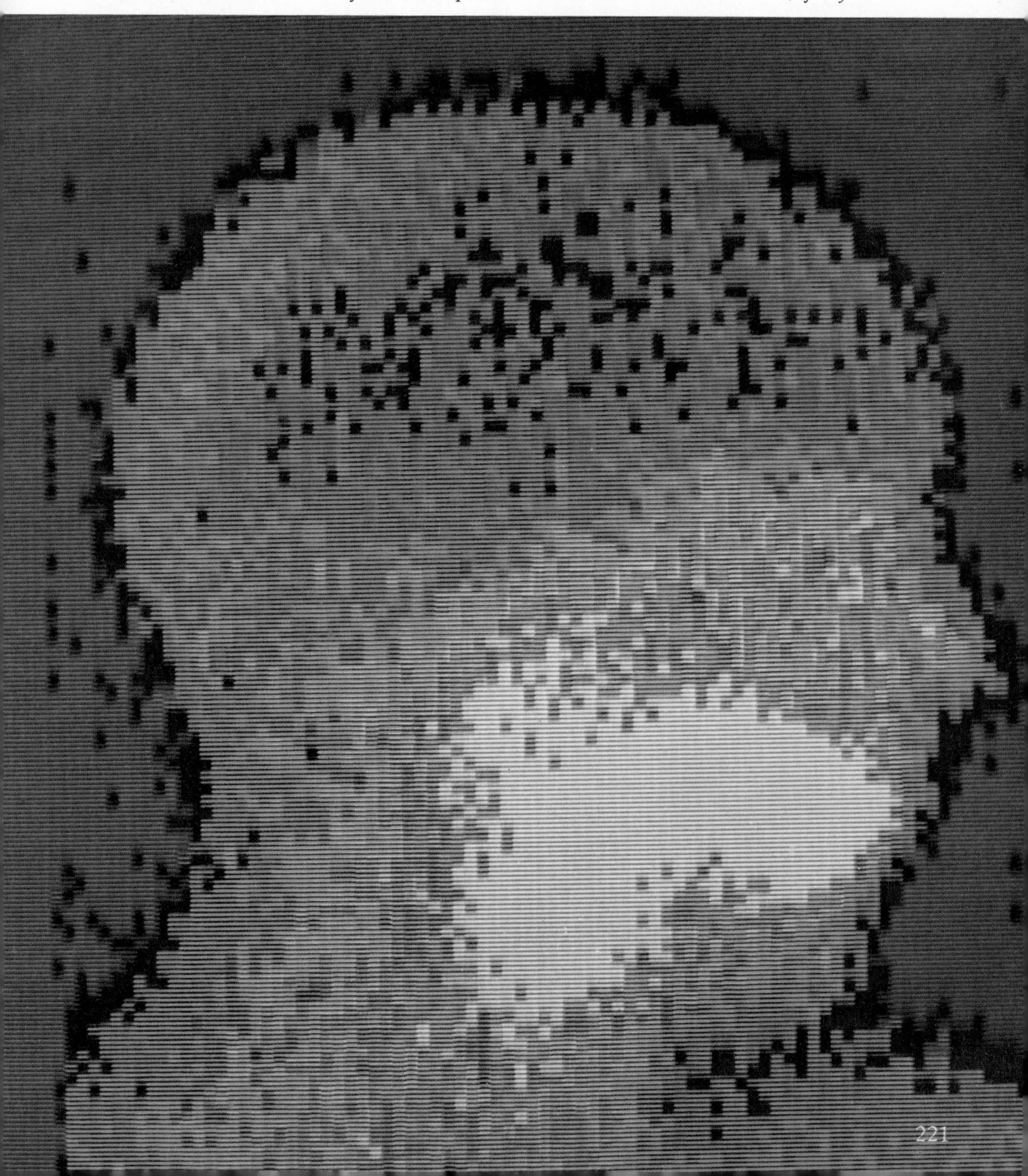

The hemalog, pictured here, is a blood analyzer that can perform one complete blood analysis each minute—with eight or ten different tests made on each blood sample. Results are automatically printed.

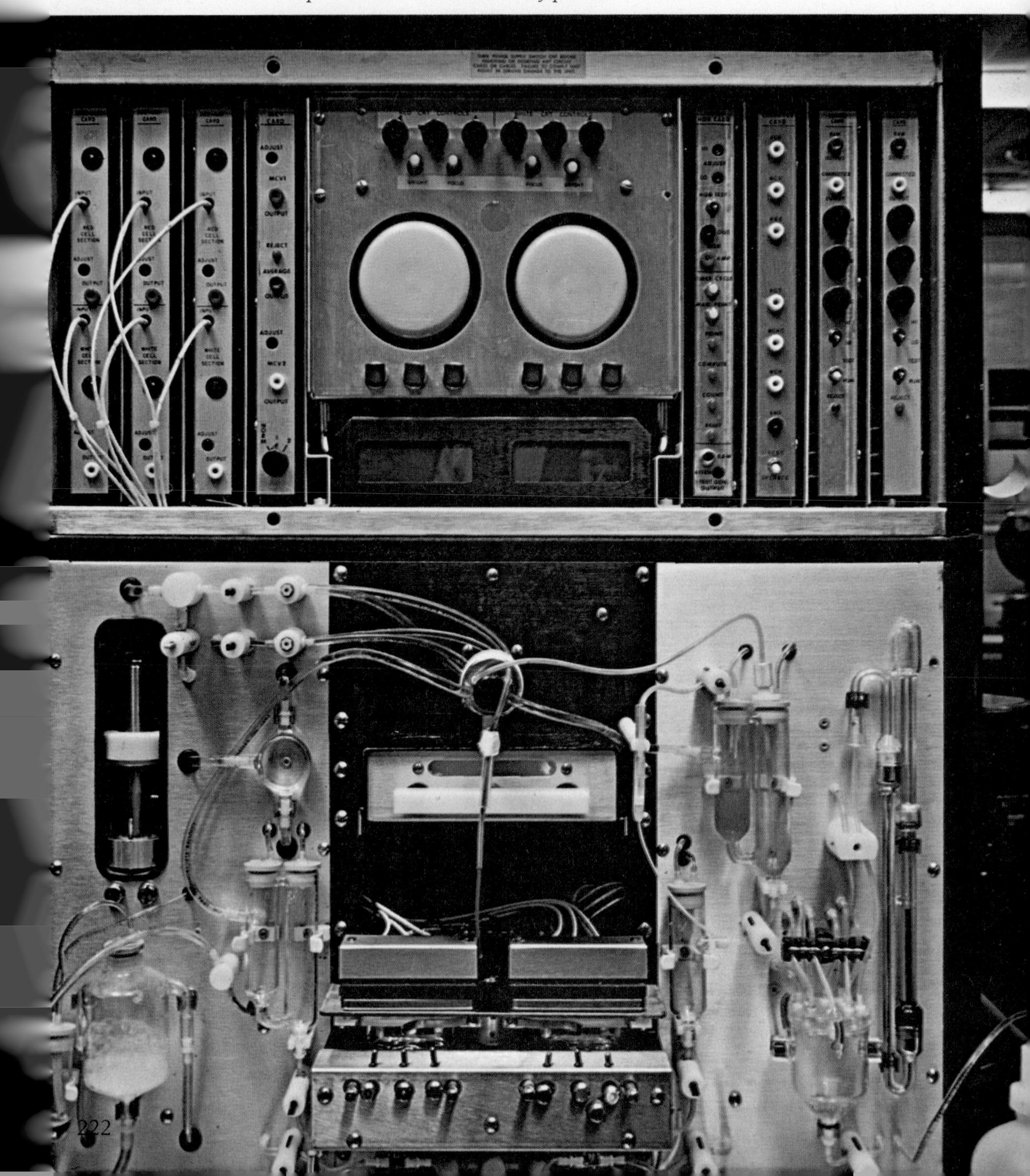

In an intensive-care unit in a modern hospital, special monitors check continuously the blood pressure, pulse, respiration, and so on of critically ill patients. Information about each patient, who is specially wired, is recorded constantly.

Artificial limbs have been greatly improved in recent years. In place of wood and steel, light materials such as plastic and aluminum are used. The artificial hand shown here operates almost like a real one by muscle power from a transistor placed in the wrist.

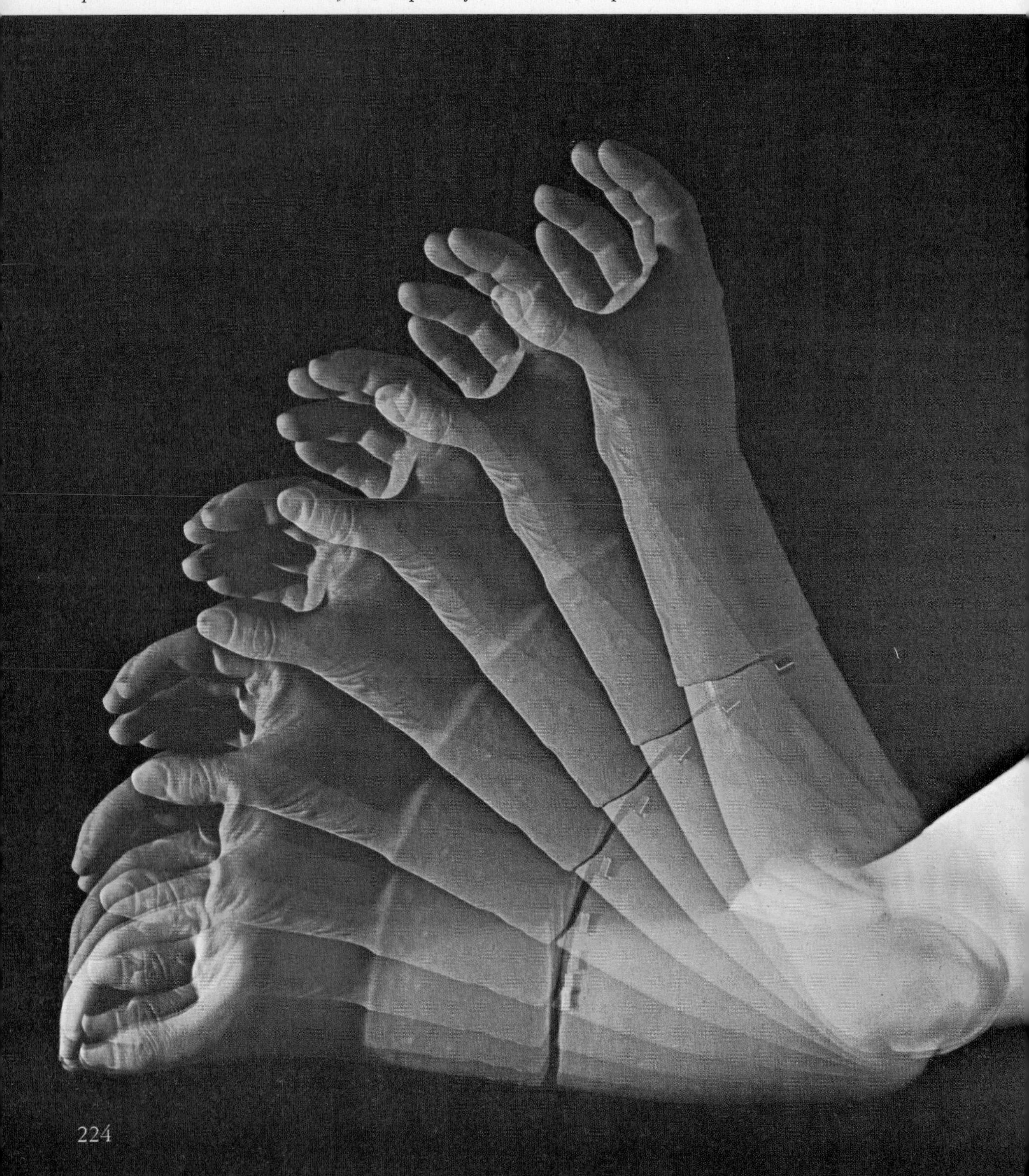

In the picture below you can see, close up, the surgeon replacing a faulty heart valve with an artificial one. Once the artificial valve is sewn in place, it will allow blood to flow only one way—as did the original heart valve.

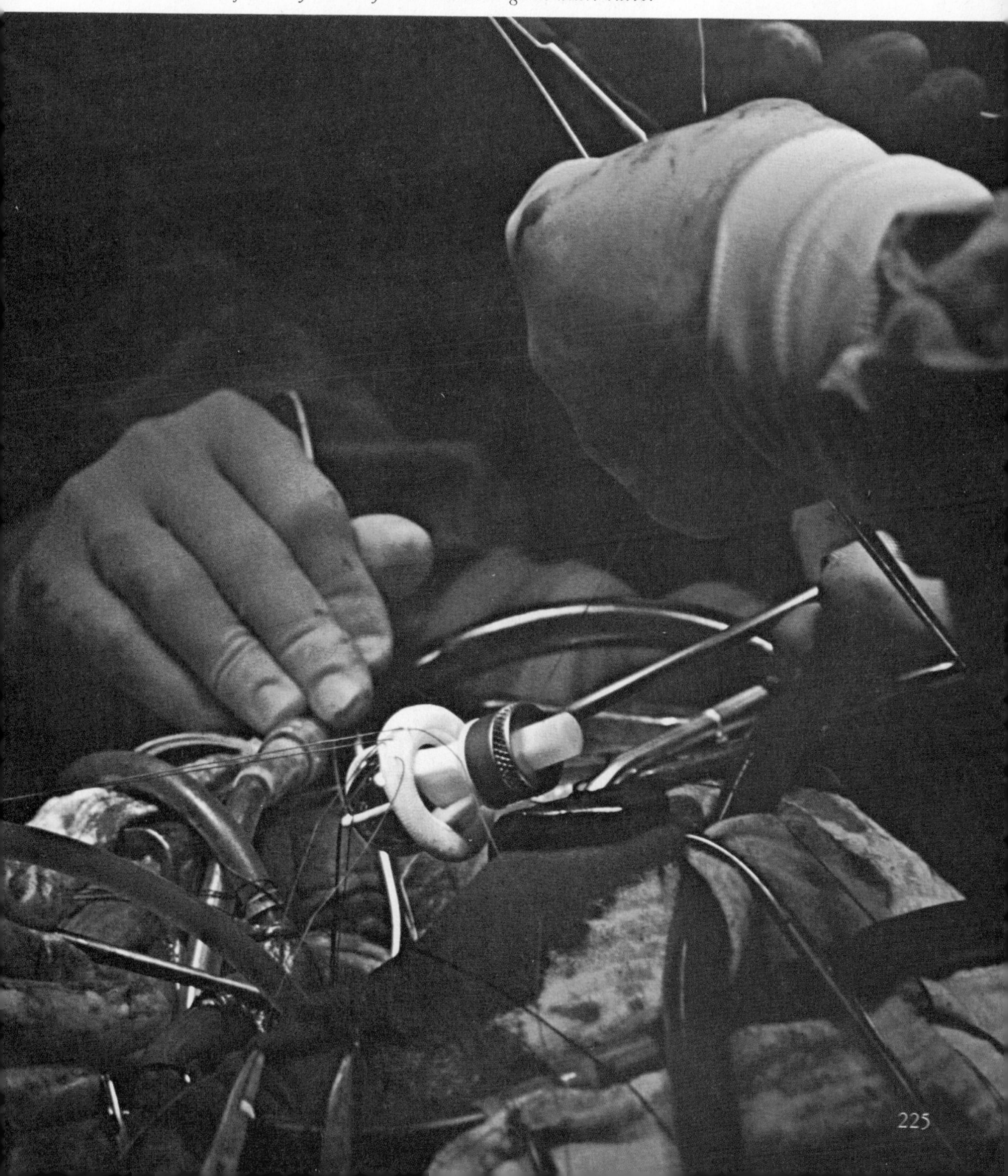

Today, significant research concerns the DNA molecules in a living cell. DNA usually consists of two long chains of atoms linked together and twisted spirally. These two spirals—shown in the DNA model below—control the growth and heredity of the cell.

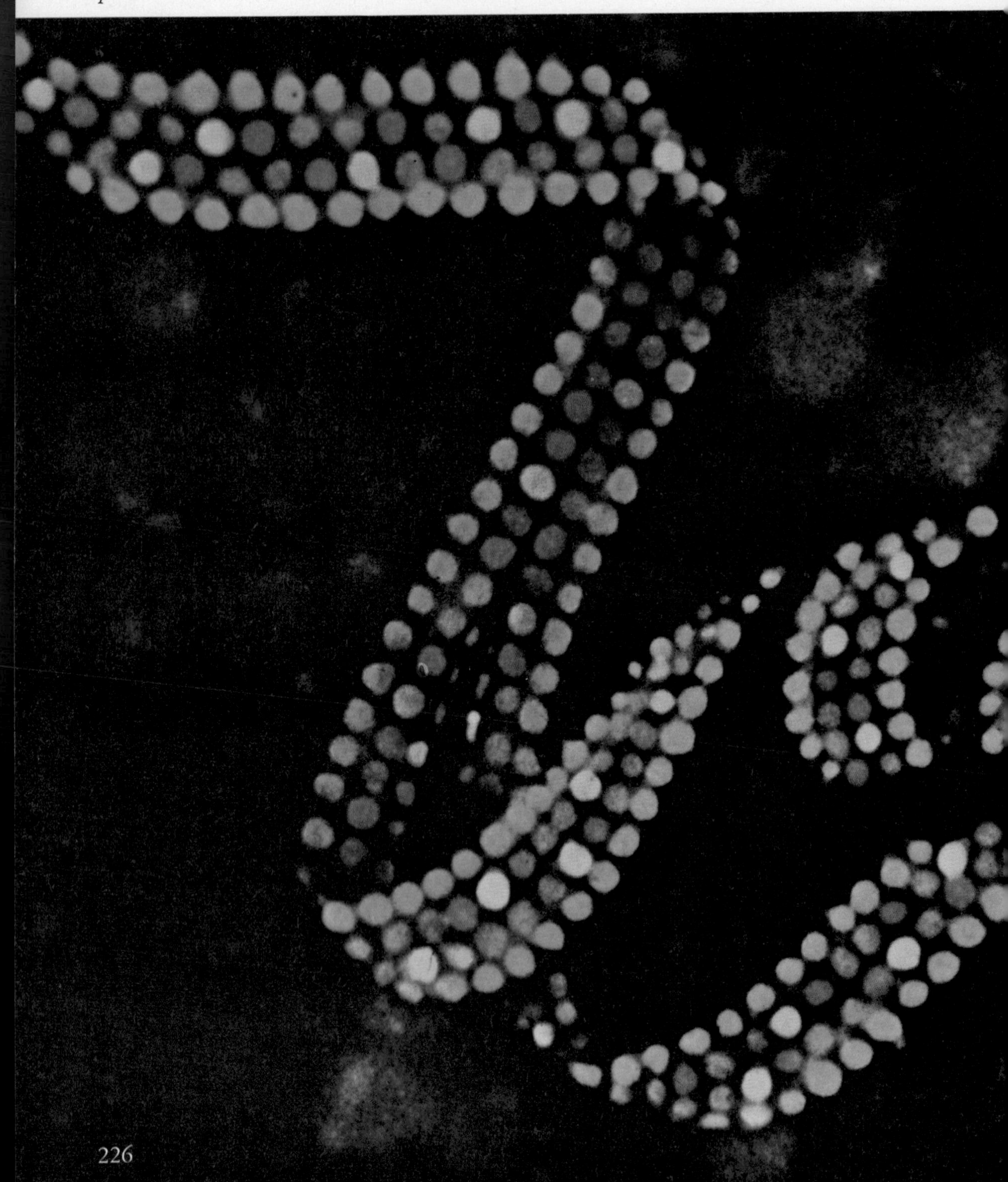

What Progress Has Taken Place in Treating Mental Illness?[1]

Mental illness and *emotional illness* are terms used to describe certain disturbances of the mind that affect the way a person thinks, feels, and behaves. There is a wide range in degree of mental illness. The range extends from the *neuroses,* or less severe personality disorders, to the *psychoses,* or mental disturbances so severe that the patient loses touch with reality for brief or long periods of time. People troubled with a psychosis may be treated in a mental hospital during their illness. Nowadays, however, many of these people are treated as outpatients in community mental-health clinics.

Neuroses

Neuroses vary in severity. People who have a very mild neurosis may go about their everyday activities with a fair amount of success. Some of these people may make very good or even outstanding contributions. Frequently they are not aware that they are neurotic—although they are quite likely to feel fatigued much of the time, anxious, rather unhappy, and somewhat at odds with life.

Some neurotic persons have symptoms that are usually connected with physical illness. The symptoms may include continual headaches, frequent indigestion, or diarrhea. Such physical symptoms are caused by the effect on the autonomic nervous system of constantly recurring emotions such as anger, fear, or worry. These illnesses are known as *psychosomatic illnesses,* and they are usually not caused by physical disorders. As you recall from your study of the digestive system, emotions such as anger, fear, and anxiety can interfere with digestion. If the digestion were disturbed in this way over a period of time, a *physical* disability could result. Sometimes, however, in psychosomatic illnesses, *no* physical disorder occurs at all. The psychosomatic illnesses may be cured by the discovery, and then removal, of their emotional causes.

[1]Adapted from the pamphlet "Some Things You Should Know About Mental and Emotional Illness." National Association for Mental Health. Read for accuracy by the Association and used by permission.

Teacher's Notes

Until this treatment in *Book 8,* the focus in the HEALTH AND GROWTH Program from the earliest levels has been on *mental health.* As children mature, however, their queries about *mental illness* increase.

Before students begin this section, you might have them jot down questions they have on mental illness. Some commonly asked questions by eighth-graders—as reported in the Connecticut Study *Teach Us What We Want to Know* by Ruth Byler, Gertrude Lewis, and Ruth Totman (Mental Health Materials Center)—are these: How can you detect—and prevent—mental illness? Cracking up? Nervous breakdown?

Students' own questions will help you identify misconceptions that may exist about mental illness. For example, some young people confuse mental illness with mental retardation.

Some Things to Do

1. A volunteer might write to the National Association for Mental Health, 1800 North Kent Street, Arlington, Virginia 22209, to ask for a list of available pamphlets on mental illness. Later, pamphlets of interest might be obtained for independent use and as the basis for reports.

2. Check to see if there is a Mental Health Association in your city or county. If so, a volunteer might write to see if a staff member from the association can come to talk to your group.

Teacher's Notes
Discuss with students the fact that everyone at times may feel shy, tense, fearful—or have some other symptom that a person with neurosis has. The important concept to be stressed is in paragraph three: "All of us have some of these symptoms some of the time, but the neurotic person has one or more of them to a great degree most of the time."

The family doctor can often help with a psychosomatic illness. Sometimes, though, the emotional causes may be difficult to discover and the help of a psychiatrist may be needed to bring to light deep-seated anxieties or fears. Once a person can be freed of his emotional conflicts, his physical symptoms, such as recurring headaches, usually go away.

Should the stresses of life become very great, a person with a mild neurosis may develop a more severe form of neurotic illness. In this event, he will most surely require some kind of psychiatric treatment.

Symptoms of neurosis may be indicated by one or a combination of the following: a feeling of being unloved, inferior, inadequate—often without apparent reason; excessive shyness; a constant sense of guilt, dread, and fear; chronic tiredness, nervous tension, or sleeplessness; or various psychosomatic illnesses. All of us have some of these symptoms some of the time, but the neurotic person has one or more of them to a great degree most of the time.

Other forms of neurotic behavior may be evidenced by such symptoms as *phobias,* or excessive fears of certain things—such as high places, enclosed spaces, or a particular kind of animal. A list of phobias is given at the left.

A person whose severe neurosis prevents him from carrying on in his job or in his family life needs to be treated by a medical specialist. Expecting a person to "snap out of it" without such help is as impossible as expecting someone with appendicitis to forget about it. Most deep-seated problems do not just "happen" suddenly. They grow over long periods of time. And it takes time for them to be removed.

Different Types of Phobias

Ophidiophobia	Fear of snakes
Agoraphobia	Fear of open spaces
Claustrophobia	Fear of being enclosed
Acrophobia	Fear of heights
Hydrophobia	Fear of water
Xenophobia	Fear of strangers
Ailurophobia	Fear of cats

For pronunciations, see the Glossary.

Psychoses

Psychoses refer to various forms of severe mental illness. A person who is suffering from a psychosis lives in an imaginary world of his own. He usually recognizes something of what is going on, however; there may even be occasions during the illness when his symptoms disappear completely.

Some ways in which a psychosis may affect a person are these: he may "hear voices," think his food is poisoned, or believe everyone is out to "get" him. He may be either quite depressed or quite excited. He may feel that something terrible is about to happen to him or that he has committed a dreadful crime for which he is being punished. He may imagine he has magical powers or that he is a famous person.

During the time of his illness, the person suffering from a psychosis has little control over what he does; therefore he needs to be cared for and treated.

People who are psychotic are not insensitive, as is often believed. Many suffer intensely; most respond gratefully to kindness and attention.

Only a few persons who are seriously mentally ill become overactive or violent; only a very small percentage are dangerous—most are quiet, unexcited people.

Organic psychoses are those that stem from physical causes. These psychoses can result from an injury to the nervous system, such as damage to the brain. They may also result from the use of poisonous chemicals, from severe alcoholism, or from advanced syphilis. Still other organic psychoses are caused by bodily changes; for example, by cerebral arteriosclerosis, which is more common in old age.

Schizophrenia is the most common of all the psychoses. It is also one of the most puzzling. The term covers a wide variety of disorders. The person suffering from this psychosis may misinterpret reality and may sometimes have delusions and hallucinations. Some scientists believe this disorder is linked to certain unusual chemical processes within the body. Therefore, it is a mental disorder in which medication is frequently used. Other scientists are trying to discover whether schizophrenia can be prevented by protecting people from various harmful experiences in childhood.

A person who suffers from a psychosis benefits from treatment. The earlier the treatment is given, of course, the better is the chance of recovery.

There has been a marked increase recently in the number of psychotic people who do recover. In addition to the improvement of care in mental hospitals, much of the credit belongs to the new, modern treatment services which are becoming increasingly available in the community. These include

Teacher's Notes

In the course of discussing the ideas presented here, talk over the meaning of such terms as these: *organic psychoses, functional psychoses, schizophrenia.*

Do You Know? (A Quiz)

Can you name members of four professions who often work as a team in community mental-health clinics and in mental hospitals to aid persons who are mentally ill? What does each member of the team do?

(Check your answers with those given in the margin on page 230.)

Teacher's Notes

Discuss some types of workers who are specially trained to help people with mental illness.

During discussion, ask:

"What are some helpful attitudes to take if there is mental illness in the family?"

In addition to discussing the kinds of research taking place in the field of mental illness, students might think about some of the pressing problems in this field. One is the problem in some areas of overcrowded facilities available for the care of the mentally ill. There is also the problem of lack of trained personnel in state mental hospitals and in community mental-health clinics. Encourage pupils to be on the alert for newspaper articles, and for radio and TV programs, that tell of special progress and special problems in this area in their own community and state.

Answers to Quiz on Page 229

1. Psychiatrist—*a physician trained in prevention, diagnosis, and treatment of emotional disorders.*

2. Clinical psychologist—*a person with special training in measuring intelligence and assessing personality strengths and weaknesses and in the understanding and modifying of human behavior.*

3. Psychiatric social worker—*a person with special training in understanding family relationships and community problems and in helping people with emotional problems.*

4. Psychiatric nurse—*a nurse with special training in caring for the mentally ill.*

psychiatric services in general hospitals; community mental-health centers which give various kinds of outpatient and inpatient care; and special treatment centers for mentally ill children.

The important thing to remember about mental illness is that it is an illness. And, with proper care and treatment, many mentally ill people can and often do make remarkably successful recoveries.

Widespread Research Today

Research on mental illness is being conducted by scientists in a wide variety of fields. Physiologists and biochemists, for example, are studying the structure and functioning of the brain and nervous system for clues about possible physical causes of mental illness. Psychiatrists and psychologists are continuing to analyze the effects of a person's life experiences on his mental health. Social scientists are trying to learn more about the effects of different environments in producing—or in reducing—tension and strain.

In addition, much research is going on to help improve the various kinds of treatment, such as individual and group psychotherapy, occupational and recreational therapy, and drug therapy. Research in this country and in other countries has resulted in some promising new methods for handling patients in mental hospitals and for giving them follow-up guidance upon their release.

Sometimes a patient may have a relapse and may have to return to the hospital. A return to the hospital can often be avoided, though, if the person has proper follow-up treatment. Understanding and acceptance on the part of his family, friends, and co-workers are important, too, in his recovery.

We all need to understand that anyone can have a bout with mental illness—and that fine, capable people can become seriously mentally ill and yet recover to lead full and productive lives.

In the picture story on pages 231–233, you can see a modern mental-health clinic in action. Young patients are being helped by trained mental-health workers to understand and to solve their problems.

The Community Mental Health Center

A promising development in recent years is the community mental health center—a convenient place where people of all ages can be helped with troublesome problems and feelings.

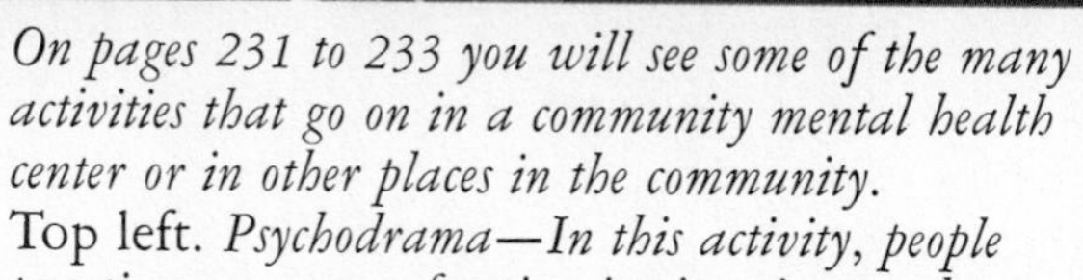

On pages 231 to 233 you will see some of the many activities that go on in a community mental health center or in other places in the community.
Top left. *Psychodrama—In this activity, people practice new ways of acting in situations so they will feel more comfortable in the future.*
Top right. *Parents receive guidance about situations that are new or worrisome to them.*
Bottom left. *Many chances are given for activity therapy—in which people can express themselves and learn new interests and skills.*
Bottom right. *Opportunities to talk things over with someone who understands are available.*

Not all activities take place at the community mental health center. Frequently, people who come for help are directed to special individuals or groups in the community which provide guidance or treatment.

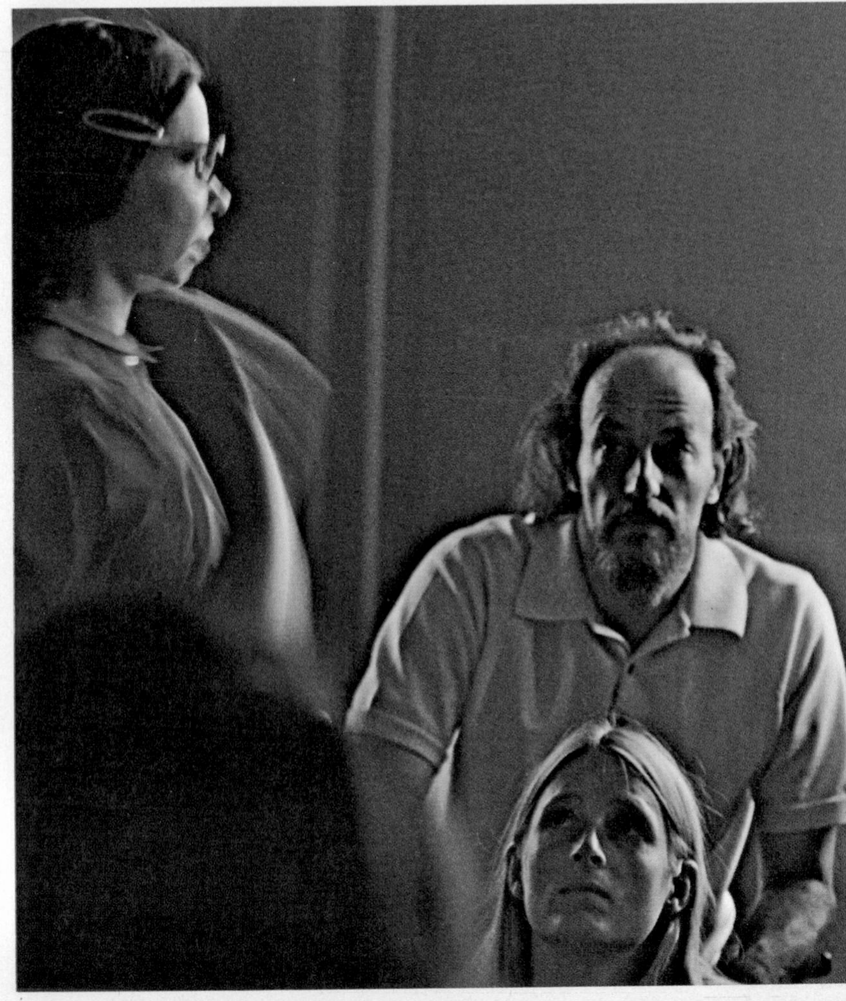

Counseling or therapy of different kinds may take place in a large modern clinic, in a church group, in a school, or in some other place—depending on the resources of the community.

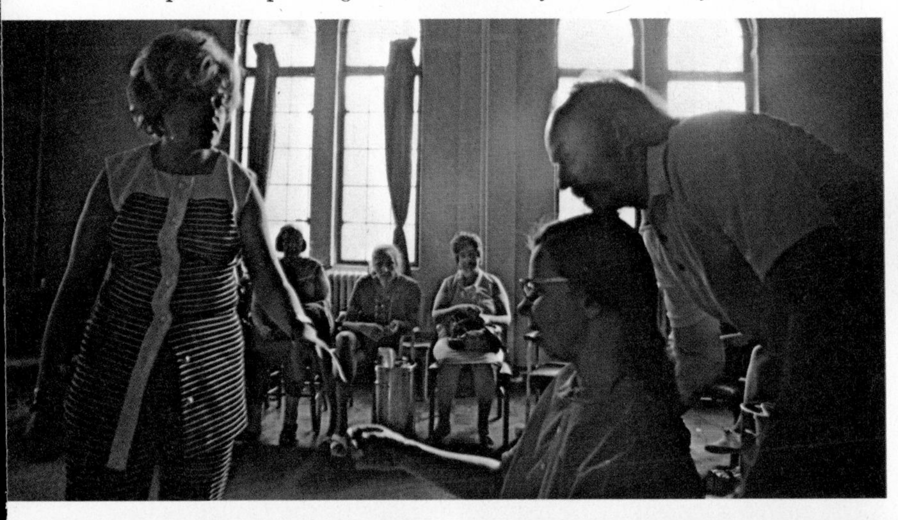

A person, for example, might talk over his problems with a therapist in the privacy of his office. Later meetings might include discussions with all of the patient's family members.

Often in a community there is an opportunity to be a member of a group in which all members share the same concerns and problems. The group may take part in psychodramas, engage in activity therapy of various kinds, or have group discussions about mutual concerns.

Prompt help provided by a mental health center often prevents severe mental health problems from developing.

People who come to a mental health clinic with severe problems, however, may be advised that they need hospitalization. With the many types of treatment that are now available, the chances for recovery are good.

Teacher's Notes

The subject of mental retardation is one that holds considerable interest for young people. It is also a subject about which many erroneous ideas are held. To help you spot erroneous ideas, you might use this procedure:
1. Have pupils jot down their questions about this topic *before* they read pages 234-236.
2. As the various subsections are considered, have them read aloud and thoroughly discussed.

What Progress Is Being Made in Treating Mental Retardation?[1]

What is meant by the term *mentally retarded?* This is a term used to describe individuals who are limited in their ability to learn. The term mental retardation should not be confused with mental illness.

Mental retardation ranges from profound conditions to mild ones. At one end of the scale are the relatively few individuals handicapped to the point of total helplessness. At the other end of the scale are those who underachieve in a regular school program but are capable of learning to become independent adults, able to work and assume family responsibilities. In the chart at the right on page 235 you can see an estimated distribution of retarded persons in the United States. The chart shows the degree of mental retardation.

Some retarded persons are placed in special institutions for the mentally handicapped. However, the vast majority live at home or independently in the community. It is now recognized that even those few with severe handicaps—if they are given adequate opportunities in childhood—can make considerable progress. They can lead happy and purposeful lives in a sheltered environment.

Mentally retarded children may be born to brilliant parents as well as to average ones, to highly educated parents and to the not-so-highly educated, to wealthy families and to poor ones. They are born to parents of every race, religion, and nationality. There should be no blame or disgrace attached to mental retardation. It is a developmental disability like cerebral palsy or epilepsy and should be accepted as such.

Did You Know?

With proper care, twenty-five out of thirty retarded children can learn how to read simple material, write, and do basic arithmetic. Some of these children may need to be enrolled in special classes with teachers trained to meet their particular needs. Others may get along in regular classrooms if they are permitted to move along at their own pace.

Causes of Mental Retardation

Although more than two hundred causes of mental retardation have been identified, and others are suspected, no clear determination of cause can be made in 75 to 85 percent of the identified cases of mental retardation.

[1]Much of this material has been adapted by permission from pamphlets published by the National Association for Retarded Children. The material has been reviewed for accuracy by the staff of the Association.

Some children are born with malformations of the brain due to hereditary factors. Other children have mental retardation because of an injury to the brain that occurs either at birth or later in life.

Glandular imbalance may prevent normal growth of the nervous system in some instances. So, too, can the lack of certain chemicals in the blood which prevents a child's tissues from using food normally.

Some conditions that affect a mother during her pregnancy, such as German measles (rubella) or glandular disorders, may result in a child's being born retarded. Retardation due to inherited or metabolic defects, diseases, injuries at birth, or brain injuries from accidents later in life generally cannot be reversed.

In much of the world, malnutrition is thought to be a common cause of poor mental functioning. Studies with animals have indicated that severe malnutrition in infancy (though not in adult life) causes changes in the chemical make-up of the brain. It seems likely that in the developing human infant, malnutrition over long periods of time can also result in changes in brain chemistry.

Increasingly, too, it is believed that mild cases of mental retardation occur in populations that are poor, malnourished, and sick. In such situations, parents are often unable to provide their children with interesting things to do, with toys and activities that stimulate their minds and their use of language. Such children are to be found in all societies; they are particularly apt to be found in areas that are devastated by war or areas in which health-education services and opportunities for education itself are poor or do not exist. A term that is used to describe mild retardation of this kind is "environmental deprivation."

Mild retardation due to environmental deprivation can often be reversed. Children can be rehabilitated by such means as stimulating preschool programs and projects, adequate food, and proper housing. Follow-up studies of children with mild mental retardation show that most of them become independent and useful citizens.

Teacher's Notes

Talk over some of the many causes of mental retardation—conditions that arise in the mother's pregnancy (like German measles), poor nutrition, brain injury at birth, injury and disease suffered in early infancy, a brain-damaging hereditary disease, and so on. Discuss, too, current ideas about causes of a mild kind of retardation known as "environmental deprivation." What can help eliminate such deprivation? (Attempts on the part of society to see that families are properly fed and housed; that parents are helped to raise healthy, active, curious children; that stimulating preschool or day-care centers are available; and so on.)

Of all those in the United States who are mentally retarded (6.1 million, or 3 percent of the population), the degree of retardation varies widely. What percent of mentally retarded people are classified as "mild"?

Adaptation of "Estimated Distribution of Retardates in the United States" from *Facts on Mental Retardation,* 1971. Reprinted by permission of the National Association for Retarded Children.

Teacher's Notes

Students may want to consider the often-asked question reported in the Connecticut Study *Teach Us What We Want to Know* (Mental Health Materials Center): "Why do children make fun of mentally retarded people?" (As a result of their study, pupils may have come to realize that those who make fun of the mentally retarded lack information on this subject. Such people also may not understand the causes of mental retardation; or they may not know how much can and is being done to enable many of the mentally retarded to become useful citizens. Sensitive, fair-minded, knowledgeable people do not ridicule those who are handicapped—whether the handicap be one of poor hearing, inadequate vision, mental retardation, poor muscular coordination or paralysis, speech problems, or a combination of handicaps.)

Some Things to Do

1. You may want to read the book called Don't Take Teddy *by Babbis Friis-Baastad (Scribner). This book describes the attempts of Mikkel to protect an older, retarded brother. Look for the book in the school or public library.*

2. A member of the group might write to the National Association for Retarded Children, 2709 Avenue E East, Arlington, Texas 76011, and ask for individual copies of available pamphlets on the subject of mental retardation.

It is important to remember that mentally retarded children and adults resemble normal persons more than they differ from them. Like everyone else, the mentally retarded need love, understanding, and acceptance. They need, too, an opportunity to grow and develop to the very best of their potential intelligence and abilities.

All except the most severely retarded *can* develop, but this development is at different rates and to different degrees. Scientists today are working to learn more about the retarded mind. They want to know the full extent of growth that mentally retarded persons can achieve when they receive a maximum amount of help.

Preventing Mental Retardation

At the present time, information is available that can help prevent retardation stemming from certain causes. Thus, some cases of mental retardation due to lack of certain blood chemicals can be prevented by special diets. Then, too, disorders in body chemistry—such as the one known as PKU (phenylketonuria)—can now be diagnosed in newborn infants. Steps can be taken, when it is diagnosed early enough, to eliminate the condition before it affects the brain.

Through surgery, a condition causing pressure on the brain, and known as "water on the brain," or *hydrocephalus,* can sometimes be prevented or minimized.

Blood transfusions at birth can check the danger which threatens the child born of parents who have incompatible blood types. Thus, all expectant mothers should be tested for the RH factor early in pregnancy.

Immunization against German measles is now available and urged for women in child-bearing years who have not had this disease. How will such immunization help?

The antibiotics now available can be used to control the high fever formerly associated with many children's diseases. Controlling high temperatures in these diseases can prevent mental retardation caused by injury to the nervous system.

It is believed that research will soon be forthcoming that will gradually provide the know-how to prevent retardation in an increasing number of cases.

Teacher's Notes

Check Yourself: After students have read and thought about these questions, use them as guides for a summary discussion.

Things to Do and *Special Research:* Pupils who so desire may wish to make independent studies on advances in medicine. Someone, for instance, might investigate a substance known as *interferon* which is manufactured by the body itself. Some studies have shown that if the body can be stimulated at times to produce interferon, a means may be at hand to help fight influenza and the common cold.

Check Yourself

1. Look back at the questions on page 198. How would you answer them now?

2. Explain the following terms:

a. immunity to a disease

b. anesthesia

c. antisepsis

d. asepsis

e. mental retardation

3. Why do many diabetics take insulin?

4. Why are radioactive isotopes valuable medical tools?

5. What steps are taken to protect the public from harmful or ineffective drugs?

6. Why are streptococcus infections not so deadly as they were before the 1930's?

7. What do you think is meant by the slogan, "The mentally ill can come back"?

8. What protects the human body from invaders such as bacteria and viruses?

9. What communicable diseases can be prevented by immunization?

10. What important medical work do you associate with each of these scientists?

a. Jenner | e. Roentgen
b. Lister | f. Ehrlich
c. Fleming | g. W. G. T. Morton
d. Banting and Best | h. the Curies

Things to Do

1. Bring in clippings for the bulletin board about recent medical advances.

2. Prepare a report on one of these unsolved medical problems:

a. cancer | c. heart diseases
b. cerebral palsy | d. muscular dystrophy

3. Report to the group about some of the pioneers in heart surgery—pioneers such as the young Black surgeon Daniel Williams. One helpful book on this subject is *The Heart Explorers* by Tony Simon (Basic Books).

4. Make a report on a promising new family of chemical compounds called *prostoglandins.*

Special Research

Investigate available kinds of health careers. One book you may want to read is *Horizons Unlimited: A Handbook Describing Rewarding Career Opportunities in Medicine and Allied Fields* (American Medical Association).

Another booklet of interest is *Jobs in Health,* No. 5-963 (Science Research).

Look, too, at the sampling of medical careers described on page 238. Notice that there are careers for medical helpers of many different talents and many differing amounts of training and education.

Professional Registered Nurse	*Training:* High-school graduate. Two years in junior college nursing course, or three years in hospital school of nursing, or four to five years in college or university with nursing major.
Nurse's Aide (or Orderly, if Male)	*Training:* No definite educational requirements, although high-school diploma preferred. One to three months on-the-job training in a hospital. Minimum age: seventeen years.
Medical Assistant	*Training:* High-school graduate. Some college is desirable, but not necessary; secretarial skills often required.
Radiologic Technologist	*Training:* High-school graduate. Two years in X-ray school or four years of college for degree in radiologic program.
Doctor, General Practitioner	*Training:* High-school graduate. Four years of college. Four years of medical school. One year internship.
Practical Nurse	*Training:* High-school graduation often required but some hospitals will admit with less training. One year in school of practical nursing, sponsored by a hospital, community agency, or junior college.
Medical Technologist	*Training:* High-school graduate. Three years of college and one year in an approved school of technology.
Dental Hygienist	*Training:* High-school graduate. A two- or three-year college program which awards certificate or associate degree; or a four-year college program.

Teacher's Notes

Pupils may work independently on this review of the unit. Encourage them to reread material in the text when necessary. Tell pupils that any sensible answer which completes the sentence correctly can be considered a "right answer."

Self-Help Review

Use a ruler or a strip of paper to cover the answer column at the right. Read the first item and write the missing word or words on a piece of paper. Then move your ruler or paper strip down to uncover the answer and see if you are right. Go on in the same way with each of the other items. Do not write in this book.

The numbers by the answers show the pages in this book that give information about the subject. For the items you miss, go back and review this information.

1. Protection against harmful or ineffective drugs is given to the public by the ______ and ______ Administration.	Food, Drug 201
2. The drugs insulin, cortisone, and ACTH are known as ______ drugs.	hormone 202
3. To fight each kind of infectious microorganism that enters it, the body produces a special kind of ______.	antibody 205
4. Some vaccines are made from live microorganisms whose disease-producing ability has been eliminated or greatly ______.	weakened 206
5. The body's reaction to a transplant of foreign tissue is sometimes called the ______ *response.*	immune 217
6. Cobalt 60 is one of the medical tracers known as radioactive ______.	isotopes 219
7. Two forms of mental illness are called neuroses and ______.	psychoses 227
8. Excessive fears of things such as high places are known as ______.	phobias 228

Teacher's Notes

After pupils have taken the test and their papers have been scored, the test items can serve as guides for summary discussion.

Health Test for Unit Seven

Copy the number of each sentence below. After it, write T if the statement is *True;* write F if the statement is *False.*

T 1. At least one form of surgery was known about and practiced in ancient times.

F 2. Before anesthesia, surgeons took long periods of time to perform operations.

T 3. In many cases, the human body rejects tissue from another body.

T 4. Corneas of the eyes can be transplanted.

F 5. Joseph Lister is known for his pioneer work with insulin.

T 6. Penicillin is a useful drug made from a type of mold.

F 7. Anybody can make and market a drug.

T 8. Insulin, cortisone, and ACTH can all be artificially produced in the laboratory.

T 9. Diabetics are people whose bodies cannot make proper use of sugars and starches.

T10. Antibodies are substances manufactured in the body to kill germs that enter it.

T11. Vaccines have been developed against smallpox, polio, measles, and German measles.

T12. Developments in atomic medicine have led to some effective treatments of cancer.

F13. One kind of germ causes every known type of communicable disease.

T14. Cobalt 60 is a radioactive isotope.

T15. The word asepsis means "absence of infection."

F16. A bronchoscope is an instrument used for examining the eyes.

F17. A pacemaker is a medical device that is used to see how fast patients can jog.

F18. Today the average life span of people in the United States is about fifty years.

T19. A "light knife," or laser, is an instrument that produces a light beam so powerful that it can cut through human tissue.

T20. It is possible to replace parts of human arteries with sections made from plastic.

F21. The brain has successfully been transplanted from the body of one human being to that of another.

T22. Mental illness is a term used to describe disturbances that affect how a person thinks, feels, and behaves.

T23. Mentally ill people can recover.

F24. The greatest years for medical progress were those from 1600 to 1700.

T25. An eye surgeon works in the field of medicine called ophthalmology.

Number of Answers	25
Number Right	______
Score (Number Right × 4)	______

8 What Progress Has Been Made In Public and World Health?

Teacher's Notes

Unit Overview: Use the message here to start a preliminary conversation about public health and the need for attention to it. During the study of the unit, remind students to refer to the Glossary for pronunciation of specialized health words and for enriching information about these words.

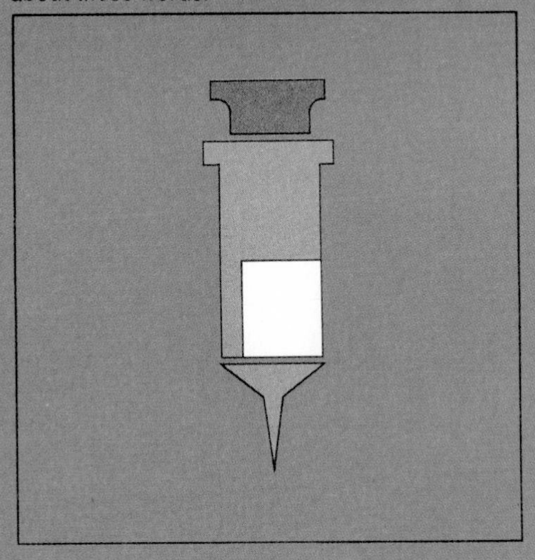

From the very earliest times, communities have tried to deal with the health problems that arise when people live in groups. Such problems include maintaining a safe and sanitary environment, controlling communicable diseases, disposing of wastes, seeing that food and water are safe for use, and supplying medical care. These are all *public health* problems. The individual in the community cannot solve them by himself; they require group action. In this unit you will learn about some of these public health problems and about scientific progress that is helping solve them. Other public health problems will be considered in Unit Nine.

Teacher's Notes

Read to Find Out: These questions stimulate interest in the main topics to be treated in the unit. Discuss them briefly—just long enough to give students a chance to commit themselves to some answers. Such commitment can be a factor in holding pupils' attention during the study of the unit. Boys and girls will want to check the accuracy of the tentative answers they have proposed.

What Was Known About Public Health in Past Times? Discuss evidences of attention to public health in ancient times—and the basic reason why, despite such attention, communicable diseases were so prevalent.

Read to Find Out

1. *What evidence is there that the early Greeks and Romans were concerned about public health problems?*

2. *What were some causes of public health problems during the Middle Ages? What steps did the people take to fight disease?*

3. *What were the contributions of each of these men in developing a scientific approach to the war against communicable disease:* Leeuwenhoek, Jenner, Pasteur, Koch?

4. *What are some* official *agencies in the United States that are concerned with keeping the public healthy? Some unofficial, or* voluntary, *agencies? Some* professional *agencies?*

5. *What are some contributions that each of these organizations makes to world health:* WHO, UNICEF, FAO?

What Was Known About Public Health In Past Times?

Ancient Greece and Rome were among the early civilizations to pay attention to matters of public health. At the time of Hippocrates, about 400 B.C., Greek physicians began to note that there was a relationship between disease and such conditions in the environment as impure water and spoiled food.

The ancient Romans used some of the ideas about public health that they had learned from the Greeks. In addition, the Romans used their engineering talents to build aqueducts—which brought pure water from distant mountains to the towns—and to construct sewerage systems. Today, visitors to countries that were once Roman provinces can see the remains of these early aqueducts and sewers. (See the picture at the left.)

Ruins of the Pont du Gard, an old Roman aqueduct, may still be seen near Nimes, France. What was the purpose of an aqueduct?

Despite the various efforts of the ancient Greeks and Romans to improve public health, communicable diseases still took a tragic number of lives. Even the wisest doctors did not know what caused such diseases and how these diseases spread. Therefore they did not know how to control them.

Public Health in the Middle Ages

In the Middle Ages, public health problems increased for many different reasons. The Crusaders, for example, took communicable diseases with them as they traveled. Many cities came into being, and people were crowded together within the city walls to protect themselves against enemies. It was not uncommon for people in the cities to shelter all sorts of animals in their homes. They also threw dead animals, garbage, and human wastes into the streets, rivers, and streams.

Like the ancient Greeks and Romans, many people in the Middle Ages believed there was some connection between filth and disease. So special officers were appointed to deal with sanitary problems. These officers issued rules, threats, and appeals to end such practices as throwing refuse into streets and rivers. In many instances these appeals were ignored because the community was not convinced of their importance.

The people of the Middle Ages were beset by diseases. Two great epidemics of bubonic plague swept through Europe in this period (A.D. 500-1450). Between the plague epidemics came outbreaks of other diseases such as smallpox, measles, diphtheria, typhoid fever, and tuberculosis.

Gradually people realized that well persons became sick just by being in contact with sick persons. *Why* this occurred, they did not know. But they did begin to fight communicable diseases by passing community laws to isolate the sick. For example, laws were passed that required people with the plague to be locked in their houses. People who had any contact with the sick carried white sticks when they went out into the streets. Ships arriving from ports where an epidemic was present were required to anchor in the harbor for forty days without contact with the people on shore. Laws like these form the basis for our present quarantine laws.

Public Health and the New Science of Bacteriology

In 1676, an event took place that foreshadowed the beginning of the scientific approach to control of communicable disease. In that year, a Dutchman named Antony van Leeuwenhoek, while pursuing his hobby of viewing things under a microscope, first observed bacteria and other microorganisms.

Teacher's Notes

Questions such as these might be used as discussion-starters:

"What were health conditions like in the Middle Ages?"

"Who *were* the Crusaders?" (Men who took part in religious military expeditions between 1096 and 1272 to recover the Holy Land from the Mohammedans.)

"What did the Crusaders have to do with communicable diseases?"

"What attempts were made in the Middle Ages to improve public health? Why were these efforts largely unsuccessful?"

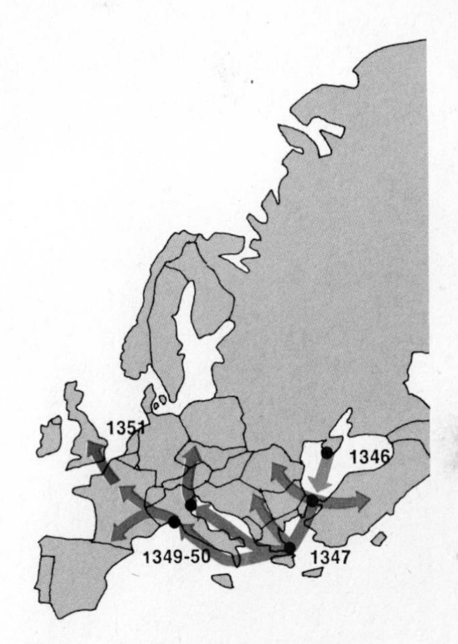

This map of Europe shows the spread of the Great Plague of the fourteenth century.

Teacher's Notes

Discuss the role of each of these "health heroes" in the battle to conquer communicable diseases: Leeuwenhoek, Jenner, Pasteur, Koch. Have students summarize, in particular, the basic understandings about communicable diseases that were contributed by Pasteur.

Many years were to pass, however, before scientists discovered the connection between Leeuwenhoek's microscopic organisms and the spread of disease.

In 1796, a very significant advance was made when Dr. Edward Jenner discovered a way to vaccinate people against smallpox. This was a step forward in bringing this dread disease under control.

The years from 1860 to 1895 were productive ones in lifting the cloud of mystery that had made it difficult to fight communicable diseases. During this period the French scientist Louis Pasteur contributed the important *germ theory* of communicable disease. He also added such basic understandings as these: *Each kind of communicable disease is caused by a special kind of germ which enters the body from the outside. When living germs get into the body, the warmth, food, and moisture there aid their growth. As the germs eat and live in the body, they throw off poisons. It is these poisons that cause a person to feel sick when he has a communicable disease.* As a result of his many experiments, Pasteur was also able to prove that vaccination could provide immunity to certain diseases.

In another country, about the same time, the German scientist Robert Koch was carrying out studies that confirmed Pasteur's ideas. Koch proved, too, that a specific germ causes a specific disease. For instance, one kind of germ causes tuberculosis and *only* tuberculosis. And it was Koch who first made the breakthrough to identify the germ causing tuberculosis. Until this discovery, doctors had no idea about the cause of tuberculosis, even though in the 1880's it was killing one out of every seven people. (You can see a picture of the tuberculosis germ at the left.)

Koch also developed methods of growing disease germs in the laboratory and then staining them so that they would be clearly visible under a microscope. In the pictures on page 246, you can see several photographs of slides on which stained disease germs have been placed.

Pasteur and Koch contributed a wealth of new knowledge that added much to the understanding of bacteria. These men are often called pioneers in the science of *bacteriology.*

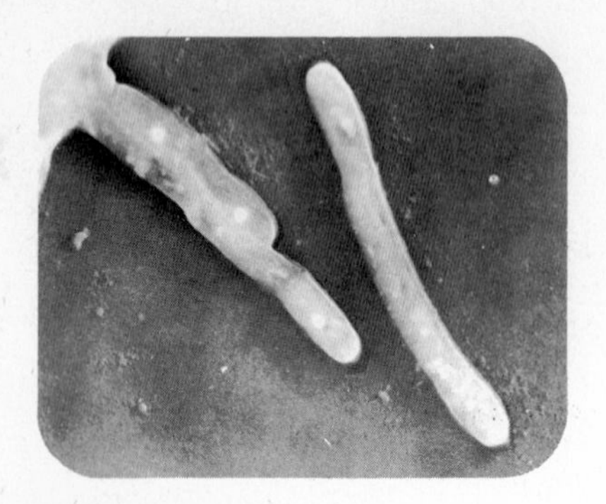

Some tuberculosis bacteria

What About Public Health Today?

In the years after Pasteur and Koch, many scientists became active in the field of bacteriology and in the field of *immunology,* the study of immunity to diseases. The specific organisms that cause diseases such as cholera, typhus, bubonic plague, diphtheria, yellow fever, tuberculosis, typhoid fever, measles, German measles, influenza, and polio were identified.

At the present time it is possible to immunize people against a great variety of communicable diseases. (See the Immunization Chart on page 208.)

Scientists have also unlocked the mystery of how disease germs are spread. The chart on page 246 summarizes some of this basic information. What *are* some ways in which disease-producing germs can be passed from person to person? After scientists learned how disease germs are spread, they could devise increasingly effective methods to prevent this spreading. In addition, public understanding grew concerning the importance of pure food, milk, and water; proper waste disposal; and control of animals and insects that transmit diseases.

Public Health in the United States

In the United States today there are various kinds of health agencies that are concerned with keeping people healthy. Some of these agencies are *official,* some are *professional,* and still others are *voluntary.*

The official agencies are those supported by the Federal, state, and local governments. The professional organizations, such as the American Medical Association, the American Dental Association, and the American Public Health Association, are supported by dues of members. The voluntary agencies are supported through donations by the public.

Some Responsibilities of the Federal Government

The Federal government in the United States is concerned with preventing the importing of disease from abroad, preventing the spread of disease from state to state, promoting the health of the nation as a whole, and working with other nations to help bring about better health for people throughout the world.

Teacher's Notes

Such questions as the following might be used as conversation-starters:

"What is meant by *bacteriology? Immunology?*"

"What had to precede the making of a vaccine to immunize people against a given disease such as smallpox?" (The specific germ that causes the disease had to be discovered.)

"What are some effective methods of protecting the public against impure milk?" (Pasteurization, sanitary methods of handling and storing.) "Against impure food?" (Sanitary handling and storing, safe canning, freezing, and other ways of preserving foods.) "Against impure water?" (Treatment by mechanical methods and chemicals at water-treatment plants.)

"What are some kinds of agencies that promote public health in the United States?"

Have students study page 246. Then discuss with them what each of the following might have to do with the spread of disease: flies, towels, cups, air, food, water, mosquitoes, "missed cases," human carriers, cows.

Something to Do

Start now to investigate careers in the field of public health. Volunteers might write to the following sources for information:

American Public Health Association, 1015 Eighteenth Street, N.W., Washington, D.C. 20036.

U.S. Public Health Service, Public Inquiries Branch, Office of Information, Washington, D.C. 20025.

How Communicable Diseases Are Spread

Chickenpox

By direct contact or indirect contact (through towels, cups, and so on) with persons who have the disease. Discharges from bowels, kidneys, nose, or mouth of sick persons may carry disease-producing bacteria and viruses.

Cholera

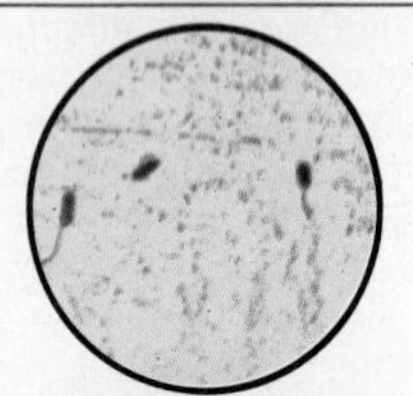

By contaminated drinking water or by contaminated water in swimming places. Contaminated water causes such diseases as typhoid fever, dysentery, and cholera.

Influenza

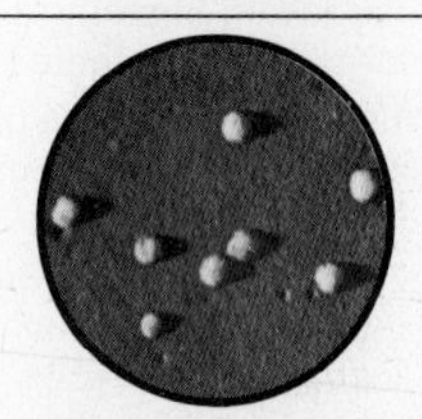

By airborne infection. Infectious droplets sneezed or coughed into the air carry contagious disease germs. Such viral diseases as colds, influenza, and other respiratory diseases can be transmitted in this way.

Diphtheria

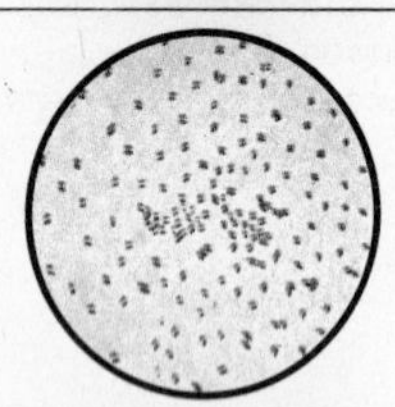

By contaminated food. Such diseases as tuberculosis, scarlet fever, diphtheria, and septic sore throat are spread by the use of contaminated milk and other foods.

Malaria

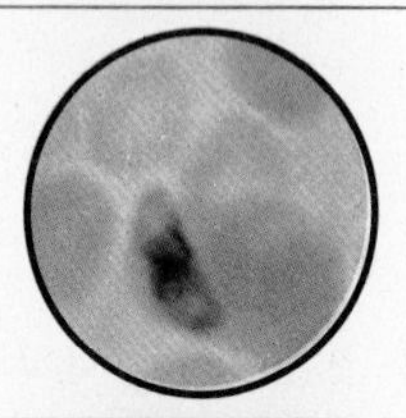

By animals, including insects. Diseased cows spread tuberculosis and undulant fever. Rat fleas may spread plague; rabbits, tularemia; flies, typhoid fever and dysentery; mosquitoes, malaria and yellow fever; lice and rat fleas, typhus.

Typhoid Fever

By carriers—persons who have germs of a particular disease in their bodies but show no signs of the disease. Carriers may spread typhoid fever, diphtheria, and scarlet fever.

Tuberculosis

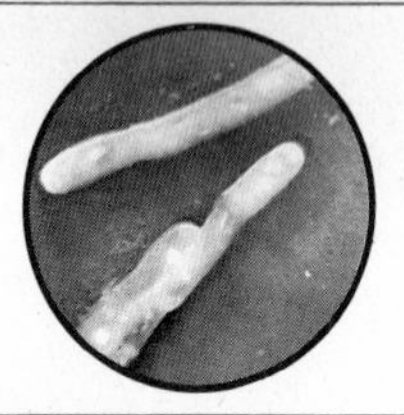

By mild or "missed" cases—persons who have a "light" case of a disease but do not seek medical care and thus are not isolated. They are called "missed" cases because the disease is not diagnosed.

Many of the important health activities of the Federal government are carried out by the Public Health Service (PHS). For example, the Public Health Service operates quarantine stations at all the seaports and airports that have foreign commerce. Every ship or plane and its passengers coming from a foreign port must get health clearance from the U.S. Quarantine Station at the first United States port entered. At the quarantine station, passengers and crew are checked for signs of dangerous communicable diseases. As the need arises, ships are fumigated at quarantine stations to kill yellow-fever mosquitoes or plague fleas carried by rats. The interiors of planes arriving from tropical countries are routinely sprayed to kill insects that may have been brought in.

The Public Health Service makes available to states and cities the very latest knowledge in health and sanitary matters. It provides specially trained people to assist states and cities in developing and maintaining efficient health departments of their own. And it lends experts to help local health authorities study and keep under control any epidemics of diseases that might occur.

The National Institutes of Health

The National Institutes of Health (NIH) are the chief medical-research agencies of the Federal government. These institutes include the ones for Allergy and Infectious Diseases, Cancer, Arthritis and Metabolic Diseases, Eye, Heart and Lung, Environmental Health Sciences, Neurological Diseases and Stroke, Child Health and Human Development, Dental Research, and General Medical Sciences. Another institute, the National Institute of Mental Health, is a part of the Health Services and Mental Health Administration. These institutes carry out extensive programs of direct research in their laboratories and clinics at Bethesda, Maryland. Research programs are designed to seek new scientific knowledge to help control killing and crippling diseases.

The National Institutes of Health also support, through various grants, medical research in such places as schools of medicine, dentistry, veterinary medicine, and nursing—as well as in universities and other research centers.

Teacher's Notes

Such questions as these might be used as discussion guides:

"What are some major public health concerns of the United States government?"

"How does the Public Health Service aid the Federal government in meeting those responsibilities?"

"What benefits come to the public from the work of the National Institutes of Health? What are some specific areas on which the institutes focus?"

Did You Know?

Medicare *is a Federal health-insurance program. It is financed through Social Security payments made during a person's working years. At age sixty-five, a person is eligible for Medicare benefits that include hospital and nursing-home care. For an additional small monthly premium payment, persons over sixty-five may receive other benefits such as help in defraying doctor bills and costs of various diagnostic tests. Has any member of* your *family benefited from Medicare? If so, how?*

Teacher's Notes

Be sure students realize that the areas of responsibility of a local health department—cited on this page and the next—are typical ones but not necessarily all-inclusive ones. Explore students' knowledge of activities that the health department in their own community carries on. Invite examples of evidence that their local health department is at work. (Public health nurses in the neighborhood, signs in food stores such as NO DOGS ALLOWED, special radio and TV programs presented by the department, and so on.)
Mention that, in large cities, departments such as the Water Department and Sewerage Department may have direct charge of water purification and sewage treatment, but that the health department checks on these activities from the standpoint of public health and safety.

Something to Do

Check to see if there are other departments or agencies in your community that help protect and promote public health. Find out, for example, if there is a Bureau of Sanitation that oversees garbage disposal and street-cleaning. Is there a Department of Air-Pollution Control? Is there a Water Department? Is there a Sewerage Department?
Be ready to tell how the various bureaus or agencies function to help keep people in the community healthy.

State Departments of Health

In the United States, each state has the responsibility for, and authority to guard, the health of its citizens. As a rule, there is a state board of health, a state health officer, and a number of bureaus. The bureaus are concerned with such matters as communicable-disease control, food sanitation, public health nursing, and health education.

The responsibility of the state health department extends over the whole state, and in most instances its services are given to the people indirectly—through aid to cities, counties, or districts.

Local Health Departments

Local health departments vary from place to place. Cities have their own health departments, and rural communities may have county or township health departments.

Whether a local health department is organized by a city, county, or group of counties, the main services provided are much the same. Because the local health department is in closest contact with the needs of a particular community, it is in a good position to do long-range planning. Its services cover for the most part the broad areas described below and on the next page.

Vital Statistics: Complete records are kept of births, deaths, marriages, divorces, and cases of communicable diseases.

Environmental Sanitation: A constant check is kept on the safety of the community's water supplies. Health department sanitarians also supervise the production and distribution of milk. Sanitarians check sanitary conditions in restaurants, too, as well as the procedures of people who handle food there. These health workers see that bacterial counts are made of water in public swimming pools and beaches to be sure that pollution is not at a dangerous level. Insect- and rodent-control programs are also part of environmental sanitation.

Communicable-Disease Control: People are encouraged to be inoculated routinely against many communicable diseases, such as diphtheria, whooping cough, measles (rubeola), German measles (rubella), and polio. Sometimes special clinics are provided if certain diseases pose problems in a community.

Maternal and Child Health: Educational programs, often carried on with the help of school personnel and facilities, may be conducted to prepare people for parenthood. Special classes may be held for expectant mothers or for both prospective mothers and fathers. The services of public health nurses may be provided when there is a baby in the family to help the new mother learn proper infant care. Health departments are also concerned with identifying handicapped children so that they may receive the special care they need.

Public Health Education: People in the community are provided with up-to-date, accurate health information by a local health department. Health experts are made available to talk on local radio and TV programs on such subjects as fluoridation and to conduct classes in home nursing, nutrition, or some other health area. Free pamphlets are distributed and films are provided on various health subjects.

Hospitals and Clinics

Many cities, towns, and counties maintain hospitals and clinics of various kinds. Some typical clinics are these: chest, cancer, well-baby (for health supervision of infant and mother both before and after the infant's birth), dental, eye, and VD. Other hospitals and clinics are operated by private groups within the community.

Today's hospitals reflect the great advances that have been made in medicine and surgery, in sanitation, and in public health care. See the photographs on pages 251–256 that show scenes in a modern hospital. What evidences of progress in medical science do you see? In such hospitals, patients are given specialized care that is not available in their homes or in their doctor's office.

Not all patients are seriously ill when they enter a hospital. Some enter for diagnostic purposes so that doctors may make special tests or observations.

In addition to the local hospitals, each state maintains special hospitals, such as those that care for the blind, deaf, and mentally ill. The Federal government supports veterans' hospitals for those who have been in military service. Many hospitals also serve as centers for scientific research.

Teacher's Notes

Discuss with students the kinds of information and services that would be lacking in a community in which no city, county, or district health department existed.

A panel discussion by volunteers might be held on the topic "Public Health Activities in Our Community."

Some Different Types of Hospitals

Some Different Types of Hospitals
Veterans' hospital
Children's hospital
Community hospital
Private hospital
Mental hospital
Drug-treatment hospital
Research hospital

Teacher's Notes
Some other voluntary health agencies, not mentioned on this page, are these: American Hearing Association, National Foundation—March of Dimes, National Society for Crippled Children and Adults, National Cystic Fibrosis Research Foundation, United Cerebral Palsy Association, National Multiple Sclerosis Society, Muscular Dystrophy Association of America. Invite students to suggest others. Encourage comments on contacts your students may have had with any of these organizations. Point out that the National Tuberculosis Association is now called the American Lung Association.

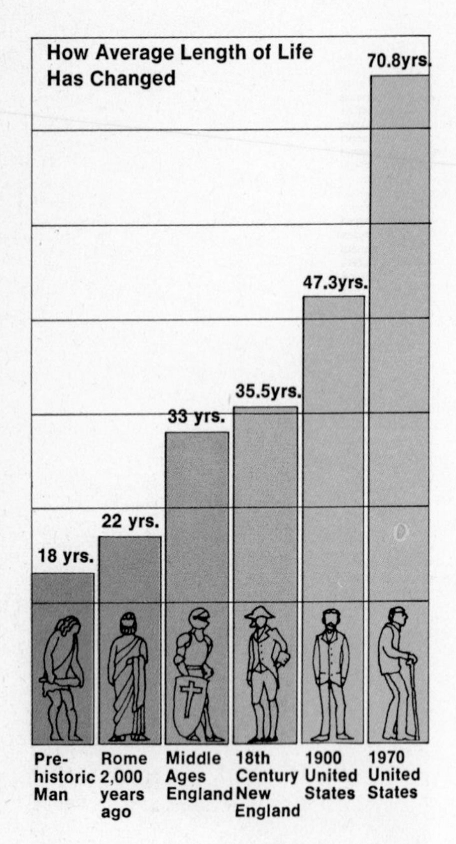

This chart shows the advances in the average length of life from prehistoric times to the present.

Statistics from the Metropolitan Life Insurance Company.

Voluntary Health Agencies

Voluntary or nonofficial health agencies also make important contributions to public health work. A voluntary health agency usually comes into existence because some citizens feel there is a need for new knowledge in a particular field. Those people who are interested then join together on a local, state, or national basis to form an organization to meet the need. Thus the National Tuberculosis Association arose in 1904. Other national organizations, each with an interest in a special field of health, also have arisen. Among them are the American Cancer Society, American Heart Association, American National Red Cross, National Association for Mental Health, National Society for the Prevention of Blindness, and National Association for Retarded Children. What other voluntary health agencies do you know about?

Many of these voluntary health agencies carry on an extensive program of support for research in the cause and prevention of the particular disease in which they are interested. In addition, all these organizations have public health education as one of their major purposes. In what ways does the public support the work of these agencies? What have *you* or your family done to aid a voluntary health agency?

Some Results of Progress in Public Health

As a result of the progress that has been made in the United States in public health, as well as in medicine, people in this country are much healthier than were people of earlier times. There has been a great reduction in the death rate of babies and young children. Great progress has been made, too, in safeguarding the lives of mothers during childbirth. Deaths following surgery have been remarkably reduced; and epidemics of communicable diseases like yellow fever, cholera, smallpox, diphtheria, typhoid fever, and polio have been practically eliminated.

Furthermore, as you have learned, the average life span of people in the United States has been increasing. While in 1900 the average length of life was about forty-seven years, at the present time the national average length of life is about seventy years.

The Community Hospital

Glimpses into the fascinating world of the community hospital are given here and through page 256. Below you can see nurses taking a patient to surgery.

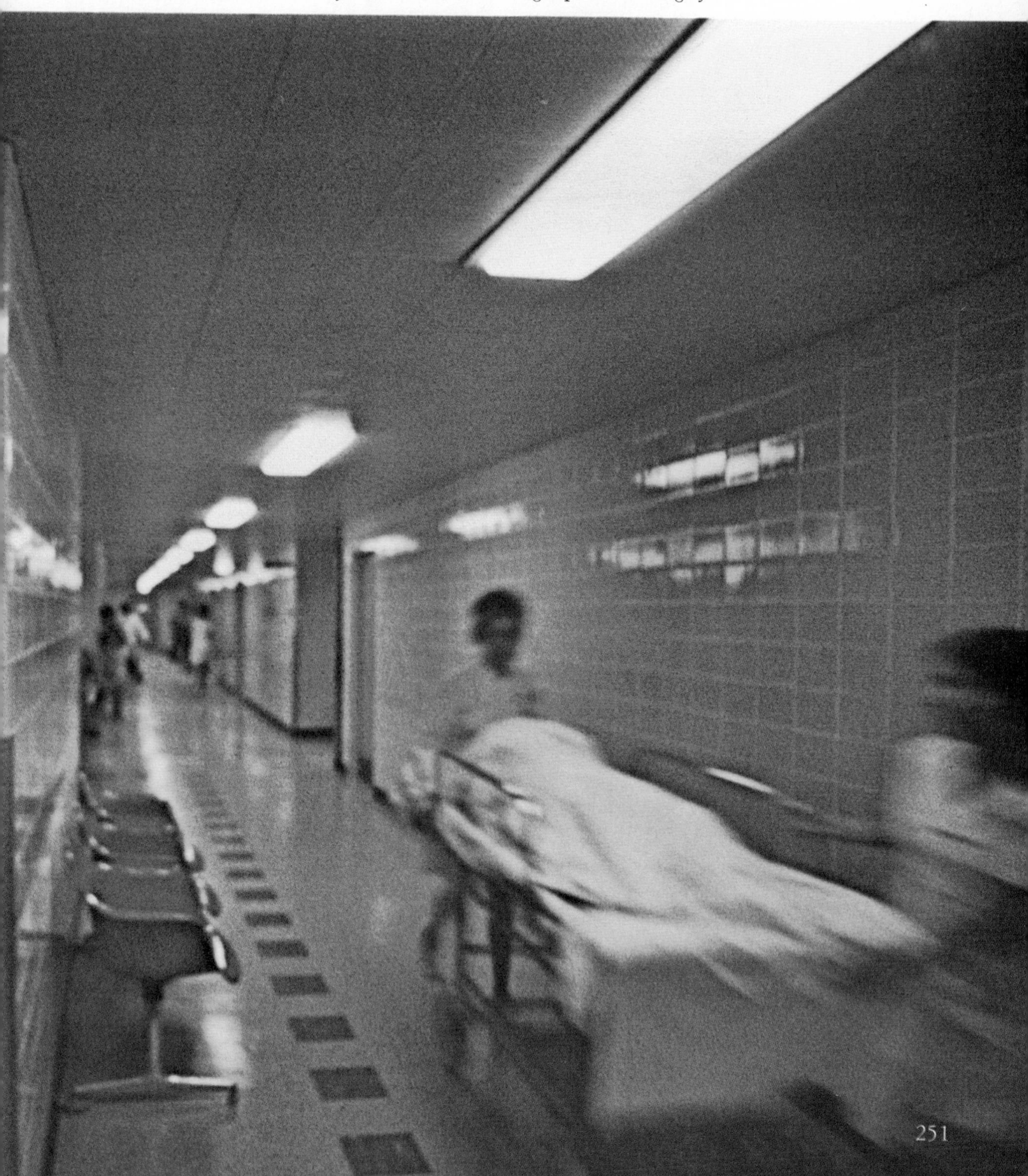

The thousands of employees and visitors who come to a large hospital are reflected by full parking lots.

This sign shows range of services offered by a modern hospital.

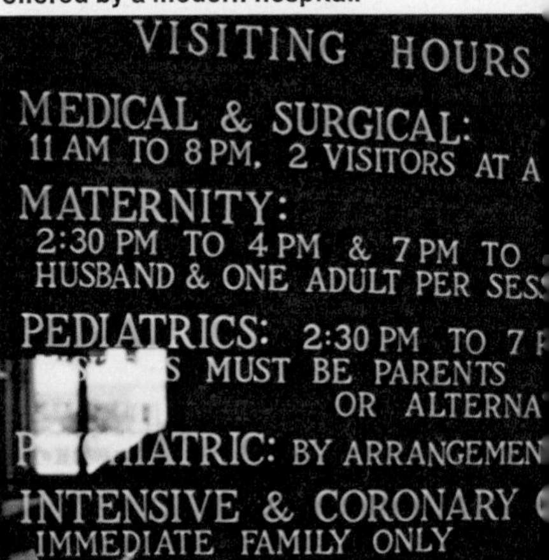

Outpatients wait in this reception area.

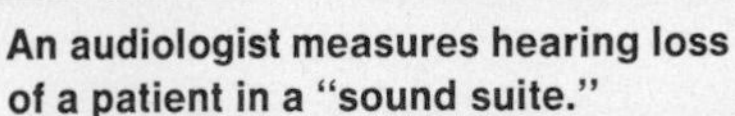

An audiologist measures hearing loss of a patient in a "sound suite."

Emergency cases go directly to this room for care.

Emergency department staff treat a coronary victim. An electrocardiogram records the patient's heart rhythm.

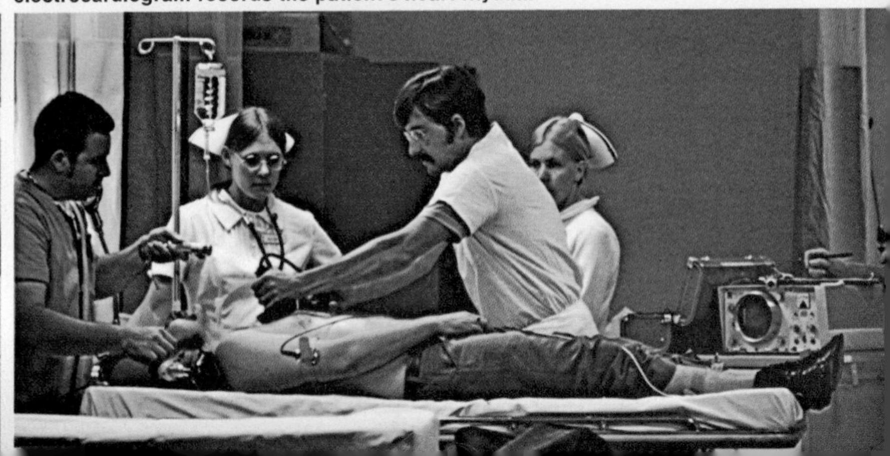

This scene is in the hospital's nuclear scanning department.

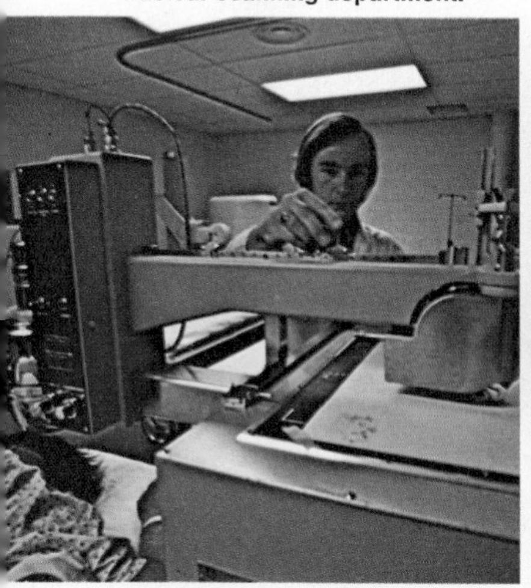

A radiologic technologist performs an X-ray procedure.

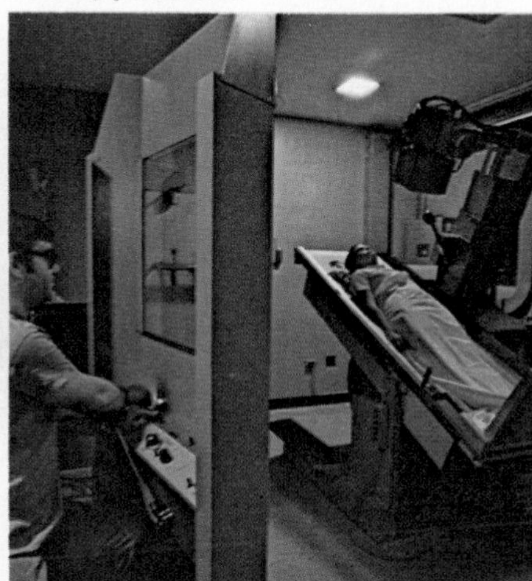

Radiologic technologists develop and prepare X-ray films.

The hemalog performs a blood analysis in one minute.

A technician prepares a stained smear of blood to study under the microscope.

A technician is always on hand to get blood data from computers.

Nurse observes children's heart rhythms on cardiac monitor.

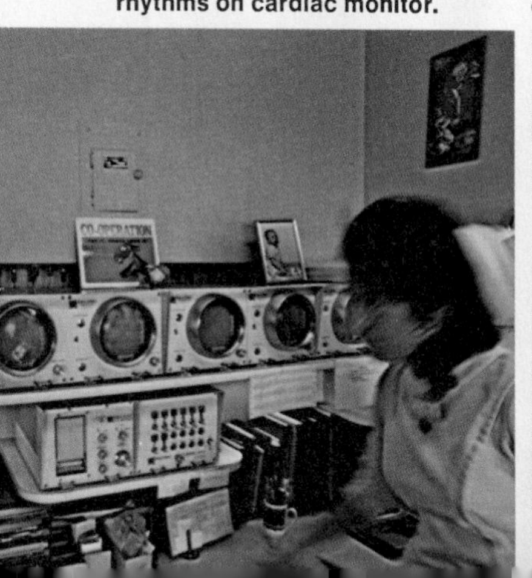

Nurse helps young patient who requires constant observation and care.

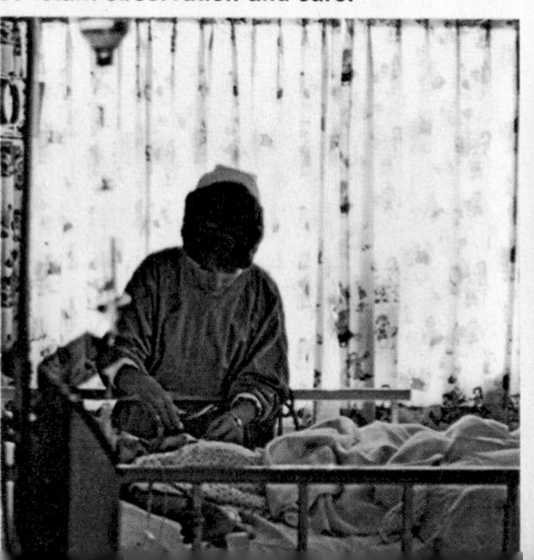

Newborn babies are kept in this nursery.

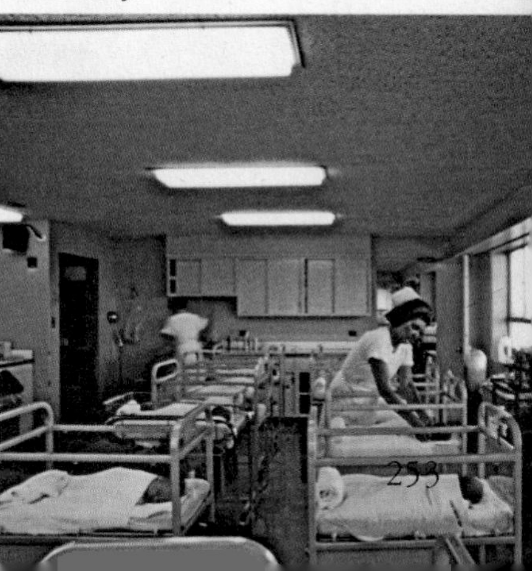

A child receives whirlpool treatment in the physical-therapy department.

Exercise in the occupational-therapy department helps rehabilitate patients.

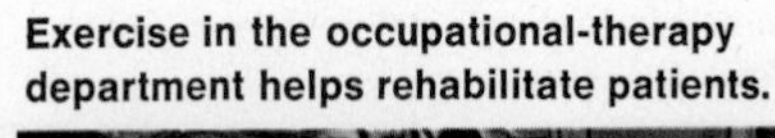

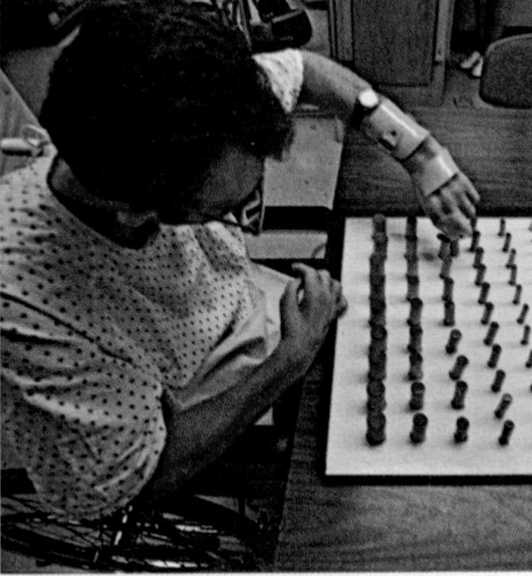

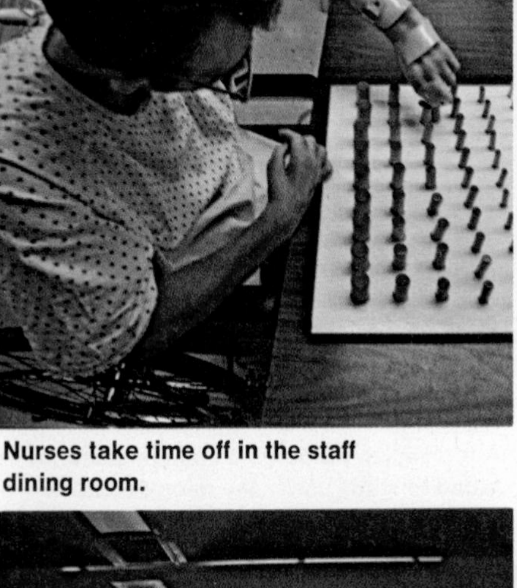

Here is a physical therapist at work in the hospital.

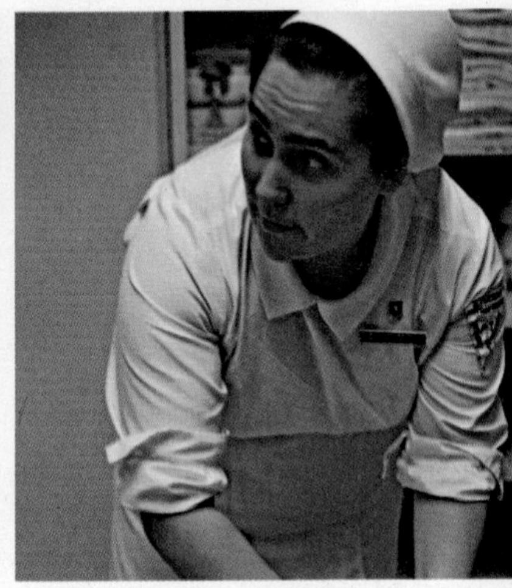

Nursing station—capped nurses are registered nurses.

Nurses take time off in the staff dining room.

This is the head nurse in the pediatric intensive-care unit.

Lighted names indicate which doctors are on duty in the hospital.

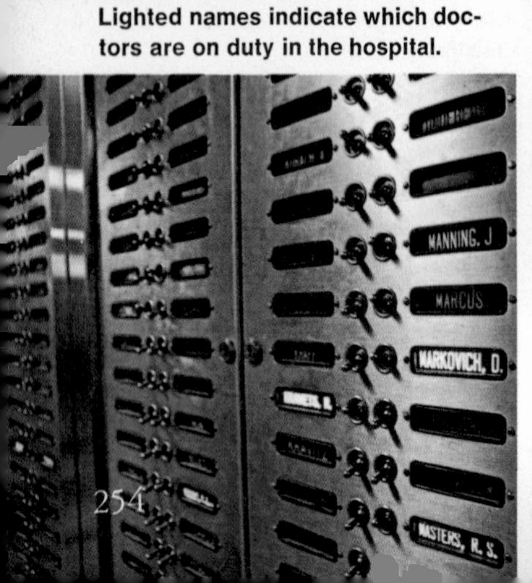

A physician and medical students discuss a patient's progress.

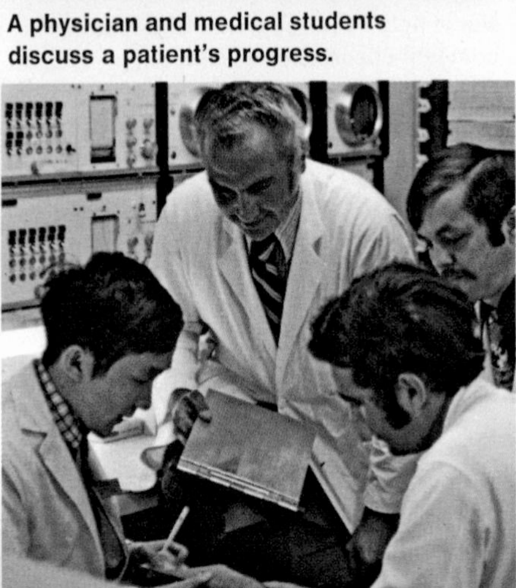

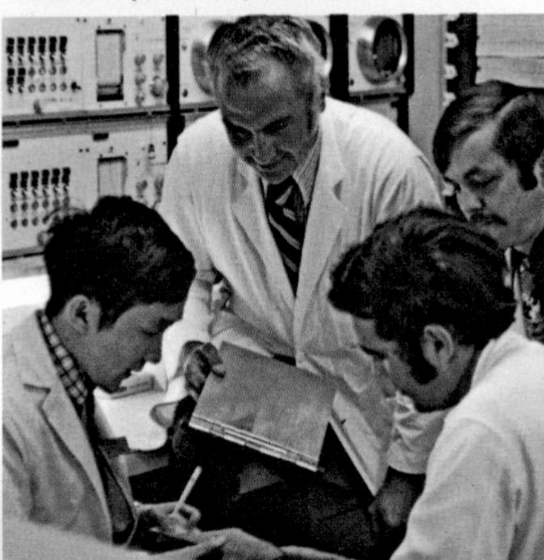

Attendants like this young man are called orderlies.

A culture is being prepared in the microbiology laboratory.

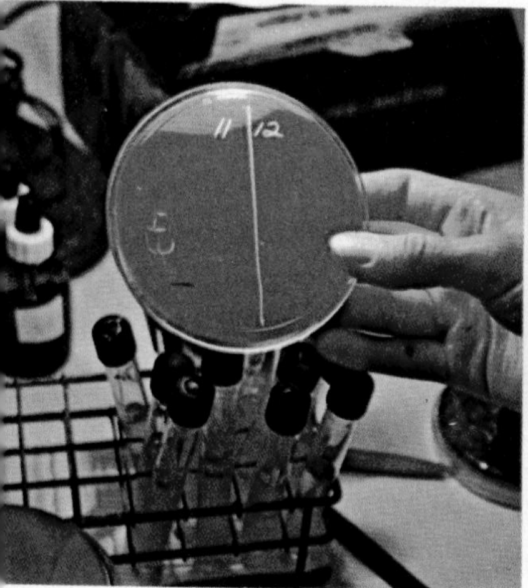

Here is a microbiology technician at work in the laboratory.

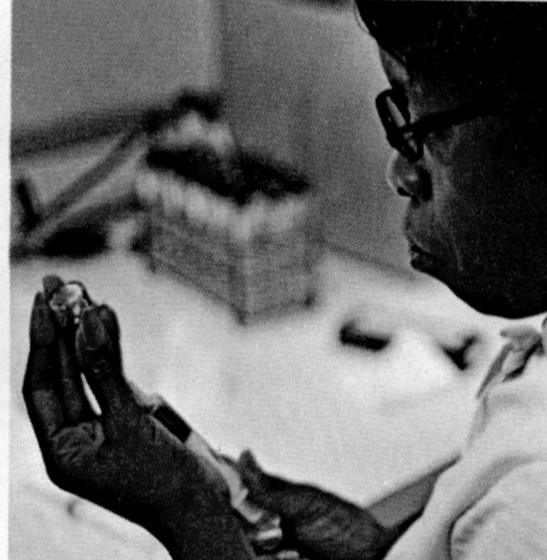

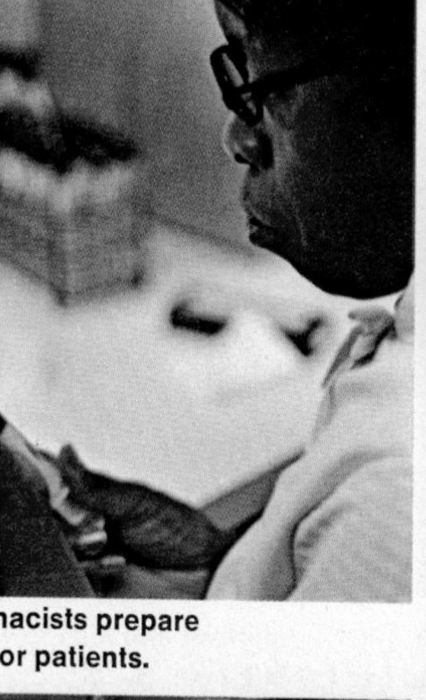

This electron microscope is a much-used research tool.

A hospital pharmacy must have a complete stock of medications.

Hospital pharmacists prepare prescriptions for patients.

A modern computer efficiently handles hundreds of jobs.

File shelves in the medical records department are bulging.

The hospital medical library contains volumes of books about medical topics.

A medical student studies in the medical library.

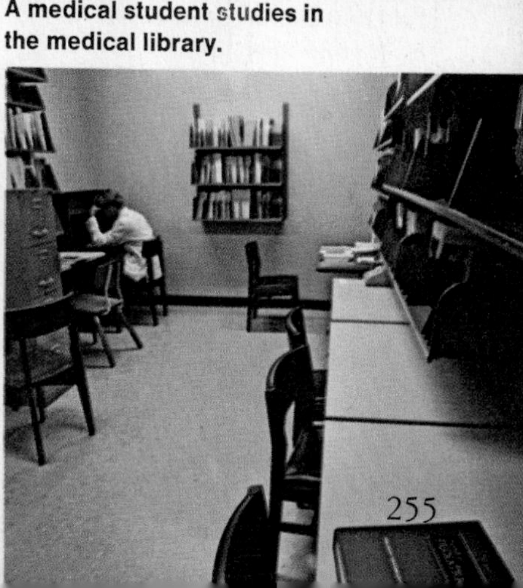

The hospital purchasing department has a huge storeroom.

Central sterile supply provides clinical materials to hospital health-care departments and nursing units.

A hospital dietary department requires much equipment and manpower. Over one hundred pies are baked in an oven at one time.

A registered dietitian checks a patient's food tray.

Two physicians confer about a patient's condition.

A teen-age girl volunteer, called a "candystriper," performs many useful services at the hospital.

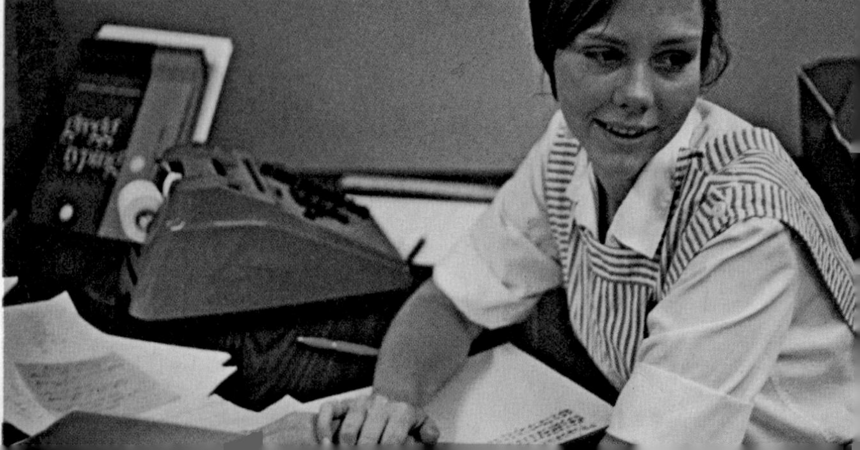

What Progress Has Been Made in World Health?

It has been estimated that half the people of the world suffer from chronic diseases that modern medicine has the knowledge and the skills to correct. Diseases such as malaria and tuberculosis are still major health problems in many areas of the world. Poor health due to poor diet is suffered by millions of people. Sanitation and clean water are unknown in many parts of the world. Do such facts as these emphasize the need for fighting disease and improving health around the world?

In recent years there have been many individuals, groups, and countries whose aim is to improve public health throughout the world. These organizations have been operating with the pooled contributions of money, equipment, drugs, and personnel of many nations.

The World Health Organization (WHO) is one agency that helps solve health problems that exist in the world today. The United Nations Children's Fund (UNICEF) is another agency which aids those countries that need and ask for help with health problems. UNICEF is especially concerned with the health of children. The Food and Agriculture Organization (FAO) also attacks problems of hunger and nutrition in various parts of the world.

Perhaps someday you may want to be a public health worker. You may want to have a part in helping to solve public health problems in the United States or in various parts of the world.

How can you decide whether or not a career in public health might be one that appeals to you? For one thing, you can read as much as you can about such careers. As a starter, you can write to the U.S. Government Printing Office, Public Documents Distribution Center, 5801 Tabor Avenue, Philadelphia, Pennsylvania 19120.

You might look for a list of available materials on careers in health. The librarian in your school or public library may be able to suggest some good reading materials. A list that describes a few of the many public health careers is shown on the next page.

Something to Do

A class member might write for information about each organization listed below. These organizations, which seek to improve world health conditions, are financed by voluntary contributions of the public.

1. Project HOPE—*a ship that spreads medical skills (2233 Wisconsin Avenue, N.W., Washington, D.C. 20007).*
2. CARE/MEDICO—*a person-to-person program to aid the sick and hungry (660 First Avenue, New York, New York 10016).*

A Sampling of Public Health Careers

Public Health Nurse	Works in health clinics or health departments, visits homes, helps families live healthfully, sometimes helps in school health-education programs.
Engineer (Sanitary)	Takes part in mosquito- and rodent-control activities. Consults about problems connected with water supply and sewage disposal.
Bacteriologist	Studies plants and animals that cause diseases. May work on some types of problems concerned with water pollution, air pollution, milk and food contamination, and treatment of industrial wastes.
Entomologist	Works with insect-control problems to prevent malaria, typhus, and other diseases in which insects are carriers.
Veterinarian	Inspects animals to be used for human consumption, before and after slaughter.
Health Inspector	Examines business and residential premises for sanitary violations. Educates people about sanitary practices in food stores, restaurants, and the like.
Health Educator	Helps educate the public about such problems as sanitation, mental health, child growth and development, and disease prevention.
Aquatic Biologist	Studies how living things may sometimes help with problems of purifying streams and may aid in sewage-treatment problems and processes. Works on some problems pertaining to water pollution.
Industrial Hygienist	Checks possible health hazards at places of business and suggests solutions. Diagnoses health difficulties that may arise from industrial processes.

Some Important Public Health Tasks in Various Parts of the World

Activities designed to help seek the highest possible level of health for all people everywhere are shown below and on pages 261-264. Below is a cholera inoculation center in India.

Many developing countries in Africa are now setting up health services in remote rural areas and are providing medical assistance as needed. Here a routine test is being made at a dispensary in the bush country.

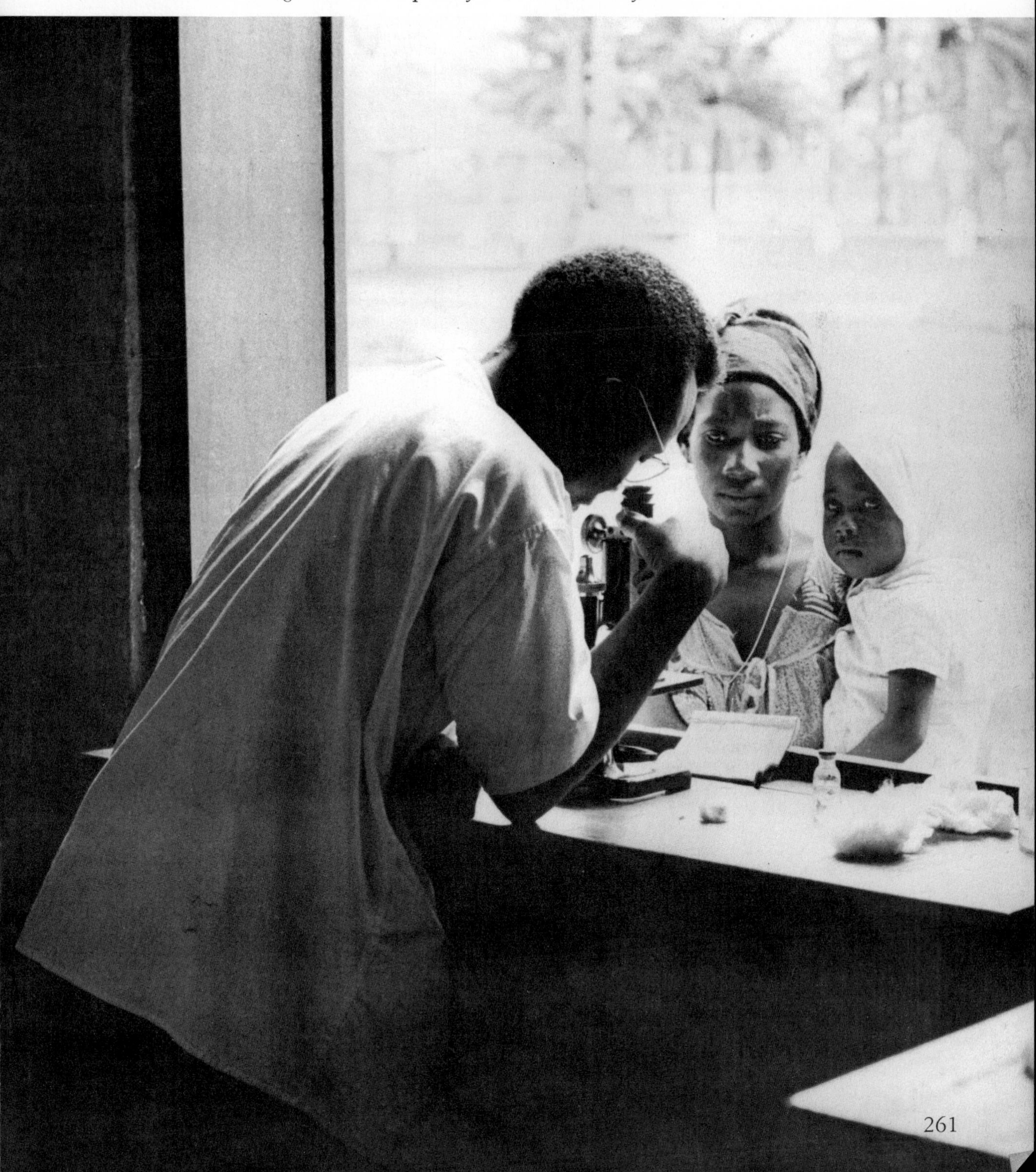

This Turkish mother finds helpful advice when she brings her baby to the Mother and Child Health Center. She and others like her make regular visits to ensure that their babies have a healthy start in life.

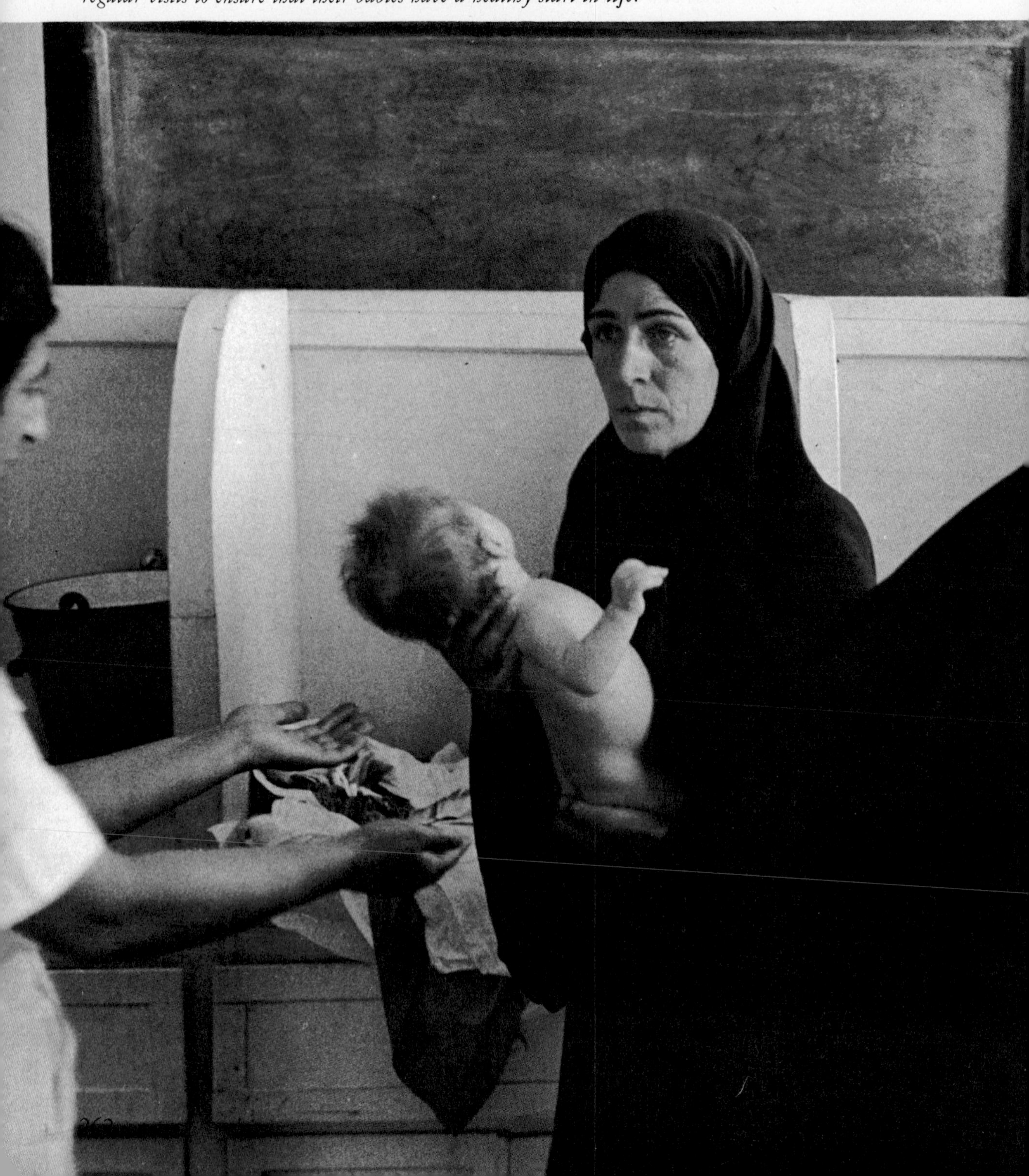

Health services around the world emphasize health education, training of health workers, and medical research. The nurse here is learning special techniques with a "dummy" patient at a hospital in the West Indies.

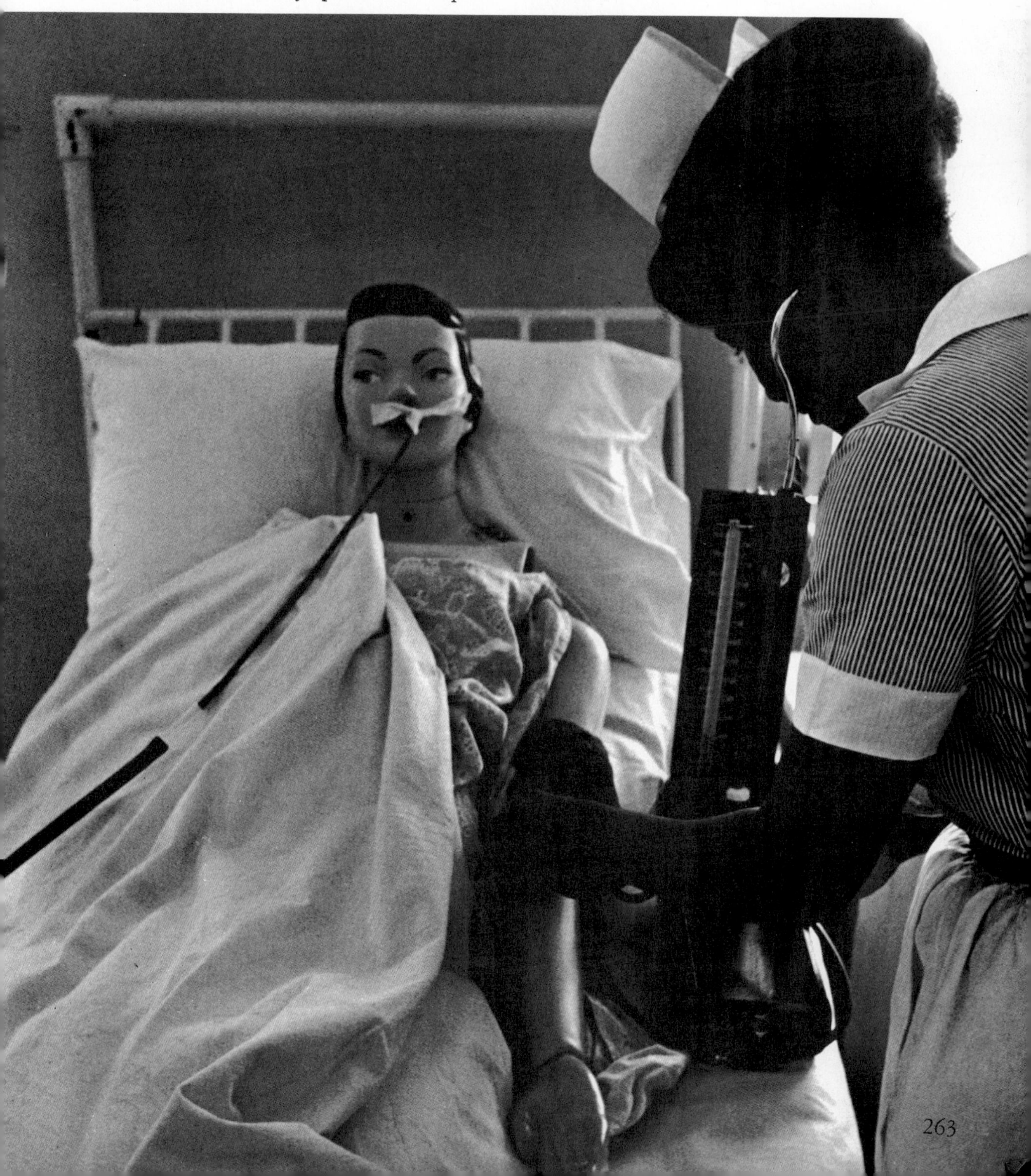

Many countries today share their health knowledge and research. Here Professor A. A. Avakyan of Russia discusses the growth of the smallpox virus in the cell.

What Are Some Challenging Public Health Problems?

Teacher's Notes

See page 15 of the *Resource Book.* Note that the U.S. Public Health Service, as well as the Joint Committee on Health Problems in Education of the National Education Association and the American Medical Association, feels that the study of venereal diseases should be initiated "not later than the seventh grade." Stress that gonorrhea and syphilis can be cured if they are treated by a physician *in the early stages.* A pamphlet that provides additional information about VD—and one that can be used for individual self-instruction—is *VD: Facts You Should Know* by André Blanzaco, M.D. (Scott, Foresman).

Tremendous progress has taken place in the improvement of public health, especially in industrially developed countries. Nonetheless, there are still problems to be solved.

Pollution Problems

Some of the most pressing of today's public health problems have grown in severity along with the increasing industrialization and expanding population of various nations. Problems of pollution of food, water, air, and landscape have worsened. Noise, too, has become a health hazard. You will learn more about these public health problems in Unit Nine.

Venereal Diseases

Among the most serious communicable-disease problems in the United States—and in other countries as well—are the venereal diseases, often referred to as VD. The two most common venereal diseases are *gonorrhea* and *syphilis.* Gonorrhea is the number-one communicable disease in the number of new cases in the United States, and syphilis ranks third. Both of these diseases are caused by *microorganisms.* And both diseases are passed from the body of one person to the body of another by intimate personal contact, such as in sexual contacts, with someone who has the disease. The Public Health Service reports that teen-age VD has increased by 350 percent during a recent ten-year period.

It is not possible to immunize people against either gonorrhea or syphilis. A person who thinks he might be infected with either disease should see a doctor at once. Many cities have clinics that operate under the supervision of the local health department—clinics to which people can go for diagnosis and treatment. The right medicine, given by a doctor, is the only cure for these diseases.

The surest way for a person to avoid syphilis and gonorrhea is to avoid intimate sexual contact with a person who might be carrying the germs. Skin-to-skin (mucous membrane-to-mucous membrane) contact is almost the only way the germs of these diseases can be passed from one person to another.

Something to Do

You can learn more about VD in any of the materials listed below. Look for these and other references on the subject in the school and public libraries:

American Medical Association. Why the Rise in Teen-age Gonorrhea? *and* Why the Rise in Teen-age Syphilis? *Leaflets.*

Blanzaco, André. VD: Facts You Should Know *(Scott, Foresman). Booklet.*

Webster, Bruce, M.D. What You Should Know About VD—and Why *(Scholastic). Paperback.*

Teacher's Notes

Check Yourself: After students have read and thought about these questions, use them to guide a group summary discussion of important ideas in this unit.

Special Research: Reports might be made on potential new sources for protein: seaweed and other algae, green leaves, and so on.

Check Yourself

1. Look back at the questions on page 242. How would you answer them now?
2. What is meant by the term *bacteriology? Immunology?*
3. What important understandings about communicable diseases did Pasteur contribute?
4. What are some ways in which communicable diseases can be spread?
5. What are some responsibilities of the Public Health Service?
6. How does the work of the National Institutes of Health benefit the public?
7. How does a state health department help the people of a state?
8. What are some services a local health department may provide?
9. What are some functions of hospitals and clinics?
10. What contributions do voluntary health agencies make to public health?
11. What are some health problems that still need to be solved?
12. What are some kinds of public health careers?
13. Explain this statement: "Different parts of the world have different health needs and different problems to be solved."

Things to Do

1. Write a paragraph or two on one of these topics:

What Is Meant by Public Health?

Careers in Health

A Modern Hospital

2. Look in the yellow pages of your local telephone directory for listings of the voluntary health organizations that are active in your community. Report your findings to the group. Someone in the group might write to various agencies and request information about their services and a list of their printed materials.

Special Research

1. To learn more about the world of medicine, today and tomorrow, look for the book *Medicine in Action,* Revised Edition, by Margaret O. Hyde (McGraw-Hill).

2. Make a report on efforts that are being made to develop new types of protein-rich foods for people in the developing nations. You might refer to the booklet *The Protein Gap,* which can be obtained from the Agency for International Development, Bureau for Technical Assistance, Washington, D.C. 20523. Look also for the book *The Race Against Famine* by Melvin A. Benarde (Macrae).

Teacher's Notes

Tell pupils that any sensible answer which completes the sentence correctly can be considered a "right answer."

Self-Help Review

Use a ruler or a strip of paper to cover the answer column at the right. Read the first item and write the missing word or words on a piece of paper. Then move your ruler or paper strip down to uncover the answer and see if you are right. Go on in the same way with each of the other items. Do not write in this book.

The numbers by the answers show the pages in this book that give information about the subject. For the items you miss, go back and review this information.

1. Health problems that arise whenever people live in groups are known as ______ health problems.	public 241
2. The concern of the early Romans for public health was evidenced by their building of ______ and ______.	aqueducts, sewers 242
3. The French scientist ______ contributed the germ theory.	Pasteur 244
4. The German scientist ______ pioneered in the field of bacteriology.	Koch 244
5. Up-to-date information on health and sanitary matters is made available to states and cities by the United States ______ ______ ______.	Public Health Service 247
6. Vital statistics in a community are kept by the local ______ ______.	health department 248
7. As a result of improvement in public health, the death rate of babies and young children has been ______.	reduced 250
8. The average life span of people in the United States has been steadily ______.	increasing 250

Teacher's Notes

After students have taken the test and their papers have been scored, let the test items serve as guides for a summary discussion. Pupils may also try orally rewording false statements to turn them into true ones.

Health Test for Unit Eight

Part I

Copy each number in List A and after it write the letter of the item in List B that best describes it. For example, 1, *h*.

List A

h 1. aqueduct
g 2. Robert Koch
e 3. Louis Pasteur
a 4. National Institutes of Health
j 5. kwashiorkor
c 6. voluntary health agency
b 7. operator of U.S. Quarantine Stations
d 8. "candystriper"
f 9. registered nurses
i 10. NIH

List B

a. Federal medical-research agencies
b. Public Health Service (PHS)
c. Nonofficial agency supported by public contributions
d. teen-age hospital volunteer
e. discoverer of the germ theory
f. capped nurses
g. discoverer of ways to stain bacteria
h. pipe that brings water from a distance
i. National Institutes of Health
j. disease caused by lack of protein

Part II

Copy each number on your sheet of paper. After the number, write the correct answer, *true* or *false*.

F 11. Quarantine laws of any kind were unknown until the 1940's.
F 12. Today the average life span for men and women in the United States is about 40 years.
T 13. An important job of the Public Health Service is to prevent importing of disease from abroad to the United States.
F 14. A voluntary health agency is one that is supported by the Federal government.
F 15. Diseases such as tuberculosis and malaria have been almost completely wiped out everywhere in the world.
T 16. In ancient Greece and Rome, people did not know what caused communicable diseases.
T 17. Each kind of communicable disease is caused by a specific kind of germ.
F 18. The first man to see microorganisms under the microscope was Edward Jenner.
T 19. Venereal diseases are communicable.
F 20. The health problems in every region of the world are exactly the same.

Number of Answers ____20____
Number Right ________
Score (Number Right × 5) ________

9 What Are Some Effects of Pollution on Health?

Teacher's Notes

Unit Overview: In considering the questions posed on this page, you might begin to develop the concepts that many pollution problems today are complex and are not completely understood as yet; they are not inexpensive to solve; they are not always capable of being "perfectly" solved; and many of the problems are interrelated.

This unit focuses on environmental health problems. It considers especially the hazards to health posed by water, air, and noise pollution and the misuse of land. The unit is based upon various aspects of the science of *ecology*, the study of the relationship of all living things to each other and to their environment.

Many people today believe that finding the best possible answers to pollution problems is one of the most important challenges we face. What do *you* think about this? What are some things involved in seeking answers to pollution problems?

Teacher's Notes

Read to Find Out: Discuss these queries just long enough to give students a chance to commit themselves to some answers. Such commitment helps ensure that readers' attention will be held during study of the unit. They will want to check the accuracy of the tentative answers they have offered.

The outset of the unit is a good time to enlist some volunteers to set up an "ecology corner" of books and pamphlets for the reading shelves; other volunteers might maintain a section of the bulletin board that will feature displays of material on ecological problems.

Something to Do

Look in the school or public library for books such as the following about pollution problems:

Aylesworth, Thomas G. This Vital Air, This Vital Water: Man's Environmental Crisis *(Rand McNally).*

Billington, Elizabeth T. Understanding Ecology *(Warne).*

Cailliet, Greg; Setzer, Paulette; and Love, Milton. Everyman's Guide to Ecological Living *(Macmillan).*

Carlson, Carl W. and Bernice. Water Fit to Use *(John Day).*

Hilton, Suzanne. How Do They Get Rid of It? *(Westminster).*

Hungerford, Harold. Ecology, The Circle of Life *(Childrens Press).*

Pringle, Laurence. The Only Earth We Have *(Macmillan).*

Van Dersal, William R. The Land Renewed: The Story of Soil Conservation *(Walck).*

Worth, Jean. Man, Earth, and Change *(Coward).*

Read to Find Out

1. What factors have led to widespread problems of pollution today?

2. Why is water pollution a health problem? Air pollution?

3. What are some different ways in which land can be misused? How can land misuse affect health?

4. What effects can noise have on health?

Why Is There So Much Concern Today About Pollution Problems?

Human beings and all other living things on this earth exist in what is known as the *biosphere.* The biosphere is the thin layer of water, air, and soil that covers the surface of the earth. Energy comes into the biosphere in the form of sunlight. Green plants need this sunlight to make food, and all life on the earth depends on these green plants for food. Without the water, air, and soil of the biosphere—and without sunlight—all life on the earth would end. It is essential then to keep the natural resources of water, air, and soil in the very best possible condition.

People have learned to leave the biosphere for short periods during space flights. However, they can do this only by taking along with them as much from the biosphere as possible in the way of air, water, and food.

The Biosphere, an Ecosystem

The biosphere is an *ecosystem,* the largest known ecosystem of all. An ecosystem is an environment in which living and nonliving things work together to exchange the materials of life and to use them over and over.

By studying an ecosystem, you begin to understand the ways in which living things depend on each other and how water, air, and soil contribute to life on earth. So long as these relationships are not broken, the ecosystem operates smoothly. Pollution, however, causes a breakdown in this system.

Changes made in an ecosystem may burden the natural processes that sustain life. And over the years people have been making changes in the ecosystems of the earth. Most changes seemed, until recently, to be useful and harmless.

For example, trees were cut down in vast numbers and used for such purposes as building and the manufacturing of paper. Coal and oil were burned for fuel and for the generation of electricity in power plants. Chemicals were developed to control insect pests. Fertilizers were used to increase the amount of food that could be grown. Automobiles made travel fast and convenient.

How People's Changes Affect the Biosphere

Lately, though, people have begun to understand that many changes they make in the biosphere can upset its ecosystem —and can lead to other unexpected and often unwelcome changes. Thus, cutting down trees in massive numbers results in the soil's being washed or blown away—since trees, by their network of roots, help hold soil in place. The soil may be washed into rivers and streams, causing them to become muddy and full of sediment. Meanwhile, the richness of the remaining soil is reduced.

Some crop fertilizers contain harmful chemicals that wash off the land into rivers, lakes, and streams where the plant and animal life may be harmed. Certain chemicals used to kill insect pests now are known also to harm birds, fish, and other animals—and at times, people. The burning of coal and oil to provide heat and to help generate electricity pollutes the air with smoke, dirt, and gases. Still greater amounts of pollution come from automobiles. Air pollution, in turn, affects the health of people, plants, and animals.

Modern technology, such as that in the United States, is bringing about changes in the ecosystem of the biosphere with a speed unique in all history. And people have begun to consider the consequences of these changes, many of which result in various kinds of pollution. Such changes, it is now generally realized, pose threats to the earth we live on and to the health of all living things on the earth. That is why there is so much concern today about pollution problems.

Teacher's Notes

Talk over what is meant by such terms as *biosphere* and *ecosystem.* Some conversation-starters might be these:

"What are some important parts of a pond ecosystem?"

"What are some factors that are upsetting the ecosystem of the biosphere?"

"Why are pollution problems increasing in many areas of the world today?"

"What is an example of a change in the earth's biosphere that once seemed harmless but today poses a threat to the environment?"

"Why are many people becoming concerned over pollution problems?"

"How would you evaluate this as a title for a book about ecological problems: *Man, Earth, and Change?*"

Something to Do

Use a book such as Elizabeth T. Billington's Understanding Ecology, *listed on page 270, to make a detailed report to the group about an ecosystem, such as a simple pond ecosystem.*

Teacher's Notes

Some follow-up discussion leads that might be used are these:

"What kinds of things pollute our waterways?"

"What examples of water pollution do you know about in *your* community?"

"What are some of the ways in which communities handle their sewage? How would you evaluate the various methods? How is sewage treated in *your* community?"

"Why do you think *tertiary treatment* is said to be the goal toward which all communities should strive?"

"What responsibility does each person have in controlling pollution of water, land, and air?"

Sources of Water Pollution

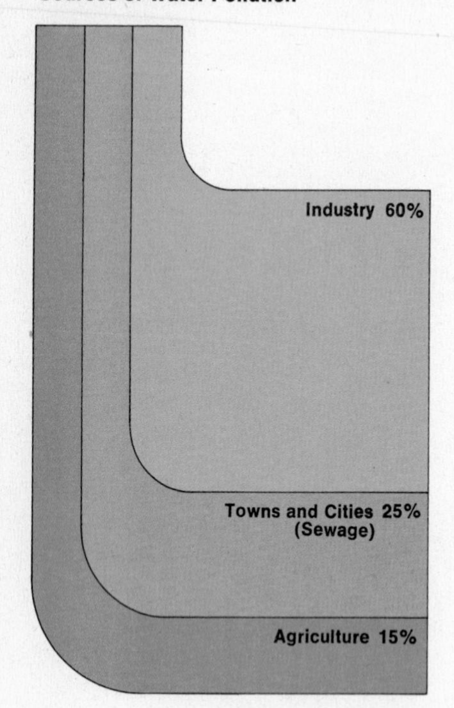

What is the foremost source of water pollution?

Chart adapted from the October-November issue of *National Wildlife Magazine*. Copyright 1970 by the National Wildlife Federation. Used by permission.

How Does Water Pollution Affect Health?

From the earliest times people have dumped various kinds of wastes into nearby waters. When populations were small—and before the great growth in the number and kind of industries—rivers, lakes, and streams could generally clean themselves of wastes. The wastes were diluted in large quantities of water, for example. Some wastes settled to the bottom of waterways. Bacteria in the water, aided by oxygen, changed certain organic wastes into harmless chemicals. Some of the wastes went off into the air as carbon dioxide. And sunlight helped destroy many harmful microorganisms in the water.

Many Kinds of Pollutants

Nowadays the ecosystems of most rivers, lakes, and streams are overburdened by the kinds and vast quantities of wastes dumped into them. Most waterways can no longer clean themselves and are becoming heavily polluted.

Wastes found today in waterways of the United States include chemical pollutants from dairies, canneries, textile plants, laundries, oil tankers, refineries, paper mills, and slaughterhouses. Sand and earth, fertilizers, and pesticides drain from the soil into the surrounding waters and pollute them. Litter and junk visually pollute the waters.

Then, too, wastes come into the waterways from sewage that is poured into them. Some of the sewage has been given *primary treatment* in sewage plants to settle out solid material. Some sewage has also been given *secondary treatment* to dissolve organic matter; chlorination is a part of this treatment. In fewer instances, the sewage has been given a third or *tertiary treatment* which does the best job of all in removing harmful substances. However, some communities still dump *untreated sewage* into nearby waters.

Thermal pollution, or heat pollution, is another problem today. Many industries use water from nearby waterways and then dump it back as hot water. The heated water may kill certain water plants and animals and upset the ecological balance. The heated water also encourages growth of green plants called *algae.* These plants decay and, in so doing, rob the water of oxygen needed to help it clean itself. There is less oxygen, too, in the water heated by thermal pollution. To prevent thermal pollution, water should be cooled and *aerated,* or exposed to the air, before industries return it to the waterways. These processes are expensive.

Health Hazards of Water Pollution

Water in very large amounts is needed daily by people. And the supply of fresh water is strictly limited, since salt water makes up 97 percent of the earth's water supplies. The fresh water available will increasingly have to be used over and over again. Unless this recycled water is kept as clean and pure as possible, the health of people using it will be affected.

For example, untreated sewage and partially treated sewage contain harmful microorganisms. So do wastes from hospitals and slaughtering plants. Diseases that can be contracted from impure drinking water containing harmful microorganisms include typhoid fever, polio, cholera, dysentery, and infectious hepatitis.

In the United States, waterborne diseases of this kind have been reduced over the years. Safety of communities' water supplies has been brought about, in part, by sewage-treatment plants and by water-purification plants. As water sources are increasingly polluted by industries and by wastes from a growing population, ever more effective water-pollution control measures have become essential. Without such measures, waterborne diseases are likely to increase greatly.

Fish from polluted waters can also be health hazards. For example, people can get hepatitis by eating clams from polluted waters. Chemicals like mercury found in polluted waters get into fish such as swordfish. The mercury, in turn, enters the bodies of people who eat the fish. Mercury, above certain levels, is harmful to humans. Fish supplies must be carefully checked by the Food and Drug Administration (FDA) to see if they are safe to eat.

Healthful kinds of recreation are curtailed in many areas because of polluted waters. Swimming may be forbidden and boating made unpleasant. What are some other types of recreation that polluted waters can spoil?

Teacher's Notes

Talk over the various health hazards of polluted water in a community. The dangers of swimming in sewage-tainted water—as well as drinking it or eating fish from it—might be considered. Discuss the dangers of swimming and sunning at a beach littered with such things as cans, bottles, and bottle tops. Discuss, too, any information students have about methods of *desalting* sea water. Ask why these methods are not used extensively as yet. (The high cost.) Another challenging topic for individual research or for a panel-discussion activity is *"How does radioactive material enter water supplies and what is being done about this problem?"*

What Can You *Do?*

Remember that supplies of usable water are not unlimited. Learn to help conserve the water supply.

1. Do not run water unnecessarily. For instance, use a bucket of water and a sponge to wash a car—not a running hose.

2. Save water by taking a shower instead of a bath, or reduce the amount of bath water used.

3. Use white toilet tissue. Colored tissues contain harmful dyes that pollute water and are difficult to remove from the water.

4. Use soap flakes or phosphate-free detergents for washing. (Phosphates in some detergents—unlike soap flakes—encourage growth of algae in water. Algae, in decaying, rob water of oxygen that water plants and animals need. Algae overgrowths upset a stream's or a body of water's ecosystem.)

Teacher's Notes

The following information makes a good starter for a discussion of the air we breathe: "We can do without water or food for days, but without air for only a few minutes. Every day we eat about two to three or so pounds of food. We drink about four pounds of water. However, in the same twenty-four-hour period we draw into our lungs about thirty pounds of air. Obviously, air that is safe to breathe is a vital human need."

Discuss reasons for the increase in air pollution over the years and some effects of air pollution in terms of expense, decrease in sunshine, nuisance, poor health, and other environmental hazards.

Note that for many years it was not understood that there was a connection between air pollution and the illnesses and deaths that occurred during periods of heavy pollution.

Some Major Sources of Air Pollution

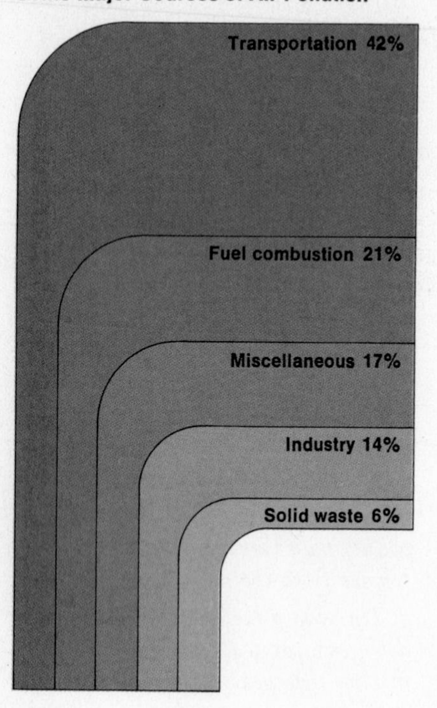

What is the chief source of air pollution?

Chart adapted from the October-November issue of *National Wildlife Magazine.* Copyright 1970 by the National Wildlife Federation. Used by permission.

Why Is Air Pollution a Threat to Health?

Just as people have made changes in the quality of the water in waterways, they have also made changes in the quality of the air. Centuries ago the changes made were not serious ones. They came about chiefly as campfires were built and smoke rose into the air.

Air pollution really began to be a problem when people started to live in towns and cities. The burning of many wood and coal fires by people living very close together caused trouble. Smoke, soot, and gases were sent into the air in quantities that interfered with people's comfort and health.

Complaints about air pollution were voiced in London as early as the thirteenth century. Air pollution worsened there and in various other parts of Europe in the early nineteenth century. This was due to the occurrence of the Industrial Revolution which involved a great growth of factories. Frequently, smoke hung like "dismal clouds" over the industrial areas. Sometimes the smoke combined with fog to create a condition that in later years was termed "smog."

Particularly unpleasant over the years were the effects of burning a low-grade soft coal containing much sulfur. When burned, such coal gives off both soot and a gas called *sulfur dioxide.* This gas irritates the nose and throat. At times in factory towns when the wind died down and polluting substances could not be blown away, smog caused more people than usual to become ill. Some people with respiratory troubles became worse and some died at such times.

Air Pollution in the United States

Air pollution problems began to appear at a somewhat later time in the United States than in Europe, because the rapid growth of population and of industries occurred at a later period in the United States. But with the increasing development of cities and industries came the problem of dirty air in the United States too. Today the problem is serious.

Within recent years air pollution caused by burning wood, coal, and oil has been fought in various ways. Efforts have been made in many communities to substitute low-sulfur coal for the even dirtier high-sulfur coal. Natural gas, a very clean fuel, is often used instead of coal and oil. Many industries have installed smoke-control devices, dust and soot collectors, and devices which trap sulfur dioxide and keep it from escaping into the air. In some communities, it is against the law to burn leaves or garbage in the open.

Although these efforts are helpful, they have by no means eliminated all smoke, soot, and ash from the air. Today, however, there is more *concern* about controlling these pollutants than ever before.

Particulate Pollutants

The soot, ash, and smoke you have been reading about, along with dust, contribute to the air what are known as *particulate pollutants.* The burning of fuels, leaves, garbage, and other refuse releases many of these small particles into the air around us.

The activities of various industries in grinding, sawing, pulverizing, crushing, and blasting send forth other particles into the air. Among these particles are bits of clay, iron, steel, rubber, asphalt, and asbestos. Particulates generally make up the very visible aspect of air pollution. These particulates get people and things dirty. Such particles also enter people's breathing systems and cause irritation, and, at times, they can produce serious illness.

Other Pollutants

Other pollutants that get into the air are mainly gases and aerosols. *Aerosols* are the products of chemical reactions that take place in hydrocarbons and various gases in the presence of sunlight.

The main source of gases and aerosols that pollute the air is transportation, chiefly automobiles. Other sources are the burning of fossil fuels (oil and coal) to heat houses and buildings and the burning of fuel to generate power. Still other pollution comes from industrial plants and from the burning of wastes of various kinds.

Most of the gases that pollute the air are invisible. Although they cannot be seen, they are nonetheless harmful. For example, carbon monoxide in the quantities often found in city

Teacher's Notes

Talk over the meaning of such terms as *high-sulfur* and *low-sulfur coal, particulate pollutants, aerosols.* You might also use such queries as these: "How would you explain the term 'a clean fuel'? Give an example. In what ways can some protection be given from various particulate pollutants?"

"If polluting gases are invisible, how do we know they are present?" (Some can be smelled; some cause coughing or smarting eyes; some cause damage to paint, statues, stockings, and the like. Carbon monoxide, however, is invisible, odorless, and does not sting the eyes—it is especially treacherous.)

Elements of Air Pollution

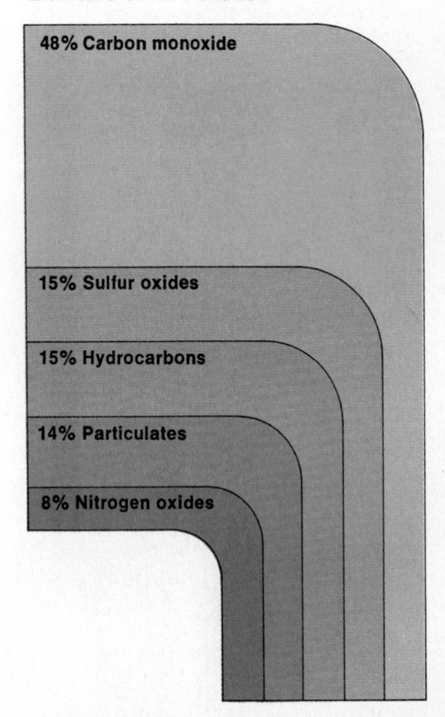

Although carbon monoxide is the biggest air pollutant, sulfur oxides and particulates rate number one on the danger scale.

Chart adapted from the October-November issue of *National Wildlife Magazine.* Copyright 1970 by the National Wildlife Federation. Used by permission.

Teacher's Notes

Some possible discussion leads are these:

"What is a photochemical smog? How can it affect human health?"

"Why is the automobile considered a major 'villain' in producing air pollution?"

"What steps are being considered to reduce air pollution caused by cars? Which steps seem the most promising?"

"When lead-free gas is available, why do you think so few people buy it?"

"Why is air pollution a problem at least to some degree in almost *every* community in the United States?" (Almost every community has large numbers of cars both in it and passing through it.)

Some interesting subjects for individual research are problems caused by air pollution and steps to combat the problems being taken in such places as Venice, Athens, Sao Paulo, Tokyo, and so on. See, for example, discussion in the book *This Vital Air, This Vital Water* by Thomas Aylesworth (Rand McNally).

What Can You *Do?*

You and your family can reduce air pollution from cars by cutting down on unnecessary car travel.

1. Walk or ride a bicycle when possible instead of riding in a car.

2. Use public transportation when you can. (Buses and trains—which carry more people at one time—contribute less to the air-pollution problem than do cars.)

3. Take part in car pools as often as possible.

4. Consider buying a small *car that emits less pollution than a large car.*

5. See that your car has regular tune-ups. (Exhaust emissions are reduced when the car is tuned up every twelve months.)

6. Buy lead-free gas, if you can use it in your car.

air can cause people to become drowsy. It is believed that some traffic accidents in cities are caused by carbon monoxide in the air that is breathed. Carbon monoxide can also worsen various ailments related to the respiratory and circulatory systems. Indeed, carbon monoxide causes death when it is breathed in great quantities. This has happened occasionally when a person has been running a car engine while in a closed or poorly ventilated garage.

Sulfur oxides can cause temporary injury to human respiratory systems. And hydrocarbons and nitrogen oxides play an important part in forming *photochemical smogs.* A photochemical smog, often termed "Los Angeles–type smog," results from the action of sunlight on these pollutants. A photochemical smog irritates the eyes and lungs and reduces people's energy.

Ways to Reduce Air Pollution

Cars are the main source of harmful gases that are released into the air. Therefore much attention is being given today to this problem. The problem arises because fuel and exhaust gases do not burn fully in the internal-combustion engines now used in cars. Exhaust-control devices have been put on new models of cars to help cut down on exhaust fumes. These devices reduce but do not eliminate pollution. What is more, the devices have to be checked often to be sure they are still working effectively. At the present time, automobile manufacturers are at work on the challenge of producing cars with built-in features that should be vastly superior to the present exhaust-control devices.

Some thought is also being given to "reinventing" and improving types of cars that existed some fifty years ago. These cars were powered by steam engines or electric batteries. A gas-turbine engine has also been considered as a low-pollution alternative to the internal-combustion engine. Although cars powered by gas-turbine engines, by steam, or by electricity produce little pollution, they have lower speed limits and less pickup than the cars people are used to driving. It is not known how acceptable such cars would be to today's buyers. What is your opinion about this?

Legislation that will limit the level of pollutants of all types emitted by power plants or industries is an effective way of fighting industrial air pollution. More of such legislation is needed at the local, state, and national levels. What are the advantages of such legislation? What factors may tend to retard legislation of this kind?

Teacher's Notes

Discuss the kinds of legislation that are likely to be most effective in successfully curbing air pollution—and suggest reasons why such legislation may be delayed in many instances. (It is very costly and may be resisted for this reason; elaborate equipment will be needed to monitor the various types of pollutants being emitted.)

You might ask:

"What evidence would you cite that air pollution is hazardous to health?" (Individuals might investigate and report to the group their findings about sources of radioactive pollutants in the air—both natural and man-made—and about such problems as the safe disposal of radioactive wastes.)

Air Pollution and Health

The high level of air pollutants in large cities on many days of the year has been shown by research to have serious health consequences. At times when pollution levels are heavy, such conditions as the following occur with greater frequency than they ordinarily do: *headache, inflamed eyes, nausea, dizziness, respiratory infections,* and *decreased athletic performance.* Particularly affected by heavy air pollution are those people who already have respiratory ailments and allergies.

The chart below indicates some ill effects of continued exposure to certain air pollutants. What are these effects?

Air Pollutants and Their Effects on Children[1]

Source of Pollutant	Symptoms
Automobile exhaust	Decreased athletic performance
Steel mills, coal and oil power plants, petroleum refineries	Growth retardation; increased respiratory infections; increased asthma attacks
Superphosphate, fertilizer-producing plants	Increased respiratory infections
Synthetic alcohol plants	Headache; loss of appetite; increased upper respiratory infections
Paper mills, viscose plants	Increase in respiratory infections; inflamed eyes; headache; nausea
Motor vehicles; ferrous, metallurgical, and hydro-electric power plants	Loss of appetite; fatigue; headache; dizziness; decreased visual threshold
Solvent factories	Irritation of upper respiratory tract with increased respiratory illnesses
Cement plants; abrasive and silicone manufacturing	Increased upper respiratory disease
Asbestos plants	Disease in the lower respiratory system and aggravation of pulmonary disease

[1]Adaptation of chart "Certain Air Pollutants and Their Effects on Children" reprinted by permission of the American Academy of Pediatrics.

Teacher's Notes

Discuss what is meant by *misuse of the land* and what factors have contributed to it over the years.

You might ask, too:

"What were some of the good ecological practices of the American Indians?"

"What factors accounted for the sometimes poor ecological practices of the settlers?"

Suggest that pupils try to find pictures of their community as it looked five, ten, or twenty years ago. They can then point out some of the land changes that have been made.

Pupils might also investigate the work of the Federal agency known as the Environmental Protection Agency (EPA).

Exploding Technology	% of Change
Synthetic fibers	+1,792
Cotton	−33
Wool	−61
Detergents	+300
Soap products	−71
Plastics	+1,024
Steel	+39
Lumber	−23
Nonreturnable beer bottles	+3,778
Returnable beer bottles	−64

Over the past twenty-five years modern technology has resulted in great increases in the use of products that contribute to solid wastes (nonbiodegradable) and other pollution problems. Note, too, the decrease in products that do not contribute so materially to pollution problems.

What Are Some Ill Effects of Poor Land Use?

Over the centuries people have made many changes in the land portions of this earth. These changes have been greatly speeded up in recent years. The changes have been brought about by an exploding technology and by an ever increasing growth in population.

What are some of these changes that have contributed to what is sometimes called *land pollution?* No doubt you can give examples from your own community or its surroundings. Can you think of situations in which land has been misused by indiscriminate clearing, by widespread paving, by unwise use of pesticides, or by unsightly junkyards and dumps?

In the following material you will read about various ways in which land can be misused. As you read, note especially how such misuse can affect people's *health* and *well-being.*

Indiscriminate Land Clearing

What has occurred in the United States over the past three hundred years illustrates some consequences of the reckless clearing of land. Think back to what this land was like at the time it was occupied solely by the Indians. The Indians were careful how they used the land. They did little cutting of trees or clearing of the land. When they killed animals, they did so for food and not for sport. At that time the land was a balanced community of grass, forests, streams, animals, wild flowers, and a small number of people.

The white settlers who came to the United States in the fifteenth century—and in ever increasing numbers thereafter—began cutting down trees for homes and plowing up the green lands to plant crops. Sometimes the settlers did not even take time to cut down the trees. The trees were burned instead. Later the development of mechanized equipment made the cutting and the plowing easier and faster than ever before.

Of course, many of these changes in the land had to be made to enable the ever growing population to survive. However, some changes were made carelessly or without knowledge of, or concern for, the consequences. Forests were cut down without a thought because it was believed there were "plenty more" someplace else. Acres of plowed-up grasslands were used for just part of the year for growing grain. The rest of the time the land was left without any protective covering.

For years people did not understand that *plant cover*—the roots of trees, grass, and other plants—is essential. It is needed to hold the earth in place and to prevent rich topsoil from being blown away by the wind or being washed away by heavy rains. This process of wind or water's removing soil from one place and putting it in another is known as *erosion.* It is estimated that in the United States the average topsoil has decreased from nine to six inches in the last three hundred years. In other words, a third of the rich topsoil has been destroyed. The decrease in topsoil may, in the future, cause a shortage of food needed by this country and may hamper efforts to solve worldwide food problems.

What have been some other results of careless or unthinking use of the land? When trees have been cut down, small animals and birds have lost their homes. In fact, some eighty different kinds of animals that once lived do not exist any more; they are extinct. Harmful insects that the birds would have eaten have survived and become pests. Some formerly rich farmlands have become places where crops grow poorly if at all.

What is more, the beauty of our surroundings has been diminished by the appearance of stretches of barren land and cut-down forests. Valuable places for outdoor recreation have become less numerous. Such factors have an effect on people's mental health and sense of well-being.

In recent years people have begun to realize the harm that can come from neglect or misuse of the land. Today many farmers have learned to keep a cover on their fields after they have harvested their crops. Thus the stubble may be left when the grain is cut. Then the roots of the stubble help keep wind and water from eroding the soil.

Nowadays, too, farmers are using *contour planting.* (See the picture on page 290.) Years ago, farmers plowed their fields straight up and down even if the land was sloping. When rain came, water rushed down the furrows and carried soil

Teacher's Notes

Such key words as the following might serve as starters for conversation about various forms or causes of land misuse: *plant cover, erosion, topsoil, unnecessary cutting of trees.*

Here are some possible individual or group research projects—to be followed by reports to the class:

Examine your own backyard or the schoolyard for evidence of soil erosion. What do you find?

Consult a county agricultural agent or a farm expert about soil problems in *your* community. What *are* the problems?

Investigate the kinds of animals that are or are in danger of becoming extinct. (Otters, polar bears, five species of leopards, whooping crane, and so on.)

1970

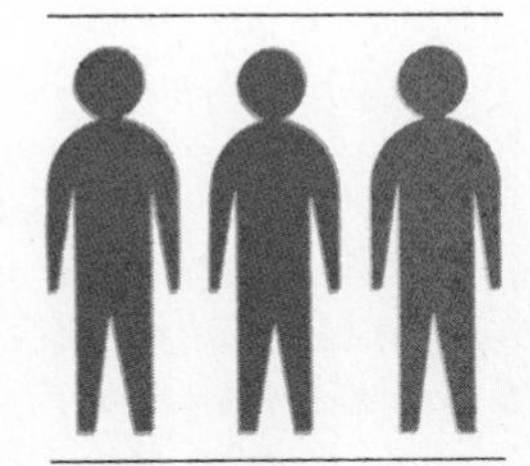

Today, two out of three persons in the world suffer from malnutrition. If the population doubles in the next thirty-five years as some people predict, what will this mean in terms of the world's food supply?

Chart adapted from the October-November issue of *National Wildlife Magazine.* Copyright 1970 by the National Wildlife Federation. Used by permission.

Teacher's Notes

Here are some interesting items of information you can inject into the discussion of such soil conservation practices as *contour planting, strip farming,* and *crop rotation:*

It is estimated that it takes Nature 500 to 700 years to build up one inch of topsoil; in erosion, Man can lose in a few years what it took Nature thousands of years to build.

Of some 500 million acres of farmland in the United States, only 100 million acres are sufficiently flat to keep erosion from being a problem.

A volunteer might investigate and report on the work of the U.S. Soil Conservation Service.

down the slopes. With contour planting, the farmers plow crosswise and curving to the slope of the land. Each raised row acts as a tiny dam and keeps rainwater from running down the slopes. Instead the water soaks into the soil.

Strip farming is another way of catching water before it rolls down slopes, carrying topsoil with it. The farmer plants one strip, or row, of grain and an alternate strip of plants like timothy hay that grow close together. When water begins rolling down a slope, the close-growing hay slows it down. The water then begins to sink into the ground.

Crop rotation is still another means that today's farmers often use to restore valuable chemicals to worn-out soil—soil in which chemicals like nitrogen have been used up because the same crop has been grown year after year. In crop rotation, crops like clover or soybeans—which restore nitrogen to the soil—are grown. Then these crops are plowed under, and grain, which needs nitrogen, is planted.

Increasingly, too, efforts are being made to remedy careless use of forested areas. A number of projects have been undertaken to replant with seedlings the areas where trees have been cut or burned down. (See page 290.)

The need to reuse, or *recycle,* products such as paper that are made from wood is also being recognized. As more and more waste paper is recycled, there is less and less need to cut down trees for paper manufacturing. What paper-recycling projects do you know about?

Some Things to Do

1. Take a walk around your community. Take a camera or notebook with you. Look for scenes that show good use of land—open spaces, parks, playgrounds, contour farming, walkways or malls in busy downtown areas, and so on. Take pictures or make notes about these scenes.

2. Be on the lookout for signs of landscape pollution—litter, junkyards, open dumps, houses crowded together without adequate green areas, and the like. Pictures or written descriptions of these places might be displayed on the bulletin board. Later, possible ways to improve these situations can be considered.

Widespread Paving of Land

Another form of land misuse is the ever increasing paving of land to build roads, parking lots, airport landing strips, housing developments, and so on. Thousands upon thousands of acres of green earth are lost each year to such construction. (See the photographs on page 291.)

The loss of green plants on the earth's surface detracts from the quality of the environment. Furthermore, a decrease in green plants can affect people's comfort as well as the quality of the air around them.

Do you know, for example, what beneficial effects grass can have around your home or school or neighborhood? Aside from its beauty, grass—like all green plants—gives off oxygen and water that people and animals need to survive. Grass also helps hold down dust and soot that would otherwise pollute the air. In the summer, water that is given off by grass and other green plants helps cool the surroundings. What is more, grass acts as a noise-absorber and cuts down the noise from sources all around us.

What can be done to minimize the misuse of land by covering green areas with concrete? Better land-use planning is one solution. For instance, when new areas are built or old areas are rebuilt, it is important that adequate space for green, growing areas be included. Provision should be made for lawns and parks and open grassy areas. What examples of this type of planning have you seen in *your* community? What examples of so-called totally planned communities have you read or heard about in the United States or other countries?

It has been suggested, too, that increased attempts be made to provide convenient train and bus service. If this is done, many people might travel by public transportation instead of using their own cars. How would that help eliminate some paving of land? How would it help minimize the problem of air pollution?

Use of Insecticides and Herbicides

Land can be polluted by *insecticides* and *herbicides.* Insecticides are used to kill insects. Herbicides are used to destroy harmful plants such as weeds that tend to reduce the quality and quantity of crops.

Some of the insecticides and herbicides lose their effectiveness rapidly—at times, within a few hours after they are sprayed. Others such as DDT and DDD are chemicals that can keep their strength over many years. Such long-lasting or persistent chemicals get into the air or they lie on the land or sink into the soil. Eventually they drain into the earth's water supplies. These chemicals can be carried great distances by air and by water. Although the chemicals can be destroyed by certain bacteria, they are taken, unchanged, into the bodies of many living things—through inhaled air, through drinking water, or through food.

Teacher's Notes

Some questions to enrich the discussion of widespread paving of land are these:

"Do you think ever increasing numbers of roads and parking lots necessarily mean 'community progress'? Explain."

"How would you justify this statement: 'In all future city planning, there should be provision for adequate parks and breathing space'?"

"Which would be more ecologically sound—a large patio or yard covered with tinted green stones, or one covered with growing grass? Why?"

A good project for a committee would be to locate on a map all the state parks, state forests, national forests, and wildlife refuges in your state. Discuss the purposes of these areas.

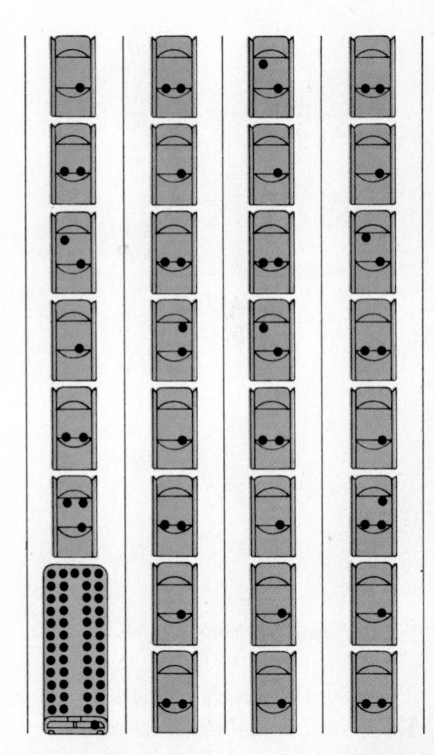

One bus, lower left, can carry fifty people. Often as many as thirty cars are used to carry the same number of people. Why might increased use of buses reduce land paving, conserve energy, and also help reduce a city's air-pollution problems?

Teacher's Notes

Among the safe practices for users of insecticides are the following ones. Discuss reasons underlying each safety suggestion.

Use the insecticide according to label directions.

Avoid getting any spray on your skin; if you do, wash it off at once.

Keep insecticides in their original containers.

Keep insecticide containers in locked places where young children cannot reach or open them.

Avoid breathing the spray or mists from insecticides.

The opossum may be poisoned by the DDT used on an elm tree—as this food chain shows. The elm tree is sprayed. The spray settles in soil and on leaves. The earthworms eat leaves. A robin eats the earthworms. The opossum eats the robin.

Adapted from *Food Chains.* Cornell Leaflet, Volume 55.

Widespread use of herbicides and insecticides illustrates how people can make certain changes in their environment that are useful ones. At the same time, however, other unexpected and sometimes harmful effects may occur. For example, pesticides—especially powerful ones like DDT that were developed in the 1940's—have prevented billions of dollars worth of crops from being destroyed.

On the other hand, DDT has been found to have harmful effects too. DDT sprayed on elm trees to kill elm-bark beetles, for instance, settles on the ground or is carried down to the ground by the elm leaves. Earthworms eat the leaves and DDT enters their bodies and remains there in body fat. Birds that eat these earthworms can be poisoned by the DDT in the worms' bodies.

Chemical Poisons in the Food Chain

A long-lasting chemical such as DDT is stored in the bodies of animals or humans that happen to consume some of it along with their food. A bug may eat a leaf with DDT on it. Next, a small bird or fish may eat the bug, and the DDT then gets into the body of the bird or fish. The small bird or fish, in turn, is eaten by a larger bird or fish. And thus the so-called "food chain" builds up. At each level of the chain, the amount of DDT increases. Large animals at the end of the food chain get the chemical concentrated from all the animals below on the chain. (Study the drawing of the food chain in the margin at the left.)

DDT in large concentrations prevents the formation of strong eggshells in certain birds. As a result, two species—the peregrine falcon and the American eagle—have been almost wiped out. DDT also has been shown to cause cancer in some warm-blooded animals.

The effects on humans of long-term, low-level contact with DDT are still being investigated in research centers in various parts of the world. There are those who believe that DDT causes actual or potential harm through accumulation in food, water, or air. Others maintain that much more study is needed and that the actual effects of long-term, low-level exposure to DDT are not known as yet.

What Can Be Done

Insecticides and herbicides can be useful. Without them, crop destruction from insects and weeds would become a threat to some of the world's food supplies. Furthermore, there would be an increase in diseases like malaria and yellow fever which are carried by certain types of mosquitoes. Other insect-borne diseases like typhus and Rocky Mountain spotted fever would also increase. The problem, then, is to make careful use of insecticides and herbicides rather than seek to eliminate them completely.

An important step taken recently is that of banning the use of DDT in the United States, except for minor public-health uses, and limiting the use of other long-lasting insecticides. New types of insecticides are being substituted. Types that are less harmful than DDT, for example, are the *botanical poisons.* Botanicals are short-lived poisons extracted from plants. Botanicals do not leave harmful remains in the environment.

People are being educated, too, to use minimum quantities of insecticides and herbicides. It has been estimated that frequently 50 to 75 percent more of these insect and weed killers are used than are needed.

Increasing attention is being given to natural ways of controlling insect pests. For example, gardeners are being reminded of the helpful role of ladybugs, toads, lizards, salamanders, and nonpoisonous snakes and spiders in eating pests that ruin plants.

Use is also being made of the ability of many plants to kill insect pests. Plants such as onion plants, asters, marigolds, and various herbs can kill certain insect pests. These plants can be interspersed in the garden among other plants.

Breeding grounds of mosquitoes are being destroyed in ever greater numbers. This is being done by removing sources of stagnant water around homes—sources such as rain-filled pails, blocked-up gutters, discarded tires, and so on. Destroying mosquitoes' breeding places in stagnant water helps eliminate the need to later use insecticides for killing adult mosquitoes. Only strong insecticides that are harmful to other forms of wildlife are successful in killing adult mosquitoes.

Teacher's Notes

Invite discussion of some of the disastrous results that might happen throughout the world if suddenly *all* use of insecticides were stopped.

Consider, too, some of the approaches to insect control—other than insecticides—that are being emphasized today.

See if students know any of the natural mosquito-eaters they may find in their own yards or gardens (birds, snakes, spiders, dragonflies, praying mantises). Such natural mosquito-eaters should not be killed.

A pamphlet that might be secured and placed with the class ecology materials is *Safe Use of Pesticides* (Safety Education Data Sheet, No. 92—price about seven cents, minimum order ten copies. National Safety Council, 425 N. Michigan Avenue, Chicago, Illinois 60611).

What Can You *Do?*

Listed below are some things you can do to cut down on the use of herbicides and insecticides. Be ready to discuss each suggestion.

1. Pull weeds by hand.

2. Eliminate sources around your home of stagnant water where mosquitoes can breed.

3. Help keep screens in good repair.

4. Kill flies with a fly swatter.

5. Encourage lizards, toads, nonpoisonous snakes, and other creatures that eat insect pests to live in your garden by providing hiding places under rocks.

6. Use feeding stations and bird houses to encourage bird life. Birds, in turn, will eat many insect pests.

Teacher's Notes

Consider some of the commonly used methods of solid-waste disposal in communities today. What are the advantages and drawbacks of each method?

It is interesting to note that currently in the United States we must dispose yearly of some 48 billion cans, 26 billion bottles and jars, and 65 billion metal and plastic caps. Add millions of junked autos, refrigerators, bedsprings, bathtubs, and so on, and the dimensions of the solid-waste disposal problem can be better visualized.

During discussion, ask:

"What is meant by this statement: 'We must learn how to change from a throw-away society to a recycle society'?"

Some Major Sources of Solid Wastes in Proportion to Weight

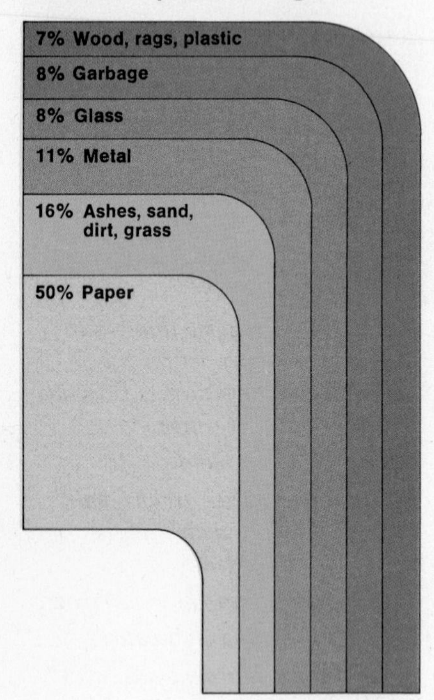

What is the chief source of solid-waste pollution?

Chart adapted from "Pollution Control Programs for U.S. Packaging Offer Too Many Promises, Too Little Planning" by Joseph M. Murtha. Used by permission of Anheuser-Busch, Inc.

Disposal of Solid Wastes

How to get rid of solid wastes is a very real problem today insofar as land use is concerned. Evidences of this problem can be seen in unsightly junkyards and dumps.

It is estimated that each day the average person in the United States discards four to seven pounds of solid waste. Included in this waste material is *rubbish* or *trash,* which consists of cartons, boxes, cans, crockery, glass, ashes, old clothing, and so on. Also included is *garbage,* which is waste resulting from growing, preparing, cooking, and serving food.

Open Dumps

One way of getting rid of solid wastes is to collect them and dump them on land in *open dumps.* This is an easy method of solid-waste disposal. But communities are using this method less frequently than they once did because it is an unsanitary practice. Open dumps are not only community eyesores; they are also health hazards. Such dumps furnish breeding places for flies and mosquitoes and homes for rats. What is more, spontaneous fires often occur in open dumps. The fires pollute nearby areas with smoke and odor. At times, open dumps are set afire deliberately to create more dumping space. Burning dumps are a major source of air pollution in communities where such burning is still permitted.

Sanitary Landfills

Another way of handling solid wastes that is generally more satisfactory than open dumps is the *sanitary landfill.* With this method, solid wastes are collected, compacted by bulldozers, and buried under many layers of soil. Often the land over buried wastes is used for public parks or playgrounds. A difficulty with this method lies in the shortage of land available for use in sanitary landfills.

High-Heat Incineration

Still another method used for solid-waste disposal is *high-heat incineration.* With this method, solid wastes are burned at high temperatures in special incinerators. As a result, only small amounts of ashes remain. These ashes, which take up very little space, are then buried in landfills. A drawback in this incineration method is that smokestacks from the incinerators send forth many particulates that pollute the air. Recently, though, special devices have been perfected that can greatly reduce air pollution from such sources.

Recycling

Perhaps the most promising method for the future will involve *recycling* solid wastes instead of burying or burning them. Universities, industries, and many cities in the United States are working on the problem of how to successfully reclaim for use various materials in solid wastes. Many recycling plants are already in operation.

Before too many years, it may be commonplace for communities to have recycling plants that can take solid wastes—from old cans to old tires—and shred the wastes into small chunks. The materials would then be separated by kind. From each kind of waste, small bits, or granules, of glass, steel, aluminum, paper, and so on, would be reclaimed. These granules would be sold and reused in various ways.

In the United States, some of the recycling plants now in the planning stages would be able to take as much as 130 thousand tons of solid wastes a year and turn them into about 52 thousand tons of raw materials. Among the recycled materials would be glass to help surface highways, paper scraps to be used as a blend for fertilizers, insulation products, and additives for pet foods. The furnaces of such recycling plants would also generate steam to sell to power plants.

Recycling of solid wastes has already made considerable progress in various European countries. For example, huge recycling plants in France, Germany, Sweden, and Denmark convert wastes of various kinds into heat, electricity, and fuel that is sold to industries and private users.

The problem of how to recycle automobiles is receiving special attention today. There is experimental equipment that breaks up old cars and sorts out scrap iron and steel for reuse, but it is not yet perfected. Why do you think successful recycling of discarded cars would be important?

No doubt there are efforts to recycle some solid wastes in *your* community. What do you know about such efforts and their effectiveness in solving the solid-waste problem?

Teacher's Notes

Talk over what is meant by *recycling,* what efforts are being made to promote recycling of materials, and what some of the challenges of the future may be in this area.

Some suggestions that have been made about what individuals can do to promote recycling and conservation of materials are the following. Discuss each one.

Avoid buying, as much as possible, products that come in containers that cannot be reused.

Encourage stores with whom you trade to use minimum amounts of packaging, wrappings, and so on.

Encourage the use of simple, biodegradable (easily broken down and reused) containers—paper instead of plastic containers, for example.

Use a metal lunch box instead of a paper bag.

Share magazines.

Write on *both* sides of a paper.

Save and reuse gift wrappings.

What Can You *Do?*

What can you do to help cut down on wastes your family throws away?

1. Reduce your use of paper products like paper towels and cups. Cut down, too, on the use of plastics such as throw-away spoons, forks.

2. Save metal or plastic hangers from dry cleaners; return hangers to the cleaner.

3. Cooperate in any paper, can, or bottle collections for recycling.

4. Reuse aluminum foil, boxes, and plastic bags.

5. Buy only returnable bottles for soft drinks and be sure to return them.

6. Take your own shopping bag to the store.

What items can you add to the list?

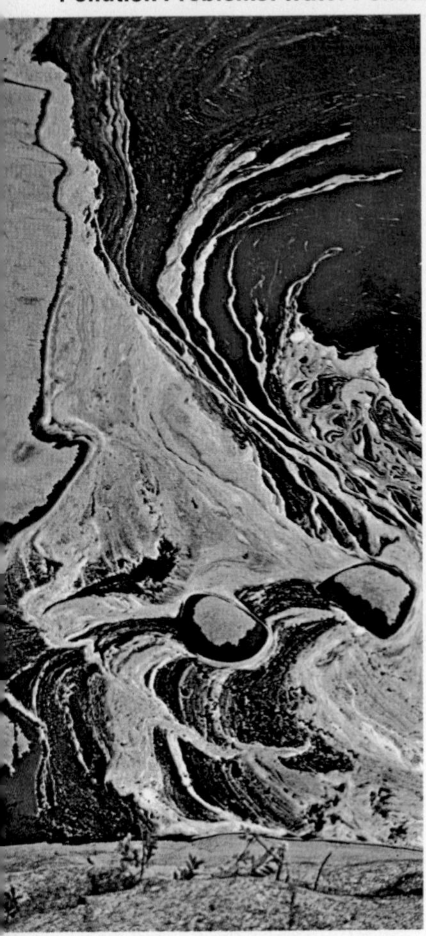

Wastes—loaded with wood dust and chemicals from a pulp mill—go into this waterway.

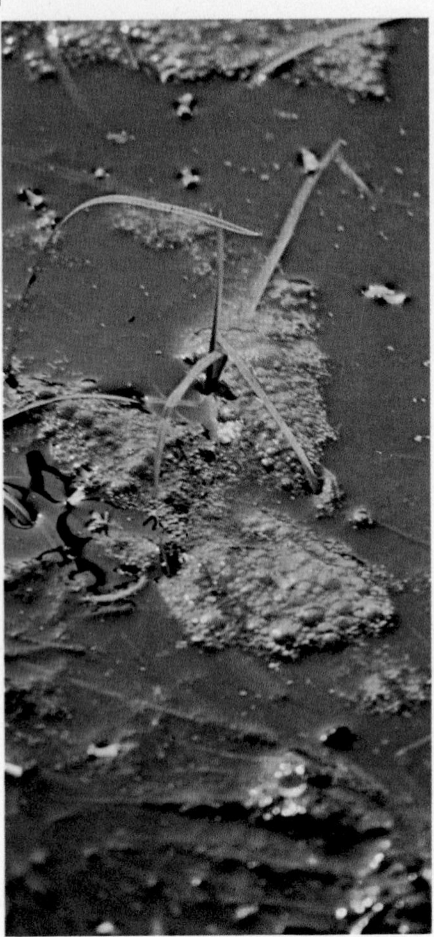

When algae growths—fostered by phosphates in wastes—die, they decay, using oxygen from the water.

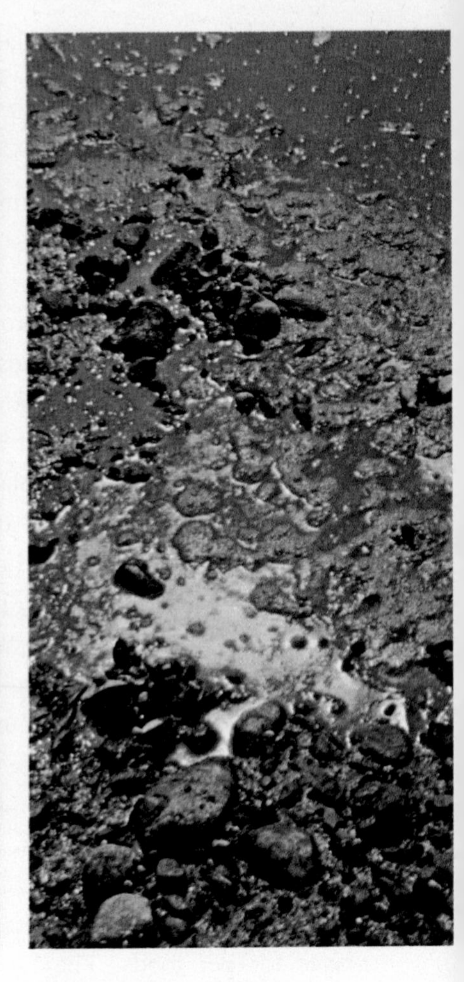

Silt, including washed-away soil, muddies waterways and at times fills them up.

Trash thrown into waterways is unsightly and constitutes an aesthetic pollution.

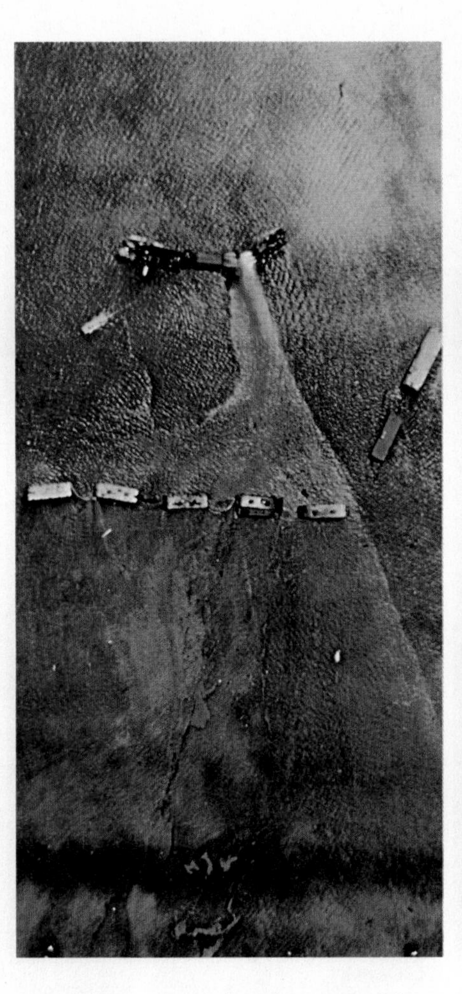

Oil pollution ruins beaches, kills fish and other marine and animal life, and is hard to remove.

Various physical effects such as foaming are considered a form of water pollution.

Page 286. Bottom far left. *Water sample is tested in a research laboratory.*
Page 286. Bottom right. *A big-city sewage-treatment plant, which helps prevent water pollution from the dumping of raw sewage.*
This page. Bottom. *Solid wastes from sewage are dried in drying beds. Later this material can be used for fertilizer.*

Boston

Louisville

Chicago

Air pollution is common now everywhere, but the greatest pollution occurs in the large cities. In most cities, cars, trucks, and buses produce more pollution than all other sources. Industries create problems, too—especially those dealing with metals, oil, pulp, paper, chemicals, and fertilizers.

Some kinds of air pollution can be controlled fairly easily, some are hard to control, and some are still impossible to control satisfactorily.
At the right is a steel-making furnace, photographed before and after use of pollution controls. What are some pollution controls you know about?

Cleveland

Los Angeles

New York

Another major cause of air pollution is electric-power generation—especially that involving the burning of fossil fuels (oil and coal). Burning of fuels to heat homes, schools, and other buildings pollutes the air also. Still another cause of air pollution is the burning of trash and garbage. How else is air polluted?

Air pollution harms plants as well as human beings. Pollution does its damage by entering through leaf pores or through the roots.
Left. *Plants grown in polluted air of a city.*
Right. *Similar plants grown in a controlled environment of nonpolluted air.*

Above. *The aftermath of a forest fire—ruined trees, dead wildlife, burned soil that can now easily be eroded.*
Below. *A needed supply of new trees will come from this reforestation project.*

Above. *An example is shown here of badly eroded soil. Notice the lack of plants and trees that would help hold the soil down.*
Below. *Contour planting is being practiced. How does this help with soil conservation?*

Above. *Large buildings fill almost all available space in this inner-city area.*
Below. *Things are less crowded and buildings are smaller in this inner-city area. In which area is more thought given to people's needs?*

Above. *What are some disadvantages of widespread paving of the land?*
Below. *In the heart of a large city is this extensive park. How can it contribute to the health and well-being of people?*

Above. *Insecticides sprayed by a plane (left) often soak into the land and may be carried with eroded soil into waterways (right).*
Below. *Biological methods offer an alternative way of controlling insect pests.* At left. *An electron microphotograph shows a parasite, known to destroy the eggs of an insect pest, emerging from the egg.* At right. *A virus known to kill the cotton bollworm is shown.*

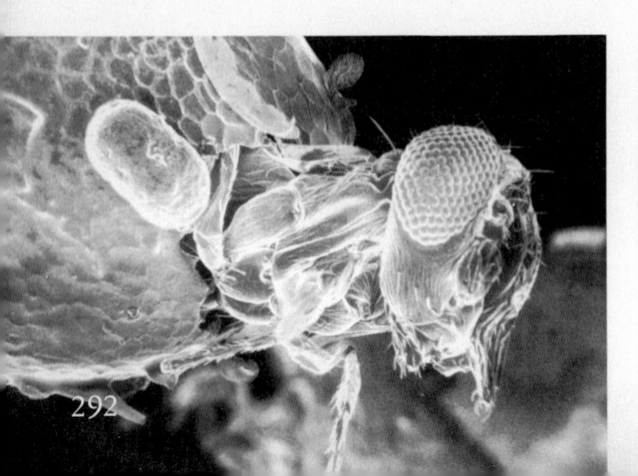

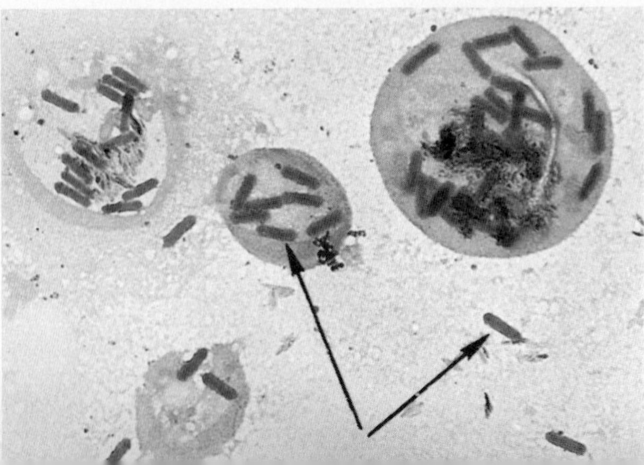

Above. *All too often solid wastes appear as litter along the highways—and as "eyesores."*
Below. *One promising use for waste glass is to collect, process, and recycle it. Here a road is being paved with "glassphalt" made of recycled glass.*

Above. *A day's failure to remove garbage indicates the solid-waste problem.*
Below. *High-heat incinerators like this efficiently burn solid wastes. Smokestacks need devices to control air pollution.*

Teacher's Notes

Check to see if students know the unit for measuring the loudness of sounds. *(Decibel.)* Some intensities of various common sounds are these:

	Decibels
Whisper	30
Ordinary conversation	60
Radio, full volume	75
City traffic	80
Vacuum cleaner	85
Food blender	93
Jackhammer	95
Farm tractor	98
Outboard motor	102
Rock band (amplified)	114
Jet plane at takeoff	150
Rocket engine	180

Loud noises are those from 60–80 decibels; very loud, from 90–100 decibels; deafening, from 100–120; from 120 and above the threshold of pain is reached.

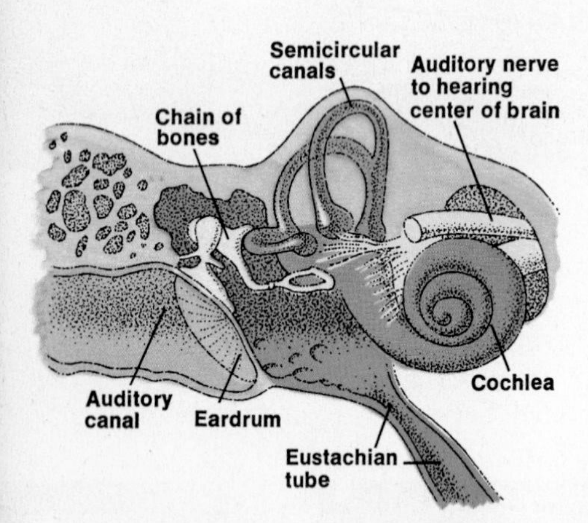

Prolonged exposure to high levels of noise affects the eardrum. Also affected are such structures in the inner ear as the cochlea *and the* auditory nerve. *Some loss of hearing is the result.*

You can read about noise pollution in the book Our Noisy World *by John Navarra (Doubleday).*

Can Noise Be Harmful to Health?

Another change that people have made in their environment over the years is to increase the kinds and levels of *noise.* Like so many other changes that have occurred, noise has accompanied the fast pace of industrialization and the ever increasing use of machines. As a result, many people in the world today—and especially people in cities—are bombarded by noise. There is the noise of machinery at home and at work, as well as the noise of sirens, buses, television sets, motorcycles, power mowers, jackhammers, and the like.

For years some of the ill effects of noise on human beings have been suspected. Now there are research studies to document these ill effects. Some of the effects that sudden or prolonged noise can produce are the following ones: The heart beats more rapidly. The blood vessels contract. Adrenalin is sent into the blood by the adrenal glands, as it is under all stressful situations. The pupils of the eyes dilate. Spasms occur in the esophagus, stomach, and intestines. People become nervous and tired. And some permanent hearing loss may occur. Noise, then, cannot be dismissed merely as being "unwanted sound" around us.

What can be done about pollution caused by noise? One step is to try to muffle loud noise as much as possible. Thus carpeting may be used on floors and acoustical tile placed on the walls and ceilings of homes, schools, and offices. In industry, new machines are being developed to replace older, noisier types. For instance, a machine called the Road-Bor or "cookie cutter" has been produced that can replace the loud pneumatic drill. The Road-Bor produces one third the noise of the pneumatic drill. Also, workers in noisy areas may be required to wear special earmuffs.

As the world grows ever more noisy, strict noise-control laws will undoubtedly become necessary. Such laws will set limits on noise levels. Individuals, too, will need to become increasingly conscious of the need to cut down on pollution from noise. What are some things *you* can do to cut down on the level of noise in your environment?

Teacher's Notes

Check Yourself: After students have read and thought about these questions, use them as guides for a summary discussion.

Things to Do: Students might enjoy seeing how they score on the National Environment Test (adapted from the CBS News broadcast) and published in the paperback *National Environment Test,* adapted by Patricia Lynch and Robert Chandler (Pocket Books).

Check Yourself

1. Look back at the questions on page 270. How would you answer them now?

2. What is meant by these terms?

a. ecology	e. food chain
b. ecosystem	f. particulates
c. biosphere	g. erosion
d. thermal pollution	h. recycling

3. How would you explain the following statement: "The automobile has become an air-pollution problem, a land-use problem, and a junk-disposal problem"?

4. Toward what goals should a community be working to help ensure the safety of its water supplies?

5. What are some things a farmer can do to help prevent soil erosion?

6. Why, with such insecticides as DDT and DDD available, are scientists searching for better ways to control insect pests?

7. What are some long-term advantages of recycling scrap paper to make it usable?

8. In what ways can some of the harmful effects of noise be minimized?

9. How would you explain this statement: "Individuals can lessen pollution in the environment by learning to live ecologically"? Give examples.

Things to Do

1. Plan a panel discussion on "Litter Is a Form of Land Pollution." As preparation, take some "litter walks" around your school and your neighborhood. Note the different kinds of litter that you see.

2. List some benefits of grass and trees.

3. Bring in for display some materials from your local newspaper that tell of special pollution problems *your* community has. Talk over what is being done about these various problems.

4. Write a report telling about some things *you* are doing to reduce pollution.

Special Research

1. Make a report on John Muir, George Marsh, or Rachel Carson, all of whom, at different times, warned about pollution. One book that tells about these people is *A World You Can Live In* by William Bixby (McKay).

2. Investigate and report on the work of such organizations as these: *The Sierra Club* (San Francisco, California 94104); *Friends of the Earth* (San Francisco, California 94133); *National Audubon Society* (New York, New York 10038); *Citizens for Clean Air* (New York, New York 10019).

Teacher's Notes

Pupils may work independently on this review of the unit. Encourage them to reread material in the text when necessary. Tell pupils that any sensible answer which completes the sentence correctly can be considered a "right answer."

Self-Help Review

Use a ruler or a strip of paper to cover the answer column at the right. Read the first item and write the missing word or words on a piece of paper. Then move your ruler or paper strip down to uncover the answer and see if you are right. Go on in the same way with each of the other items. Do not write in this book.

The numbers by the answers show the pages in this book that give information about the subject. For the items you miss, go back and review this information.

1. An environment in which living and nonliving things work together to exchange the materials of life and to reuse them is called an ______.	ecosystem 270
2. Most of the harmful gases that are released into the air come from ______.	automobiles 276
3. Some harmful insects that destroy crops are eaten by ______.	birds 279
4. Reuse of products such as paper is known as ______.	recycling 285
5. Chemicals used to destroy weeds are called ______.	herbicides 281
6. One example of a long-lasting or persistent chemical insecticide is ______.	DDT 281
7. Spontaneous fires often occur in open ______.	dumps 284
8. The biosphere is made up of the thin layer of ______, ______, and ______ that covers the earth's surface.	water, air, soil 270
9. Energy comes into the biosphere in the form of ______.	sunlight 270

Teacher's Notes

After pupils have taken the test and their papers have been scored, the test items can serve as guides for a summary discussion.

Health Test for Unit Nine

Part I

Copy the number of each sentence below. After each number, write the word or words that complete the sentence correctly.

1. The science that deals with living things and their environment is **ecology**.

2. People may become nervous and more tired than usual as a result of excessive or prolonged **noise**.

3. Heated water poured into a waterway is known as **thermal** pollution.

4. When a resource is used over and over again, such as paper or water, we say it is being **recycled**.

5. Greenish plants that often become too abundant in polluted waters are **algae**.

6. The thin layer of water, air, and soil that covers the earth's surface is the **biosphere**.

7. Soot, ash, smoke, and dust are known as **particulate** pollutants.

8. Some main sources of gases and aerosols that pollute the air are **fossil** fuels, **autos**, and **industrial** plants.

9. The wearing away of topsoil by wind or water is known as **erosion**.

10. Putting solid wastes in open **dumps** is an unsanitary practice.

Part II

Copy each number on a piece of paper. After the number write the correct answer, *true* or *false*.

F 11. The only pollution found in rivers, lakes, and streams today comes from industrial chemicals.

T 12. The most desirable goal in sewage treatment is the tertiary treatment.

F 13. It is perfectly safe to eat fish that come from polluted waters.

F 14. Air pollution is annoying but poses no real threat to anyone's health.

T 15. Many of the gases that pollute the air are invisible.

T 16. Sunlight is necessary to produce a photochemical smog.

F 17. Crop rotation involves planting the same crop on the same soil year after year.

F 18. Insecticides have no important uses and should all be discontinued.

T 19. Stagnant water encourages mosquito breeding.

F 20. Liquid wastes can be recycled but solid wastes cannot be so treated.

Number of Answers	20
Number Right	______
Score (Number Right × 5)	______

End-of-Book Test

Part I

Copy each number on a piece of paper. After each number, write the letter that represents the *best* answer.

1. An ophthalmologist is a doctor who (a) takes care of the skin, (b) is a specialist in the care of the eyes, (c) administers anesthetics, (d) is a specialist in the care of the ears.

2. Blackheads in acne are caused by (a) excess oil from the oil glands, (b) dirty skin, (c) dandruff, (d) too many layers of skin.

3. An orthodontist is a doctor who (a) specializes in ear surgery, (b) properly aligns the teeth, (c) is a mental health counselor, (d) treats diseases of the heart.

4. An organ that has been safely transplanted from one person to another is (a) the brain, (b) a kidney, (c) the entire eye, (d) the urinary bladder.

5. Germ-killing drugs made from molds or mold products are (a) antibiotics, (b) hormones, (c) lasers, (d) narcotics.

6. The discoverer of the germ theory was (a) Lister, (b) Jenner, (c) Pasteur, (d) Best.

7. The United Nations agency concerned primarily with the health of children is (a) UNICEF, (b) FAO, (c) HOPE, (d) WHO.

Part II

Copy the number of each sentence below. After it, write *T* if the statement is *true;* write *F* if the statement is *false.*

F 8. All body processes speed up in sleep.

T 9. Heroin is outlawed in the United States.

T 10. Cigarette smoking has been proved to be a cause of lung cancer.

F 11. Alcohol is a stimulant.

T 12. Alcoholic drinks can affect a person's reason and judgment.

F 13. Mumps is a deficiency disease.

T 14. Inactivity can be a factor in a person's being overweight.

F 15. The best doctors are those who advertise.

T 16. Young people your age need four cups of milk—or its equivalent—daily.

F 17. Sweet, sticky foods protect the teeth by crowding out bacteria that might cause decay.

T 18. Neuroses and psychoses are two forms of mental illness.

T 19. Many mentally ill people recover and go on to lead happy, productive lives.

F 20. The greatest single cause of air pollution today is open burning of dumps.

Number of Answers	20
Number Right	______
Score (Number Right × 5)	______

Part III

Copy the number of each sentence below. After each number, write the word or words that complete the sentence correctly.

1. Burning of food in the body is called **oxidation**.

2. The same chemicals found in the human body are also found in **food**.

3. Butter is a **fat**-rich food.

4. Meat, eggs, and fish are good sources of the nutrients called **proteins**.

5. Health fakers are called **quacks**.

6. A doctor must order **prescription** drugs.

7. Over-the-counter drugs are ones that are meant for temporary and **minor** ailments.

8. Many gun accidents occur because a person mistakenly thinks a gun is not **loaded**.

9. A hunter should wear red or **fluorescent orange**.

10. **shock** may accompany severe injury.

11. When you enter a public building, check for the nearest **exit**.

12. Forming opinions about a person without really knowing him is a form of **prejudice**.

13. You can communicate with people through your **actions** as well as through your words.

14. There is no disgrace in **failure** if you have honestly tried to meet a goal.

15. At the present time, the average life span of people in the U.S. is about **seventy** years.

16. A controversial drug made from the Indian hemp plant is **marijuana**.

17. Drugs that speed up the work of the central nervous system are classed as **stimulants**.

18. Depressant drugs, when taken in large doses or with alcohol, can interfere with a person's ability to **breathe**.

19. Sniffing **glue** and other volatile chemicals can be very hazardous to health.

20. There may be recurrent effects several months later of a single dose of the hallucinogenic drug **L S D**.

21. FDA stands for **Food** and **Drug** Administration.

22. Excessive fears of certain things such as high places or cats are known as **phobias**.

23. Modern technology in developed countries is a cause of much **pollution**.

24. An example of a persistent or long-lasting insecticide is **D D T**.

25. The greatest challenge to eliminating air pollution today is the development of a **car** that will emit fewer pollutants.

Number of Answers 25

Number Right ______

Score (Number Right × 4) ______

Books of Information[1]

Health Needs and Interests of Teen-agers

*American Dental Association. *Teeth, Health, and Appearance.*

American Medical Association. *The Look You Like.*

Foulkes, David. *The Psychology of Sleep.*

*Gallagher, J. Roswell. *You and Your Health.*

*Gregg, Walter H. *A Boy and His Physique.*

*Leverton, Ruth. *A Girl and Her Figure.*

Drug Abuse, Alcohol, and Smoking

*Houser, Norman. *About You and Smoking.*

——. *Drugs: Facts on Their Use and Abuse.*

Hyde, Margaret, Editor. *Mind Drugs.*

Madison, Arnold. *Drugs and You.*

*McCarthy, Raymond C., and Pasciutti, John J. *Facts About Alcohol.*

Public Health Service. *The Health Consequences of Smoking. A Report of the Surgeon General: 1973.* Paperback.

Consumer Education and Quackery

*Love, Barbara. *Buyers Beware.*

*Seaver, Jacqueline. *Fads, Myths, and Quacks—and Your Health.*

Nutrition

Arnold, Pauline, and White, Percival. *Food Facts for Young People.*

Benarde, Melvin. *The Race Against Famine.*

Helfman, Elizabeth S. *This Hungry World.*

Leverton, Ruth. *Food Becomes You.* Paperback.

Sebrell, William H.; Haggerty, James J.; and the Editors of *Life* Magazine. *Food and Nutrition.*

Stare, Frederick J. *Eating for Good Health.* Paperback.

Mental Health and Human Relations

Alexander, Arthur. *The Hidden You.*

Goldenson, Robert. *All About the Human Mind.*

Hall, Elizabeth. *Why We Do What We Do—A Look at Psychology.*

Noshpitz, Joseph. *Understanding Ourselves: The Challenge of the Human Mind.*

Safety and Accident Prevention

Bendick, Jeanne. *The Emergency Book.*

Benjamin, Bry, M.D., and Annette F. *In Case of Emergency.*

Medicine, Public Health, and Disease Control

*Blanzaco, André, M.D. *VD: Facts You Should Know.*

Dodge, Bertha. *Hands That Help: Careers for Medical Workers.*

Englebardt, Stanley L. *Jobs in Health Care.*

Rosenberg, Nancy, and Rosenberg, Lawrence, M.D. *The Story of Modern Medicine.*

Rosenberg, Nancy, and Snyderman, Reuven, M.D. *New Parts for People: The Story of Medical Transplants.*

Ecology

Bixby, William. *A World You Can Live In.*

Cailliet, Greg; Setzer, Paulette; and Love, Milton. *Everyman's Guide to Ecological Living.* Paperback.

McCoy, J. J. *Shadows Over the Land.*

Navarra, John. *Our Noisy World: The Problem of Noise Pollution.*

Pringle, Laurence. *The Only Earth We Have.*

Van Dersal, William R. *The Land Renewed: The Story of Soil Conservation.*

Worth, Jean. *Man, Earth, and Change.*

[1]Asterisk * indicates pamphlet or booklet.

Books to "Grow On"

Bell, Margaret. *Watch for a Tall White Sail.* The courageous adjustment of a sixteen-year-old to the hardships of Alaska in the 1880's.

Bontemps, Arna. *Chariot in the Sky.* The story of the Jubilee Singers and the founding of Fiske University.

Butler, Beverly. *Light a Single Candle.* How a young girl adjusts to blindness.

Cavanna, Betty. *Jenny Kimura.* A Japanese-American girl visits her grandmother in the United States and has some difficult adjustments to make.

Colman, Hila. *Classmates by Request.* Carla and several of her friends learn something about prejudice when they transfer to an older, previously all-Black high school.

Curcija-Prodanovic, Nada. *Ballerina.* A young Yugoslavian girl has a tragic accident but recovers and learns to dance again.

Frick, C. H. *Five Against the Odds.* Although crippled by illness, Tim finds he can still make a contribution to the high-school basketball team.

George, Jean. *The Summer of the Falcon.* June, a thirteen-year-old girl, learns about freedom and discipline as she trains a sparrow hawk.

Gilbert, Nan. *The Unchosen.* Three girls who feel "out of things" seek a place in the "in" world of their age-mates.

Heaps, Willard. *Wandering Workers.* Through taped interviews, young readers learn about the life and the problems of some of today's migrant workers.

Hinton, S. E. *That Was Then, This Is Now.* A direct, believable story of how an older friend —at the expense of seeming betrayal—reports Mark, who is not only using drugs but is a pusher.

Ish-Kishor, S. *A Boy of Old Prague.* How ghetto life affects a peasant boy in Prague in the 1540's.

Johnston, Johanna. *A Special Bravery.* Brief biographical sketches of fifteen black men and their specific acts of courage.

Kingman, Lee. *The Year of the Raccoon.* Being an "average" boy among talented brothers is Joey's problem.

Krumgold, Joseph. *Henry III.* Thirteen-year-old Henry takes some important steps in growing as a person.

Mather, Melissa. *One Summer in Between.* The diary of a southern student teacher records her experiences in caring for six energetic Vermont youngsters.

Ogilvie, Elizabeth. *Blueberry Summer.* A summer of responsibility brings about changes in selfish Cass.

Preston, Edward. *Martin Luther King: Fighter for Freedom.* An excellent biography of this civil rights leader, which stresses his ideals.

Rodman, Bella. *Lions in the Way.* A realistic novel about school integration.

Shannon, Monica. *Dobry.* A Bulgarian peasant boy fulfills his ambition to leave the farm and become a sculptor.

Stevenson, Janet. *Women's Rights, A First Book.* An account of the history of the feminist movement.

Stoutenburg, Adrien. *Out There.* A science-fiction story in which some young people in the 21st century seek to save the few remaining plants and animals in the highly polluted environment.

Van Leeuwen, Jean. *A Time of Growing.* A collection of short stories about thirteen-year-old girls and their typical problems.

Glossary

The pronunciation of each word is shown just after the word, in this way: ab bre vi ate (ə brē′vē āt). The letters and signs used are pronounced as in the words below. The mark ′ is placed after a syllable to show a primary or heavy accent. The mark ′ is placed after a syllable to show a secondary or lighter accent, as in the word ab bre vi a tion (ə brē′vē ā′shən).

a hat, cap	e let, best	o hot, rock	u cup, butter
ā age, face	ē equal, be	ō open, go	u̇ full, put
ä father, far	ėr term, learn	ô order, all	ü rule, move
		oi oil, voice	yü use, music
	i it, pin	ou house, out	
	ī ice, five		

ə represents: *a* in about, *e* in taken, *i* in April, *o* in lemon, *u* in circus. TH is pronounced as *th* in this. *Foreign Sound:* N as in French *bon*. The N is not pronounced but shows that the vowel before it is nasal.

Pronunciation key is from *Thorndike-Barnhart High School Dictionary* (Scott, Foresman and Company).

ab scess (ab′ses), a collection of pus in the tissues of some body part, usually due to infection.

ab sorp tion (ab sôrp′shən), the act or process of taking in or sucking up liquids.

ac ne (ak′nē), a skin condition in which the oil glands and ducts become clogged and inflamed, causing pimples, whiteheads, and blackheads.

ac ro pho bi a (ak′rə fō′bē ə), a morbid fear of great heights.

ACTH (*ad re no cor ti co trop ic hor mone*) (ad-rē′nō kôr′ti kō trop′ik hôr′mōn), hormone, secreted by the pituitary gland, that stimulates the outer portion of the adrenal glands.

ad dict (ad′ikt), person who is a slave to a habit, especially to the taking of some drug.

ad re nal gland (ə drē′nl gland′), either of the two endocrine glands, one on the upper part of each kidney, that secrete adrenalin, cortisone, and certain other hormones.

a dren al in (ə dren′l ən), a hormone secreted by the adrenal glands.

aer ate (er′āt *or* ar′āt), expose to and mix with air.

aer o sol (er′ə sol *or* ar′ə sol), very fine particles of a solid or liquid substance which are suspended in the air or in some other gas.

ag o ra pho bi a (ag′ər ə fō′bē ə), a morbid fear of being in open places.

ai lu ro pho bi a (ā lür′ə fō′bē ə), a morbid fear or hatred of cats.

al com e ter (al kom′ə tər), a device used by law-enforcement agents to determine whether a driver is intoxicated.

al gae (al′jē), group of water plants that can make their own food. Algae contain chlorophyll, but lack true stems, roots, or leaves.

a mi no ac id (ə mē′nō *or* am′ə nō as′id), any of a group of organic compounds containing nitrogen into which proteins are broken down during digestion; the chief building blocks of protein.

am phet a mine (am fet′ə mēn *or* am fet′ə min), stimulant drug used medically to increase the activity of the brain or other part of the body.

an es the sia (an′əs thē′zhə), entire or partial loss of such feelings as pain, touch, and cold.

an es the si ol o gy (an′əs thē′zē ol′ə jē), science that deals with the uses and effects of anesthetics.

an ti bi ot ic (an′ti bī ot′ik), substance produced by a living organism which destroys or weakens germs; as a drug, it fights disease.

an ti bod y (an′ti bod′ē), substance produced in the body which can destroy or weaken bacteria or neutralize poisons produced by them.

an ti sep sis (an′tə sep′sis), prevention of infection by destroying or hindering growth of infectious agents.

an ti ven in (an′tē ven′in), 1. an antitoxin (antibody) present in the blood of an animal after repeated injections of venom. 2. the antitoxic serum obtained from such blood.

ar thri tis (ar thrī′tis), inflammation of a joint or joints.

a scor bic ac id (ə skôr′bik as′id), chemical name for vitamin C, found in foods such as citrus fruits.

a sep sis (ə sep′sis *or* ā sep′sis), method of maintaining absence of disease-producing organisms.

a stig ma tism (ə stig′mə tiz′əm), irregularity in the surfaces of the cornea or the lens of the eye so that light rays are not focused correctly and vision is blurred or indistinct.

au to graft (ô′tō graft), a graft of skin or other tissue taken from the body of the grafted person rather than from another person.

bac ter i a (bak tir′ē ə), very tiny and simple plants, so small that they can usually be seen only through a microscope.

bac ter i ol o gy (bak tir′ē ol′ə jē), science that deals with the study of bacteria.

Ban ting (ban′ting), **Sir Frederick,** 1891-1941, Canadian research physician who discovered the hormone insulin, now used to treat diabetes.

bar bit ur ate (bär bich′ər it *or* bär bich′ə rāt′), depressant used medically for relaxation and sleep.

bas al me tab o lism (bā′səl mə tab′ə liz′əm), energy produced by an individual during physical, digestive, and emotional rest, measured directly by the heat given off and indirectly by the oxygen consumed and carbon dioxide given off.

Ben ze drine (ben′zə drēn′), trademark for one of the stimulant drugs.

Best (best), **Charles,** born 1899, Canadian physiologist associated with the discovery of insulin.

bi o sphere (bī′ə sfir), the region surrounding the earth—including the soil, water, and air—which can be inhabited by living things.

blood let ting (blud′let′ing), the act of opening a vein to take out blood.

bomb cal o rim e ter (bom′ kal′ə rim′ə tər), a metal chamber in which a measured quantity of food or fuel undergoes complete combustion, its calorie value being determined by exact measurement of the heat given off during this process.

bo tan i cal (bə tan′ə kəl), any of several short-lived poisons extracted from plants.

brain stem (brān′ stem′), lower portion of the brain, where many automatic functions are centered; the extension upward from the spinal cord.

bron chi tis (brong kī′tis), inflammation of the mucous membrane that lines the bronchial tubes.

bron cho scope (brong′kə skōp), a thin tube by which a doctor can see into the bronchi, administer treatment, or remove foreign objects or mucus.

bu bon ic plague (byü bon′ik plāg′), a very dangerous, contagious disease, accompanied by fever, chills, and swelling of the lymph glands.

cal cu lus (kal′kyə ləs), *see* **tartar.**

cal o rie (kal′ə rē), unit of heat used to measure energy supplied by food.

can cer (kan′sər), harmful growth of body cells that tends to spread and destroy healthy tissues.

car bo hy drate (kär′bō hī′drāt), substance composed of carbon, hydrogen, and oxygen. Carbohydrates furnish heat and energy for the body.

car bol ic ac id (kär bol′ik as′id), a very poisonous acid obtained from coal tar and used in solutions as a disinfectant and antiseptic.

car bon mon ox ide (kär′bən mo nok′sīd), a colorless, odorless, very poisonous gas. It is part of car exhaust and tobacco smoke.

car ti lage (kär′tl ij), a tough, elastic substance forming parts of the skeleton. Cartilage is more flexible than bone and not as hard.

ce men tum (sə men′təm), hard, thin substance covering the roots of a tooth up to its neck.

cer e bral ar ter i o scle ro sis (ser′ə brəl är tir′ē ō-sklə rō′sis), an arterial disease of the brain occurring especially in the elderly.

chem o ther a py (kem′ō ther′ə pē), the treatment of infections by means of chemicals.

cho les ter ol (kə les′tə rol′ *or* kə les′tə rōl′), a white, fatty substance found in the blood and other tissues of the body and also in foods such as eggs and meat.

chro mo some (krō′mə sōm), one of the microscopic threadlike bodies that are evident in the nucleus of a cell during cell division. Chromosomes carry the genes that transmit traits from parents to offspring.

cil i a (sil′ē ə), tiny, hairlike projections that grow on the surface of respiratory mucous membranes.

claus tro pho bi a (klô′ strə fō′bē ə), an abnormal fear of enclosed spaces.

co caine (kō kān′), stimulant drug once used to deaden pain.

co deine (kō′dēn), a narcotic derived from opium and prescribed medically for relief of pain.

Col lip (kol′ip), **James,** 1892-1965, Canadian biochemist known for his work on internal secretions of the parathyroid and pituitary glands.

con vul sion (kən vul′shən), a violent, involuntary contracting and relaxing of the muscles.

cor ne a (kôr′nē ə), the transparent part of the outer coat of the eyeball.

cor tex (kôr′teks), outer layer of an internal organ, such as the cortex of the adrenal gland.

cor ti sone (kôr′tə zōn), hormone obtained from the cortex of the adrenal glands or produced synthetically; it is used in the treatment of arthritis and other ailments.

cry o sur ger y (krī′ō sėr′jər ē), surgery utilizing extremely low temperatures to permit removal of diseased tissue.

Cur ie (kyůr′ē *or* kyů rē′), **Marie,** 1867-1934, Polish-French chemist who, with her husband Pierre, discovered radium in 1898.

Cur ie (kyůr′ē *or* kyů rē′), **Pierre** (pē er′ *or* pē ar′), 1859-1906, French chemist, co-discoverer of radium in 1898.

cys to scope (sis′tə skōp), an instrument which permits examination of and operation on the urinary bladder.

de lir i um (di lir′ ē əm), temporary disorder of the mind that occurs during fevers, insanity, drunkenness, and so on.

den tal car ies (den′tl ker′ēz *or* kar′ēz), decay of dental tissues; tooth decay; cavity.

den tin (den′tən), hard, bony material beneath the tooth enamel. It forms the main part of the tooth.

de pres sant (di pres′ənt), drug that quiets the nerves, relieves worries, and sometimes encourages sleep.

der ma tol o gist (dėr mə tol′ə jist), a doctor who treats the skin and its diseases.

der mis (dėr′mis), the sensitive layer of skin beneath the outer skin where many blood vessels and nerve endings are located.

Dex e drine (dek′sə drēn), trademark for a stimulant drug used for controlling mental depression and appetite.

di a be tes (dī′ə bē′tis *or* dī′ə bē′tēz), disease in which body cells are unable to utilize normal amounts of sugar and starch.

dis pen sar y (dis pen′sər ē), place where medicines, medical care, and medical advice are given free or for a very small charge.

DMT (*di meth yl tryp ta mine*) (dī meth′əl trip′tə-mēn), an hallucinogenic drug, usually smoked, that produces a short, intense experience similar to that of LSD.

DNA (*de ox y ri bo nu cle ic ac id*) (dē ok′sə rī′bō-nyü klē′ik as′id), complicated molecules, present in most chromosomes, which control the growth and heredity of the cell.

drug de pen dence (drug′ di pen′dəns), condition in which a person has become completely dependent upon a drug either physically or psychologically or both.

e col o gy (ē kol′ə jē), branch of biology that deals with the relation of living things to their environment and to each other.

e co sys tem (ē′kō sis′təm), an environment in which living and nonliving things interact and in which materials are used over and over again.

Ehr lich (er′lik *or* ār′lik), **Paul,** 1854-1915, German bacteriologist who discovered the drug "606" (Salvarsan).

el e ment (el′ə mənt), one of the simple substances, such as oxygen, hydrogen, nitrogen, and carbon, that cannot be broken down chemically into other known materials and still keep its identity.

em phy se ma (em′fə sē′mə), disease in which the lungs become expanded and inefficient in supplying oxygen to and removing carbon dioxide from the blood.

en do crine gland (en′dō krin *or* en′dō krīn gland′), any of the various glands that produce secretions which pass directly into the bloodstream or lymph instead of into a duct.

en do crin ol o gy (en′dō krin ol′ə jē), science that deals with the endocrine glands.

en er giz er (en′ər jī′zər), drug that elevates a person's mood and stimulates his activity.

en vi ron men tal dep ri va tion (en vī′rən men′tl dep′rə vā′shən), mild mental retardation often found in poor, malnourished, and sick populations.

en zyme (en′zīm), chemical substance produced in living cells, that can cause changes in other substances within the body without being changed itself. Pepsin is an enzyme.

ep i de mi ol o gy (ep′ə dē′mē ol′ə jē), the branch of medicine dealing with epidemic diseases.

ep i der mis (ep′ə dėr′mis), the thin outer layer of the skin.

ep i lep sy (ep′ə lep′sē), a chronic disorder of the nervous system marked by complete or partial loss of consciousness and sometimes convulsions.

e ro sion (i rō′zhən), a gradual eating or wearing away by glaciers, running water, waves, or wind.

e ther (ē′thər), a colorless, strong-smelling liquid that burns and evaporates readily. Its fumes cause unconsciousness when deeply inhaled.

Flem ing (flem′ing), **Sir Alexander,** 1881-1955, Scottish bacteriologist who discovered penicillin.

flu o ride (flü′ə rīd′), fluorine compound that may be added to community water supplies in small amounts, or applied directly to the teeth by a dentist, to help prevent tooth decay.

fol li cle (fol′ə kəl), a small cavity, sac, or gland.

Ga len (gā′lən), **Claudius** (klô′dē əs), A.D. 130?-210?, Greek physician who is famous for his theory of body "systems."

gas tro scope (gas′trə skōp′), an instrument for inspecting the interior of the stomach.

glu cose (glü′kōs), the end product of the digestion of starches and sugars; the body's chief source of energy.

gly co gen (glī′kə jən), starchlike form in which excess sugar is stored in the body, largely in the liver but also in the muscles. It can be changed quickly back into sugar as needed.

goi ter (goi′tər), disease of the thyroid gland characterized by swelling in the neck.

gon or rhe a (gon′ə rē′ə), a contagious venereal disease caused by the gonococcus germ.

hal i to sis (hal′ə tō′sis), bad breath.

hal lu ci na tion (hə lü′sn ā′shən), a sensory experience which does not exist outside an individual's mind and is a false perception of reality.

hal lu cin o gen (hə lü′sn ə jən′), drug that produces hallucinations.

hash ish (hash′ēsh′), the dried flowers, top leaves, and tender parts of some kinds of hemp prepared for use as a narcotic.

he ma log (hē′mə lôg), new blood analyzer that performs a complete blood analysis in one minute.

he mo glo bin (hē′mə glō′bən), the protein matter in the red blood cells that is composed of globin and hematin. It carries oxygen from the lungs to the tissues and some carbon dioxide from the tissues back to the lungs.

Hench (hench), **Philip,** 1896-1965, United States physician who used cortisone and ACTH for treating rheumatic diseases.

hep a ti tis (hep′ə tī′tis), a liver inflammation.

her bi cide (hėr′bə sīd), a toxic chemical used to kill weeds.

her o in (her′ō ən), poisonous, habit-forming narcotic drug made from opium; it can cause physical and psychological dependence.

HGH, a synthetic human growth hormone developed in 1971.

Hip poc ra tes (hi pok′rə tēz), 460?-357? B.C., a Greek physician, called the father of medicine.

hor mone (hôr′mōn), chemical substance formed in certain parts of the body which enters the blood and affects activities of organs.

hy dro ceph a lus (hī′drō sef′ə ləs), accumulation of fluid within the cranium, especially in infancy, often causing great enlargement of the head.

hy dro chlo ric ac id (hī′drə klôr′ik as′id), normal constituent of the gastric juice in man and other mammals.

hy dro pho bi a (hī′drə fō′bē ə), an abnormal fear of water.

hy per ven ti la tion (hī′pər ven′tə lā′shən), excessive or forced respiration, causing a lowering of the normal amount of carbon dioxide in the blood.

hy po thal a mus (hī′pə thal′ə məs), the part of the brain under the thalamus, controlling temperature, hunger, thirst, and the pituitary gland.

hy po ther mi a (hī′pə thėr′mē ə), a condition of reduced body temperature that slows the flow of blood during surgery.

im mune re sponse (i myün′ ri spons′), production of special white blood cells by the body which attack and destroy foreign tissues introduced into it.

im mu ni za tion (im′yü nə zā′shən), method by which the body is made resistant to disease.

im mu nol o gy (im′yü nol′ə jē), the science dealing with the nature and causes of immunity to diseases.

in sec ti cide (in sek′tə sīd), agent that destroys insects.

in su lin (in′sə lən), hormone secreted by the islets of Langerhans in the pancreas which enables the body to use sugar and other carbohydrates.

i ris (ī′ris), colored part around the pupil of the eye. It contains muscles which regulate the amount of light entering the eye.

ir ra di a tion (i rā′dē ā′shən), the use of X rays or other radiation for the treatment of disease.

is lets of Lang er hans (ī′lits əv läng′er häns), groups of cells in the pancreas that have an endocrine function and that secrete insulin.

i so tope (ī′sə tōp), any of two or more forms of a chemical element that have the same chemical properties but different atomic weights.

Jen ner (jen′ər), **Edward,** 1749-1823, English physician who discovered smallpox vaccine.

Koch (kôk), **Robert,** 1843-1910, German physician and pioneer bacteriologist who proved that a specific germ causes a specific disease.

kwa shi or kor (kwä′shē ôr′kôr), an often fatal disease of infants and young children, caused by a protein deficiency in the diet. It occurs especially in developing nations of the world.

lar ynx (lar′ingks), upper end of the windpipe, where the vocal cords are located and where voice is produced.

la ser (lā′zər), device that produces a very narrow and intense beam of light of only one wavelength going in only one direction. Laser beams are sometimes used to remove diseased body tissues.

Leeu wen hoek (lā′vən hu̇k), **Antony van,** 1632-1723, Dutch scientist who was the first to study blood cells and tiny organisms through magnifying lenses.

leu ke mi a (lü kē′mē ə), cancer found in the blood-forming tissues; it is characterized by a large excess of white blood cells.

Lis ter (lis′tər), **Joseph,** 1827-1912, English surgeon called the father of antiseptic surgery.

LSD (*ly ser gic ac id di eth yl am ide*) (lī sėr′jik as′id dī eth ə lam′īd), hallucinogenic compound of lysergic acid that has highly dangerous properties.

lymph (limf), nearly colorless liquid that surrounds and bathes all the body cells, somewhat like blood without red blood cells.

lymph node (limf′ nōd′), one of the glandlike structures occurring along the course of lymph vessels which serve as traps to remove bacteria and other particles from the bloodstream.

mal nu tri tion (mal′nü trish′ən *or* mal′nyü trish′-ən), poor nourishment; lack of nourishment.

mal oc clu sion (mal′ə klü′zhən), condition in which teeth are poorly aligned.

mar i jua na (mar′ə wä′nə), drug made from the dried leaves and flowers of the hemp plant. It is a mild hallucinogen but is dealt with legally as a narcotic.

me dul la (mi dul′ə), central part of an organ, such as the medulla of the adrenal glands.

men tal health (men′tl helth′), state of being in which one feels comfortable about oneself and others and is able to meet life's demands.

mes ca line (mes′kə lēn), hallucinogenic drug found in the peyote cactus.

met a bol ic de fect (met′ə bol′ik dē′fekt), a physical or mental defect, present at birth, which resulted from faulty metabolism.

me tab o lism (mə tab′ə liz əm), sum of the chemical work done by the body cells, including the changing of food into living tissue and energy and the breaking down of worn-out tissue.

meth a done (meth′ə dōn), a synthetic narcotic used to relieve pain. It is sometimes used to treat heroin addiction.

Meth e drine (meth′ə drēn), trade name for methamphetamine hydrochloride, a stimulant drug.

mi cro bi ol o gy (mī′krō bī ol′ə jē), science dealing with microorganisms.

mi cro or gan ism (mī′krō ôr′gə niz′əm), plants or animals too small to be seen without a microscope.

mi cro sur ger y (mī′krō sėr′jer ē), the performing of an operation on organs or tissues, using a microscope or a magnifying lens.

min er al (min′ər əl), class of nutrients occurring in food in the form of water-soluble salts which furnish building materials and help keep the body working well. Calcium is a mineral.

mol e cule (mol′ə kyül), the smallest particle into which an element or compound can be divided without changing its chemical properties.

mor phine (môr′fēn), narcotic made from opium, used medically to lessen pain and cause sleep.

Mor ton (môr′tən), **W. T. G.,** 1819-1868, United States dentist who experimented with sulfuric ether as an anesthetizing agent.

mu cous mem brane (myü′kəs mem′brān), the lining of the body cavities that open to the air.

mu cus (myü′kəs), slimy substance secreted by and moistening the mucous membranes.

nar co lep sy (när′kə lep′sē), abnormal sleepiness.

nar cot ic (när kot′ik), drug that is capable of causing drowsiness, sleep, unconsciousness, or stupor. Such drugs blunt the senses and can cause physical and psychological dependence.

neu ro sis (nu̇ rō′sis or nyu̇ rō′sis), a mental disorder that is a sign of some maladjustment or a symptom of some conflict with reality. It is characterized by depression, anxiety, and fears.

ne vus (nē′vəs), a discolored or pigmented spot on the skin from birth, as a mole; birthmark.

ni a cin (nī′ə sən), chemical name for one of the group of B vitamins, found in such foods as lean meat, liver, wheat germ, milk, and eggs.

nu cle us (nü′klē əs *or* nyü′klē əs), mass of specialized protoplasm found in most plant and animal cells without which the cell cannot grow and divide.

nu tri ent (nü′trē ənt *or* nyü′trē ənt), nourishing substance, such as a vitamin or protein, found in foods and having specific functions in the nourishment of the body.

oc clu sion (o klü′zhən), proper alignment of teeth so that the teeth of both jaws fit together.

oc cu pa tion al ther a py (ok′yə pā′shə nəl ther′ə pē), the treatment of persons having physical disabilities through creative activities.

o phid i o pho bi a (ō fid′ē ō fō′bē ə), an abnormal fear of snakes.

oph thal mol o gist (of′thal mol′ə jist), doctor who specializes in the treatment of all diseases, defects, and injuries of the eye.

oph thal mol o gy (of′thal mol′ə jē), branch of medicine dealing with the structure, function, and diseases of the eye.

o pi um (ō′pē əm), a narcotic obtained from the opium poppy and from which various other narcotics are extracted.

or tho don tics (ôr′thə don′tiks), branch of dentistry that deals with aligning teeth.

or tho don tist (ôr′thə don′tist), dentist who specializes in aligning teeth.

or tho pe dic sur ger y (ôr′thə pē′dik sėr′jər ē), the branch of surgery that deals with the deformities and diseases of bones and joints.

os si fy (os′ə fī), to change into bone.

o var y (ō′vər ē), the organ of a female in which eggs are produced.

ox i da tion (ok′sə dā′shən), the combining of oxygen with another element to form one or more new substances.

pace mak er (pās′mā′kər), an electric device implanted in the wall of the heart to maintain or restore the rhythm of the heartbeat.

pal pi ta tion (pal′pə tā′shən), very rapid beating of the heart.

par a thy roid glands (par′ə thī′roid glanz′), small glands near or in the thyroid gland. Their secretion, which enables the body to use calcium and phosphorus, is necessary for life.

Pa ré (pə rā′), **Ambroise** (äɴ brwaz′), 1517-1590, French surgeon often called the father of modern surgery.

Pas teur (pa stėr′), **Louis** (lü′ē), 1822-1895, French chemist and bacteriologist who is often called the founder of the science of microbiology.

pat ent med i cine (pat′nt med′ə sən), 1. any medicine that may be purchased without a doctor's prescription. 2. medicine sold by a company which has a patent on its manufacture and trade name.

pel lag ra (pə lag′rə), disease marked by spinal pain, digestive upset, skin rash, and sometimes mental disturbances.

pen i cil lin (pen′ə sil′ən), first antibiotic, obtained from a kind of mold; it hinders development of many kinds of microorganisms.

Pen to thal (pen′tə thôl′), trademark for thiopental. A barbiturate used as an anesthetic.

per i o don tal dis ease (per′ē ə don′tl də zēz′), condition in which gums, bones, and tissues supporting teeth are affected and the teeth become loose.

per i o don tal mem brane (per′ē ə don′tl mem′-brān), soft covering surrounding a tooth and holding it in place in the jaw.

pe yo te (pā ō′tē), a variety of cactus containing the hallucinogenic ingredient mescaline.

phag o cyte (fag′ə sīt), a white blood cell capable of absorbing and destroying waste or harmful material, such as bacteria that produce disease.

pho bi a (fō′bē ə), an abnormal fear of something.

phos phate (fos′fāt), a substance containing the chemical element phosphorus.

phys i cal de pen dence (fiz′ə kəl di pen′dəns), a condition characterized by bodily tolerance to a drug which requires progressively larger doses of the drug to produce the desired effect.

phys i cal ther a py (fiz′ə kəl ther′ə pē), treatment of diseases and defects by physical and mechanical means, as by exercise, massage, heat, and light.

pig ment (pig′mənt), substance that occurs in and colors the tissues of an animal or plant. The color of a person's skin is due to pigment in the body cells.

pin e al bod y (pin′ē əl bod′ē), small, cone-shaped body of unknown function located in the brain.

pi tu i tar y gland (pə tü′ə ter′ē *or* pə tyü′ə ter′ē gland′), small, oval endocrine gland situated beneath the brain. It produces several hormones necessary to life.

PKU (*phen yl ke to nu ri a*) (fen′əl kē′tə nyůr′ē ə), an inherited abnormal condition usually first characterized by signs of mental retardation in infancy.

plan tar wart (plan′tər wôrt′), wart found on the sole of the foot.

plaque (plak), thin, transparent film composed of saliva, bacteria, and food debris, which is constantly being formed on the surface of the teeth.

plas ma (plaz′mə), the clear, almost colorless liquid part of the blood or lymph in which blood or lymph cells float.

plas tic sur ger y (plas′tik sėr′jər ē), surgery that restores or improves the body's outer appearance.

pol lu tion (pə lü′shən), addition of man-made products to the environment which can be a danger to the health and survival of all living things.

prej u dice (prej′ə dis), opinion formed without taking time and care to judge fairly.

proc to scope (prok′tə skōp), an instrument for visual examination of the interior of the rectum.

pro tein (prō′tēn), one of the many substances containing nitrogen which are a necessary part of the cells of animals and plants.

pro to plasm (prō′tə plaz′əm), essential, living, colorless, jellylike material of which every plant and animal cell is composed.

psy che del ic (sī′kə del′ik), revealing the mind or psyche; producing a mental state of extremely intensified perception; consciousness-expanding.

psy chi a trist (sī kī′ə trist), doctor trained in the branch of medicine that deals with the prevention and treatment of mental disorders.

psy cho dra ma (sī′kō drä′mə), a method of group psychotherapy taking the form of a play in which the patients assume and dramatize roles relevant to their problems.

psy cho log i cal de pen dence (sī'kə loj'ə kəl di pen'dəns), a condition characterized by a persistent emotional need for a drug which may border on compulsion.

psy chol o gist (sī kol'ə jist), person skilled or trained in the science that deals with the study of mental processes and behavior.

psy cho sis (sī kō'sis), any severe mental illness.

psy cho so mat ic ill ness (sī'kō sō mat'ik il'nis), a physical disorder that is caused by or influenced by the emotional state of the patient.

quack (kwak), someone who practices medicine without the proper qualifications; an ignorant pretender to knowledge or skill of any sort.

quar an tine (kwôr'ən tēn'), keeping a person, animal, plant, ship, and so on away from others for a time to prevent the spread of disease.

ra di o ac tive fall out (rā'dē ō ak'tiv fôl'out'), radioactive particles of dust that fall to the earth after an atomic explosion.

ra di o ac tive i so tope (rā'dē ō ak'tiv ī'sə tōp), isotope that is naturally radioactive, or that is produced artificially by bombardment with nuclear particles in an atomic reactor. Radioactive isotopes are useful in medical diagnosis and treatment.

ra di o ac tiv i ty (rā'dē ō ak tiv'ə tē), the property of giving off rays that can pass through solid matter.

ra di o graph (rā'dē ō graf'), picture produced by X rays or other rays on a photographic plate.

re cy cle (rē sī'kəl), to put through a cycle again or through a new cycle.

re tar da tion (rē'tär dā'shən), act of making slow.

ret i na (ret'n ə), inner layer of nerve cells at the back of the eye which is sensitive to light and receives the images of things viewed.

rheu ma toid ar thri tis (rü'mə toid är thrī'tis), inflammation and stiffness of the joints, often crippling in its effects.

Rh fac tor (fak'tər), substance often found in the blood of human beings. Blood containing this substance (Rh positive) does not combine favorably with blood lacking it (Rh negative).

ri bo fla vin (rī'bō flā'vən), chemical name for vitamin B_2, found in such foods as liver and eggs.

RNA (*ri bo nu cle ic ac id*) (rī'bō nü klē'ik *or* rī'bō nyü klē'ik as'id), a complex chemical compound found in all living cells. It acts as a messenger for DNA.

Roent gen (rent'gən), **Wilhelm Konrad,** 1845-1923, German physicist who discovered X rays.

ru bel la (rü bel'ə), a contagious disease resembling measles; German measles.

ru be o la (rü bē'ə lə), infectious virus disease, usually attacking children; measles.

san i tar i an (san'ə ter'ē ən), specialist in sanitary science and public health.

sca ler (skā'lər), a steel instrument for removing tartar from the teeth.

scan ner (skan'ər), a radiation-sensitive instrument that moves back and forth over a body organ and produces a picture (scan) showing diseased areas, if any, in a patient who has first been given radioactive isotopes.

scape goat (skāp'gōt'), person made to bear the blame for the mistakes or faults of others.

schiz o phre ni a (skit'sə frē'nē ə *or* skit'sə frēn'yə), psychotic disorder, often beginning in young adulthood, that is characterized by unpredictable disturbances in stream of thought and behavior; a tendency to withdraw from reality.

se ba ceous gland (si bā'shəs gland'), gland in the skin that supplies oil to the skin and hair.

sed a tive (sed'ə tiv), *see* **depressant.**

sig moid o scope (sig moi'də skōp), an instrument for examination of the sigmoid colon, or lower part of the large intestine.

small pox (smôl'poks'), a very contagious disease characterized by fever and blisterlike eruptions on the skin that often leave permanent scars.

spleen (splēn), organ behind and at the left of the stomach which destroys diseased red blood cells and manufactures certain of the white blood cells needed by the body to fight infection.

stim u lant (stim'yə lənt), food or drug that temporarily increases the activity of the brain or some other part of the body.

STP (es′tē′pē′), a synthetic hallucinogenic drug.

stra bis mus (strə biz′məs), a vision disorder due to the turning of one eye or both eyes from the normal position, so that both cannot be directed at the same point or object at the same time.

strep to coc cus in fec tion (strep′tə kok′əs in-fek′shən), infection caused by a group of spherical bacteria which usually grow in twisted chains.

strep to my cin (strep′tō mī′sn), a powerful antibiotic, similar to penicillin, that is effective against such diseases as tuberculosis.

sul fa drugs (sul′fə drugz′), family of drugs derived from a compound called sulfanilamide, effective against many infections.

syph i lis (sif′ə ləs), a contagious venereal disease caused by a spirochete.

tar tar (tär′tər), a hard substance formed by the action of saliva on food and deposited as a crust on the teeth.

tel e ther a py (tel′ə ther′ə pē), treatment with X rays or radiant energy of a high intensity, applied at a distance from the body or affected organ.

tes ti cle (tes′tə kəl), gland in a male animal that produces sperm; testis.

ther mal pol lu tion (thėr′məl pə lü′shən), contamination resulting from the discharge of an excess of heated water into a body of water.

thi a min (thī′ə mən), chemical name for vitamin B_1, found in such foods as green vegetables and cereals or prepared synthetically.

thy mus (thī′məs), a small ductless gland of uncertain function, located in the upper chest, that grows steadily from birth through childhood but begins to shrivel during the teens and may even disappear.

thy roid gland (thī′roid gland′), endocrine gland in the neck which secretes thyroxin.

thy rox in (thī rok′sən), hormone, rich in iodine, produced by the thyroid gland; it helps regulate the rate at which the body uses its store of energy.

trac er (trā′sər), agent by which something can be followed or identified. Radioactive tracers used in medicine can be introduced into the body and their course and distribution followed.

tran quil iz er (trang′kwə lī′zər), a drug that may be prescribed by doctors to relieve tension or lower blood pressure; it may also be used to calm psychotic patients in mental hospitals.

tre pan ning (trə pan′ing), oldest known surgical procedure in which a hole was cut in the skull either to relieve pressure from a fracture or remove foreign objects from the brain; used also to let out "evil spirits."

tu ber cu lo sis (tü bėr′kyə lō′sis *or* tyü bėr′kyə-lō′sis), infectious disease affecting various tissues of the body, but most often the lungs.

vac ci na tion (vak′sə nā′shən), act or process of inoculating with vaccine.

ve ner e al dis ease (və nir′ē əl də zēz′), or **VD** (vē′dē′), an infectious disease passed on by close intimate contact, usually though not necessarily always by sexual contact.

vil li (vil′ ī), tiny, hairlike parts growing out of a membrane, especially those projecting from the mucous membranes of the small intestine, that aid in absorbing certain substances.

vi ta min (vī′tə min), one of a group of substances occurring naturally in many foods which in relatively small amounts are essential for life and growth.

vo cal cords (vō′kəl kôrdz′), two pairs of membranes in the larynx. The lower pair can be pulled tight or let loose to help make the sounds of the voice.

vol a tile chem i cal (vol′ə təl kem′ə kəl), a liquid or a solid substance that changes rapidly and easily into a vapor or gas.

Waks man (waks′man), **Selman,** born 1888, Russian-American microbiologist who discovered the antibiotic streptomycin.

with draw al sick ness (wiᴛʜ drô′əl sik′nis), extremely painful symptoms that a drug abuser suffers when a substance upon which his system has become physically dependent is withheld.

xen o pho bi a (zen′ə fō′bē ə), an abnormal fear of strangers or strange things.

Index

Index of Health and Safety Ideas[1]

[1]Selected behavioral objectives for this level are given in the *Resource Book,* pages 25-26.

Credits

Cover: The color scan shown here was performed on a prototype rectilinear video scanner developed by ElScint, Inc., Haifa, Israel. The image was produced at the Nuclear Medicine Service, Veterans Administration Hospital, Hines, Ill. Used courtesy of Ervin Kaplan, M.D.

Unit 1: 9—Drawing by George Suyeoka. 11—X rays from *Medical Care of the Adolescent,* 1960, by J. Roswell Gallagher. Courtesy of Appleton-Century-Crofts, Inc. 12, 13—Drawings by George Suyeoka. 15—Drawing by Arnold Ryan Chalfant, AMI. 18-21—Photographs by Ray Komorski. 24, 25—Drawings by George Suyeoka. 26-27—Photographs by Myles DeRussy. 28—Drawing by Cynthia Fujii. 29, 31—Drawings by Lou Barlow, AMI. 33—Drawing by George Suyeoka. 35—X rays courtesy of Dr. Norman Olsen. 37-40—Anatomical drawings by Lou Barlow, AMI. 41—Drawing by George Suyeoka. 45—Drawings by Lou Barlow, AMI. 46-47 (Pictures 1, 2, 4, and 8)—Photographs by Archie Lieberman; (Picture 3)—Photograph by Myles DeRussy; (Pictures 5, 6, and 7)—Photographs by Lyle Mayer.

Unit 2: 64-65—Photographs by Archie Lieberman taken with the cooperation of staff and residents of Gateway Houses Foundation Inc., Chicago, Ill. 66 (Top)—Photograph by R. Engh from Photo Researchers. 66 (Bottom)—Photograph from United Press International. 67 (Top Left)—Photograph by Pierre Berger from Photo Researchers. 67 (Top Right)—Photograph from United Press International. 67 (Bottom)—Photograph by Syd Greenberg from Photo Researchers. 68-69—Photographs courtesy of Hinsdale Sanitarium and Hospital, Hinsdale, Ill. 71—Drawing by George Suyeoka. 76-77—Drawings by Lou Barlow, AMI. 78—Drawing by George Suyeoka.

Unit 3: 85—Engraving from The Bettmann Archive, Inc. 88, 89—Collages by Franz Altschuler. 91-94—Photographs by James L. Ballard taken at the National Museum of Medical Quackery with the cooperation of the St. Louis Medical Society and the FDA. 96, 101—Drawings by George Suyeoka.

Unit 4: 107—Drawing by George Suyeoka. 108, 109, 110—Drawings by Lou Barlow, AMI. 111, 112, 113, 114, 115, 121—Drawings by George Suyeoka. 123-126—Photographs by Ralph Cowan. 128, 132—Drawings by George Suyeoka. 134—Photograph by Marilyn Silverstone from Magnum. 135 (Top Left)—Photograph by Stern/Hopker from Black Star. 135 (Top Right)—Photograph courtesy of United Nations. 135 (Bottom)—Photograph by Marc Riboud from Magnum. 136 (Top)—Photograph by Stern/Hopker from Black Star. 136 (Bottom Left)—Photograph by Erich Hartmann from Magnum. 136 (Bottom Right)—Photograph courtesy of United Nations. 137—Photograph by Tor Eigelund from Black Star.

Unit 5: 148—Drawing by George Suyeoka. 151-154—Photographs by Ralph Cowan. 156, 157, 158, 159, 160, 161, 162, 165—Drawings by George Suyeoka.

Unit 6: 173, 176, 178—Photographs by Michel Ditlove. 181—Drawing by George Suyeoka. 184-185—Drawings by George Suyeoka based on design photographs supplied by Fairchild Industries. 186-188—Photographs courtesy of General Motors Corporation. 190—Drawing by George Suyeoka. 193—Photograph courtesy of U.S. Department of Commerce, National Environmental Satellite Service.

Unit 7: 199—Microphotograph courtesy of Dieter Sussdorf, Ph.D. 200—Drawings courtesy of The New York Botanical Garden. 202, 203—Drawings by George Suyeoka. 205—Drawing by Lou Barlow, AMI. 206—Photograph from National Library of Medicine. 207—Drawing by George Suyeoka. 210, 212—Photograph and etching from National Library of Medicine. 213, 216, 217—Drawings by Lou Barlow, AMI. 219—Drawing by George Suyeoka. 220—Etching from National Library of Medicine. 221—(See Cover credit.) 222—Photograph by James L. Ballard taken at Lutheran General Hospital. 223—Photograph by Dan McCoy from Black Star. 224—Photograph by James L. Ballard taken courtesy of Dudley S. Childress, Ph.D., Northwestern University Prosthetic Research Laboratory. 225—Photograph by Joe Sterling. 226—Photograph courtesy of Abbott Laboratories. 231-233—Photographs by Archie Lieberman taken at Chicago-Read Mental Health Center with the cooperation of Mrs. Della Klevs, M.A., Director of Children and Adolescent Services, Subzone I; Mr. John T. Retterer, M.A., Program Chief of Adolescent Program, Subzone I; Mr. Robert Tamura, M.A., Director of Central Activities. 235—Drawing by George Suyeoka.

Unit 8: 242—Engraving from The Bettmann Archive, Inc. 243—Drawing by George Suyeoka. 244—Microphotograph by Margret I. Sellers, Ph.D., Assistant Professor, Department of Infectious Diseases, University of California Medical Center, Los Angeles. Used courtesy of The National Tuberculosis and Respiratory Disease Association. 246 (Picture 1)—Microphotograph courtesy of American Society for Microbiology; (Picture 2)—Microphotograph courtesy of National Medical Audiovisual Center; (Picture 3)—Microphotograph courtesy of Virus Laboratory, University of California, Berkeley, Calif.; (Picture 4)—Microphotograph courtesy USPHS, Center for Disease Control; (Pictures 5 and 6)—Microphotographs courtesy of S. Stanley Schneierson, M.D., and Abbott Laboratories; (Picture 7)—See credit for page 244. 250—Drawing by George Suyeoka. 251-256—Photographs by Archie Lieberman taken with the cooperation of Lutheran General Hospital, Park Ridge, Ill. 259—Drawings by George Suyeoka. 260—Photograph by Homer Page, courtesy of World Health Organization. 261—Photograph by D. Henrioud, courtesy of World Health Organization. 262—Photograph courtesy of World Health Organization. 263—Photograph by E. Rice, courtesy of World Health Organization. 264—Photograph by T. Farkas, courtesy of World Health Organization.

Unit 9: 272, 274, 275, 279, 281, 282, 284—Drawings by George Suyeoka. 286 (Top Left)—Photograph by Mary Thacher from Photo Researchers. 286 (Top Middle)—Photograph by Syd Greenberg from Photo Researchers. 286 (Top Right and Bottom Left)—Photographs courtesy of Environmental Protection Agency. 286 (Bottom Right)—Photograph courtesy of Department of Streets and Sanitation, City of Chicago. 287 (Top Left, Middle, and Right)—Photographs courtesy of Environmental Protection Agency. 287 (Bottom)—Photograph courtesy of Chicago Sanitary District. 288 (Top Left)—Photograph courtesy of Massachusetts Audubon Society and Environmental Protection Agency. 288 (Top Middle, Bottom Left and Right)—Photographs courtesy of Environmental Protection Agency. 288 (Top Right)—Photograph by John Launois from Black Star. 289 (Top Left)—Photograph by Farrell Grehan from Photo Researchers. 289 (Top Middle)—Photograph by Tom McHugh from Photo Researchers. 289 (Top Right, and Bottom)—Photographs courtesy of Environmental Protection Agency. 290 (Top Left)—Photograph by Joern Gerdts from Photo Researchers. 290 (Top Right)—Photograph by Russ Kinne from Photo Researchers. 290 (Bottom Left)—Photograph courtesy of American Forest Institute. 290 (Bottom Right)—Photograph by Joseph Sterling. 291 (Top Left)—Photograph by Joseph Sterling. 291 (Top Right)—Photograph by Archie Lieberman. 291 (Bottom Left and Right)—Photographs by Joseph Sterling. 292 (Top Left)—Photograph courtesy of Environmental Protection Agency. 292 (Top Right)—Photograph by Norman Perman. 292 (Bottom Left and Right)—Microphotographs courtesy of Carlo M. Ignoffo, Director, Biological Control of Insects Research Laboratory, USDA, Agriculture Research Service, Columbia, Mo. 293 (Top Left)—Photograph by Tom Meyers from Photo Researchers. 293 (Top Right)—Photograph by Larry Mulvehill from Photo Researchers. 293 (Bottom Left)—Photograph courtesy of Glass Container Manufacturers Institute, Inc. 293 (Bottom Right)—Photograph by Archie Lieberman. 294—Drawing by Lou Barlow, AMI.

1 2 3 4 5 6 7 8 9 10 11 12 13 14 15 16 17 18 19 20 21 22 23 24 25 80 79 78 77 76 75 74

Book Eight
Resource Book

Health and Growth

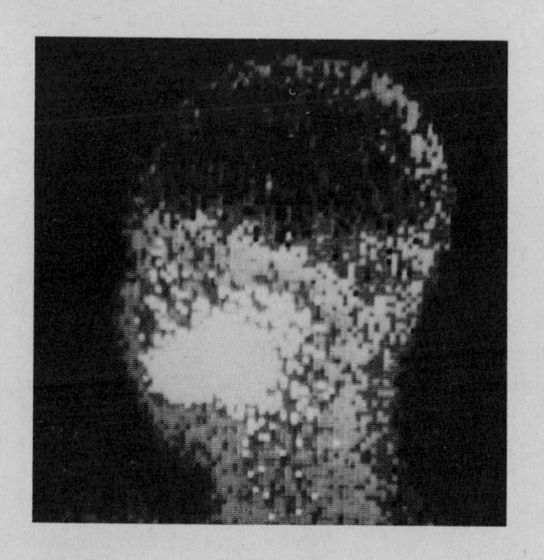

Julius B. Richmond, M.D.
Elenore T. Pounds, M.A.
Gladys Gardner Jenkins, M.A.
Dieter H. Sussdorf, Ph.D.

In consultation with
Irma B. Fricke, R.N., M.S.
Orvis A. Harrelson, M.D., M.P.H.
Norman H. Olsen, D.D.S.
Wallace Ann Wesley, Hs.D.

Designed by Norman Perman
Anatomical Art by Lou Barlow, AMI

Scott, Foresman and Company

Authors

Julius B. Richmond, M.D. Professor of Child Psychiatry and Human Development, Harvard University; Director, Judge Baker Guidance Center; Chief of Psychiatric Service, Children's Hospital, Medical Center; Professor and Chairman, Department of Social and Preventive Medicine, Harvard Medical School.

Elenore T. Pounds, M.A. Writer; lecturer; former Directing Editor, Health and Personal Development Program; classroom teacher; author of *Drugs and Your Safety* and other *Health and Growth Enrichment Booklets.*

Gladys Gardner Jenkins, M.A. Lecturer in Education and Home Economics, University of Iowa, Iowa City, Iowa; former member National Advisory Council on Child Growth and Human Development; author of *Helping Children Reach Their Potential;* coauthor of *These Are Your Children.*

Dieter H. Sussdorf, Ph.D. Associate Professor of Microbiology, Cornell University Medical College and Cornell University Graduate School of Medical Sciences, New York, New York; coauthor of *Methods in Immunology.*

ISBN: 0-673-04863-2

Regional offices of Scott, Foresman and Company are located in Dallas, Texas; Glenview, Illinois; Oakland, New Jersey; Palo Alto, California; Tucker, Georgia; and Brighton, England.

Consultants

Irma B. Fricke, R.N., M.S. Former Director of School Nursing, Evanston Public Schools, District 65, Evanston, Illinois; recipient of the 1971 William A. Howe Award in school health.

Orvis A. Harrelson, M.D., M.P.H. Director of Health Services, Tacoma Public Schools, Tacoma, Washington.

Norman H. Olsen, D.D.S. Chairman of the Department of Pedodontics and Dean of The Dental School, Northwestern University, Chicago, Illinois.

Wallace Ann Wesley, Hs.D. Director, Department of Health Education, American Medical Association, Chicago, Illinois; former teacher at primary through college levels.

Advisors

Thea Flaum, B.A. Former editor, *Safety Education,* National Safety Council, Chicago, Illinois.

Willie D. Ford, Ph.D. Professor, Nutrition and Home Economics, Grambling College, Grambling, Louisiana.

Richard E. Hudson, M.A. Eighth-grade teacher, Blowing Rock Elementary School, Blowing Rock, North Carolina.

Ruth Leverton, Ph.D. Science Advisor, Agricultural Research Service, United States Department of Agriculture, Washington, D.C.

Richard Norgaard, M.A. Health and Physical Education teacher, Mannheim Junior High School, Melrose Park, Illinois.

John D. Withers, Ph.D. Assistant Director of Education, American Institute of Biological Sciences, Education Division, Washington, D.C.

Designer

Norman Perman, B.F.A. Graphic Designer, Chicago; Guest Lecturer, University of Illinois, Circle Campus, Chicago, Illinois; past President, Society of Typographic Arts.

Contents

The HEALTH AND GROWTH Program includes *Off to a Good Start* (Junior Primer Activity Sheets), and *Book One* through *Book Eight* with accompanying *Teachers' Editions.* Also available is a preprimary health program, *Health and Safety Highlights: Pictures and Songs for Young Children.*

Goals of a Modern Health Program

The goals of today's health curriculum are directed toward teaching the health and growth sciences, those sciences that are closely related to human beings. Today's health teaching is concerned with youngsters' physical and mental health: with their understandings of the body, its structure and functioning; with care of the body; with nutrition; with consumer health and dental health; with community health and medical research; with youngsters' attitudes toward themselves, their families, and their friends; and with each young person's responsibility for helping achieve a healthful environment and for trying to improve the quality of life in the world in which he or she lives.

With the goals of modern health teaching in mind, the authors of the HEALTH AND GROWTH Program have incorporated into materials for preschool through the junior-high level a broad conceptual approach based on the physical, mental, and emotional needs of youngsters at each successive maturity level. To help teachers and students see how well the goals of health teaching are being achieved, some Behavioral Objectives are included on pages 25-26 of this *Resource Book.*

Suggested Areas of Content for a Junior-High Health Program[1]

Body Structure, Function, and Growth
Presentation of information about and development of wholesome attitudes toward the human body—its structure, function, and growth patterns; help in understanding individual differences.

Fitness, Care of the Body, and Dental Health
Guidance in building body strength and endurance; motivation for proper care of the body by getting necessary sleep, adequate diet, sufficient exercise; help in acquiring habits of good posture, cleanliness, sanitation, and grooming; knowledge of how to foster oral health.

Nutrition
Guidance in understanding that nutrition affects total health; awareness of what is an adequate daily diet for teen-agers; knowledge that nutrition is a significant factor in weight control; help in recognizing food fallacies; awareness of food problems throughout the world and of attempts to solve them.

Mental Health, Emotional Growth, and Human Relations
Guidance in helping young people grow in self-understanding and in ability to develop satisfying relationships with others; development of attitudes necessary to good citizenship, moral well-being, and the ability to take responsibility for one's own actions.

Consumer Health
Help in acquiring scientific knowledge necessary for effective evaluation and utilization of health information, products, and services.

Family Health
Development of wholesome attitudes for good family relationships; guidance in helping young people fulfill their responsibility as family members; awareness of the contributions the family makes to the health of its members.

Community Health and Medical Research
Awareness that health is a shared responsibility of individuals, families, and the community as a whole; development of knowledge about contributions of scientists, past and present, to health improvement; help in learning about local, state, and national contributions to public health; awareness that nations need to cooperate to identify and solve world health problems.

Drugs, Alcohol, and Tobacco
Awareness of beneficial uses of drugs; help in understanding that many factors influence misuse of drugs; knowledge of some effects on the body of various drugs, alcohol, and tobacco; help in appreciating the individual's responsibility for preventing misuse of drugs, alcohol, and tobacco.

Environmental Health (Ecology)
Guidance in understanding that there are ever changing hazards in our environment; that these hazards can influence the individual's total health; and that the individual, the family, and society have a responsibility for helping work for an aesthetic and healthful environment.

Safety and First Aid
Development of knowledge and attitudes necessary to help young people take responsibility for their own and others' safety; awareness of correct first-aid procedures to follow in accidents or emergencies.

[1]Selected behavioral objectives for this level are given on pages 25-26 of this *Resource Book.*

How Boys and Girls Grow and Develop: The Junior-High Years[1]

Junior high school boys and girls are neither children nor are they yet grown-ups

These are important years of transition during which youngsters are leaving the dependency of childhood behind and are moving toward greater independence of thought, action, and decision making of their own. By the end of adolescence they should be capable of becoming responsible adults. During these years there will be heightened growth and change in many areas of personality development.

These years are self-centered ones

Thoughts are turned inward on the self. "Who am I?" becomes the big question. These young people need much help in finding "themselves."

Our culture is not always kind to this age group

They are well aware of the tensions of the nuclear age and of the cultural conflicts within our society. These pressures add to the difficulties already faced in finding themselves.

Just as they are trying to find their own identity, they are engulfed with social demands for which not all of them are yet ready. Some are often expected to handle social situations and emotional reactions which belong to another and later period of life. This accelerated pseudosocial development of many junior-high pupils may become a problem. Because of the pressure to conform to the group, many of these youngsters are so absorbed in their personal problems and anxieties that their attention is drawn away from studying. It is increasingly felt that much of the emotional stress and turmoil of these early adolescent years is caused by pressure to conform to peer standards, peer culture, and the expectations of the adult society.

Another problem focuses on the different maturity levels of junior-high pupils

At the beginning of the junior-high years, many girls and some boys have already reached the adolescent level in their development. Others are in the preadolescent period; a few are still immature children. Because of this wide range of maturity levels, it is a challenge to plan a program which fits all youngsters' needs.

Adolescence has no definite beginning or end

It involves the completion of those physical changes which make a young man or woman ready for the process of reproduction; it also involves a psychological, emotional, and social readiness to assume and carry out adult responsibilities.

Some youngsters show signs of approaching the physical changes of adolescence as early as eight or nine, others as late as thirteen or fourteen. Girls usually become physically mature one and a half to two years before boys. About two thirds of the girls menstruate by the time they are thirteen, whereas about two thirds of the boys are still physically immature at that age. This poses yet another problem for the teacher. There is a difference not only in the maturity level of the pupils in the classroom but also in the developmental level between boys and girls.

About two years before the onset of puberty, physical changes begin to take place both in boys and in girls. Before these changes begin, there is usually a slowing up of growth for about six months. Periods of rapid growth follow—first in height and then often in weight, with girls frequently making dramatic gains. Boys show less-pronounced gains but over a longer period of years. This means that boys are usually smaller and slighter than girls at the beginning of the junior-high years. By the end of high school, however, most of the boys will have outdistanced the girls in both height and weight. Usually girls have

[1]The material on pages 6-12 is adapted from *These Are Your Children,* Third Edition, by Gladys Gardner Jenkins, Helen S. Shacter, and William W. Bauer. Scott, Foresman and Company, 1966.

attained their full growth by the time they are sixteen and a half years old, and boys by the time they are eighteen and a half or nineteen. There are, of course, exceptions.

This period is often called the awkward age

The rapid growth which many youngsters are experiencing does not occur simultaneously in all parts of the body. The legs usually grow long, then the trunk and arms. There follows a broadening of the chest and shoulders in boys and of the hips in girls. Hands or feet, nose or ears, may seem temporarily out of proportion. Children may trip or drop things or stand with a slouch or stoop, as they try to control their unevenly growing bodies.

The internal organs are changing too. The stomach, for example, becomes larger. The heart does not keep pace with the rest of the body, and as a result the blood pressure may fall. This should be watched in early adolescence so that the youngster does not get overtired in competitive sports. Usually between fourteen and sixteen, the heart begins increasing greatly in size.

Adolescence marks the beginning of sexual maturity

At this time, the sexual organs increase rapidly in size and development due to the greater activity of the pituitary gland. The secretions from the pituitary gland stimulate the testes in the boy and the ovaries in the girl so that hormones are released. These hormones speed up growth and development of the sexual organs and cause secondary sex characteristics to appear.

In girls the hips grow rounder and wider, the breasts fill out, the pubic and underarm hair begins to grow, and there are changes in the texture of the skin and an increase in the production of oil in the oil glands which may lead to acne. (The latter is true of boys also.) The eggs within the ovaries become ready to mature; one egg reaches maturity and is discharged about every twenty-eight days. This is the beginning of the menstrual, or reproductive, cycle, which will end only with the menopause.

In boys the release of the hormones causes an increase in the size of the penis and testes and the production of sperm cells, which make the boy capable of reproduction. Changes such as the appearance of the pubic hair, the first signs of the beard, and the deepening of the voice occur. Paralleling these changes are the broadening of the shoulders and chest and the development of the masculine figure. The boy may also experience his first nocturnal emissions for which he should have been fully prepared, so that he realizes they are a natural and normal part of growing up.

Bodily changes can be disturbing

The importance of these bodily changes to both boys and girls cannot be overestimated. During childhood, the youngster became used to his body. As he looked into the mirror he saw "himself." The changes he experienced during his grade-school days were gradual, and so he had time to get used to each one. With the coming of adolescence, however, the changes are sudden and rapid. The young person is no longer sure of his physical self. He looks into the mirror and thinks, "Is this me? I sure look funny!"

The generally recognized developmental tasks concerned with physical growth during early adolescence are these:

- ☐ Learning to manage a rapidly growing body
- ☐ Learning to accept the kind of physique that comes with reproductive maturity
- ☐ Learning to understand and manage the new concerns about body functions that emerge with full gonadal development.

The problems of the adolescent often center on these physical changes that accompany the growing-up process. Things which seem superficial and of minor importance to the adult seem very serious to the developing young person. Some young people worry about being too tall or too short, about weighing too much or too little. Some may be embarrassed about the size of the breasts or the penis, the depth or sudden squeakiness of the voice, the growth of the beard or the lack of it. Other youngsters worry about acne, freckles, birthmarks, prominent moles or scars, hair that is too straight, or body odor caused by an increase in perspiration.

Parents and teachers need to realize that, because of the rapid changes in his body, the youngster is focusing upon it—often for the first time. He wants to be perfect and is deeply concerned. He needs help in adjusting to this new outward self. He should be reassured by knowledge about the reasons for his acne, his increased perspiration, his too-large feet, his shortness, or his seeming immaturity. He must be helped also to accept his body as it is, rather than as he might wish it to be.

There are indications that a fast-maturing girl may have more difficulties than one who matures at a more moderate pace. Particularly in the sixth or seventh grade, such a girl may be embarrassed by her height; she may have an interest in boys which brings criticism from some adults and alienation from former friends. However, by the eighth or ninth grade, the fast-maturing girl is often a model for those girls who are now anxious to move into friendships with boys.

The fast-maturing boy is frequently a leader, particularly in athletics and social activities. It is the slow-maturing boy, unable to compete, who has problems.

This is a period of emotional change too

Just as there is an unevenness of body growth during early adolescence, there is also, with the onset of puberty, a greater intensity of emotional reactions. Intense friendships, crushes, and hero worship are common. Moods fluctuate, so that the teacher can rarely count on creating an even atmosphere in the classroom. A youngster who one day may seem very happy and cooperative may, on the next day, be gloomy and difficult to reach, and for no apparent cause. He may be self-confident at one time but timid and insecure at another. This week he may like his teacher or a friend very much and next week show an opposite reaction. The young adolescent is alternately generous and selfish, with surprising evidences of both maturity and immaturity.

Naturally these moods are very difficult for the teacher and the family as well as for the adolescent. Such moods yield neither to scoldings nor pleadings but gradually will be worked out as the young person gains greater understanding of himself and as he finds his place among his peers and in the adult world.

Adults can often help if they have the confidence of a young person, so that he or she will talk about these anxieties, fears, and perplexities. These confidences can never be forced, but it is wise for adults to try to keep the channels of communication open. It is important to be a good listener with an ear tuned to what the young person is trying to express.

The adult who works with boys and girls of this age must be patient—patient enough to realize that although the young adolescent is not yet adult, he is beginning to identify with adults and wants to be treated like a grown-up. Teachers and parents need the ability to ignore the moods, to encourage steadily the acceptance of responsibility, to help the youngster develop skill in meeting new situations, and to foster his increasing independence in making decisions.

Because the youngster is beginning to look so grown-up, it is often hard to be patient when he sprawls or slumps, becomes moody and irritable, is defiant, or withdraws into his daydreams. Adults are often baffled because the youngster seems to want their interest and affection, yet often rejects both. It is difficult but essential to help him achieve a self which is acceptable to others and yet satisfying to himself.

The group helps the individual find himself

The young adolescent is often unsure of himself as he tries to break away from the patterns of his childhood. Because of this feeling of insecurity, he finds support and gains confidence by trying to develop close relationships with others of his own age.

The group becomes a very strong support and influence during most of the adolescent years. Most adolescents, particularly boys, retain a loyalty to a group of friends of their own sex, but very often they will also become members of groups made up of both boys and girls. Since boy-girl friendships change frequently at this age, the mixed groups are often less stable than the all-boy or all-girl groups.

The close group relationships of early adolescence have many values in helping boys and girls grow up. The adult looking on from the outside often sees only the copying of superficial patterns. However, the attempts to look alike, act alike, and talk alike do serve as a kind of support and security to the youngster trying to find himself.

Toward the end of adolescence, as the youngster becomes more sure of himself, the influence of the group often lessens. Then the young person becomes more of an individual in his actions, his choice of friends, his decisions, and his interests.

The problem of "conforming" is ever present

Because the young adolescent is not yet sure of himself, he not only tries to resemble closely the other members of his group; he is also intolerant of those who do not conform. He may reject the classmate who wears different clothes, who has different manners, or who comes from a different background. He may not accept the boy or girl who is slow or less competent, nor, on the other hand, the one who is far ahead intellectually or very talented. He may think such children are strange because they like to study or practice or spend a lot of time in the art studio. Sometimes there is resentment against the boys or girls who are especially popular with members of the opposite sex.

These boys and girls who are rejected for various reasons—who do not belong to a group—need special help and understanding. Often they can be drawn into an organized group or class activity and gradually become better accepted by the others. The alert teacher will try to spot the young person who needs help and encourage him to take part in an activity in which he can make some contribution. On the other hand, some highly talented children may need support in retaining their individuality and continuing their individual interests.

The more popular boys and girls may also need help in becoming more understanding and tolerant of differences in others. One of the vital things all adolescents must learn is how to accept differences in other people instead of feeling threatened by these differences.

Insecurity may cause behavior problems

The more secure a young person has been in his relationships with his family and friends, usually the better will be his adjustment to his own age-mates during these junior-high years. If a youngster has rather poor relationships with others, it is wise to consider these questions: First, does he have outstanding differences that set him off from other young people? Second, does he have a background of insecurity in his home life which has made him unsure of himself?

It is not always easy for a young person to live up to the demands of his group, even if he is accepted by them. Many youngsters have feelings of anxiety and inferiority when they are with members of their own group. Often children become tense and irritable when they are not sure that they can hold their own with others.

Sometimes young people who are a bit uncertain about their social abilities will try to attract attention by doing or saying startling things. Clowning is a familiar example of insecurity. Gossiping, especially among the girls, is another frequent and immature sign of trying to belong. Some girls will always have something to whisper to others, even though it may hurt someone. Other girls may become snobbish.

Some insecure young people will try to be popular by agreeing with everything the leader or the popular members of the group say or do. They are the youngsters who seem to have no minds of their own, who float along with the crowd. Such young people are afraid to express their own opinions; they listen first to see which way the wind is blowing. There are youngsters, too, who are critical of everything—of their acquaintances and of any group plans. They may demand things loudly, often strutting and boasting.

These are not desirable traits, but condemning them or being irritated by them will not effectively curb them. The adolescents who are reacting in this way need help in becoming more secure. A skillful teacher can often give these youngsters a greater sense of belonging. The teacher can encourage them to take part in class activities which give them a little prestige or an opportunity to gain attention in positive ways. Again, some of these youngsters may have a deeper underlying problem which is adding to their insecurity. If this seems to be the case, they may need special help from the school guidance counselor or from a psychologist.

Another way young people have of trying to cope with insecurity is by withdrawing from reality into daydreams. Most adolescents daydream. Many of their daydreams are constructive and lead to positive contributions in adult life. If an adolescent daydreams but remains well related to real situations and takes part in the life of the classroom and the school activities, there is little cause for concern. But if a young person withdraws into daydreams as an escape from life around him, he may need help in working out an adjustment. It is not wise to prod such a youngster continually in an attempt to make him focus on his work. The problem is often something he cannot voluntarily control or handle because it involves deep-rooted personality difficulties.

Active adolescents who have an opportunity for stimulating work and for recreation in an environment in which they feel liked and accepted do not often become delinquent. On the other hand, the patterns of a delinquent group may be adopted by a youngster if his home environment has been punishing or so severe that he has felt rejected instead of loved and accepted—or if the pressures of the school have so disregarded individual differences that the young person has experienced continual rejection or academic failure.

In early adolescence boys and girls become more and more interested in being together

This interest in one another is a normal part of their development. It is a necessary step toward the adult task of choosing a mate and establishing a family. During their junior-high years, boys and girls will begin to increasingly seek opportunities to do things together. Because of the differences in physical maturity, the time at which this heterosexual interest develops will vary with the individual child. For this reason, in the junior-high years it is particularly wise to have some activities for girls and others for boys, as well as opportunities for boys and girls to do things together. In their informal activities, boys and girls will increasingly find themselves in boy-girl groups, while they also retain their interest in and need for friends and activities with their own sex.

One of the problems of this age group is that friendships which had been close and loyal during elementary-school years may now begin to break up. Differences in physical maturity often make previously good friends no longer compatible. The early-maturing girl finds that her former friend—who is not yet adolescent—is uninterested in the growing concerns she feels about herself and her developing interest in boys. The fast-maturing boy who is able to take part in athletics leaves behind his friend who is not yet sufficiently developed physically to have the height or weight needed in junior-high sports. It is well to be aware of these shifting friendship patterns, since many youngsters worry and feel guilty when they leave a former friend out of their new interests and activities.

Because of the social pressures surrounding them, some boys and girls do develop unwholesome attitudes toward one another at a time when boy-girl contacts should be on a wholesome, friendly basis. Thus many girls and boys may develop feelings of inferiority and anxiety because they are not yet ready to become socially adept in boy-girl activities, even of an informal nature. A girl may feel she is a "failure" if she is not included in the activities of a boy-girl group or if she is dropped by a friend who is now included. Or a boy may feel there is something wrong with him because he is shy and awkward around girls.

A girl's problems, when she reaches the eighth grade, may be complicated by the fact that although many boys are now being pushed into a pattern of social activities, a majority still remain basically uninterested. There are not enough socially aware boys to meet the demands of the more socially mature girls. As a result some girls take the initiative toward the boys and often become aggressive in their demands. This is poor preparation for later and more mature relationships. Or if their desire to meet boys is not met by boys of their own age, some may turn to hero-worship of older boys or men. At even thirteen or fourteen, some girls may start serious dating with an older boy. If this happens, over-stimulating dating patterns, such as car dating, and the mature development of the older boy may lead to sexual intimacies and a possible pregnancy.

Wise school people and parents will try to provide as many wholesome opportunities as possible for boys and girls of the junior-high age to participate in mixed-group activities. The normally developing interest in one another can be fostered when grown-ups encourage activities that involve group participation instead of those activities that call for individual pairing off.

At the junior-high age, picnics, hikes, swimming parties, wiener roasts, roller-skating parties, or informal get-togethers after school at home or at a recreation center can offer fun for both mature and immature boys and girls. The majority of young adolescents respond best to informality—to a casual approach both in dress and in plans. A place to get together with their friends becomes important.

In addition to social activities, the need of boys and girls to begin to know each other can be met through hobby groups, dramatics, orchestra, chorus, photography, and other small-group activities. By the end of junior high school, some boys and girls will be sufficiently mature socially to begin dating in groups.

Because these boys and girls are passing through a transition period in junior high school, some good students may slump in their schoolwork

They may grow careless and appear uninterested in their studies. This naturally distresses both parents and teachers. The tendency is to put pressure on the young person to do better. It must be remembered that the youngster is engrossed in all the changes that are happening to him both physically and emotionally. He is trying to find himself and create new patterns. If his schoolwork can be correlated with his growing interests, if school helps him learn about himself and his environment, he will often respond and be motivated to study. This is especially true if he is not expected to give stereotyped answers but is encouraged to formulate and express opinions in a sympathetic environment where mistakes are viewed as a part of the learning process.

Adolescence cannot be singled out

It is a phase in the child's total development from birth to adulthood. It is unfortunate that so many grown-ups seem to think of the teen years as if they were separate from the rest of life. What the boy or girl is today is affected by those things which have happened to him in the past, those relationships and experiences which he has had during his earlier years. It is important for the teacher to be aware of the different backgrounds which have been part of the development of the individual boy or girl. Adolescents cannot be considered as a homogeneous group. Their reactions to the same situations may be very different indeed. Behavior which may seem deviant to the teacher may, for instance, be acceptable or even desirable in the community where the youngster is growing up. It is often difficult but necessary for the junior-high teacher to become aware of the many varying cultural backgrounds of the children who are in any one particular junior high school. Only by recognizing the influences of the past can the child of the present be understood and helped to move forward in his growth and his development.

Adolescence is a time of heightened growth activity —physically, emotionally, and cognitively—but this growth must be seen in context, as related to the past and as preparation for the future.

The young adolescent today is exposed to many more external pressures and conflicts than the young adolescent of even a decade ago. Drugs, openly expressed changes in sexual morality, increasing challenges to the influence of the church, disregard for law and order, and an increasing emphasis on "doing your own thing" all impinge on the growing young person. Youngsters from homes which have given them loving support and security—as well as youngsters who have not had adequate home support—may feel the impact of social change. This adds to the difficulty of choices which must be made. Young adolescents need adults who can help them think through the perplexities of our rapidly changing society rather than grown-ups who simply give thoughtless condemnation to the young.

Books and a Pamphlet for Further Reading[1]

Bernard, Harold W. *The American Adolescent.* McGraw-Hill, 1970.

Greenblatt, Augusta. *Teen-Age Medicine, Questions Young People Ask About Their Health.* Cowles, 1971.

Hartmann, Ernest, Editor. *Adolescence.* Stratton, 1969.

Hill, John, and Shelton, J., Editors. *Readings in Adolescent Development and Behavior.* Prentice-Hall, 1970.

Jenkins, Gladys G.; Shacter, Helen S.; and Bauer, William W. *These Are Your Children.* Scott, Foresman, 1966. (Paperback.)

McCandless, Boyd. *Adolescents: Behavior and Development.* Holt, 1970.

Schwartz, June V., M.D. *Health Care for the Adolescent.* Public Affairs Pamphlet #463. Public Affairs Committee, 1971.

Sebald, Hans. *Adolescence: A Sociological Analysis.* Appleton, 1970.

[1]For directories of sources, see page 48 of this *Resource Book.*

Family-Living Education

A unit such as "What Are Your Personal Health Concerns?" in *Book Eight* is a reminder that pupils may have questions about body structure and function that are not generally answered in classroom texts. They may have questions centering on the reproductive organs and on sexuality.

It is important for parents and teachers to be aware that today's young adolescents are growing up in a culture which overemphasizes sexuality. Many of these youngsters do have knowledge, interest, and curiosity that go beyond what is usually attributed to boys and girls of this age group. Their questions are evidence of this growing awareness.

The television shows, the commercials, the movies that boys and girls attend are openly sexually stimulating and they show patterns that may influence adolescents' own behavior. Articles in magazines discuss types of sexual behavior engaged in by adults and older adolescents both within and outside of marriage. The standards and values of the relationships between the sexes are openly questioned. Junior-high boys and girls are more aware of changing attitudes than many teachers and parents are willing to believe.

The majority of junior-high boys and girls are not experimenting together in any intimate sexual way. But the number of thirteen- and fourteen-year-olds who are experimenting is increasing. And other boys and girls are well aware of this.

The many pressures that impinge on our boys and girls at an ever younger age make it imperative that home and school work together in the area of sex and family-life education. All junior-high boys and girls should be helped to obtain knowledge needed to guide them wisely as they grow up. They also need opportunities to talk out their problems.

School-Home Cooperation

It is generally accepted today that a modern health program will take responsibility for helping develop an appreciation of the family and the youngster's place in it. Relationships with parents and other family members and the development of self-understanding are emphasized. Concepts on responsible family living are built into the Scott, Foresman HEALTH AND GROWTH Program at every level.

When, however, family-life education at school moves into such areas as the details of human reproduction, it is essential that parents be informed and their cooperation sought. Many schools schedule special meetings or sponsor study groups—open to all interested parents—at which proposed concepts are discussed. At such meetings, materials to be used, such as films, filmstrips, and booklets, can be made available for examination and evaluation. Professional resource people may be called on to help lead group discussions. The teacher should be sure to become thoroughly familiar with local policy on sex education in the classroom. The teacher should check to see if the school system has a course of study or guidelines in this area.

At times, individual parents may ask the teacher to suggest books and pamphlets either for their own use or for use by their youngsters. Materials such as those listed on page 14 can aid parents in gaining familiarity with facts they wish to discuss with their youngsters. Materials that young people can read themselves are also included.

Explaining Menstruation

Although some girls begin to menstruate around the age of twelve or thirteen, others begin much earlier and still others much later. Some girls may have their first period as early as the fifth or sixth grade; others may begin in junior high.

In the event that menstruation should occur for the first time at school, a possible course of action should be thought out in advance. Perhaps the school nurse or counselor can be called upon to provide a sanitary pad and to offer explanation and reassurance. If necessary, the teacher may be called upon to explain briefly such facts of menstruation as these:

Physical maturity for a girl means that her reproductive organs (ovaries) are ready to release mature ova or egg cells. The egg cell, in union with a male reproductive cell, the sperm, produces a fertilized egg cell which is the beginning of a new life. An egg leaves one of the ovaries each month and travels down the Fallopian tube to the uterus. The uterus is especially designed to serve as a sort of nest where a baby can grow if the egg is fertilized.

As soon as the egg leaves the ovary, the blood supply to the uterus is increased so that in case the egg is fertilized, there will be plenty of nourishment for the developing baby. When the egg is not fertilized, the extra blood sent to the uterus is not needed, so it is discharged through the vagina. This is the menstrual flow, which usually lasts from three to five days.

Questions should be encouraged and answered in a straightforward manner, without hint of mystery or embarrassment. Menstruation is a healthy aspect of normal development for a girl.

Books and Pamphlets for Teachers and Parents[1]

Arnstein, Helene S. In consultation with the Child Study Association of America. *Your Growing Child and Sex.* Bobbs-Merrill, 1967.

Child Study Association of America. *What to Tell Your Children About Sex.* Revised Edition. Pocket Books, 1968. (Paperback.)

Eckert, Ralph G. *Sex Attitudes in the Home.* Association, 1956. (Paperback, Popular Library, 1963.)

Gruenberg, Sidonie M., Editor. *The New Encyclopedia of Child Care and Guidance.* Doubleday, 1968. (See especially the chapter on attitudes toward sex.)

Hofstein, Sadie, et al. *Sex Education: A Working Design for Curriculum Development and Implementation. Grades: Pre-Kindergarten through Twelve.* The Education Council for School Research and Development, Mineola, New York, 1968. (Paperback.)

Kilander, H. Frederick. *Sex Education in the Schools.* Macmillan, 1970.

Lerrigo, Marion, and Southard, Helen. *Facts Aren't Enough.* (Milton J. E. Senn, M.D., medical consultant.) AMA and NEA, 1971. (Pamphlet.)

Schultz, Esther D., and Williams, Sally R. *Family Life and Sex Education: Curriculum and Instruction.* Harcourt, 1968. (Paperback.)

Southard, Helen F. *Sex Before Twenty: New Answers for Young People.* Revised Edition. Dutton, 1971.

Books and Pamphlets for Young People

Day, Beth, and Liley, Margaret, M.D. *The Secret World of the Baby.* Random House, 1968.

Hofstein, Sadie. *The Human Story: Facts on Birth, Growth, and Reproduction.* Revised Edition. Scott, Foresman, 1972. (Pamphlet.)

Lerrigo, Marion, and Southard, Helen. *Finding Yourself.* (Milton J. E. Senn, M.D., medical consultant.) AMA and NEA, 1970. (Pamphlet.)

Levinsohn, Florence, and Kelly, G. Lombard, M.D. *What Teenagers Want to Know.* Budlong, 1971. (Available only through professional sources from Milex Corp., 5917 North Northwest Highway, Chicago, Illinois 60631.) (Booklet.)

Power, Jules. *How Life Begins.* Simon & Schuster, 1968.

Films for Classroom Use

As Boys Grow. Medical Arts.

Boy to Man. Churchill.

The Day Life Begins. Carousel.

Girl to Woman. Churchill.

How Life Begins. McGraw-Hill.

Human Growth. Second Edition. Wexler.

It's Wonderful Being a Girl. Revised Edition. Association. (About menstruation.)

The Story of Menstruation. Association.

[1]For directories of sources, see page 48 of this *Resource Book*.

Teaching About Venereal Diseases

Many adults are not fully aware of how widespread and how dangerous the venereal diseases are. *Because of the seriousness of the epidemic among teen-agers today, it is crucial that teachers and parents cooperate with the public-health authorities in helping check and reduce the incidence of these communicable diseases.*

The U.S. Public Health Service states that more than 20 percent of reported venereal diseases occur among young people under twenty. *More than 500,000 teen-agers between fifteen and nineteen are infected annually.*

The U.S. Public Health Service, as well as the Joint Committee on Health Problems in Education of the National Education Association and the American Medical Association, feels that the study of venereal diseases should be a systematic part of communicable-disease education during early adolescence, and that it should be initiated "not later than the 7th grade."[1]

When boys and girls come into junior high school, they are not only entering a new school experience but also a new period of their development. Boys and girls must be correctly informed about venereal diseases, since they must make important decisions when they begin going out together. Indeed, in one large city, the highest rise in venereal-disease incidence was found among thirteen-year-olds. The U.S. Public Health Service states that only about 10 percent of our youth have any adequate knowledge of either syphilis or gonorrhea and their effects.

Unfortunately, many parents and teachers have taken an "it can't happen here" attitude toward the problem, only to be shocked out of their complacency when it *did* happen. The present-day increase in sexual relations among boys and girls of all social levels at an earlier age is resulting in an increased danger that a chain reaction of venereal-disease infection may occur in any community.

In teaching about venereal diseases—leads for which are provided on page 265 of the pupil's book—there are certain essential facts to stress:

☐ The venereal diseases of syphilis and gonorrhea are spread almost entirely by sexual intercourse with someone who has the disease. There is a rare exception: syphilis may occasionally be spread through kissing, if one of the young people has on the lips or in the mouth a sore containing the germs of syphilis.

☐ The germs of syphilis and gonorrhea are unable to live outside the body. So there is little possibility of contracting either disease from toilets, drinking cups, eating utensils, or doorknobs.

☐ Both syphilis and gonorrhea can be cured if they are detected and treated in their early stages. Untreated syphilis can cause blindness, deafness, heart disease, insanity, paralysis, and death. Gonorrhea, if untreated, can cause damage to the sex organs, sterility, crippling arthritis, blindness, and death.

☐ Just because a person has one of these diseases does not mean he cannot have the other. He may even have both at the same time. And there is no immunity following a cured infection; both gonorrhea and syphilis can be contracted again and again after exposure to the disease.

☐ The first symptom of syphilis—which takes from 10 to 90 days to develop—is the chancre (shang′kər), a painless sore which may appear on any part of the body, but usually in or around the sexual organs. If it is inside the body, it may go undetected; and it will eventually disappear even if untreated. But the germs continue to spread

[1]From *Report of Public Advisory Committee on Venereal Disease Control* of the U.S. Public Health Service. Copyright by Venereal Disease Branch, Communicable Disease Center, Atlanta, Georgia 30333.

through the body. They may cause damage particularly to the heart, brain, liver, or bones.

- Some weeks after the appearance of the syphilis chancre, a measleslike rash of pink spots may break out all over the body, including the abdomen, sides, and limbs. Many young people confuse this rash with the pimples of acne. There is no connection between the two—a point that needs careful emphasis.
- Gonorrhea is more difficult to detect in girls than in boys, since in its early stages the infection produces no pain in the female sex organs. A girl may pass the disease on to a boy without even realizing she herself is infected. Boys who contract gonorrhea will have, usually within a few days, such warning symptoms as a burning sensation on urination and the presence of pus.
- If a youngster suspects that he or she has a venereal disease, a report should be made immediately to a physician or to a clinic. Parents should be confided in at once; but if the youngster cannot tell them, he may feel he can talk more easily to the family doctor. Or he may go directly to a public health clinic. If money is a problem, most health departments have free diagnostic and treatment clinics. Treatment by a physician is essential, preferably by one known to the patient.
- Teen-agers should be impressed with the fact that if they do contract a venereal disease they must cooperate with the health authorities by identifying any boys or girls with whom they have had sexual contact. This information is of extreme importance since it often provides the only means by which help can be given to other infected boys and girls. Many boys and girls look upon the act of identifying their contacts as a betrayal of their friends. But they should know that this information is kept confidential by health authorities.

Books and Pamphlets for Teachers and Parents[1]

American Medical Association. *Venereal Disease Is Still a World Problem.* AMA, 1965.

American Social Health Association. *Today's VD Control Problem—1971.* ASHA, 1971. Published annually.

Brooks, Stewart M. *The V.D. Story.* Barnes, 1971.

Brown, Abe A., and Podair, Simon. *Venereal Diseases —The Silent Menace.* Public Affairs Pamphlet #292B. Public Affairs Committee, 1970.

A Curriculum Guide on Venereal Disease for Junior High School Teachers. The Commonwealth of Massachusetts Department of Public Health, Division of Communicable Disease, State House, Boston, Massachusetts, 1968.

Schwartz, William F. *Teacher's Handbook on Venereal Disease Education.* NEA, 1965.

U.S. Dept. of HEW. *The Eradication of Syphilis.* PHS Pub. #918. Sup't of Documents, 1962.

________. *VD Fact Sheet.* Sup't of Documents. Published annually.

Books and Pamphlets for Young People[1]

(Asterisk * indicates pamphlet.)

*American Medical Association. *Why the Rise in Teen-age Gonorrhea?* AMA, 1966.

*________. *Why the Rise in Teen-age Syphilis?* AMA, 1966.

*Blanzaco, André, M.D. *VD: Facts You Should Know.* Scott, Foresman, 1970.

Landers, Ann. *Ann Landers Talks to Teen-Agers About Sex.* Crest. Fawcett World, 1970. (Paperback.)

*U.S. Dept. of HEW. *About Syphilis and Gonorrhea.* PHS Pub. #410. Sup't of Documents, 1962.

*________. *Strictly for Teenagers.* PHS Pub. #913. Sup't of Documents, 1962.

Webster, Bruce, M.D. *What You Should Know About VD—and Why.* Scholastic, 1967. (Paperback.)

[1]For directories of sources, see page 48 of this *Resource Book.*

Physical Education in the Curriculum

Physical education activities are often the responsibility of a specialist at the junior-high level. In many schools, however, the classroom teacher is responsible for both health and physical education instruction. For teachers with this dual responsibility, some helpful hints are included here.

The degree to which the values of physical education are realized depends upon the teacher. Few values, except the physiological, accrue unless definite instruction is provided.

The variations in size, strength, and skill among young adolescents are especially noticeable in physical education and must be taken into account in planning activities. For pupils at upper maturity levels the teacher can help hold their interest by using them as officials, team captains, and helpers in general. Students at all levels of maturity should be shown how they are improving in comparison with their own previous performances. Although differences in skill are obvious to the students, emphasis should be on each student's performing at the highest level possible for him.

Most students by the junior-high level should have a minimum proficiency in game skills, but they still need instruction in the more advanced skills and in the behavioral skills and personal relationships that foster desirable social growth.

Because of the differences in physique, in interests, and in performance ability, separate physical education activities for boys and girls are generally recommended at this level.

Some Appropriate Goals

Goals suggested as appropriate for the majority of students are growth in the ability:

- ☐ To understand that exercise promotes health
- ☐ To learn rules of appropriate games
- ☐ To master skills basic to sports, such as running, jumping, throwing, batting, kicking, catching
- ☐ To recognize weaknesses and to try to improve one's own ability in sports
- ☐ To practice rules of safety
- ☐ To appreciate one's own strengths, as well as the strengths of others
- ☐ To understand and learn to control emotions which often build up during competitive games
- ☐ To assume the role of captain, team member, referee, winner, or loser whenever appropriate.

Activities That Should Be Included

Movement-exploration activities, relays, team games, and lead-up activities for various sports are important aspects of the physical education program at the junior-high level. Self-testing activities are valuable too. (See the references under "Tests and Measurements," page 24.) Activities in all these areas can measure and help improve the students' endurance, flexibility, coordination, and strength, as well as other aspects of physical fitness.

Group loyalty is very apparent at this age, and lead-up games and team games offer a means of learning to cooperate and work with others. Students now show an increased willingness to concentrate on the intricacies of team games and the basic skills involved.

During the junior-high years, strength and endurance are of prime importance to boys, and there is great interest in highly organized team games, such as touch football.

Girls tend to be less competitive than boys, and their interests gradually turn from team games to the dual and individual sports, such as tennis and bowling. Girls tend, too, to be more interested than boys in improving their poise and grace, and the opportunity for posture training and dance is enhanced.

Although separate physical education classes for boys and girls are recommended, provision should be made for coeducational activities. For example, various forms of dance—ballroom, folk, and square dancing—offer opportunities for improving health, for developing valuable game skills, and for camaraderie. Also, a team game like volleyball is excellent for mixed groups and teaches recreational skills that can be used later in adult life. Coeducational activities are important, because much "awkwardness" of adolescence is due to social insecurity, as well as to imbalance of body parts.

The activities presented here are appropriate for both boys and girls, unless otherwise indicated. Individual differences in the performance of a skill should be expected. Before vigorous activities are engaged in, a gradual warm-up is desirable. This may be through mild participation in the less vigorous skills of a sport or dance, or through formal exercises. The more directly the warm-up movements are related to the subsequent skills, the better—physiologically—is the warm-up. For example, the pitcher warms up by relaxed throws to a catcher; the golfer warms up by practice swings with his club; and the tennis player, by easy shots across the net with his opponent.

Movement-Education Approaches[1]

Movement education, or movement exploration, as a basis for instruction in physical education was introduced in England around 1950. Since then movement-exploration approaches have become typical in elementary schools in many countries, including the United States. In secondary schools also, applications of movement concepts have developed in both gymnastics and dance.

With movement-education approaches, the individual development of each student is paramount. Every student has many opportunities to experience satisfaction from successful use of his body. Thus, success contributes to the improved self-image and provides the basis for his seeking more challenging tasks. Problem solving is a basic method used in movement exploration. This method requires total involvement of students in their own learning situations. Students structure their own movements, within the restrictions of the problem, in ways that are meaningful to them. In so doing, each student develops understanding and appreciation of movement and also improves his skills. Creativity is encouraged, since there is no single response to the problem.

Movement education centers around such concepts as *the use of the body* (what you move), *the use of space* (where you move), and *the quality of the movement* (how you move). Themes to develop concepts of body awareness include transfer of weight, reception of weight, and shaping of movements by such means as curling, stretching, and twisting. In addition to individual work, use of the body is developed through partner and group work in problems involving matching movement, contrasting movement, meeting and parting, and passing around, over, and under. Ability to use a variety of directions and levels serves as the core for spatial concepts. The quality of movement is described in terms of the "strength," marked by strong or light; the "time," marked by quick or slow acceleration or deceleration; and the "flow," marked by continuous, broken, successive, or simultaneous movement.

The teacher using movement-exploration approaches to physical education presents a problem emphasizing a single concept, or, with older students, a combination of concepts. Each student then responds with movements that enable him to improve control of his body while also expanding his understanding of how this concept affects his ability

[1]Adaptation of "The Movement Education Approach to Teaching in English Elementary Schools: A Report Based on Observations of Participants in the Second Anglo-American Workshop on Movement Education" by Shirley Howard from *Journal of Health, Physical Education, & Recreation* (January 1967). Reprinted by permission of American Association for Health, Physical Education, and Recreation.

to move. The problem-solving situation enables each student to gain satisfaction from moving within his own capacities.

In elementary schools, as well as in secondary schools, these movement experiences are further developed in relation to apparatus.

Initially, students are given free choice of how they use the apparatus. They are encouraged to move continuously, still with free choice of movement. Gradually the students are directed toward supporting and suspending their bodies on different parts of the apparatus and toward developing a variety of ways for mounting, dismounting, and moving on the apparatus. The teacher then further structures problems by specifying the path of the movement, the types of movement, or the quality of movement.

Parallel to modern gymnastics, modern educational dance has developed from movement education in the elementary school. As in gymnastics, the emphasis is on freedom of movement as well as on creative and expressive movement response to dance stimuli. Dance themes are developed from music, rhythm instruments, and dramatics.

In general, the physical education program is enhanced by the large variety and quantity of equipment available for instructional use. Balls, paddles, jumpropes, beanbags, hoops, stilts, and wands provide students with maximal activity during each class period.

A representative lesson, for example, might begin with individual practice in tossing and catching, each student with his own ball. Next the students might throw the ball to moving partners.

Boys might then try such a problem-solving task as stopping the ball with different parts of the body, putting the ball into the air from the floor without using the hands, passing the ball with the feet, or keeping the ball in the air with different parts of the body. These skills have application in games such as soccer and speedball.

Girls might work individually to keep the ball in the air with their hands without catching and throwing. They might also work in groups of three, volleying the ball back and forth while moving around the room. Skills gained are useful in volleyball.

Skills that emerge in ball handling are an outgrowth of carefully structured problem-solving experiences and can be accomplished without specific instruction as to how to develop these skills. The skills gained are later put to use in various game situations.

Movement-education approaches also have application with physically handicapped youngsters. Emphasis is placed on the development of physical skills in spite of the varying restrictions of each student's physical capabilities.

Physical fitness is a natural outcome of the continuous movement and vigorous action inherent in movement-exploration approaches to physical education teachings.

(Some references giving more detailed help in movement-exploration approaches are listed on page 24 of this *Resource Book.*)

Some Relays for Junior-High Students

Relays are excellent for meeting the competitive needs of adolescents and can contribute to the development of good sportsmanship. The following safety precautions should be observed:

☐ Be sure teams are far enough apart to avoid collision. (At least 15 feet of space between teams is recommended.)

☐ Have players keep to their right when running, in order to avoid a collision in the middle of the course.

☐ Have a definite stopping and starting line. (Do not use a wall, since players may collide with the wall and be injured.)

Obstacle Relay

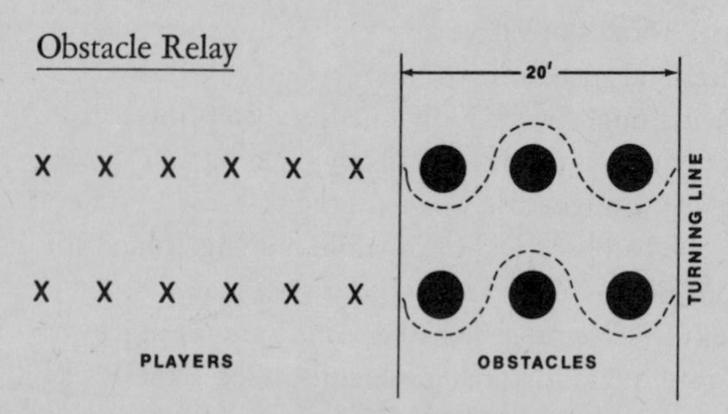

Equipment: Obstacles such as Indian clubs
Players: Teams of 6 members
Place: Gymnasium or playground

There are as many ways to set up the obstacles as there are materials and conditions available. One way is shown above.

After the obstacle course is marked off, the teams line up in file formation behind the starting line. At a signal, the first team member begins the obstacle course. When this player reaches the turning line, he turns and sprints back to the starting line and his team, avoiding all obstacles. When he reaches the starting line, he touches the next runner's left hand with his left hand, and the next runner begins the course. Each player repeats the relay process. If a player fails to follow the instructions, he must begin again. The first team to get its last player across the starting line wins.

Kangaroo Relay

Equipment: Soccer or playground ball for each team
Players: Teams of 6 to 8 members
Place: Gymnasium or playground

Teams line up in parallel lines behind a starting line. A turning point is marked 20 feet in front of each team. The first team member grips the ball between his ankles, keeping it off the ground. At a signal, he starts hopping toward and then around the turning point. When he returns to his team, he drops the ball. Each player repeats the relay process. The team that finishes first wins. If the ball drops to the ground, the player must replace it and resume hopping from the point where the ball was dropped.

Basketball-Pass Relays

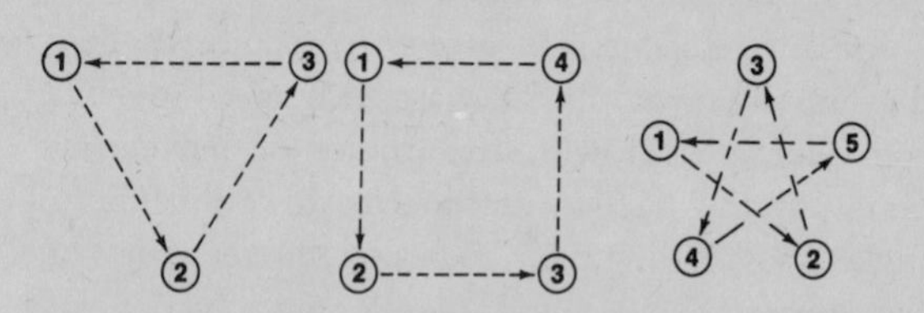

Equipment: Basketball for each squad
Players: Small squads of 3 to 5 members
Place: Gymnasium or playground

Relays make fine warm-ups while providing practice in the various types of basketball passes. Three sample formations are shown above. In one of these formations, several squads of players line up with 3 to 5 yards between players. At a signal, team members begin passing the basketball in the prescribed order. The first squad to pass the basketball around three times wins. Stress the importance of not rushing through the relay; rushing might cause the players to sacrifice the fundamentals they are working on.

Dribble-Up, Throw-Back Relay

Equipment: Basketball for each team
Players: Teams of 6 to 8 members
Place: Gymnasium or playground

Teams line up in parallel lines behind a starting line. A turning point is marked with chalk 20 feet in front of each team. The first team member dribbles up to the turning point, pivots, and passes the ball back to the next player on his team. He then runs to the end of the line. This procedure continues until all team members have returned to their original places. The team that finishes first wins.

Some Favorite Lead-up Games and Activities

The following activities give students an opportunity to develop skills in basketball, softball, soccer, volleyball, and football. (Official rule books for these sports are available from the American Association for Health, Physical Education, and Recreation.)

Following are some *basketball* activities—Twenty-One, Freeze-Out, and Basketball Keep Away—that are popular among young people.

Twenty-One

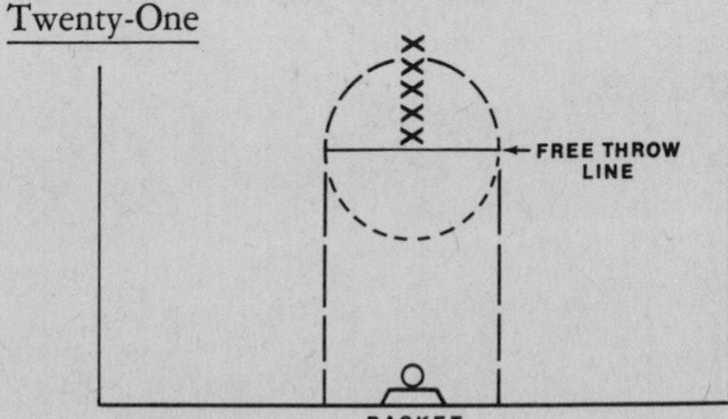

Equipment: Basketball for each group
Players: 5 or so in each group
Place: Basketball court

One game is organized around each basket. Teams line up behind the free-throw line (15 feet from the basket). Each of the players takes a shot from the free-throw line; then he recovers the ball for a short shot. Shots from the free-throw line earn 2 points; short shots earn 1 point. The first player to earn 21 points wins. Any type of shot is permissible, but short shots must be made at the point of rebound of the long shot. In a variation of the game, a player must earn exactly 21 points. In this case, a shot giving the player more than 21 points would not count.

Freeze-Out

Equipment: Basketball for each group
Players: Up to 10 in each group
Place: Basketball court

One game is organized around each basket. The first player selects a spot and shoots any way he wishes—underarm, chest, dribble and lay-up, and so on. If the player is successful, the next player must attempt to make the same shot from the same spot on the court in order to stay in the game. If he fails, the next player is free to make any shot he wishes. The last player remaining in the game wins.

Basketball Keep Away

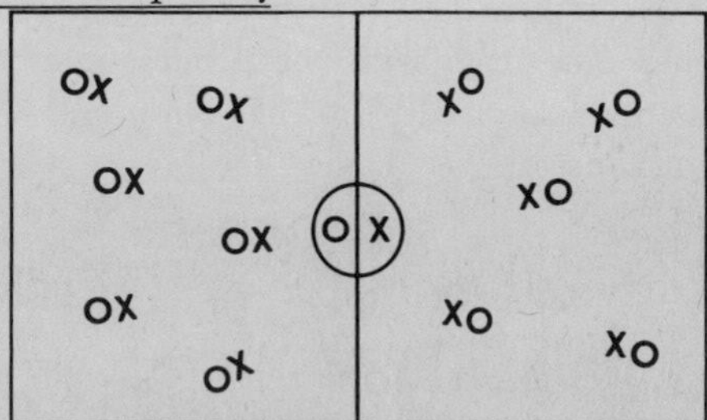

Equipment: Basketball; shoulder bands of different colors for 2 teams
Players: 2 teams of up to 12 members each
Place: Basketball court

The ball is tossed up in the center of the court between two opposing team members. The team member that gets the ball begins to pass it to his teammates, and the team attempts to make five consecutive passes. They call aloud the number of each pass. A player with the ball may not take more than one step in any direction and must release the ball within three seconds. Members of the opposing team try to intercept the ball. If they fail to do so, and the team with the ball makes five consecutive passes, a point is scored. The first team reaching a previously decided score wins.

Following are the rules for two *soccer* activities—Mickey Soccer and Diamond Soccer.

Mickey Soccer

Equipment: Soccer ball for each team
Players: 2 or more teams of even numbers, 6 or so per team
Place: Gymnasium or playground

Each team is arranged in a circle, and team members are numbered. The game leader calls a number. The player in each circle with that number runs to the center of his circle, picks up the ball, and dribbles it out through his open place in the circle. He continues around the circle, back through his place, and returns the ball to the center of the circle. The first player to complete these maneuvers earns a point for his team. The team with the greatest number of points after a specified period of time wins.

Diamond Soccer

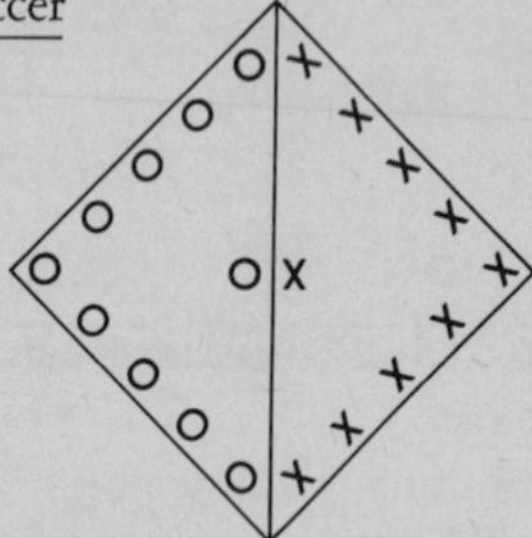

Equipment: Soccer ball
Players: At least 2 teams of 8 to 10 members each
Place: Gymnasium or playground

One player from each team plays in the center position, while all other players are guards and defend their side of the diamond—as shown in the diagram above. The center player tries to kick the ball through the opposing team's line. Each team plays in its own half of the diamond. The guards may block, trap, or kick the ball but may not use their hands to stop it. The team scored against puts the ball back in play. After each score, players are rotated, and two new players take the center positions. A point is scored each time the ball goes through the opponents' line (below shoulder level for boys, below waist level for girls). The team with the most points at the end of a specified time wins.

Two softball activities—Grounders and Flies, and Touch-Bases Ball—are given in the next column.

Grounders and Flies

Equipment: Bat, 6 balls
Players: 1 batter; 5 players in field
Place: Gymnasium or playground

The batter hits one ball after another into the field. Each time a fielder is in position to field a ball, he must call "mine" and attempt the play. He receives 3 points if he catches the ball on a fly, 2 points for a fly caught on the first bounce, or 1 point for a grounder. The first fielder who gets 15 points takes the place of the batter who then goes into the field.

Touch-Bases Ball

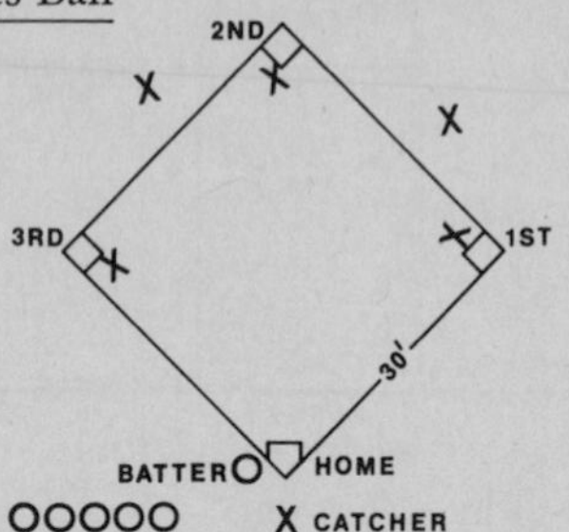

Equipment: Softball, bat, 4 bases
Players: At least 2 teams of 6 to 8 members per team
Place: Gymnasium or playground

The batter tosses the ball into the air and tries to hit it into fair territory. The opposing team members try to catch the ball and throw it to the catcher. The batter tries to run as many of the four bases as possible before the catcher gets possession of the ball and calls "stop." There are no outs in this game. An inning consists of a turn at bat for each team member. A caught fly ball is played as any other ball fielded. A foul ball counts as a turn at bat. One point is scored for each base touched before the catcher calls "stop"; for example, four points are scored when a batter touches all four bases before the catcher calls "stop." The game is over when each team's members have had a turn at bat; team with highest score wins.

Directions for two *volleyball* activities—One-Line Volleyball and Serve It By Yourself—are given here.

One-Line Volleyball

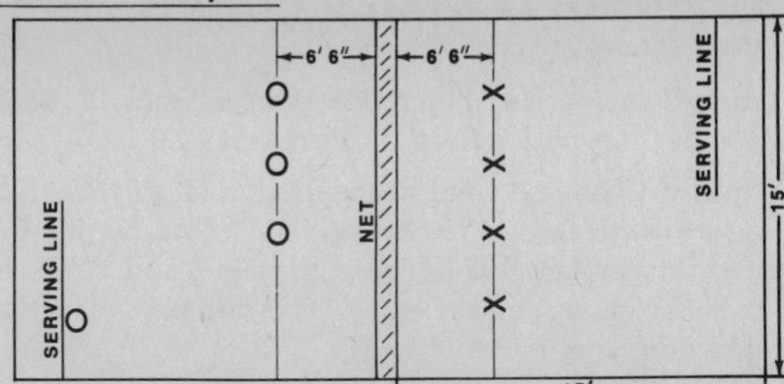

Equipment: Volleyball, net
Players: 2 teams of 4 or more players each
Place: Gymnasium or playground

Team members stand on a line on either side of the net, as shown above. Player on the right-hand corner of line serves the ball. The serve must go over on the first try. The ball is hit back and forth across the net until it goes out of bounds—or until one team is unable to return it or makes a foul. The serving team wins a point if the opponents fail to return the ball over the net or if the ball goes out of bounds on return. If the serving team does not return the ball or if it goes out of bounds on return, the opposing team wins the serve. The ball may be hit any number of times by a team, but no single player may hit the ball twice in succession. Players rotate to the left when their team wins the serve. The end player goes to the head of the line and becomes the server. The server must state the score before serving. The team that reaches ten points first wins.

Serve It By Yourself

Equipment: Several volleyballs
Players: Any number
Place: Gymnasium or playground with wall

Individual players repeatedly serve volleyball to a point on a wall five feet high. The serving is done at varying distances from the wall.

Some *touch football* activities for boys—Runout, Sneak Ball, and Center-Number Pass—are given here.

Runout

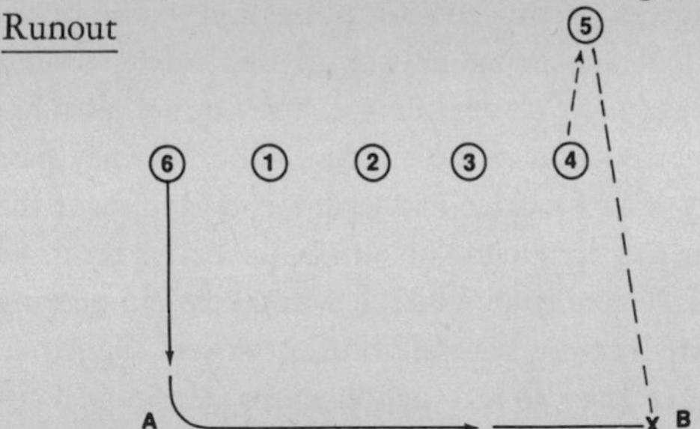

Equipment: Several footballs
Players: At least 2 squads, 6 boys per squad
Place: Playground

Each squad is lined up as shown in the diagram above. The boy in the fourth position passes the football to the boy in the fifth position. The boy in position six runs to point A, then to point B, where he attempts to catch the football thrown by the boy in the fifth position. All boys then rotate one position with the sixth boy becoming the first. Each complete pass counts as one point for the squad. The squad with the most points after a specified period wins.

Sneak Ball

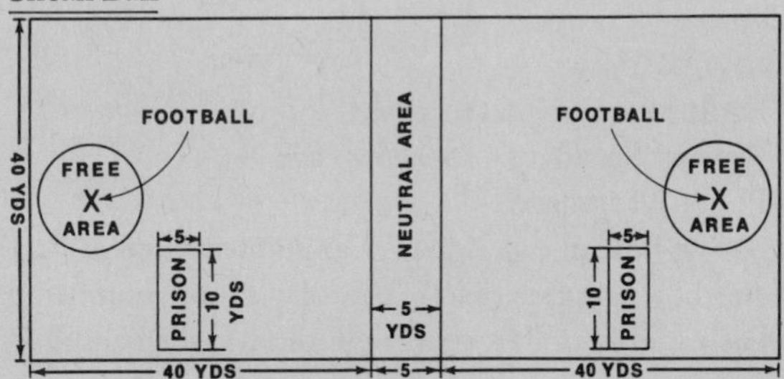

Equipment: 2 footballs
Players: 2 teams of any number
Place: Field, 40 yards × 85 yards

A football is placed in each team's free area. Teams are divided into guards and attackers. Attackers for each team line up facing each other in the neutral area. Guards for each team stay in their half of the field to protect the ball in their own free area.

Attackers attempt to gain possession of the opponents' ball and bring it back to their area without being tagged by an opponent guard. Once a team has gained possession of the enemy's ball, they may pass or carry it. If a carrier (attacker) is tagged, or if the ball touches the ground on a pass, the ball is returned to the free area from which it was taken. No tagging is allowed in the neutral zone. Attackers tagged in enemy territory go into prison in that territory. Prisoners may be freed by an attacking teammate who reaches the prison without being tagged. Ex-prisoners must return to their own half of the field before resuming play. When a team brings the enemy's ball back into its own territory without being tagged, a point is scored. The team with most points after a specified time wins.

Center-Number Pass

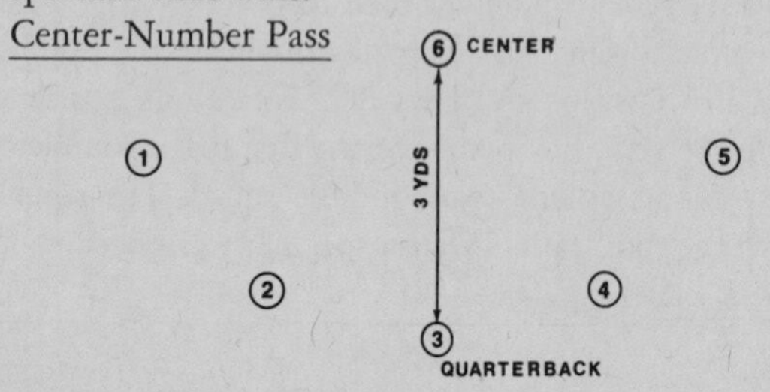

Equipment: Several footballs
Players: Squads of 4 to 8 boys each
Place: Playground

One boy on each squad is appointed as center and one boy as quarterback. The players are numbered. Each squad forms a semicircle three yards behind its center. The quarterback calls a number and the center must snap the football to the player whose number is called. After five passes, the players rotate positions so that there is a new center and a new quarterback. Each completed pass counts as one point. The squad with the most points after a specified time wins.

References for Physical Education Activities[1]

Movement Exploration, Games, and Dance

American Association for Health, Physical Education, and Recreation. *Knowledge and Understanding in Physical Education.* AAHPER, 1969.

Anderson, Marian; Elliot, Margaret E.; and La Berge, Jeanne. *Play with a Purpose.* Harper, 1972.

Bucher, Charles A., and Reade, Evelyn M. *Physical Education and Health in the Elementary School.* Second Edition. Macmillan, 1971. (See Chapters 3 and 20-27 for material on movement experiences for physical education programs.)

Edgren, Harry D., and Gruber, Joseph J. *Teacher's Handbook of Indoor and Outdoor Games.* Prentice-Hall, 1963.

Krauss, Richard. *A Pocket Guide of Folk and Square Dances and Singing Games for the Elementary School.* Prentice-Hall, 1966.

Latchaw, Marjorie, and Pyatt, Jean. *A Pocket Guide of Dance Activities.* Prentice-Hall, 1958.

Schurr, Evelyn L. *Movement Experiences for Children: Curriculum and Methods for Elementary School Physical Education.* Appleton, 1967.

Souder, Marjorie A., and Hill, Phyllis J. *Basic Movement: Foundations of Physical Education.* Ronald, 1963.

Vannier, Maryhelen, and Fait, Hollis F. *Teaching Physical Education in Elementary Schools.* Third Edition. Saunders, 1969.

Tests and Measurements

American Association for Health, Physical Education, and Recreation. *AAHPER Youth Fitness Test Manual.* Revised Edition. AAHPER, 1965.

American Association for Health, Physical Education, and Recreation. *Skills Test Manual.* AAHPER. Manual available for each sport, current year.

Clarke, Henry H. *Application of Measurement to Health and Physical Education.* Fourth Edition. Prentice-Hall, 1966.

[1]For directories of sources, see page 48 of this *Resource Book.*

Selected Behavioral Objectives in Health and Safety

Unit 1: What Are Your Personal Health Concerns?

Discusses individual differences in rate, time, and extent of growth in boys and girls during the teen years.

Lists some sound, sensible hints for those who want to gain weight and those who want to lose weight.

Discusses some beneficial effects of exercise on the body.

Explains the term physical fitness and *discusses* the advantages of being physically fit.

Demonstrates some daily exercises that can contribute to physical fitness.

Tells why acne is common during the teen years.

Lists some general practices for care of acne.

Discusses dandruff and what can be done about it.

Explains some modern methods of preventing and combating tooth decay.

Discusses some things research tells us about sleep.

Evaluates ads about products designed to "cure" such conditions as acne and bad breath.

Describes some typical procedures in a health checkup and *tells* why the procedures are undertaken.

Unit 2: What Are the Facts About Drug Abuse, Alcohol, and Smoking?

Distinguishes between use and abuse of drugs.

Explains the difference between prescription drugs and nonprescription, or over-the-counter, drugs.

Identifies the kinds of drugs most likely to be abused and the effects on the body of misuse of each of these classes of drugs.

Lists ways in which alcohol affects the body.

Tells why the use of alcoholic beverages may be particularly hazardous to young people.

Explains why smoking, especially cigarette smoking, is hazardous to health.

Describes what happens when smoke from a cigarette enters the body and is drawn down into the lungs.

Discusses how one's personal values and goals can influence his decisions about the use of alcohol, tobacco, and drugs.

Unit 3: Are You Alert to Health Quackery?

Explains what is meant by health quacks and quackery.

Tells why people may at times be fooled by quackery.

Cites examples of health quackery taken from reliable sources.

Lists ways to recognize a health quack.

Discusses why quackery is often dangerous.

Summarizes some of the sales "pitches" of food quacks.

Explains how education helps avoid food quackery.

Identifies the various Federal agencies and departments that help fight health quackery.

Describes how to choose a doctor and a dentist.

Gives examples of food fallacies versus food facts.

Unit 4: What Do You Know About the Science of Nutrition?

Plans a daily diet that is adequate for a thirteen- or fourteen-year-old.

Discusses the fact that the human body and food are made of the same chemical elements.

Cites the important functions of food in the body.

Explains the process of digestion of food by the body.

Lists the four food groups in the Food for Fitness guide and the number of servings from each group that are needed daily.

Tells why a variety of foods is needed in the daily diet.

Explains what is meant by a calorie.

States reasons why breakfast is an essential meal.

Discusses some of the common weaknesses in the diets of teen-agers.

Describes what is meant by basal metabolism.

Reports upon food problems and potential food shortages throughout the world.

Unit 5: How Can You Improve in Your Human Relations?

Describes what is meant by human relations.

Discusses the importance of improving human relations in the home, school, community, and world.

Lists important human needs that all individuals have.

Describes how failure to have important human needs adequately met can affect behavior.

Lists important steps in the problem-solving method of facing a difficult situation.

Identifies some commonly used defense mechanisms.

Describes what is meant by prejudice.

Demonstrates ways to communicate ideas or feelings by means other than words.

Explains the importance of effective communication in fostering good human relations.

Discusses the importance of recognizing and accepting the contributions of others.

Evaluates traits of the mentally healthy individual.

Lists some aids to achieving good mental health.

Unit 6: How Much Do You Know About Safety and Accident Prevention?

Explains why safety instruction is of particular importance to thirteen- and fourteen-year-olds.

Gives examples of the importance of knowing the why's as well as the what's of safety practices.

Lists factors that sometimes cause accidents among people even though they know the proper safety practices.

Describes proper procedures to take in many emergency situations.

Unit 7: How Is Medical Knowledge Advancing?

Lists some of the advances made in the beneficial use of drugs since the early 1900's.

Cites some of the uses and the drawbacks of such drugs as the sulfas, antibiotics, cortisone, and ACTH.

Discusses some ways in which the public is protected from harmful or ineffective new drugs.

Summarizes major milestones in the progress of surgery over the years.

Explains how various vaccines function to immunize people against infectious diseases.

Cites examples of modern medical tools and techniques.

Defines the terms neuroses and psychoses.

Identifies some of the professional workers who may treat those with mental illness.

Distinguishes between mental illness and mental retardation.

Cites some of the causes of mental retardation.

Unit 8: What Progress Has Been Made in Public and World Health?

Explains what is meant by the term public health.

Discusses some important responsibilities of the Federal government in the field of public health.

Describes some of the health activities carried on by the Public Health Service (PHS).

Explains the responsibilities of the National Institutes of Health (NIH).

Discusses what local and state departments of health do.

Cites examples of how advances in public health have benefited people in the United States today.

Discusses the need for worldwide efforts to fight disease and improve health.

Discusses why gonorrhea and syphilis pose serious public health problems.

Unit 9: What Are Some Effects of Pollution on Health?

Explains what is meant by the terms ecology, ecosystem, and biosphere.

Identifies some environmental hazards that are a result of technological progress.

Cites some of the chief sources of water pollution.

Lists the chief sources of air pollution.

Investigates air and water pollution problems in local communities.

Describes what is meant by the term poor land use and *gives* examples.

Cites some of the positive contributions as well as some of the hazards in using insecticides and herbicides.

Tells why disposal of solid wastes presents problems to communities today.

Lists some sources of noise in our environment.

Discusses the effects of excessive noise on human health.

Enrichment Suggestions for Unit One: What Are Your Personal Health Concerns?[1]

Books and Pamphlets for Students

American Dental Association. *Between You and Me... Is Your Smile* (ADA). Pamphlet.

Gregg, Walter H. *A Boy and His Physique* (NDC). Pamphlet.

Haupt, Enid A. *The Seventeen Book of Fashion and Beauty* (Macmillan).

Leverton, Ruth M. *A Girl and Her Figure* (NDC). Pamphlet.

Levinsohn, Florence, and Kelly, G. Lombard, M.D. *What Teenagers Want to Know* (Budlong). Available only through professional sources from Milex Products, Inc., 5917 N. Northwest Highway, Chicago, Illinois 60631.

Lubowe, Irwin I., M.D., and Huss, Barbara. *A Teen-Age Guide to Healthy Skin and Hair* (Dutton).

Luce, Gay G., and Segal, Julius, M.D. *Sleep* (Coward).

President's Council on Physical Fitness. *Vim, A Complete Exercise Plan for Girls 12 to 18* and *Vigor, A Complete Exercise Plan for Boys 12 to 18* (Sup't of Documents). Pamphlets.

Materials for Teachers

Byler, Ruth; Lewis, Gertrude; and Totman, Ruth. *Teach Us What We Want to Know* (Published for the Connecticut State Board of Education by the Mental Health Materials Center). Paperback.

Greenblatt, Augusta. *Teen-Age Medicine: Questions Young People Ask About Their Health* (Cowles).

Schwartz, June V., M.D. *Health Care for the Adolescent*, Pamphlet #463 (Public Affairs).

Films

Improving Your Posture (Coronet).

Physical Performance Test (Aims).

Sleepwatchers (McGraw-Hill).

Specific Sports Skills (Documentary).

Your Hair and Scalp (BFA).

Your Skin (BFA).

[1]For directories of sources, see page 48 of this *Resource Book.*

Unit Overview

For the learning objectives of the unit, see page 7 of the pupil's text.

Important Ideas Developed in the Unit

During the teen years, individual differences in rate, time, and extent of growth are to be expected among girls and boys.

As physical changes leading to manhood and womanhood begin, there will be a period of fast growth known as the growth spurt.

A young person's heredity is a factor in determining potential growth and whether or not a young person is an early- or late-grower.

The endocrine glands, especially the pituitary, play an important part in the teen-age growth spurt.

A doctor should be consulted, if possible, before a young person takes steps to either lose or gain weight.

Activity, or exercise, and the amount of food eaten are key factors in controlling body weight.

Exercise is a factor in achieving physical fitness, including adequate energy for physical and mental tasks, as well as improved strength, endurance, and coordination.

Acne is a skin disorder of the teen years triggered by a temporary overactivity of the oil glands.

Dandruff in the teen years is generally the result of an oily scalp.

Athlete's foot is caused by a common fungus that flourishes in moist conditions.

Periodic dental checkups are important in furthering dental health.

Near-sightedness in the teen years results from lengthening of the eyeball as it grows.

Sleep needs are individual; 9 to 10 hours of sleep at night are needed by many teen-agers.

Teen-agers should have periodic health checkups.

7 What Are Your Personal Health Concerns? (Unit Title Page)

Introducing the Unit

Students might write on unsigned papers their own special health concerns.

8-17 How Do You Know If You Are Growing As You Should?

In a summary, consider all the things pupils have learned about how growth takes place during the teen years.

18-21 Picture Essay: Individuality in Growth

This material enriches by both pictures and text the concepts developed in this section.

22-23 What Can Be Done About Weight Problems?

A volunteer might write for the U.S. Department of Agriculture Pocket Guide *Calories and Weight, Home and Garden Bulletin No. 153.* It is available from the Sup't of Documents.

24-28 How Can You Improve Your Posture? *and* The Basic Workout

A volunteer committee might work at assembling reference materials on posture and exercise.

29-32 What Can Be Done About Skin Problems?

Individual reports might also be made on moles, calluses, corns, and blisters.

33-39 How Can Teeth Be Kept in Good Condition?

Individuals or a committee might investigate and report on what is being done with tooth transplantation today. Reports might also be given on new ideas about brushing and flossing the teeth to remove plaque.

40-42 What Causes Near-sightedness and Other Eye Defects?

A panel discussion might be held on the proper care of the eyes and on special precautions for contact-lens wearers.

43-44 How Much Sleep Is Needed?

Reports might be made on the subject of *dreams.* See the books *Dreams* by Larry Kettlekamp (Morrow) and *Sleep: The Mysterious Third of Your Life* by Marianna and Jonathan Kastner (Harcourt).

45 Why Does the Voice Change During the Teen Years?

You might want to clarify these terms: *larynx* (an oblong hollow organ at the top of the windpipe—with a framework made of bone and cartilage, bound together by ligaments, membranes, and muscles); *vocal cords* (two thin-edged bands of elastic tissue running from the front to the rear of the larynx); *Adam's apple* (the projection in the front of the neck formed by the largest cartilage of the larynx).

45 What Can Be Done About Bad Breath?

Have pupils bring in ads about mouthwashes as aids for bad breath. Evaluate the ads in light of these facts: Mouthwashes cannot treat infections in the mouth, nasal passages, or throat; they cannot remove decay from teeth; nor can they cope with digestive disturbances.

46-47 Why Are Health Checkups Needed?

Discuss whether periodic health checkups are required for school-age children in your state—and if so, at what intervals.

48-50 Review Material, Activities, Tests

Enrichment Suggestions for Unit 2: What Are the Facts About Drug Abuse, Alcohol, and Smoking?[1]

Books and Pamphlets for Students

Diehl, Harold S. *Tobacco and Your Health: The Smoking Controversy* (McGraw-Hill). Paperback.

Greenberg, Harvey R., M.D. *What You Should Know About Drugs & Drug Abuse* (Scholastic). Paperback.

Houser, Norman W. *About You and Smoking* (Scott, Foresman). Paperback.

________. *Drugs: Facts on Their Use and Abuse* (Scott, Foresman). Paperback.

McCarthy, Raymond G., and Pasciutti, John J. *Facts About Alcohol* (SRA). Pamphlet.

National Institute of Mental Health. *Thinking About Drinking* (Sup't of Documents). Pamphlet.

Ochsner, Alton, M.D. *Smoking: Your Choice Between Life and Death* (Simon & Schuster).

Materials for Teachers

American School Health Association and Pharmaceutical Manufacturers Association. *Teaching About Drugs: A Curriculum Guide, K-12* (ASHA). Paperback.

Mariken, Gene, and Scheimann, Eugene, M.D. *A Doctor's Sensible Approach to Alcohol and Alcoholism* (Budlong). Available only through professional sources from Milex Products, Inc., 5917 N. Northwest Highway, Chicago, Illinois 60631.

U.S. Dept. of HEW. *The Health Consequences of Smoking: A Report of the Surgeon General: 1972* (Sup't of Documents). Paperback.

Films

Drinking: How Will Charlie Handle It? (McGraw-Hill).

Drugs, Drinking and Driving (Aims).

Focus on Drugs (Avanti). Series of five films.

Keep Off the Grass (Sid Davis).

Marijuana: The Great Escape (BFA).

Smoking: It's Your Choice (Alfred Higgins).

Smoking: Past and Present (ACS).

[1]For directories of sources, see page 48 of this *Resource Book.*

Unit Overview

For the learning objectives of the unit, see page 51 of the pupil's text.

Important Ideas Developed in the Unit

Drugs, in legal products, are medical tools that have many benefits when used properly.

A person who fails to take a drug according to directions or who takes a drug for other than medical purposes is a drug abuser.

Drugs that are most often abused are the stimulants, depressants, and hallucinogens.

Stimulant drugs speed up the work of the nervous system; if they are abused, they can lead to psychological dependence.

A person who is psychologically dependent on a drug has formed the habit of taking that drug; he becomes jittery and even panicky without it.

Depressants slow down the work of the nervous system and can lead to physical dependence if they are abused.

A person who is physically dependent on a drug builds up a tolerance for the drug and suffers withdrawal symptoms without it.

Hallucinogens cause distorted sensations and intensified awareness of these sensations.

Marijuana often affects a person's sense of time and distance; it can also affect reflexes and dull the thinking.

Alcohol in the body does not have to be digested; it is absorbed directly into the bloodstream.

Smoking is a factor in the development of lung cancer, heart diseases, chronic bronchitis, and emphysema.

Accurate knowledge about the effects on the body of drugs, alcohol, and tobacco is necessary before people can make wise decisions about using these substances.

51 What Are the Facts About Drug Abuse, Alcohol, and Smoking? (Unit Title Page)

Introducing the Unit

Use the message on the unit title page to initiate preliminary discussion of the topics treated in this unit and the need for having accurate information about them.

52-63 What Drugs Are Often Abused?

A committee might be appointed to assemble books from the library on drugs and drug abuse.

A series of Public Health Service pamphlets entitled *Marihuana: Some Questions and Answers; Stimulants: Some Questions and Answers; Sedatives: Some Questions and Answers; LSD: Some Questions and Answers;* and *Volatile Substances: Some Questions and Answers* might be obtained from the Sup't of Documents for a cost of 10 cents each.

Insofar as possible, students should be encouraged to discuss and share information gained in the course of studying this unit. Here are some possible activities your class might like to try:

Panel discussions on drug abuse prepared for presentation to their own group and perhaps to groups of younger students.

Posters or cartoons made for display on bulletin boards in the school hall.

Bulletin-board displays of newspaper clippings or magazine articles on hazards of misuse of drugs.

Surveys of radio and television guides for forthcoming programs on drugs—their use and misuse.

64-69 Picture Essay: Gateway House: Drug Rehabilitation Center; Alcohol and Accidents; *and* Cigarette Smoking and Respiratory Problems

This material enriches by both pictures and text the concepts developed in the unit.

70-74 What Is Known About Alcoholic Beverages?

Special reports might be given by individuals on the history of alcoholic beverages.

A good source of material for the class library is the National Institute on Alcohol Abuse and Alcoholism, National Institute of Mental Health, P.O. Box 2345, Rockville, Maryland 20852.

A committee might be appointed to investigate the part played by alcohol in economic problems; for example, economic loss through inefficient workmanship, lower output of work, underdeveloped and unused talents and skills, destruction of property by fire, absenteeism from jobs.

A panel discussion might center around alcohol's part in social problems (unhappy family life, broken homes, job losses, and so on).

75-78 What Should You Know About Smoking?

Individuals or committees might make special research reports on the history of pipe, cigar, and cigarette smoking.

Some good sources for pamphlets about the effects of smoking on health are given below:

American Cancer Society, 219 East 42nd Street, New York, New York 10017

American Heart Association, 44 East 23rd Street, New York, New York 10010

American Lung Association, 1740 Broadway, New York, New York 10019

National Clearinghouse for Smoking and Health, P.O. Box 2345, Rockville, Maryland 20852

National Interagency Council on Smoking and Health, Suite 1301, 419 Park Avenue South, New York, New York 10016.

79-82 Review Material, Activities, Tests

Enrichment Suggestions for Unit 3: Are You Alert to Health Quackery?[1]

Books and a Pamphlet for Students

American Medical Association. *Facts on Quacks—What You Should Know About Health Quackery; Health Quackery; Mechanical Quackery;* and *Merchants of Menace* (AMA).

Deutsch, Ronald M. *Nuts Among the Berries: An Exposé of America's Food Fads* (Ballantine). Paperback.

Hemphill, Josephine. *Fruitcake and Arsenic* (Little).

Maple, Eric. *Magic, Medicine, and Quackery* (Barnes).

Seaver, Jacqueline. *Fads, Myths, Quacks—and Your Health,* Pamphlet #415 (Public Affairs).

White, Philip, Editor. *Let's Talk About Food: Answers to Your Questions About Foods and Nutrition* (AMA).

Materials for Teachers

Block, Irvin. *How to Get Good Medical Care,* Pamphlet #368 (Public Affairs).

Consumer Education for High Schools (Bureau of Curriculum Development, Board of Education, City of New York).

Gardner, Martin. *Fads and Fallacies in the Name of Science* (Dover). Paperback.

Jones, Kenneth; Shainberg, Louis; and Byer, Curtis. *Consumer Health* (Canfield).

U.S. Dept. of Agriculture. *Consumers All: The Yearbook of Agriculture, 1965* (Sup't of Documents).

Young, James Harvey. *Medical Messiahs: A Social History of Health Quackery in Twentieth-Century America* (Princeton University Press).

________. *Toadstool Millionaires: A Social History of Patent Medicines in America Before Federal Regulation* (Princeton University Press).

Films

Health Fraud Racket (U.S. Dept. of HEW).

Label Logic (Aims).

Nutritional Quackery (Aims).

Read the Label (Alfred Higgins).

[1]For directories of sources, see page 48 of this *Resource Book.*

Unit Overview

For the learning objectives of the unit, see page 83 of the pupil's text.

Important Ideas Developed in the Unit

Health quackery involves worthless and often dangerous treatments, medicines, and gadgets.

A harmful and illegal form of health quackery is mail-order "doctoring."

Many foods "pushed" by food quacks are good foods in themselves; it is the false claims about these foods that constitute the quackery.

A safeguard against food quackery is sound nutrition knowledge.

A quack advertises and uses "case histories" and testimonials to impress people.

A quack usually promises a quick "cure."

The quack refuses to use tried and proved methods of medical research and proof.

The quack downgrades surgery, X-ray treatments, and drugs prescribed by qualified physicians; he often opposes immunizations.

Federal agencies and departments that fight health quackery are the Federal Trade Commission (FTC), the Food and Drug Administration (FDA), and the U.S. Postal Service.

Some of the organizations that fight health quackery are the American Medical Association, the American Cancer Society, and the National Better Business Bureau.

An over-the-counter drug is one that can be obtained without a doctor's prescription.

Over-the-counter drugs—as well as prescription drugs—should be taken only when needed and used exactly according to directions.

A food fallacy is a mistaken idea or half-truth about food. Food fallacies may cause poor nutrition practices or lead people to spend money needlessly.

83 Are You Alert to Health Quackery? (Unit Title Page)

Introducing the Unit

Use the message on the unit title page to initiate discussion about why people need to be safeguarded against health quackery.

84-90 What Is Health Quackery?

A committee might be appointed to seek available books and pamphlets on health quackery from the school and public libraries.

Panel discussions might be held on the major types of quackery today: cancer quackery, arthritis quackery, food quackery, and "reducing without dieting" programs.

In connection with "reducing without dieting" programs, it is essential that students realize weight losses result from eating less and/or increasing one's activity level. Following are some other concepts that should be stressed:

Spot reducing: It is impossible to control where fat will be lost in the body.

Vibrators: It is not possible for body fat to be vibrated off.

Massaging: Fat cannot be massaged away.

Reducing creams: They have no effect.

In talking over why people are "taken in" at times by health quackery, consider with your students the part played by *fear, ignorance,* and *gullibility.* Note, also, that poor people may be receptive to quackery because good medical services may be scarce or too expensive in their low-income areas.

91-94 Picture Essay: The St. Louis Medical Society's Museum of Medical Quackery

This material enriches by both pictures and text the concepts developed in the unit.

95-97 How Do You Recognize Health Quackery?

Students might make posters or think up slogans that could help educate people about health quackery.

Students might also make booklets in which articles, clippings, pictures, and warnings concerning health quackery are displayed.

Other students might make reports on the legal protection that is available in the different areas of quackery. They might also find out what these Federal and private agencies do to help fight quackery: Federal Trade Commission, U.S. Postal Service, American Medical Association, and National Better Business Bureau.

Another project would be for students to present dramatic skits on how a quack might present his case and on the hazards of such quackery.

98-101 What Are Your Questions?

In connection with the section on choosing a doctor, you might explain that there are board examinations for specialists. A person who is either *board eligible* or an *Academy Fellow* is well trained. The local or state medical society can provide this information about a specialist.

Students might make a display of various labels and instructions from containers of over-the-counter drugs and note the precautions printed on the labels. For example, the following information is often listed on a container: the number of pills to be taken, by whom the medicine can be taken, whether it is safe for one to operate machinery while using the medicine, and the maximum dosage to be taken.

Students probably have heard of food fallacies other than the ones listed. They might make a chart of them, showing the facts that go with the fallacies.

102-104 Review Material, Activities, Tests

Enrichment Suggestions for Unit 4: What Do You Know About the Science of Nutrition?[1]

Books and Pamphlets for Students

Adams, Charlotte. *The Teen-Ager's Menu Cookbook* (Dodd).

Ames, Gerald, and Wyler, Rose. *Food and Life* (Creative Educational Society).

Arnold, Pauline, and White, Percival. *Food Facts for Young People* (Holiday).

Helfman, Elizabeth. *This Hungry World* (Lothrop).

Leverton, Ruth. *Food Becomes You.* Third Edition (Iowa State University Press).

Lewis, Alfred. *The New World of Food* (Dodd).

Mickelsen, Olaf. *Nutrition Science and You* (Scholastic). Paperback.

Riedman, Sarah R. *Food for People* (Abelard).

White, Philip L., Editor. *Let's Talk About Food: Answers to Your Questions About Foods and Nutrition* (AMA). Paperback.

Materials for Teachers

Bogert, L. Jean; Briggs, George M.; and Calloway, Doris Howes. *Nutrition and Physical Fitness.* Eighth Edition (Saunders).

Family Food Budgeting for Good Meals and Good Nutrition (Sup't of Documents). Pamphlet.

Nutrition Today, 101 Ridgely Avenue, P.O. Box 465, Annapolis, Maryland 21404. Magazine.

Pattison, Mattie; Barbour, Helen; and Eppright, Ercel. *Teaching Nutrition.* Second Edition (Iowa State University Press).

Films

Food, Energy and You (Wexler).

Food for Life (Wexler).

Food for a Modern World (Wexler).

G for Goldberger (Teaching Films).

How a Hamburger Turns into You (Wexler).

Vitamins from Food (Wexler).

[1]For directories of sources, see page 48 of this *Resource Book.*

Unit Overview

For the learning objectives of the unit, see page 105 of the pupil's text.

Important Ideas Developed in the Unit

The body gets the substances it needs for building and maintaining body tissues from food.

Food furnishes the chemical substances that act to regulate body processes.

Food furnishes chemical substances the body can burn for energy. The burning of food in the body is known as *oxidation.*

The process by which the body changes food into living tissue and energy is known as *metabolism.*

Digestion involves changing food into a form the body can use.

The six main classes of nutrients are proteins, fats, carbohydrates, minerals, vitamins, and water.

Digested food is carried by the blood and left wherever cells are growing or need to be repaired—or wherever the different parts of the body need energy to do work.

To get the nutrients the body needs, it is necessary to eat a variety of foods.

Proteins build and maintain body tissues.

Minerals serve as body regulators and furnish some building materials.

Water is essential to the body's transportation system; it aids in digestion and helps regulate body temperature.

Vitamins are essential to growth and health.

Carbohydrates and fats produce the energy to help the body keep warm and do work.

A daily food guide can help you choose foods for an adequate diet.

The calorie is the unit of energy used in nutrition.

Finding food for a growing world population is an important problem for now and the future.

105 What Do You Know About the Science of Nutrition? (Unit Title Page)

Introducing the Unit

Use the opening message on page 105 to initiate preliminary conversation.

106-107 Why Do You Need Food?

A committee might be appointed to assemble books and booklets on food from the school and public libraries and from other sources.

One student might write to the Food and Drug Administration, Office of Consumer Affairs, Consumer Inquiry Branch, P.O. Box 2345, Rockville, Maryland 20852, for a single copy of the pamphlet *Facts About Nutrition.*

Another student might write to the U.S. Department of Agriculture, Office of Information, Washington, D.C. 20250, for *How to Buy*..., a set of 12 booklets on buying meats, fruits, vegetables, dairy products, and so on.

108-110 What Happens to All the Food You Eat?

Here students solve the mystery posed on the unit-opening page—the mystery about why a person does not weigh as much as the food he eats and what happens to the food taken into the body.

111-115 What Kinds of Foods Do You Need?

Students might prepare talks for younger children on *why* a variety of foods is needed in the daily diet.

Consideration might be given, too, to how variety may be obtained in the serving of a given food. Thus bread may be served plain, toasted, French fried, or in sandwiches; it may be varied in kind, such as rye, whole wheat, white, or the like. Ethnic and regional favorites might be explored too—Italian, French, pumpernickel, sourdough, corn bread, and so on.

116-117 How Does a Daily Food Guide Help?

Ask, "Do you think school lunchrooms use a food guide? Explain." (A copy of "Food for Fitness—A Daily Food Guide," Leaflet #464, USDA, can be obtained from the Sup't of Documents for a few cents.)

118-122 How Much Should You Eat?

Pupils might bring to class some more extensive calorie guides for examination.

123-126 Picture Essay: Different People, Different Menus

This material enriches by both pictures and text the concepts developed in this section.

127-133 What Are Your Questions About Nutrition?

Another question often asked is, "Why do people overeat?" There are many reasons; for example:

Some people get into the habit of overeating because of sociability. They like to sit around and talk and eat; they go with friends for snacks; they absentmindedly munch nuts, popcorn, and candy while watching television.

Some people are bored and become constant nibblers because eating is a pleasant way to pass the time.

Other people have feelings of loneliness, discontent, or unhappiness that persist; these people may turn to food for comfort and as a way of satisfying unmet needs.

When simple methods of controlling overeating do not work, a doctor may be able to help.

134-137 Picture Essay: Food for Hungry People

This material enriches by both pictures and text the concepts developed in this section.

138-140 Review Material, Activities, Tests

Enrichment Suggestions for Unit 5: How Can You Improve in Your Human Relations?[1]

Books for Students

Alexander, Arthur. *The Hidden You: Psychology in Your Life* (Prentice-Hall).

Goldenson, Robert M. *All About the Human Mind: An Introduction to Psychology for Young People* (Random).

McBain, William N., and Johnson, R. C. *The Science of Ourselves: Adventures in Experimental Psychology* (Harper).

Noshpitz, Joseph D., M.D. *Understanding Ourselves: The Challenge of the Human Mind* (Coward).

Books for Teachers

Allport, Gordon. *Pattern and Growth in Personality* (Holt).

Aruspiger, Rucker. *Human Values* (W. C. Brown).

Bernard, Harold W. *Mental Health in the Classroom* (McGraw-Hill).

Clark, Kenneth B. *Prejudice and Your Child* (Beacon).

Erickson, Eric. *Youth: Change and Challenge* (Basic).

Jenkins, Gladys; Shacter, Helen S.; and Bauer, William W. *These Are Your Children.* Third Edition (Scott, Foresman).

Maslow, Abraham H., Editor. *Motivation and Personality* (Harper).

Mussen, Paul H.; Conger, John Janeway; and Kagan, Jerome. *Child Development and Personality* (Harper).

Seidman, Jerome. *Education for Mental Health* (Crowell).

Films

I Am (Wombat).

Acting with Maturity (Coronet).

Black and White: Uptight (BFA).

It's Your Move: Decisions for Discussion (Coronet).

Parent Problems (King Screen).

Right or Wrong? (Coronet).

[1]For directories of sources, see page 48 of this *Resource Book*.

Unit Overview

For the learning objectives of the unit, see page 141 of the pupil's text.

Important Ideas Developed in the Unit

Human relations can be described as "what goes on between people."

One commonly accepted theory about why we behave as we do is that we are trying to satisfy important human needs.

Our primary, or physiological, needs are for air, water, food, clothing, sleep, and shelter.

Our secondary, or psychological, needs are for love, self-respect, and the right to be ourselves.

Much of our behavior is learned.

A mature way of meeting difficult situations is to try the problem-solving approach.

All of us unconsciously try to protect ourselves and our feelings about ourselves and our behavior; we use what are sometimes called "defense mechanisms."

Some common ways we protect ourselves are through rationalization, compensation, daydreaming, repression and suppression, displaced aggression, projection, and denial.

Human relations are improved when we remember that the other fellow needs kindliness, friendliness, and a feeling of self-respect.

Prejudging a person before the facts are known about him is called prejudice.

Prejudice is damaging both to the person against whom it is directed and to the person who holds it.

Communication takes place through actions as well as words.

Mental health involves the ability to feel comfortable about ourselves, kindly in our feelings about other people, and able to meet life's demands.

Mental health is influenced by many factors—family, friends, work, recreation, and so on.

141 How Can You Improve in Your Human Relations? (Unit Title Page)

Introducing the Unit

Before starting the unit, students might write their own definitions of what they think is meant by human relations.

142 What Is Meant by Human Relations?

Discuss whether there is a Human Relations Council in the students' community and what activities it carries on.

143-148 Why Do People Behave As They Do?

Before reading this material, explore the ideas students hold about what factors influence people's actions and whether there are reasons underlying their behavior.

149-150 *and* 155-162 How Can You Meet the Demands of Life?

Pupils might cite examples from books they have read in which various characters at times used different ways to protect themselves.

Small groups might also plan and present skits based on these various examples from library books they have read.

The following description of people who are able to meet life's demands may help students work toward this important goal of mental health. It is from the pamphlet *Mental Health Is 1, 2, 3* (National Association for Mental Health):

They plan ahead and do not fear the future.

They try to think for themselves and make their own decisions.

They do something about their problems as these problems arise.

They accept their responsibilities.

151-154 Picture Essay: Some Problem Situations: What Would You Do?

This material enriches by both pictures and text the concepts developed in this section.

On unsigned papers, students might briefly outline other everyday problems that are often troublesome or perplexing. These suggested problems can serve as the basis for continued discussion of productive ways of coping with difficult situations. Consider how problem-solving techniques can help.

163-165 How Can You Improve in Your Relationships with Others?

On unsigned papers, students might write accounts of prejudice they have observed, together with their analyses of how the situations could be changed and improved.

Later students might also write about—and talk over—instances in which good human relations have been evident. These situations might be drawn from the classroom, the playground, the community, or the national or international scene.

166-167 What Is Good Mental Health?

Another definition of mental health is this one: "When we speak of satisfaction with one's life, of concern for the well-being of others, of the ability to meet problems arising in daily living, then we are usually talking about mental health."

Suggest that students look through available reference materials on mental health to find still other definitions.

Reports might also be given on ideas presented in William Menninger's book *How to Be a Successful Teen-ager* (Sterling).

168-170 Review Material, Activities, Tests

Enrichment Suggestions for Unit 6: How Much Do You Know About Safety and Accident Prevention?[1]

Books and Pamphlets for Students

The American National Red Cross. *Basic First Aid: Books 1, 2, 3, 4* (Doubleday). Paperbacks.

Bendick, Jeanne. *The Emergency Book* (Rand McNally).

Benjamin, Bry, M.D., and Annette F. *In Case of Emergency: What to Do Until the Doctor Arrives* (Doubleday).

Hyde, Margaret. *Driving Today and Tomorrow* (McGraw-Hill).

National Safety Council. *Family Emergency Almanac* (NSC). Pamphlet.

You and Safety (Bete). Pamphlet.

Materials for Teachers and Students

The following are among the many Safety Education Data Sheets that can be obtained from the National Safety Council: *Bicycles, Firearms, Highway Driving, Let's Hunt Safely, Motor-Vehicle Speed (Revised), Night Driving, Pedestrian Safety, Poisonous Plants, Poisonous Snakes, Promoting Safety Through School Newspapers, Swimming, (Bad) Weather.*

School Safety World (NSC). Magazine.

Books for Teachers

American Association for Health, Physical Education, and Recreation. *Annual Safety Education Review* (AAHPER). Published annually.

Seaton, Dan; Stark, Herbert; and Loft, Bernard. *Administration and Supervision of Safety Education* (Macmillan).

Yost, Charles P., Editor. *Sports Safety* (AAHPER).

Films

Accidentally Yours (IFB).

The Baby Sitter (AT & T).

Read the Label (Alfred Higgins).

Self-Defense for Girls (BFA).

Your Clothing Can Burn (Alfred Higgins).

[1]For directories of sources, see page 48 of this *Resource Book.*

Unit Overview

For the learning objectives of the unit, see page 171 of the pupil's text.

Important Ideas Developed in the Unit

Safety instruction for thirteen- and fourteen-year-olds is more important than ever because of the rising accident rate for this group.

To live safely, a person must both know and practice safe ways of doing things.

Knowing the why's of safety practices helps one remember them.

Water accidents rank among the most frequent and serious ones for junior-high-age students.

Factors that may cause accidents among people who really know the proper safety practices are emotional upsets, carelessness, foolhardiness, lack of necessary skills, and overestimation of one's strength or skill.

Accidents with firearms rank high among young people; these accidents are about equally divided between home and hunting accidents.

Take a course in safe gun-handling, treat every gun as if it were loaded, check to make sure any gun is unloaded before it is brought into the house, never keep a loaded gun in the house, and never point a gun at anyone or at yourself are important firearms-safety practices.

The single most effective safety guide a car driver or passenger can follow is to always buckle the safety belts.

Many accidents can be prevented by foresight.

Young people can learn what to do—and can perform competently—in such emergency situations as contact with poison ivy, frostbite, a burn, a bruise, hiccups, dog bite, chemicals in the eyes, snake bite, fire in the oven, grease fire, shock, floods, hurricanes, and nuclear explosions.

171 How Much Do You Know About Safety and Accident Prevention? (Unit Title Page)

Introducing the Unit

The message on the unit title page can be used to initiate interest in the subject of safety and why it still needs to be taught at the junior-high level.

172 What Is Involved in Living Safely?

Discuss ways by which people learn important safety practices: through direct teaching in school; radio and television programs; posters; newspaper and magazine articles; parent instruction and example; and so on.

173-175 What Do You Know About Water Safety?

Discuss what to do if you see someone in trouble in the water. Remind students that only someone trained in lifesaving should attempt a swimming rescue of a drowning person. Most drowning people have panicked, which makes a swimming rescue very dangerous to the would-be rescuer. Since most drownings occur close to shore, help can usually be given by such means as throwing the person a life preserver, an oar, a plank, or anything that will keep the person afloat until the rescuer can reach him. Or, if the person is near a pier or the side of a pool, the rescuer can lie down and extend a hand, leg, stick, or towel to aid him.

If a boat is available for the rescue, the person should be instructed to grasp and hang on to the side of the boat.

Consider, too, what should be done if one is in a boat and needs help. (Any of these distress signals may be used: a constant horn, bell, or whistle; someone waving a shirt, towel, or the like; a flag flying upside down; a flare; a light blinking SOS—3 short, 3 long, 3 short blinks.)

176-177 How Much Do You Know About Firearms Safety?

Discuss what should be done with a gun if a hunter is going over or under a fence. (Pass the gun under or over the fence first. If two hunters are together, one partner holds the guns, then hands them to the other partner before following him over or under the fence.)

178-183 How Much Do You Know About Auto Safety?

Consider what should be done when a car on a highway is not working properly. (If possible, the driver should get the car off the highway before stopping. Then he can signal for help by raising the hood and by tying something white to the radio antenna or to the door handle on the traffic side.)

Ask about the kinds of information young people need to help them become good drivers in the future.

Discuss the different ways in which people view a car—as a means of transportation, as an instrument of personal prestige, as a means of self-expression, and so on. How do young people regard a car? Have pupils bring in car advertisements and analyze them to see what aspects are featured (pride, prestige, economy, safety, and so on).

184-188 Picture Essay: Experimental Safe-Car Design Programs *and* Experimental Testing Programs

This material enriches by both pictures and text the concepts developed in this section.

189-193 Do You Know What to Do in Emergencies?

Common emergency and first-aid treatments that young people might find useful are featured here.

194-196 Review Material, Activities, Tests

Enrichment Suggestions for Unit 7: How Is Medical Knowledge Advancing?[1]

Books and a Pamphlet for Students

Calder, Ritchie. *The Wonderful World of Medicine* (Doubleday).

Epstein, Samuel, and Williams, Beryl. *Medicine from Microbes: The Story of Antibiotics* (Messner).

Ladimer, Irving. *The Challenge of Transplantation,* Pamphlet #451 (Public Affairs).

Levine, I. E. *The Discoverer of Insulin: Dr. Frederick G. Banting* (Messner).

Mann, John. *Louis Pasteur: Founder of Bacteriology* (Scribner).

Nolen, William A., M.D. *Spare Parts for the Human Body* (Random).

Poole, Lynn and Gray. *Electronics in Medicine* (McGraw-Hill).

Rosenberg, Nancy and Lawrence, M.D. *The Story of Modern Medicine* (Norton).

Rosenberg, Nancy, and Snyderman, Reuven K., M.D. *New Parts for People: The Story of Medical Transplants* (Norton).

Silverstein, Alvin and Virginia B. *The Endocrine System: Hormones in the Living World* (Prentice-Hall).

Simon, Tony. *The Heart Explorers* (Basic).

Sylvester, D. S. *The Story of Medicine* (St. Martin's).

References for Teachers

Sinacore, John S. *Health, A Quality of Life* (Macmillan).

Starbinski, Jean. *A History of Medicine* (Hawthorn).

Films

Conquest of Pain (Teaching Films).

How Much Is a Miracle? (Modern).

Incredible Voyage (McGraw-Hill).

Riddle of Heredity (McGraw-Hill).

Surviving in Space (McGraw-Hill).

The Wild Cell (McGraw-Hill).

[1]For directories of sources, see page 48 of this *Resource Book.*

Unit Overview

For the learning objectives of the unit, see page 192 of the pupil's text.

Important Ideas Developed in the Unit

Since primitive times, drugs have been used for treating diseases of various kinds, for healing sores, and for relieving pain.

Systematic efforts to find new drugs began with Paul Ehrlich, who discovered "606" in 1909.

A milestone in fighting infection came with the sulfa drugs of the 1930's—followed by the antibiotics.

Today's physician has many useful drugs for preventing and treating diseases; these include the sulfas, antibiotics, tranquilizers, energizers, and hormone drugs.

The Food and Drug Administration (FDA) helps protect the public from harmful drugs.

Today, vaccines exist to protect people from a wide variety of epidemic-producing diseases.

Anesthesia ushered in a new era in surgery in the mid-1800's; newly developed instruments, machines, and techniques have given further impetus to advances in surgery today.

The major aim of current research in organ transplantation is to make the recipient tolerant to tissue from unrelated donors—and to find ways of using artificial organs.

Mental illness describes disturbances of the mind which affect the way a person thinks, feels, and behaves.

Mental illness may range from mild neuroses to severe mental disturbances known as psychoses.

With proper care, many mentally ill people recover to lead full and productive lives.

Much research is underway to prevent mental retardation—and to help the retarded achieve the best possible performance for them.

197 How Is Medical Knowledge Advancing? (Unit Title Page)

Introducing the Unit

Use the message to explore, through preliminary conversation, the information students already have about milestones in medicine in the past and in the world today.

A committee might also be appointed to assemble from the school or public library books on modern medical advances.

Students might be encouraged to begin collecting clippings, pamphlets, and books on careers in medicine. A member of the group might write for information on this subject to the Department of Program Services, American Medical Association, 535 North Dearborn Street, Chicago, Illinois 60610.

198-201 What New Drugs Have Been Developed?

Students might start a scrapbook of clippings about new drugs that have been developed.

202-204 What Is Hormone Therapy?

Volunteers might prepare dramatic skits in which highlights of the work of the team of Banting and Best or of Dr. Philip Hench are portrayed.

205-208 What Progress Has Been Made in Immunization?

Students might contribute their own questions to be used in a quiz on the topic "Immunization—Yesterday and Today."

209-217 What Progress Has Been Made in Surgery?

Students might make reports on various surgical specialties such as plastic surgery, orthopedic surgery, heart surgery, and others, and the special problems and tools related to each specialty.

218-219 What Progress Has Been Made in the Use of Radiation?

Volunteers might make reports that give additional information on the work of Roentgen and the Curies—and on the many uses of radioactive isotopes in the diagnosis and treatment of disease.

220 What Progress Has There Been in Developing Mechanical Aids?

Students might report on progress in developing improved mechanical aids such as artificial limbs. One book that will prove helpful is *New Parts for People: The Story of Medical Transplants* by Nancy Rosenberg and Reuven K. Snyderman, M.D. (Norton).

221-226 Picture Essay: Modern Medical Tools and Research Help Doctors Help Their Patients

This material enriches by both pictures and text the concepts developed in this section.

227-230 What Progress Has Taken Place in Treating Mental Illness?

A good topic for a summary discussion is "What I Have Learned About Mental Illness That I Did Not Know Before."

231-233 Picture Essay: The Community Mental Health Center

This material enriches by both pictures and text the concepts developed in this section.

234-236 What Progress Is Being Made in Treating Mental Retardation?

Volunteers might work together to present a panel discussion on mental retardation. A committee might assemble materials for a reading shelf.

237-240 Review Material, Activities, Tests

Enrichment Suggestions for Unit 8: What Progress Has Been Made In Public and World Health?[1]

Books and Pamphlets for Students

Agency for International Development. *The Protein Gap* (AID). Pamphlet.

American Medical Association. *Why the Rise in Teen-age Gonorrhea?* and *Why the Rise in Teen-age Syphilis?* (AMA). Pamphlets.

Benarde, Melvin. *The Race Against Famine* (Macrae).

Blanzaco, André, M.D. *V.D.: Facts You Should Know* (Scott, Foresman). Paperback.

Epstein, Sam and Beryl. *The First Book of the World Health Organization* (Watts). Easy.

Savage, Katharine. *The Story of the United Nations* (Walck).

Smith, Ralph. *Getting to Know the World Health Organization* (Coward). Easy.

Speiser, Jean. *UNICEF and the World* (John Day). Easy.

Walsh, William B. *A Ship Called HOPE* (Dutton).

Webster, Bruce, M.D. *What You Should Know About VD—and Why* (Scholastic). Paperback.

Materials for the Teacher

Health Is a Community Affair (APHA). Pamphlet.

Sinacore, John S. *Health, A Quality of Life* (Macmillan).

Turner, Clair E. *Personal and Community Health.* Fourteenth Edition (Mosby).

Films

A Half-Million Teenagers (Churchill). About VD.

Legacy of HOPE (Modern).

Little Man—Big City (Produced by Pannonia Studios, Budapest; distributed by WHO). About city health.

Man Alive (United Nations). About WHO.

V.D. Every 30 Seconds (Alfred Higgins).

[1]For directories of sources, see page 48 of this *Resource Book.*

Unit Overview

For the learning objectives of the unit, see page 241 of the pupil's text.

Important Ideas Developed in the Unit

Public health problems center around health concerns that the individual cannot solve by himself.

The Greek and Roman civilizations were among the first to pay attention to public health matters.

Public health problems concerned people in the Middle Ages, and crude attempts at sanitation and quarantine were undertaken.

Each kind of communicable disease is caused by a special kind of germ which enters the body from the outside.

The warmth, food, and moisture found inside the human body encourage the growth of germs.

As germs eat and live in the body, they throw off poisons; it is these poisons that cause a person to feel sick from a communicable disease. Today, there are vaccines that can provide immunity for many communicable diseases.

Disease germs are spread by direct or indirect contact with a person who has the disease.

Diseases can be spread by contaminated drinking water, by coughs or sneezes, by contaminated food, by animals and insects, by human carriers, and by mild or "missed" cases.

Many of the important health activities of the Federal government are carried out by the Public Health Service (PHS).

Advances in public health and medicine have resulted in reducing the death rate of babies and young children, in safeguarding the health of mothers during childbirth, in eliminating epidemics of most communicable diseases, and in extending the average length of life in the United States to about seventy years.

241 What Progress Has Been Made in Public and World Health? (Unit Title Page)

Introducing the Unit

Invite speculation on what benefits have come to people in the United States as a result of improvement in public health. The answer is spelled out later —on page 250 of this unit. Use this discussion to provoke curiosity.

242-244 What Was Known About Public Health in Past Times?

Volunteers might do research to find out about death tolls of the epidemics during the Middle Ages. For example, an epidemic of plague in Europe in the mid-fourteenth century killed 25 million people, or one fourth of the population!

245-250 What About Public Health Today?

Discuss how public health activities are financed. (By taxpayers' money.) What are some important returns in the way of health services and benefits that the taxpayers receive on this investment?

Have the class begin to compile a list of careers in public health. A book by Stanley L. Englebardt that may be helpful is *Jobs in Health Care* (Lothrop, Lee & Shepard Company).

Students might be interested to know that data from the National Center for Health Statistics of the U.S. Public Health Service shows that in 1967 there were about 3.4 million persons employed in the major health professions and occupations. It is estimated that by 1977 there may be twice that number of employees in these areas.

251-256 Picture Essay: The Community Hospital

This material enriches by both pictures and text the concepts developed in this section.

257-259 What Progress Has Been Made in World Health?

Your pupils may be interested in the comment of a Peruvian surgeon to an American doctor who had served as a teaching surgeon on the S.S. HOPE. "Tomorrow you will be in your own United States, but you will still be here in my country. Tomorrow when I go into the operating room, you and what you taught me go there too."

Note that there are other agencies besides those mentioned here that help promote worldwide health. Some of them are given below:

The United Nations Educational, Scientific, and Cultural Organization (UNESCO). This agency is interested in education, including health education.

The International Labor Office (ILO). This agency is concerned with the health of workers.

The Peace Corps. Volunteers have supplied a corps of needed health workers in countries until native workers could be trained.

260-264 Picture Essay: Global Health

This material enriches by both pictures and text the concepts developed in this section.

265 What Are Some Challenging Public Health Problems?

Be sure to read the section on venereal diseases on pages 15-16 of this *Resource Book.*

You may be interested in obtaining a copy of *A Curriculum Guide on Venereal Disease for Junior High School Teachers* (The Commonwealth of Massachusetts, Department of Public Health, Division of Communicable Diseases, State House, Boston, Massachusetts 02133).

266-268 Review Material, Activities, Tests

Enrichment Suggestions for Unit 9: What Are Some Effects of Pollution on Health?[1]

Books for Students

Aylesworth, Thomas G. *This Vital Air, This Vital Water: Man's Environmental Crisis* (Rand McNally & Co.).

Bixby, William. *A World You Can Live In* (McKay).

Cailliet, Greg; Setzer, Paulette; and Love, Milton. *Everyman's Guide to Ecological Living* (Macmillan). Paperback.

Hilton, Suzanne. *How Do They Get Rid of It?* (Westminster).

Hungerford, Harold. *Ecology, The Circle of Life* (Childrens Press).

Navarra, John G. *Our Noisy World: The Problem of Noise Pollution* (Doubleday).

Pringle, Laurence. *The Only Earth We Have* (Macmillan).

Van Dersal, William R. *The Land Renewed: The Story of Soil Conservation.* Revised Edition (Walck).

Worth, Jean. *Man, Earth, and Change* (Coward).

Books for Teachers

De Bell, Garrett, Editor. *The Environmental Handbook* (Ballantine). Paperback.

Jones, Kenneth; Shainberg, Louis; and Byer, Curtis. *Environmental Health* (Canfield). Paperback.

Swatek, Paul. *The User's Guide to the Protection of the Environment* (Ballantine). Paperback.

Films

Alone in the Midst of the Land (NBC).

Down Decibel Down (King Screen).

From the Face of the Earth (King Screen).

The Garbage Explosion (EBE).

Heritage of Splendor (Alfred Higgins).

The Litter Monster (Alfred Higgins).

The Noise Boom (NBC).

Runaround (American Lung Association).

[1]For directories of sources, see page 48 of this *Resource Book.*

Unit Overview

For the learning objectives of the unit, see page 269 of the pupil's text.

Important Ideas Developed in the Unit

Ecology is the study of the relationship of all living things to each other and to their environment.

An ecosystem is an environment in which living and nonliving things work together to exchange the materials of life and reuse them.

The biosphere is an ecosystem, the most complete ecosystem of all.

Over the years, people have been making changes in the biosphere; these changes result in pollution problems which threaten human health and the health of all living things.

Waters polluted by such contaminants as chemicals and other industrial wastes, sewage, and heat pose a threat to human health and to the health of living things in the waters.

Major pollutants in the air are carbon monoxide, sulfur oxides, hydrocarbons, nitrogen oxides, and particulates.

High levels of air pollution have been shown to have ill effects on human health.

Misuse of land includes indiscriminate land clearing, poor farming methods, widespread paving of land, unwise use of insecticides and herbicides, and inadequate disposal of solid wastes.

A promising method of solid-waste disposal that will no doubt be increasingly used in future years is recycling.

Noise is a form of environmental pollution and ways are being sought to control it.

Research studies have clearly indicated that excessive noise can cut down on hearing acuity, can affect the human nervous system, and can diminish the quality of life.

269 What Are Some Effects of Pollution on Health? (Unit Title Page)

Introducing the Unit

Invite discussion of aspects of pollution that students will be considering in this unit. This preliminary discussion might conclude with the compiling of a list of questions on pollution problems that students especially want to have answered.

A committee might assemble books such as those listed on page 43 for group reference.

270-271 Why Is There So Much Concern Today About Pollution Problems?

See what evidence students can cite that there *is* concern today about pollution problems. (Frequent articles in newspapers and magazines, television and radio programs, community action programs to help solve pollution problems, and so on.)

272-273 How Does Water Pollution Affect Health?

If possible, the entire group—or a committee—might visit the local water-treatment plant and later summarize the information gained on the trip.

274-277 Why Is Air Pollution a Threat to Health?

Following are some related topics that individuals or committees might research and later present to the group in the form of talks, television-type "documentaries," posters, bulletin-board displays, or panel discussions:

The Effects of Air Pollution on Plants
Soot As a Financial Problem in Large Cities
Effects of Air Pollution on Livestock
Pollution-Free Cars of the Future
Measuring Pollutants in the Air
Air Pollution and Public Statues
Forest Fires As a Source of Air Pollution

278-285 What Are Some Ill Effects of Poor Land Use?

Another form of land pollution that should be considered is that of *salting* icy walkways and roads. The salts used are somewhat damaging to the undersides of cars and to footwear, floors, and other places where the salts are tracked—unless they are washed off promptly.

Salt can also have a damaging effect on the environment. Salts from walkways and roads can drain off into the soil and waterways. Salty soil can weaken the resistance of some plants to insect pests. Salt has even been known to contaminate the community water supply.

Instead of salt, a substance like sand might be used. Sand is nonpolluting, is effective at very low temperatures, and can be recovered and used again.

286-293 Picture Essay: Pollution Problems: Water Pollution; Pollution Problems: Air Pollution; Land Use: Country and City; *and* Land Use: Insecticides and Solid Waste

This material enriches by both pictures and text the concepts developed in this section.

294 Can Noise Be Harmful to Health?

Help students compile a list of undesirable effects that excessive noise can have in the United States today—accidents, sleeplessness, nervousness, inefficiency on the job, health ailments, loss in hearing acuity, and so on.

Individuals or committees might prepare reports on efforts being made by various cities to curb noise. *Our Noisy World: The Problem of Noise Pollution* by John G. Navarra (Doubleday) is a useful reference for the class.

295-297 Review Material, Activities, Tests

Reference Aids[1]

Books and Pamphlets for Teachers and Parents

American Association for Health, Physical Education, and Recreation. *What Educators Can Do About Cigarette Smoking.* AAHPER, 1971. Pamphlet.

American School Health Association and Pharmaceutical Manufacturers Association. *Teaching About Drugs: A Curriculum Guide, K-12.* ASHA, 1970. Paperback.

Bernard, Harold W. *The American Adolescent.* McGraw-Hill, 1970.

Benarde, Melvin A. *Our Precarious Habitat: An Integrated Approach to Understanding Man's Effect on His Environment.* Norton, 1970. Paperback.

Brown, Abe A., and Podair, Simon. *Venereal Diseases—The Silent Menace.* Public Affairs Pamphlet #292B. Public Affairs, 1970.

Byler, Ruth; Lewis, Gertrude; and Totman, Ruth. *Teach Us What We Want to Know.* Published for the Connecticut State Board of Education by the Mental Health Materials Center. Mental Health Materials Center, 1969. Paperback.

Cox, George W., Editor. *The Crisis in Environment.* Scott, Foresman, 1970. Paperback.

Cuban, Larry. *To Make a Difference: Teaching in the Inner City.* Free Press, 1970.

De Bell, Garrett, Editor. *The Environmental Handbook.* Ballantine, 1970. Paperback.

Gallagher, J. Roswell, M.D. *Medical Care of the Adolescent.* Second Edition. Appleton, 1966.

Hill, John, and Shelton, J., Editors. *Readings in Adolescent Development and Behavior.* Prentice-Hall, 1971.

Jenkins, Gladys G.; Shacter, Helen S.; and Bauer, William W. *These Are Your Children.* Third Edition. Scott, Foresman, 1966. Paperback.

Joint Committee on Health Problems in Education. *Health Appraisal of School Children.* Fifth Edition. AAHPER and AMA, 1970. Booklet.

Jones, Kenneth; Shainberg, Louis; and Byler, Curtis. *Consumer Health.* Canfield, 1971. Paperback.

[1]See page 48 for Directories of Sources.

Kaplan, Louis. *Education and Mental Health.* Harper, 1971.

Mariken, Gene, and Scheimann, Eugene, M.D. *A Doctor's Sensible Approach to Alcohol and Alcoholism.* Budlong, 1969. Available only through professional sources from Milex Products, Inc., 5917 N. Northwest Highway, Chicago, Illinois 60631. Paperback.

Maslow, Abraham H., Editor. *Motivation and Personality.* Harper, 1970.

McCandless, Boyd. *Adolescents: Behavior and Development.* Holt, 1970.

Pattison, Mattie; Barbour, Helen; and Eppright, Ercel. *Teaching Nutrition.* Second Edition. Iowa State University Press, 1963.

Read, Donald, and Greene, Walter. *Creative Teaching in Health.* Macmillan, 1971.

Schwartz, June V., M.D. *Health Care for the Adolescent.* Public Affairs Pamphlet #463. Public Affairs, 1971.

Seaton, Don; Stack, Herbert; and Loft, Bernard. *Administration and Supervision of Safety Education.* Macmillan, 1968.

Sebald, Hans. *Adolescence: A Sociological Analysis.* Appleton, 1970.

Sinacore, John S. *Health: A Quality of Life.* Macmillan, 1968.

Stare, Frederick J. *Eating for Good Health.* Simon & Schuster, 1969.

Swatek, Paul. *The User's Guide to the Protection of the Environment.* Ballantine, 1970. Paperback.

Turner, C. E. *Personal and Community Health.* Fourteenth Edition. Mosby, 1971.

USDA. *Food for Us All: The Yearbook of Agriculture, 1969.* Sup't of Documents, 1969.

U.S. Dept. of HEW. *The Health Consequences of Smoking: A Report of the Surgeon General: 1972.* Sup't of Documents, 1972. Paperback.

White, Philip L., Editor. *Let's Talk About Food: Answers to Your Questions About Foods and Nutrition.* Second Edition. AMA, 1970. Paperback.

Films for Teachers and Parents

Accidentally Yours. IFB. Shows how common accidents at home can be prevented; the safe use of consumer products is stressed.

The Beautiful River. NBC. The story of water pollution and the Connecticut River.

Black and White: Uptight. BFA. Excellent film on how prejudice develops.

Fathers and Sons and *Mothers and Daughters.* Carousel. Two open-ended companion films provide an insight into the different ideas held by the younger and older generations.

Focus on Drugs. Avanti. This series of five films focuses attention on LSD, "downers," "uppers," heroin, and marijuana.

Health Fraud Racket. U.S. Dept. of HEW. Exposes the schemes of the fraud, the quack, and the charlatan.

How's School, Enrique? Aims. Award-winning film points out the differences in two educational philosophies as taught in Enrique's Mexican-American school.

Invention of the Adolescent. NFBC. Penetrating look at how the twentieth-century adult views the adolescent.

Me and About Twenty Others. Brigham Young. Dramatizes the need for school health programs and suggests how such programs can be started.

On Guard—Bunco. Aims. Good consumer-education film, though not primarily health-oriented.

Pas de Deux. NFBC. Award-winning film on locomotor and nonlocomotor movements as shown by a ballet dancer.

The Time to Stop Is Now. ACS. This film emphasizes that if a smoker quits, gradual repair of damage to body tissues will begin.

Up to Our Necks. NBC. Film explores some solutions to the solid-waste problem.

VD: A Call to Action. Association. Provides up-to-date information on venereal diseases and tells how one community faced the problem.

The Wild Cell. McGraw-Hill. Recent research on cancer—diagnosis, treatment, and causes—is detailed.

Films for Classroom Use

Acting with Maturity. Coronet. Many situations give young people the opportunity to show their maturity.

Drinking: How Will Charlie Handle It? McGraw-Hill. Open-ended film which considers the social factors that influence an individual's decision concerning alcohol.

From the Face of the Earth. King Screen. Science-fiction film showing what the world will be like in 1999 if pollution is not controlled.

Genetics: Functions of DNA and RNA. Coronet. Film shows the roles of DNA and RNA in heredity.

A Half-Million Teenagers. Churchill. Explains how venereal disease can be recognized and stresses the need for proper treatment.

Heritage of Splendor. Alfred Higgins. Film shows what people can do to prevent landscape pollution.

The Incredible Voyage. McGraw-Hill. Film dramatizes the workings of the human body.

Keep Off the Grass. Sid Davis. Open-ended film which gives the facts on marijuana.

Label Logic. Aims. Designed to promote intelligent buying through learning to read the labels.

The Litter Monster. Alfred Higgins. Young people are encouraged to see what they can do about litter.

National Health Test. McGraw-Hill. Four-part film presents questions on health which are answered in detail later.

Nutritional Quackery. Aims. Simple facts of nutrition are explained as are means to combat food faddism.

Parent Problems. King Screen. Teen-age girl faces a problem of conflicting loyalties.

Smoking: Pete Ennis Doesn't Smoke Yet. McGraw-Hill. Discusses various personal and social factors which affect a young person's decision on smoking.

Surviving in Space. McGraw-Hill. Introduces the field of bioastronautics—a new branch of medical science.

Thinking About Drinking. Alfred Higgins. Open-ended film presents some social factors that influence an individual's decisions about the use of alcohol.

Books for Young People[1]

Books of Information

The American National Red Cross. *Basic First Aid: Books 1, 2, 3, 4.* Doubleday, 1971. Paperbacks.

Bixby, William. *A World You Can Live In.* McKay, 1971. Describes various types of pollution and ways of combating them.

Blanzaco, André, M.D. *VD: Facts You Should Know.* Scott, Foresman, 1970. Presents basic information in step-by-step fashion; useful for self-instruction. Paperback.

Gabel, Margaret. *Sparrows Don't Drop Candy Wrappers.* Dodd, 1971. What individuals can do to lessen deterioration of the environment.

Houser, Norman W. *Drugs: Facts on Their Use and Abuse.* Scott, Foresman, 1969. Effects of drug abuse on the individual and society are considered. Paperback.

Larsen, Peter. *The United Nations at Work Throughout the World.* Lothrop, 1971. Note especially the chapters on UNICEF, WHO, and FAO.

Levinsohn, Florence, and Kelly, G. Lombard, M.D. *What Teenagers Want to Know.* Budlong, 1969. Available only through professional sources from Milex Products Inc., 5917 N. Northwest Highway, Chicago, Illinois 60631. Written for teen-agers, this pamphlet focuses on social problems and attitudes confronting the adolescent.

McCarthy, Raymond G., and Pasciutti, John J. *Facts About Alcohol.* SRA, Sixth Printing, 1970. Readable booklet on alcohol for junior-high students.

Nolen, William H., M.D. *Spare Parts for the Human Body.* Random, 1971. Good modern reference on transplants and their future.

Noshpitz, Joseph D., M.D. *Understanding Ourselves: The Challenge of the Human Mind.* Coward, 1964. How our minds work and why we behave as we do.

Rosenberg, Nancy and Lawrence, M.D. *The Story of Modern Medicine.* Norton, 1966. Major advances in medicine are recounted.

[1]See also "Enrichment Suggestions" for each unit on pages 27, 29, 31, 33, 35, 37, 39, 41, 43 of this *Resource Book.*

Books to "Grow On"

Arundel, Honor. *Emma's Island.* Hawthorn, 1971. Thirteen-year-old Emma, an orphan, comes to live with her aunt. She becomes a mainstay of the household and balks at leaving to continue her schooling.

Burnett, Hallie, Compiler. *Sometimes Magic: A Collection of Outstanding Stories for the Teenage Girl.* Platt, 1966. Fifteen stories about girls in the teen years.

Campbell, Hope. *Why Not Join the Giraffes?* Grosset, 1967. The teen-age desire to conform is treated in a humorous manner in this readable book.

Clark, Tom E. *The Big Road.* Lothrop, 1965. Vic leaves home during the Depression. After living as a hobo for three months, he returns home—with a new maturity and outlook.

Frick, C. H. *The Comeback Guy.* Harcourt, 1961. Overconfident Jeff eventually learns the true meaning of sportsmanship.

Glasgow, Ellen. *Vein of Iron.* Harcourt, 1965. A character study of Ada, the daughter of a proud southern family.

Honig, Donald. *Johnny Lee.* McCall, 1971. A Black boy of seventeen goes from Harlem to a Virginia mountain town to play on a minor-league baseball team.

Kingman, Lee. *The Year of the Raccoon.* Houghton, 1966. Being an "average" boy among talented brothers is Joey's problem.

Krumgold, Joseph. *Henry III.* Atheneum, 1967. Thirteen-year-old Henry, growing up in a suburb, develops his own philosophy of life.

Richardson, Grace. *Douglas.* Harper, 1966. Douglas tends to "get by" in his teen years because of his superficial charm.

Waite, Helen E. *Valiant Companions.* Macrae, 1939. Story of the understanding relationship between Helen Keller, who learned to live without sight or hearing, and her teacher, Ann Sullivan.

Walsh, Jill Paton. *Fireweed.* Avon, 1972. A wholesome friendship develops between a boy and a girl who meet during a London blitz.

Directory of Publishers

AAHPER. American Assn. for Health, Physical Education, and Recreation, 1201 16th St., N.W., Washington, D.C. 20036. **Abelard-Schuman Ltd.,** 257 Park Ave. S., N.Y., N.Y. 10010. **ADA.** American Dental Assn., 211 E. Chicago Ave., Chicago, Ill. 60611. **AID.** Agency for International Development, Bureau for Technical Assistance, Washington, D.C. 20523. **AMA.** American Medical Assn., 535 N. Dearborn St., Chicago, Ill. 60610. **APHA.** American Public Health Assn., Inc., 1015 18th St., N.W., Washington, D.C. 20036. **Appleton.** Appleton-Century-Crofts, 440 Park Ave. S., N.Y., N.Y. 10016. **ASHA.** American School Health Assn., 107 S. Depeyster St., Kent, Ohio 44240. **ASHA.** American Social Health Assn., 1740 Broadway, N.Y., N.Y. 10019. **Association Press,** 291 Broadway, N.Y., N.Y. 10007. **Atheneum Publishers,** 122 E. 42 St., N.Y., N.Y. 10017. **Avon Books,** The Hearst Corp., Hearst Magazines Div., 959 Eighth Ave., N.Y., N.Y. 10019. **Ballantine Books,** Inc., 201 E. 50 St., N.Y., N.Y. 10022. **Barnes.** A. S. Barnes & Co., Inc., Forsgate Dr., Cranbury, N.J. 08512. **Basic Books,** Inc., 10 E. 53 St., N.Y., N.Y. 10022. **Beacon Press,** 25 Beacon St., Boston, Mass. 02108. **Bete.** Channing L. Bete Co., Inc., Greenfield, Mass. 01301. **Bobbs-Merrill Co.,** Inc., 4300 W. 62 St., Indianapolis, Ind. 46268. **W. C. Brown Co.,** 135 S. Locust St., Dubuque, Ia. 52001. **Budlong.** Milex Products, Inc., 5917 N. Northwest Hwy., Chicago, Ill. 60631. **Bureau of Curriculum Development,** Board of Education of the City of New York, 110 Livingston St., Brooklyn, N.Y. 11201. **Canfield.** (See Harper.) **Childrens Press,** 1224 W. Van Buren St., Chicago, Ill. 60607. **Commonwealth of Massachusetts,** Dept. of Public Health, Div. of Communicable Diseases, State House, Boston, Mass. 02133. **Coward.** Coward, McCann & Geoghegan, Inc., 200 Madison Ave., N.Y., N.Y. 10016. **Cowles.** (See Regnery.) **Creative Educational Society,** 515 N. Front St., Mankato, Minn. 56001. **Crest.** Fawcett World Library: Crest, Gold Medal & Premier Books, 1515 Broadway, N.Y., N.Y. 10036. **Crowell.** Thomas Y. Crowell Co., 666 Fifth Ave., N.Y., N.Y. 10019. **Dodd, Mead** & Co., 79 Madison Ave., N.Y., N.Y. 10016. **Doubleday** & Co., Inc., Garden City, N.Y. 11530. **Dover Publications,** Inc., 180 Varick St., N.Y., N.Y. 10014. **Dutton.** E. P. Dutton & Co., Inc., 201 Park Ave. S., N.Y., N.Y. 10003. **Education Council for School Research and Development,** 131 Mineola Blvd., Mineola, N.Y. 11501. **Farrar.** Farrar, Straus & Giroux, Inc., 19 Union Sq. W., N.Y., N.Y. 10003. **Free Press,** 866 Third Ave., N.Y., N.Y. 10022. **Grosset & Dunlap,** Inc., 51 Madison Ave., N.Y., N.Y. 10010. **Grune & Stratton,** Inc., 111 Fifth Ave., N.Y., N.Y. 10003. **Harcourt.** Harcourt Brace Jovanovich, Inc., 757 Third Ave., N.Y., N.Y. 10017. **Harper & Row,** Publishers, 10 E. 53 St., N.Y., N.Y. 10022. **Hawthorn Books,** Inc., 260 Madison Ave., N.Y., N.Y. 10016. **Holiday House,** Inc., 18 E. 56 St., N.Y., N.Y. 10022. **Holt.** Holt, Rinehart and Winston, Inc., 383 Madison Ave., N.Y., N.Y. 10017. **Houghton Mifflin Co.,** 2 Park St., Boston, Mass. 02107. **Iowa State University Press,** Ames, Iowa 50010. **John Day.** The John Day Co., Inc., 257 Park Ave. S., N.Y., N.Y. 10010. **Knopf.** Alfred A. Knopf, Inc., 201 E. 50 St., N.Y., N.Y. 10022. **Little.** Little, Brown and Co., 34 Beacon St., Boston, Mass. 02106. **Lothrop, Lee & Shepard Co.,** 105 Madison Ave., N.Y., N.Y. 10016. **McCall.** (See Saturday Review Press.) **McGraw-Hill** Book Co., 1221 Ave. of the Americas, N.Y., N.Y. 10020. **McKay.** David McKay Co., Inc., 750 Third Ave., N.Y., N.Y. 10017. **Macmillan.** The Macmillan Co., 866 Third Ave., N.Y., N.Y. 10022. **Macrae.** Macrae Smith Co., 225 S. 15 St., Philadelphia, Pa. 19102. **Mental Health Materials Center,** 419 Park Ave. S., N.Y., N.Y. 10016. **Messner.** Julian Messner, 1 W. 39 St., N.Y., N.Y. 10018. **Milex.** (See Budlong.) **Morrow.** William Morrow & Co., Inc., 105 Madison Ave., N.Y., N.Y. 10016. **Mosby.** C. V. Mosby Co., 11830 Westline Industrial Dr., St. Louis, Mo. 63141. **NDC.** National Dairy Council, 111 N. Canal St., Chicago, Ill. 60606. **NEA.** National Education Assn. Publications, 1201 16th St., N.W., Washington, D. C. 20036. **Norton.** W. W. Norton & Co., Inc., 500 Fifth Ave., N.Y., N.Y. 10036. **NSC.** National Safety Council, 425 N. Michigan Ave., Chicago, Ill. 60611. **Platt & Munk,** 1055 Bronx River Ave., Bronx, N.Y. 10472. **Pocket Books.** (See Simon & Schuster.) **Prentice-Hall,** Inc., Englewood Cliffs, N.J. 07632. **Princeton University Press,** Princeton, N.J. 08540. **Public Affairs Committee,** Inc., 381 Park Ave. S., N.Y., N.Y. 10016. **Rand McNally** & Co., 8255 Central Park Ave., Skokie, Ill. 60076. **Random House,** Inc., 201 E. 50 St., N.Y., N.Y. 10022. **Henry Regnery** Co., 114 W. Illinois St., Chicago, Ill. 60610. **Ronald Press** Co., 79 Madison Ave., N.Y., N.Y. 10016. **St. Martin's Press,** Inc., 175 Fifth Ave., N.Y., N.Y. 10010. **Saturday Review Press,** 380 Madison Ave., N.Y., N.Y. 10017. **Saunders.** W. B. Saunders Co., W. Washington Sq., Philadelphia, Pa. 19105. **Scholastic Book Services,** 50 W. 44 St., N.Y., N.Y. 10036. **Scott, Foresman** and Co., 1900 E. Lake Ave., Glenview, Ill. 60025. **Scribner.** Charles Scribner's Sons, 597 Fifth Ave., N.Y., N.Y. 10017. **Seabury Press,** Inc., 815 Second Ave., N.Y., N.Y. 10017. **Simon & Schuster,** Inc., 630 Fifth Ave., N.Y., N.Y. 10020. **SRA.** Science Research Associates, Inc., 259 E. Erie St., Chicago, Ill. 60611. **Sterling** Publishing Co., Inc., 419 Park Ave. S., N.Y., N.Y. 10016. **Sup't of Documents.** (See U.S. Govt. Printing Office.) **Time Inc.,** Rockefeller Center, N.Y., N.Y. 10020. **U.S. Government Printing Office.** Order from: Public Documents Distribution Center, 5801 Tabor Ave., Philadelphia, Pa. 19120. **Walck.** Henry Z. Walck, Inc., 19 Union Sq. W., N.Y., N.Y. 10003. **Warne.** Frederick Warne & Co., Inc., 101 Fifth Ave., N.Y., N.Y. 10003. **Watts.** Franklin Watts, Inc., 845 Third Ave., N.Y., N.Y. 10022. **Westminster Press,** Witherspoon Bldg., Philadelphia, Pa. 19107.

Directory of Audio-Visual Sources

ACS. American Cancer Society, 219 E. 42 St., N.Y., N.Y. 10017. **Aims.** Aims Instructional Media Services, Inc., P.O. Box 1010, Hollywood, Calif. 90028. **Alfred Higgins.** Alfred Higgins Productions, 9100 Sunset Blvd., Los Angeles, Calif. 90069. **American Lung Association,** 1740 Broadway, N.Y., N.Y. 10019. **Association.** Association-Sterling Films, 600 Grand Ave., Ridgefield, N.J. 07657. **A T & T.** American Telephone & Telegraph Co., 195 Broadway, N.Y., N.Y. 10007. **Avanti Films,** Inc., 8271 Melrose Ave., Los Angeles, Calif. 90046. **BFA.** BFA Educational Media, 2211 Michigan Ave., Santa Monica, Calif. 90404. **Carousel Films,** Inc., 1501 Broadway, N.Y., N.Y. 10036. **Churchill Films,** 662 N. Robertson Blvd., Los Angeles, Calif. 90069. **Coronet.** Coronet Films, 65 E. South Water St., Chicago, Ill. 60601. **Documentary Films,** 3217 Trout Gulch Rd., Aptos, Calif. 95003. **EBE.** Encyclopaedia Britannica Educational Corp., 425 N. Michigan Ave., Chicago, Ill. 60611. **Holt.** Holt, Rinehart and Winston, Inc., Media Sales Service Dept. KS, 383 Madison Ave., N.Y., N.Y. 10017. **IFB.** International Film Bureau, Inc., 332 S. Michigan Ave., Chicago, Ill. 60604. **King Screen.** (See BFA Educational Media.) **McGraw-Hill.** (See Directory of Publishers.) **Medical Arts Productions,** Box 4042, Stockton, Calif. 95204. **Modern Talking Picture Service,** Inc., 2323 New Hyde Park Rd., New Hyde Park, N.Y. 11040. **NBC.** NBC Educational Enterprises Inc., 30 Rockefeller Plaza, N.Y., N.Y. 10020. **NFBC.** National Film Board of Canada, 680 Fifth Ave., N.Y., N.Y. 10019. **Perennial Education,** Inc., 1825 Willow Rd., Northfield, Ill. 60093. **Sid Davis.** Sid Davis Productions, 1046 S. Robertson Blvd., Los Angeles, Calif. 90035. **Teaching Film Custodians,** 25 W. 43 St., N.Y., N.Y. 10036. **United Nations Films,** Films and TV, N.Y., N.Y. 10017. **U.S. Dept. of HEW,** National Medical Audiovisual Center, Atlanta, Ga. 30334. **Wexler.** (See Perennial.) **WHO.** World Health Org., U.N. Bldg., N.Y., N.Y. 10017. **Wombat Productions,** Inc., 77 Tarrytown Rd., White Plains, N.Y. 10607. **Brigham Young University,** Film Marketing Dept. of Motion Picture Production, Provo, Utah 84601.

1 2 3 4 5 6 7 8 9 10 11 12 13 14 15 16 17 18 19 20 21 22 23 24 25 80 79 78 77 76 75 74